The
LOST
FLEET

The
LOST
FLEET

*A Yankee Whaler's Struggle
Against the Confederate Navy
and Arctic Disaster*

Marc Songini

St. Martin's Griffin
New York

Excerpts from *One Whaling Family* by Harold Williams. Copyright © 1964, renewed 1992 by Houghton Mifflin Company. Reprinted by permission of Houghton Mifflin Co. All rights reserved.

www.stmartins.com

Book design by Michelle McMillian
Map illustration by Jackie Aher

Library of Congress Cataloging-in-Publication Data

Songini, Marc L.
    The lost fleet : a Yankee whaler's struggle against the Confederate Navy and Arctic disaster / Marc Songini.
        p. cm.
    Includes bibliographical references.
    ISBN-13: 978-0-312-38095-3
    ISBN-10: 0-312-38095-X
1. Whaling—United States—History. 2. Whalers (Persons)—United States—History. 3. Williams, Thomas W. (Thomas William) 4. Whaling—Arctic Ocean—History. I. Title.

SH383.2.S66 2007
639.2'8092273—dc22   2007012056

First St. Martin's Griffin Edition: August 2008

10 9 8 7 6 5 4 3 2 1

To my parents—who couldn't be here to see
this book but who made it possible.

To my wife and helper Terry, who has contributed to this work
extensively, and who is to me like Eliza to Thomas.

And above all:
To the brave fishermen of New England,
New Bedford especially, a breed apart, then as now.

Contents

Map   ix
Acknowledgments   xi
Prelude   1

BOOK ONE: BRAVE MEN AND BRAVER WOMEN

1. Lonely but Not Alone   11
2. A Lighthouse Keeper   74
3. In Wild and Distant Seas   78
4. Journey's End   87

BOOK TWO: THE FIRST IRON

5. The Daring Fishermen of New England   99
6. Old Rodney   113
7. An Indifferent Screw Steamer   125
8. A Pirate Deed   134
9. Like Pursuing a Coy Maiden   152
10. The Other *Alabama*   189

11. Come on My Deck and Fight Me   217

12. Terrible Havoc   256

BOOK THREE: THE LANCE STRIKES

13. Idle Wharves and Dismasted Ships   267

14. Death Stared Us in the Face   274

15. In the Topmost Frost-Killed End of Creation   287

16. How Many Will See the Last Day of Next August?   308

17. The Most Crushing Blow   324

BOOK FOUR: ROLLING OUT ON THE FIN

18. Enough to Fill a Book   345

19. Appreciable Deterioration   356

20. Looking for a Modern Joshua   373

21. A Dreary and Uncertain March   381

Epilogue: The Clear-eyed Men of the Sea   398

Bibliography   405

Index   415

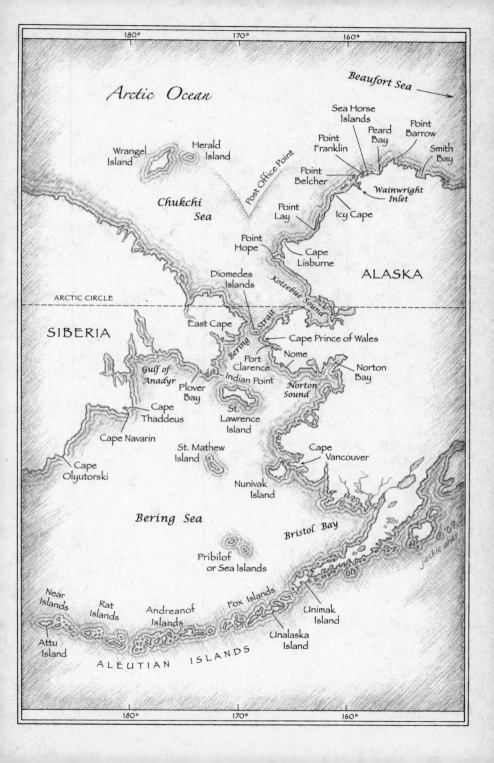

Acknowledgments

This book is a narrative meant to entertain the general—and specialized—reader, but it's also a work of nonfiction. Nothing has been written that isn't backed by research and documentation. Wherever possible, I have relied on primary sources. The dialogue as well is quoted directly as recorded—I have only made necessary changes for grammatical reasons.

Edward Gibbon conceived of his masterpiece *The Decline and Fall of the Roman Empire* while contemplating some of Rome's ruins. Through the written page he decided to follow the path of a great empire as it became a few scattered rock fragments through the ages. While I'm no Gibbon, similarly, I've seen harpoons and other whaling gear hanging in many waterfront bars throughout the Bay State, or the remnants of the whaling industry's facilities in New Bedford. I've read accounts of the whalers since I was a boy and have been aware of some great maritime enterprise that has gone out on the ebb tide. An outsider with no direct connection to the whaling industry, I decided to trace a course through the past to discover its essence—and the result is in your hands.

However, this treatment, this attempt to get at the decline and fall of whaling, is also primarily a story. It's not a philosophical or economic history of the events closing out the whaling industry in the latter 19th century. Thus for those readers interested in an in-depth discussion of Arctic whaling, I recommend the excellent *Whales, Ice, and Men* by John Bockstoce. Another well written treatment of New Bedford and its whaling fleet is *Children of the Light*, by Everett Allen, which covers the circumstances around the

1871 freeze-in extensively. For those who would like a firsthand account of the time, I also recommend *One Whaling Family* by Harold Williams, which contains the Eliza and William Fish Williams accounts.

In a work of this size and covering so many events, errors are all but inevitable, and for any, I take all the blame. The names and spellings of ships and places vary considerably between ships logs and newspaper accounts. And it must be said, many great stories are locked in nearly illegible ship logs that at time are like trying to read smoke.

Luckily, I had patient and helpful experts to assist me—and their input and error catching have been invaluable. In particular I am indebted to such gracious experts as whaling historian and author Judith Navas Lund and Paul Cyr, Curator of Special Collections at the New Bedford Free Public Library. Both people proved to be tireless and extensive resources to me. Also special thanks to Michael Dyer and Laura Pereira, librarians at the New Bedford Whaling Museum, which contains perhaps the most comprehensive collection of whaling documents in the world. Without their cooperation, this book could not have been written.

Also special thanks to Sam Craghead, a member of the staff of the Museum of the Confederacy in Richmond, who read the sections of the book that concerned the Civil War and helped correct errors.

At times, I felt like a whaler myself attempting to fill the pages just as they tried to fill their ships' holds with caskets. In the six years of working on *The Lost Fleet*, I have frequented public libraries in San Francisco, Los Angeles, Boston, Wayland, Foxboro, New Bedford, San Diego, Orlando, and other places. A debt of gratitude is due to our library system—truly one of our greatest assets.

My friend, professor Stephen Dooner, worked with me tirelessly to edit this book and make the prose tolerable. Also, I owe a special debt of gratitude to my two editors at St. Martin's Press, Tim Bent, who gave me the opportunity to write this book and let it grow, and to Marc Resnick, who adopted this project as his own and saw it through to completion. I also want to thank my agent, Jane Dystel, for taking the chance with me.

To the many other friends and associates who have read sections of the book and offered comments, encouragement and consolation, I also offer humble gratitude.

Before parting from him, he gave us his experience as a whaleman, and advised us not to be gulled by fair promises. He said he knew a thing or two about it; that he would sooner be in the penitentiary any time; and, if we had any regard for ourselves, we ought to turn our backs upon New Bedford, for it was the sink-hole of iniquity; that the fitters were all blood-suckers, the owners cheats, and the captains tyrants.

—ADVICE OF A SEASONED WHALEMAN TO J. ROSS BROWN,
JUST PRIOR TO HIS FIRST VOYAGE. FROM "ETCHINGS OF A WHALING CRUISE"

And pray, sir, what in the world is equal to it?. . . look at the manner in which the New England people carry on the whale fishery. While we follow them among the trembling mountains of ice, and behold them penetrating into the deepest frozen recesses of Hudson's and Davis's Straits—while we are looking for them beneath the Arctic circle, we hear that they have pierced into the opposed region of the polar cold—that they are at the antipodes, and engaged under the frozen serpent of the south. . . . Nor is the equinoctial heat more discouraging to them than the accumulated winter of both poles. We learn that, while some of them draw the line or strike the harpoon on the coast of Africa, others run the longitude, and pursue their gigantic game along the coast of Brazil. No sea but what is vexed with their fisheries, no climate that is not witness of their toils. Neither the perseverance of Holland, nor the activity of France, nor the dexterous and firm sagacity of English enterprise, ever carried this most perilous mode of hardy industry to the extent to which it has been pursued by these recent people—a people who are still in the gristle, and not hardened into manhood.

—ENGLISH STATESMAN EDMUND BURKE

LUCEM DIFFUNDO—I spread the light.
—CITY MOTTO OF NEW BEDFORD

I feel that you are the only sincere Friend that I have in the world, and I cant bear to part with you.

—EXCERPT FROM A LETTER FROM ELIZA WILLIAMS
TO HER HUSBAND THOMAS BEFORE HE SET OUT ON A WHALING VOYAGE

The

LOST
FLEET

Prelude

Whaling, gentlemen, is tolerably hard at first, but it's the finest business in the world for enterprising young men. If you are determined to take a voyage, I'll put you in the way of shipping in a most elegant vessel, well fitted: that's the great thing, well fitted. Vigilance and activity will insure you rapid promotion. I haven't the least doubt but you'll come home boatsteerers. I sent off six college students a few days ago, and a poor fellow who had been flogged away from home by a vicious wife. A whaler, gentlemen," continued the agent, rising in eloquence, "a whaler is a place of refuge for the distressed and persecuted, a school for the dissipated, an asylum for the needy! There's nothing like it. You can see the world; you can see something of life!

—*Speech given by a recruiter to whaling prospects,*
from Etchings of a Whaling Cruise

NOVEMBER 11, 1861,
NEW BEDFORD HARBOR, ACUSHNET RIVER

When the Fairhaven, Massachusetts, whaleship *Ansel Gibbs* dropped anchor here, she carried 560 barrels of oil and 19,500 pounds of whalebone taken from the Arctic. The *Gibbs*'s master also carried the news she was minus seven of the crewmen who'd sailed out on April 1860 on her voyage to the Davis Straits whaling grounds. Apparently, the prior August they'd deserted with two hands from another ship, the *Daniel Webster,* of New Bedford. The absence of these mariners didn't cause much fuss—whalers invariably arrived back from their voyages missing men who'd either died, jumped ship, or been discharged. The hands still surviving on board only got paid if they made it back home, and the fewer men to compensate meant that the shipowners got to keep a greater share of the profits in their pockets.

What made this situation unique was that the ill-fated band of nine had gone overboard off the coast of the misnamed glacier-covered rock called Greenland, a particularly inhospitable place. Because of the general conditions in the fishery, desertion was common enough in the seductive climes of the South Seas or Hawaii—but doing so in Arctic regions wasn't. Unsurprisingly, as the *Gibbs* reported, the men hadn't been heard of since: They'd vanished as if, Jonah-like, they'd been swallowed whole.

But for anyone who might've taken an interest in the affair, a month after the *Gibbs*'s docking, six gaunt survivors surfaced in the fishing town of St. Johns, Newfoundland. They'd an unusually grisly story to tell— shocking even in the annals of whaling, where tales of shipwreck, starvation, mutiny, and murder weren't rare. One of the more vociferous members of the troop was a John F. Sullivan. Prior to shipping out on the *Daniel Webster,* he'd been passing an obscure life in the small village of Hadley Falls, about one hundred miles west of Boston in the green, rolling hills of western Massachusetts. Although the facts available about him are few, we can reasonably guess that like many other whaling recruits, he'd probably never seen the ocean before he visited New Bedford. Assuming he wasn't a criminal on the run or looking to evade his debtors, we may guess most likely he'd been bored with a life in a field or factory distant from any large city and chanced to lay eyes on an alluring recruiting advertisement that contained somewhat misleading boasts of the profitability and excitement of a whaling adventure. Like so many other "green hands," after signing the ship's papers and sailing out, apparently Sullivan became rapidly discouraged and disillusioned by the misery that was life aboard a whaler. Also, like many of these most hardy of mariners, he was lucky to have escaped the career alive.

The facts, as he later claimed, were these: On August 4, 1861, the *Daniel Webster* was in Cumberland Sound, near Greenland, with the hunting season ending and the long, man-killing Arctic winter about to start. Sullivan feared a slow death by scurvy and felt he didn't have enough warm clothes to face the cold northern climate. A seaman could get almost anything he needed from the ship's slop chest—a kind of onboard company store—particularly if he was willing to pay a few times what it would have cost on land. But rather than squander whatever miserable lay (the portion of the vessel's profit) he was entitled to, Sullivan decided to jump ship. He and a companion from the forecastle, William Dutton, managed to fall in with seven deserters from another whaler, the *Ansel Gibbs,* who found their captain's treatment of them so intolerable they wanted to escape as well.

Among those enrolled in this grand scheme was a boatsteerer, whose job was to make first contact with a whale by fastening a harpoon, or iron, into its back in preparation for the kill. One of the most important tasks on a whaler, it required a steady hand, fine aim, and uncommon courage. There were also two cousins, Joseph and Samuel Fisher, whose situation on board could've been likened to two kinsmen simultaneously serving their respective jail sentences in the same prison cell. To escape, the ship-jumping band squirreled away seventeen pounds of hardtack, a pair of pistols, and some ammunition in a whaleboat, secretly lowered it from its davits, or cranes, and cast off.

To try their luck in such a place when so badly equipped, the sailors were clearly desperate. The *Gibbs* was due to sail home shortly in any case, so their logic was comparable to that of a convict who escapes the penitentiary by going directly to the gallows. The band originally planned to land on Cape Chidlay, a fogbound rocky bulge on the northernmost tip of Labrador that formed part of the southern edge of Hudson Strait. It was an odd choice, because so empty and harsh was Labrador, the French explorer Jacques Cartier had decided it was God's gift to Cain as punishment for having introduced murder into the world by slaying Abel. The dry climate could support little more vegetation than lichen, moss, and small shrubs, and the uneven rocky coast was coated in ice even in August. Spring and summer were potentially lethal, too, for when the temperature was its warmest, massive ship-killing Arctic bergs, calved from glaciers, floated south in their greatest numbers. The party had to sail to the south as quickly as possible to avoid winter's arrival, when the thermometer's mercury stays permanently below freezing, violent gales blow for a month at a time, and the chance to survive is slim, indeed.

After sailing another four days, Sullivan and his party "spoke" the New London whaling bark *George Henry*. Her master was Captain Sidney

O. Budington, an experienced Arctic whaleman who'd wintered over here the prior year, having been caught in the ice and unable to return to Connecticut. The *Henry* carried as passenger the explorer Charles Francis Hall, who was futilely searching for the bones of the missing explorer Sir John Franklin. (Coincidentally, Budington's uncle, James Buddington, while commanding the same whaler in 1855, found and safely recovered the H.M.S. *Resolute,* which had been part of Franklin's doomed squadron.) Despite the deserters' obvious inclinations to wander, the Inuit-speaking Budington offered to take them on as crewmen. Although they refused, Budington, in an act of whaler's generosity, gave them some provisions. Sustained by the master's gift, along with duck meat and a polar bear's "hind quarter" acquired hunting, the band pressed on across Hudson Strait. (Although Henry Hudson hadn't discovered it, this icy channel bore the name of the explorer who, like so many northern explorers, had paid with his life for the privilege of littering the landscape with his surname. He died after his own mutinous crew cast him adrift in the also eponymous Hudson's Bay, which at least he *had* discovered.) After a brief stop at Resolution Island, the food was gone, and the party sailed on through waters prone to mirages and thick fogs that made navigation deadly. Around August 20, they could see the rugged outline of Cape Chidlay, but its low-lying shoreline was too steep to make a proper landing, and they sailed thirty miles south through strong currents, putting briefly in at whatever low-lying spot they could find.

When possible, the men scavenged some of the few wild mushrooms and berries that grew on this otherwise desolate land. The prospects must've been grim, as one morning the party woke up to find its number reduced by two: Hiram Davis, called the "Doctor," and another conspirator decided to take their chances together and fled in the night with "everything that was useful." By now, Sullivan must've regretted his decision to jump ship. In addition to all else, he was unpopular with his fellow shipmates because of his habit of quarreling and faultfinding—the Fisher cousins in particular loathed him. Hunger was growing ever greater, and the deserters were now fighting an imaginary clock whose every tick brought them closer to death through starvation and exposure. Desperate, they launched the boat to escape from this new prison, but a violent gust of wind snapped the mast in two, and they had to run back to shore to splice it together again.

That night, perhaps because of the day's exertions, Sullivan's shipmate Dutton was relieved from the pains of starvation, courtesy of the grim reaper. So weak they could hardly move, the survivors weren't much better off, and the following evening, Samuel Fisher proposed they eat Dutton's body. It wasn't an idle suggestion, as he took his knife, cut off a piece of the dead man's thigh, and using the blade as a skewer, roasted it over the camp fire. By the next day, hunger had overcome whatever qualms anyone else might've entertained about eating a former shipmate.

Each starving man in his turn scraped a slice of meat from the corpse and ate it. After the bones were broken into small pieces, they were dropped into a kettle with water for boiling into soup. The dissections being a model of economy and thrift, after smashing the skull, someone even scooped out the now-unthinking brain for roasting. The men had won a brief reprieve from starvation, but the wind rose threateningly as they launched the boat into the Labrador Sea. Fighting what had become a gale, they located a small island that might've served as shelter, but they were too weak to haul the boat ashore. The men continued to struggle on in the water until striking a rock that stove the craft in.

After landing, for the next three days everyone managed to stay alive—a condition that soon changed. As Sullivan later said, he was kneeling down about to cook a freshly picked mushroom when something smashed him hard on his head. Looking up, he saw his enemy, Joseph Fisher, standing over him, club in hand. Joseph claimed later it had been his would-be victim's sharp tongue that had provoked the blow. If so, Sullivan must've said something especially galling, because Joseph struck him three more times. Possibly because starvation had made him too weak and dizzy to do the job right, Joseph was unable to kill him. Sullivan finally got to his feet as Samuel Fisher entered the fray, grabbing hold of Sullivan's right arm for Joseph to club three times, perhaps trying to keep the would-be victim from drawing his knife. Despite the onslaught, Sullivan broke away from his assailants.

"For God's sake, spare my life!" he said again and again.

"We want meat and we are bound to kill you," replied the cousins.

Sullivan drew a knife and held it in front of him as the cousins mounted a two-pronged attack. Armed with a large dirk, Samuel struck from one side, while Joseph, wielding the club and a stone, came from the other.

Samuel grabbed Sullivan's shoulder, but before he could strike, Sullivan lifted his own knife and stabbed him in the throat. After Samuel collapsed, Sullivan turned and stepped toward Joseph, who ran to where the other castaways were. Sullivan stooped alongside the dying Samuel and cried; on hearing the other party members calling to him promising their protection, he took them at their word.

When he reentered the camp, his mates cleaned the gashes to his head and washed the caked blood from his face. Samuel, bleeding from the throat, proved a blessing to his fellow castaways by quickly expiring: The one-time cannibal leader now became a meal himself. It was Joseph, Sullivan later claimed, who was the first to cut into the body and eat it the same way as they had Dutton's, scraping off the flesh and smashing the bones and skull. For his part, Joseph said he feared if he didn't eat his cousin, he would've been the next item on the menu, dying either from hunger or, weakened by starvation, at the hands of his companions.

Perhaps because of the fresh meat, the men found the strength to repair the whaleboat and sail it to what they thought was the shore of Labrador. They landed, left the boat, and struck out for help, but possibly because of the ruggedness of the terrain or their own weakness or both, their pace was agonizingly slow. After four days, making a mile a day, they arrived at the far side of what they realized was only an island. Another possibly lethal error made, they took another four days to walk back and found their boat again had been crushed. Sullivan didn't say how, but perhaps they had unknowingly placed it in the path of an unusually large wave that had picked it up off the beach and smashed it on some rocks. After performing some makeshift repairs, they launched the boat and climbed inside, after which it slipped under the waves. The sinking delivered the final blow to whatever resolve they still possessed to escape to the mainland. Leaving the craft behind, the men trudged back to the other side of the island, where, as Sullivan noted, "we should die or be picked up."

With the grim outcome of their trip becoming obvious, they consumed every piece of seal and bearskin gear they carried, and even their belts, boots, and sheaths. To add to their abundant misery during this death vigil, it rained for three days, a condition relieved only when snow began to fall. Their fortunes brightened on September 29, when a band of Inuit unexpectedly stumbled over the dying men and took them by boat to

Okak, yet another puny, insignificant island off Labrador. Here, on the edge of a desolate bay, was a century-old lonely ramshackle missionary outpost that supported the slow, hard work of the Moravian Brethren in their attempts to convert the local Inuit. The dour Moravians adhered to a strict Calvinist creed, and accepted literally and with great zeal Christ's commission to spread the Gospel from their homelands of Bohemia and Moravia to the farthest corners of the world. But in addition to saving errant souls, these apostles were also willing to rescue ailing bodies, and they gave the ragged, emaciated wretches food and clothing.

After their arrival, the survivors told a Moravian brother what they claimed was the whole ugly tale. The heart we roasted, and from the bones we made soup, they recounted very "coolly," as the missionary noted. The Brethren eventually sent the men to the village of Nain, closing out a small chapter in the brief history of their mission, which within a few decades would see disease erase it, along with the rest of Okak itself. Surprisingly, the double-deserter Doctor Hiram Davis had mysteriously survived, even beating the rest of the party's survivors to Nain by three days. Davis was minus the coconspirator with whom a month before he'd abandoned the party. He told "false stories" about why he'd left and how he'd endured the ordeal, Sullivan recounted. The actual truth might've been a bit difficult for the Doctor to manage, given that his companion was dead—possibly murdered—and almost certainly had become a meal somewhere in the wastelands of Labrador.

Shortly after, the onetime whalers returned to their homes in New England and elsewhere, lighter in weight but bearing heavy, not to mention contradictory, tales. Safely back in Stoughton, Massachusetts, Joseph Fisher denied there'd been any plan to kill Sullivan—he'd just hit him in a moment of anger. Although admitting he'd eaten his cousin, he claimed the act was so loathsome he was the last to partake. "People may blame us for doing as we did; but place anyone in our circumstances, with death staring them in the face, and probably they would have done the same," said Fisher. Here the immediate story, as the Boston and New Bedford papers told it later, closed.

But more than a year later, on January 5, 1863, Sullivan might've felt vindicated to learn the state of the *Daniel Webster*'s crew when she put in at Aberdeen, Scotland. She had sailed there instead of New Bedford to avoid crossing paths with the warships of the Confederate States of America, then prowling the seas. The vessel was minus two men and the second mate, who'd died of scurvy; however, she'd managed to send home 6,500 pounds of whalebone. The refusal to join Captain Budington also may have seemed a wise one, as the *George Henry* was frozen-in accidentally for an additional year. In hindsight, Budington probably should've kept the food he'd shared with the deserters, for every bite of even the poor-tasting pickled or salted ship fare must've mattered on his ship during that long dark Arctic winter.

Ultimately, rendering the deserters' tale, along with everything else, into particular insignificance was the blossoming War Between the States. Already in 1861, the journals were full of news from places such as Port Royal, Charleston, and Savannah. As the whalers navigated their way through seas on fire with battle, they, too, would find that their courses steered them into the newspaper columns. For the captains, owners, and sailors of the fleet, there would soon be much to read about—and almost all of it bad.

BOOK ONE

Brave Men and Braver Women

1

Lonely but Not Alone

The ship's agent whispered to the master, already on board, "Captain Jones, you've forgotten to kiss your wife good-bye!" Without so much as a look down, the captain replied: "What's ailin' her? I'm only going to be gone six months."

—*Old whaling story*

SEPTEMBER 7, 1858,
NEW BEDFORD HARBOR

At about two hours before noon on this mild day, a thirty-one-summers old and pregnant Eliza Azelia Williams left one of the many wharfs connecting to Water Street and entered a waiting pilot's schooner. About to embark on what she knew might be a three-year whaling voyage, her destination was the *Florida,* anchored five miles downstream the Acushnet River—an estuary that pulled double duty as New Bedford's harbor. Mrs. Williams's lot wasn't enviable: Not only five months with child, she was also a green hand—and so, a soon-to-be-sorry wretch who'd never been to sea. Among those in the sailboat with Eliza for her last trip as a lubber were her husband and soon-to-be-captain Thomas William Williams and his four mates. Also coming for the ride were two of her brothers and Roland Fish, a principal at Fish, Robinson & Co., the firm that owned the *Florida.* The passengers all aboard, the boat left its mooring and began to glide down the wide, deep, slow-moving greenish-gray waters of the relatively safe confines of the city's upper harbor toward Buzzards Bay and the Atlantic Ocean beyond.

Casting off from and arriving at the waterfront both were attended by a near-sacred ceremony, with the appearance of shore-side congregations part of the ritual. Here an onlooker saw great joy and heartbreak as people were sundered, sometimes forever, while others were reunited, if not permanently, then at least for a while. Eyeing the harbor was a popular pastime, with many in the city watching from a rooftop or tower to see what ship might be arriving. Some merchants paid a lookout to watch the lighthouse on Dumpling Rock off nearby Dartmouth shore in Buzzards Bay. When a vessel was heading to port, the keeper there extended the lighthouse's signaling arm. At the cry, "The arm is out!" hundreds headed down to the waterfront to greet the ships, listen to the stories, and find out how greasy (successful) or clean (poor) the voyage was. Some in the crowd might also learn they had lost their investment in the cruise—others, they were minus a brother, son, or father.

A departing party such as Eliza's was common enough at the edge of the busiest whaling port in the world, but, it was impressive-looking as well. She was in good company by the reckoning of this city. It was tall and brawny Williams and his formidable officers who were going down to the sea in ships to do a great work there. Heroes of the port and the fleet's backbone, they were the envy and object of emulation of every boy they passed. Those who'd survived long enough to become mates and masters were physically strong, brave, and handy, as well as skilled at fighting both men and whales. Their sweat, daring, muscle, and blood had made the City of Light what it was, rich for its size beyond compare with any other city in America, if not the world. Through their toil, New Bedford had grown into a global whaling enterprise, a massive octopus whose tentacles reached every ocean, sea, river, lagoon, and bay that had a whale worth taking.

Just yards away from Eliza was the proof: The city blocks by the waterfront formed a hive of activity, with nearly all those who worked there serving the queen bee of whaling. The more primitive of these toilers included blacksmiths, coopers, sailmakers, carpenters, mechanics, and spar makers; at the higher end were the bankers, merchants, and provisioners. The fleet kept ten thousand men busy hunting leviathans, and some said if the combined ships of New Bedford and her little sister Fairhaven, across the river, had been laid out end to end—not that such an arrangement was likely to happen—they would have provided ten miles of dry walking. At any given time in the harbor, a forest of skeletal masts sprouted up from ships just returned from all over the world—the Davis and Bering Straits, the South Seas, the Indian Ocean, the North Atlantic.

Here were the sounds of a busy waterfront: the ominous, pleading cries of gulls, the clink of a windlass's pawls as a crew raised an anchor, the creak of a ship riding a swell, the slap of drying sails and rigging, and the cries of mates and men. Vessels were tied up at dock or swung at anchor as they waited to disgorge their cargoes and be hove down for refitting before sailing again to harvest their varied fields. As their bosses yelled and screamed them on, stevedores manned the ship's windlass or, reining draft horses, used block and tackle to raise from a ship's airless hold the treasures of the deep—sheaves of whalebone taller than a tall man and casks of oil by the dozen. Teamsters carted these whale remnants away for the next step to their final destinations: Perhaps the oil became a fine bright light to be lit at a wedding, or the bone became embedded in a corset to keep fashionably small a matron's oversized waist.

By the wharves, covered in wet seaweed to keep the staves from shrinking and prevent leakage, the oil casks might rise up into small mountains awaiting shipment through the world. Despite precautions, some of the precious fluid always seeped out, staining the soil and giving the waterfront its unmistakable, unforgettable, and, not to mention, profitable stench. A fool could see and a blind man could sniff at New Bedford's wealth, or, to be more precise, that of its ruling and owning class. The distinctive and defining fragrance prevailed over all other aromatic rivals. These included the scent of the fresh cordage, white oak, and pine lumber, pungent sea brine, and the perfume of the pathetic thorn-bush blossoms in Rose Alley, grown as a futile buttress against the fishy smell. The whalebone was stacked to dry in yards near the waterfront, in row after row, where, collected together, it resembled a small, bristling forest. On the waterfront were outfall pipes (one was even celebrated in a painting), through which flowed raw sewage, and the poisons of industry, such as mercury, lye, and arsenic. These substances ran into the great vein of the Acushnet and mingled with the saltwater blood that sustained the city's commercial heart.

The schooner carrying Eliza and her party sailed, leaving behind the small city that rose up from the water's edge and covered the gently rolling hills beyond. With public lighting, large gardens, fine buildings, and paved streets, it was one of the grander communities in New England. Just then, it also was enjoying that time of year when the weather is a perfection of moderate temperature and mellow sunshine. The city, growing indistinct in the distance, with its fine "patrician-like" mansions, long avenues of green and gold, and fine maples, horse chestnut trees, and terraces of flowers, was "sweet to see," noted Herman Melville. Visible on the other side of the river was the low-lying town of Fairhaven and its church spires, where Fish, Robinson had its countinghouse and where the *Florida* was registered. (New Bedford had its own *Florida*.) The two rival banks of the Acushnet, set against one another forever, both geographically and economically, were united by a bridge so ugly some wondered if employing ferryboats wouldn't have been preferable.

A whaling voyage tended to be a rather effective portal into the next life, and it's likely Eliza, a devout Congregationalist, had attended some sort of a service. New Bedford, largely founded by religious dissenters, not to mention fanatics, had its share of fine edifices, like the imposing First Baptist Church on William Street. The elegant white Greek Revival structure didn't just assist in the guidance of men's souls to heaven— mariners used its tall and highly visible steeple as a landmark to help them navigate the harbor. Closer to the water—and hence, to the thousands of sailors, whores, thieves, murderers, and drunks who passed through the port each year—was the Seamen's Bethel on the slight rise called Johnny Cake Hill.

Some forward-thinking patricians with an eye to moral improvement (and the social order that followed) had erected the church to divert the wayward sailor from the many pleasures of the flesh readily available on the waterfront and make him think about death and hell. To add to the effect, set into the walls of the bethel were marble cenotaphs carrying a few of the names of the many unlucky sailors who'd died hunting whales. One such memorial was to Wm. [William] Swain of the *Christopher* of Nantucket: "This worthy man, after fastning to a whale, was carried overboard by the line, and drowned May 19th 1844 in the 49th Year of his age. Be ye also ready, for in such an hour as ye think not the son of man cometh." Clearly not the cheeriest of places—but on Sundays it was a refuge that a whaler destined for dangerous waters could seek comfort in.

A block away from the bethel was the granite-faced federal Customs House, shaped like a Greek temple. To clear his ship, Williams had trod the cobblestones on Second Street, climbed the house's rock steps, and passed through its tall Doric columns to enter. Inside, he obtained the papers needed to sail out on the face of the deep. God and death, commerce and treasure, government and power: the structures that grandly housed or signified them lay side by side here in the small, neatly ordered universe that was the city's downtown.

To Eliza, with the city gliding by her and in company with friends and family, it seemed a pleasant cruise. Yet it was more appropriate to view this trip as a funeral procession for her now-dead onshore life. Ahead in the distance was the new home her husband would soon present to her: the *Florida,* a black-hulled whaler and "a very fine sight," from Eliza's vantage point. However, with the wind light, the pilot's schooner was unable to make much headway toward the vessel, and Williams, impatient to reach her, hailed a nearby rowboat to tow them the rest of the way. The schooner began picking up speed, and soon Eliza was looking up the side of what would be her penitentiary-house. The vessel seemed quite large to her now.

The *Florida* was a 123-foot-long, 523-ton, three-masted square-rigged ship—that is, her yards were at right angles to her keel, as opposed to a fore-and-aft rigged vessel. She was 30 feet 10 inches in beam. Her keel was laid in 1821 in New York, and given the streamlined hull, the builders apparently had intended her to be something along the lines of a fast-sailing packet ship. In contrast, most whalers were bluff-bowed and broad-beamed, built for sturdiness rather than celerity—a quality generally useless in the whaling fishery, unless one was running from pirates, angry natives, or hostile warships. Despite the *Florida*'s speed, her owners had converted her for whaling, a vocation at which she'd managed to survive for thirteen years. As part of the transformation, they built a tryworks (two huge try-pots of 200-gallon capacity each, mounted on a brick furnace to boil blubber into oil) on the main deck amidships. They'd also installed davits to hang whaleboats over the side for easy launching—three on the port, or left side, and two on the right, or starboard side. To give the entirely useful a touch of elegance, the ports in her black hull had been painted white to give her a longer, more rakish look—something popular with older captains like Williams.

There remained the ticklish problem of getting Eliza on board without using a gangplank. In contrast to her tall husband, the woman, who was under a hundred pounds, was tiny—standing straight, she could fit under his outstretched arm without touching it. With a deck, on average, ten or more feet above the waterline, depending on the water's mood, usually a mariner precariously climbed up the chain plates hand over hand to the shrouds (the ropes fastened to the mastheads). Completing this transaction sounds simpler than it was to execute, particularly on a swelling sea when a boat might rise up as high as the ship's bulwarks, and in a second fall halfway back down again to the keelson. Boarding demanded a great deal of skill and split-second timing. These were quickly developed, otherwise if a strong wave smashed into the boat and sent it flying against the hull, a whaleman risked having a limb pinched or smashed between them. To keep the operation simple and safe, the crew employed block and tackle to hoist Eliza in an armchair, which seemed to her "quite a novel way" of entrance and increased her sense of awkwardness. Already she'd accurately guessed how hard it would be for her on a whaler with "so many Men and not one Woman beside myself."

On board, Eliza was in sight of nearby Clark's Point, a small flat promontory jutting into Buzzards Bay—she was just off the edge of New Bedford and the dry, fixed world she'd known all her life. In addition to the city poorhouse, the point also supported a rubblestone lighthouse to help mariners plow through the often misty and dangerous waters nearby. The officers held the roll call immediately, and all hands were found on board, which wasn't surprising. Usually the crew came over the side the day before sailing, after which the vessel left the wharf and anchored in the harbor, which had the advantage of discouraging any anxious mariners from last-minute flight.

Just like Williams, these recruits were plucked mostly from the small towns of New England, although there was a troublesome blacksmith from New York City. There was also one of the near-ubiquitous Irish, a doomed race that was engaged in perhaps the largest diaspora in history while trying to stay a step ahead of starvation—it wasn't surprising that one or two displaced Hibernians landed in any given ship's forecastle.

Later, the *Florida* would acquire some Cape Verdeans and Hawaiians to fill out the roster, men whose complete poverty made the absurdly tiny lays that whalers paid seem reasonable compensation.

For the low wages and other reasons, professional merchant mariners typically despised whalers, not wholly without cause, as filthy, incompetent unfortunates incapable of real seamanship and occupying the lowest rung on the maritime ladder. So much of what the blubber hunters did was different, including how they dressed. Rather than uniforms, whalers wore whatever they pleased or could afford, and didn't exactly look like sailors. Moreover, any given ship typically had a share of dupes who'd signed on while drunk—it was said a bottle of gin was good for a signature or an X on a contract. "And many an old Yankee skipper just as soon got his man by liquor as to say his prayers on a Sabbath morning," as one whaler noted. Some captains, it was said, even resorted to using the black-jack to persuade a reluctant prospect to join.

Now one such intoxicated or kidnapped crewman might be coming out of a stupor to find himself on a pitching ship. Head pounding, stomach churning, and about to be divorced from anything like the life he'd known for the next several years, the green hand wouldn't be in the best frame of mind for the voyage's start. Not surprisingly, forlorn countenances on the ship's deck would be common on the day of setting out.

The greenhorns required a rapid breaking-in period. This included training not just in the simplest and most essential tasks, such as how to pull the lines, which itself was an art, but also tutoring in how to ignore the most commonsensical and sanest instincts to hunt with an iron lance the biggest creatures inhabiting the planet. Thus, at least at the start, the men had to be more in awe of the officers than of the sea and the whale. To complete this makeover among his crew, it didn't hurt that Williams was a substantial physical presence whose appearance and temperament would've been appropriate to a Viking chieftain or an Elizabethan swashbuckler. (He was actually the scion of a family of weavers from a tiny inland village in Wales then toiling away in a Connecticut woolen mill.)

Despite youthful bad health, he was strong and quick enough to be a match for a half-dozen men or more at once, as he proved. His son Willie, also a whaleman, later claimed of Williams he was the finest type of man he'd ever known, six feet three in his socks, a giant in those days, broad-shouldered with long, muscular arms that functioned like human pistons. He stood straight as an arrow, or perhaps to be more accurate, the deadly lance that he wielded. At two hundred pounds, he was unburdened of any extra flesh, years of whaling having taken out all excess. If it were any comfort for the recruits, they had a successful master, who at thirty-seven had a reputation that stood out like his height. Williams had already survived whaling for nearly two decades, itself not a small feat, and proven himself worthy of the trust the owners had placed in him to manage their fat investment. A natural leader, he was fearless without being reckless, and if anyone could get the ship out and back in the least time with fewest deaths and most whales taken—it was him.

At the beginning of every voyage, as tradition demanded, the mate walked back to the quarterdeck to tell the captain the crewmen were assembled in the waist, (the section of deck before the mainmast on either side of the main hatch). Putting aside his role as husband to become master of men, Williams left his wife to begin the ritual that was the setting out on a ship, which included arranging the boat crews and watches. The four mates and the captain, one after the other, selected the men for their boat crews in the same way boys pick a team to play baseball (which, at that time, was a fairly obscure game awaiting the Civil War to give it a massive boost in exposure and popularity). The older, more veteran whalers were the best candidates, and after they'd been picked, there was nobody left but the green hands, who generally knew no more about sailing or whaling than they did about flying to the moon. A master or other officer sized up the recruit on the spot to decide whether his presence in the officer's boat might mean his death and that of everyone else in it.

As part of the ceremony, Williams delivered a speech to lay down the law of the sea, which, according to some, went back to Noah. Certainly it was as harsh and inflexible as the instructions of Jehovah to the Hebrews of antiquity; accordingly, infractions were punished in an Old Testament fashion. Williams let the men know what he expected of them: each boat crew would serve a watch, usually about four hours long, during which they would carry out duties such as steering the ship or standing lookout. A Williams litany ran like this: Orders must be executed promptly and without question—on this depended the safety of the ship and all in her. Every command would be enacted, and every punishment enforced, no matter what the consequences to the man who disobeyed. There were rules of etiquette, for instance, when on deck and not on duty, a crewman must stay forward of the waist, or the after end of the tryworks. To speak to the captain, he must get the permission of the officer of the deck—even if the master was standing nearby. The master would offer them such sensible advice as learning the complexities of the ship's rigging, and assure them they'd have fair treatment. The watches on the *Florida* fixed, the speech given, the adventure, for those who viewed a whaling voyage as such, had begun.

The schooling for the largely helpless, pathetic, and bewildered greenhorn just entering the threshold of his mariner's career was brief and rough. The officers went to work hard and fast to provide for these novices a nautical education, and in a short time, these "greenies," as first mate Samuel Morgan called them, could make sense of the spider's web of rigging that powered the ship. They'd know the names of the many lines and sails and would be steeled to chase leviathans in every water and clime. Looking on, Eliza found the ship's unfolding operations just as meaningless and confusing as the rest of the new recruits, and decided she would've proved a "dull scholar."

Still plagued by a light wind but not wanting to go back ashore for the night, Williams chartered a tug steamer to hook on to the *Florida* and pull her out of Buzzards Bay into open ocean. Buzzards Bay was thirty miles long, with two dangerous high and low tides daily, as well as fogs and shoals. Its north side ran up to the armpit of Cape Cod, where a canal now lies. The bay's southeastern side was shielded by the small, scraggly chain of Elizabeth Islands, each separated by treacherous channels, the most ferocious of which divided Woods Hole on the mainland of Cape Cod from Nonamessett Island; daily, the gut there ran with unpredictable currents and ever-changing and dangerous rapids.

Forming the final southwestern link of the sixteen-mile-long chain sat the small, dangerous, and flat island of Cuttyhunk, which, when not obscured by the frequent mist, rises up starkly from the Atlantic. A mile to the west of Cuttyhunk, hovering lethally just under the surface of the choppy waters, ran the long, narrow Sow and Pigs Reef. Its presence helped make this region of ocean a graveyard for mariners. The fact that the unwary or unlucky sailor could easily meet his fate here didn't go unnoticed by the residents of Cuttyhunk. Its inhabitants had earned a somewhat dark reputation for moving their beacon lights to deceive mariners and to try to make them crash their vessels on the reef or on their own shore where they might be either killed or robbed. A practice known locally as "moon-cussing" developed: This involved a would-be wrecker trying to move the beacons under the cover of night; if the moon happened to shine down and reveal him, he cursed it.

On the bay's landward side, the rocky coast was a series of wild-looking jagged indents that on a map resembled a jigsaw puzzle half completed. Some explorer, having seen the ospreys and other birds flying over its waters, had given the bay its unflattering and inaccurate name. Behind lay Clark's Point and its lighthouse: the vanishing sight of the latter's white towering sides and lantern top surrounded by its iron network stuck with a whaler for the rest of his life. At 5:00 P.M., the fumbling crew managed to drop sails and the ship entered the open sea, all the while the officers very publicly and rapidly pointed out the neophytes' mistakes. The new hands were tormented by those from the front of the ship, as well as the back—the greenies said odd things that made the old salts laugh at them, as Samuel Morgan noted in his log. When the green hands began to fall prey to seasickness, as they invariably did, the mirth of the veteran sailors only increased. To add to their woes, new sailors working the tar-covered lines with their tender hands often left blood on the ropes and canvas.

Going downstairs to the aft cabin and leaving the busy deck behind, Eliza found a living space that was shrunken into an area only a portion of the size of what she'd enjoyed back in Wethersfield. The ship had two cabins, with the rear farthermost holding a built-in upholstered sofa, mounted on the ship's transom (the beams that ran across the sternpost and supported the stern frame). Next to the sofa on the port side was a stateroom that housed the only other touch of voluptuousness on board: the bed. It was fairly large, given the tight space, and the bedstead was mounted on some sort of runner, so that if the weather wasn't too rough, it could swing to mask the rocking of the ship from the sleeper. Behind the berth was a water closet to serve the body's necessities in private.

The ceiling was low, as in all whalers, and while that didn't affect Eliza, her tall husband must have found it an ever-present challenge not to whack his great head. The main cabin had an overhead skylight for illumination and air, and through the glass Williams could call down to her from the deck. He tried to civilize and make comfortable these quarters for his wife, managing to fit a rocking chair inside, although it was lashed down to prevent skidding when the ship was in rough seas. Lodged in the ship's bowels, Eliza, in a type of shock, didn't quite feel like she was in a home yet. Making the situation more poignant for her, she'd also left behind two young sons, Thomas Stancel, a smart lad attending school up in Boston, and Henry Williams. Every time she thought of the abandoned home in New England, her heart ached painfully for them, her parents, and friends. The family dog had run away somewhere in New Bedford, and she comforted herself that now, at least, she'd a geranium to pet; there was also a kitten on board. She concluded that "the little Cabin that is to be all my own is quite pretty; as well as I can wish, or expect on board of a Ship."

But she'd be sharing this floating several-story rooming house with thirty men as well. As was customary, the first officer had a small cubby space to himself, while the lesser mates shared quarters. These lodgings weren't much to brag about—but they were more spacious and comfortable than what the crew shared among themselves in the forecastle. The steward who'd usurped Eliza's position as head of domestic affairs called her to dinner in a private saloon amidships in the stern. This area was reserved for the officers and the captain, and given the small quarters, if the mates and Eliza didn't get along, it could be hell for everyone. It was odd for her to be eating a meal prepared by a cook who toiled away in a galley on deck far aft, instead of by her own hand. She noted immediately the bread was hard—whaling biscuit could break teeth unless softened. The drinking water was poor, and would take a long time to get used to, but, overall, the food would be not unlike what she ate in Connecticut, with rice and beans and whatever other provisions on hand constituting the menu. For fresh meat, whalers carried a small pen on deck where hogs and chickens spent their days awaiting slaughter for the exclusive digestion of the "after gang" of master, officers, and harpooners.

As in the lodgings, the crew's fare was different. They sat around a wooden tub on the floor of the forecastle or on deck and used their knives to cut out and gobble down hunks of "salt horse." This dish, the main staple of whaling men, depending on the agent doing the outfitting, was sometimes made of the worst cuts of beef or pork—including the pig's snout. In order to preserve it at sea, it was reputedly as salty as Lot's wife. The stories of captains, often at the urging of the owners, skimping on food when provisioning the ship, were common, and the fare often provoked complaints from the men. When the meat casks were opened, the contents, years-old, might be rancid and greenish or even downright putrid, and the stench could infiltrate the entire ship. One Rhode Island whaler said after dipping his bread in his coffee, he could skim weevils from it. On that ship, the captain reportedly was especially mean. Wishing to deny his men the pleasure of the rare treat of butter, he poured sperm oil into the butter keg so that he could at least claim the stuff was on board even if it was inedible.

On the other hand, some men didn't mind nautical fare. According to one old salt: "Yer may talk of flumadiddlers and fiddlepaddles, but when it comes down to gen-u-ine grub, there ain't nothing like good old salt hoss that yer kin eat afore yer turns in and feel it all night a-laying in yer stummick and a-nourishing yer." When lucky, if the captain and owners were generous, and often they weren't, the men were treated to duff—a steamed pudding made of flour, shortening, and dried fruit, served with molasses or other sweetener, and sometimes baked into a pastry. So desirable was this nautical confection, stopping the crew's ration of it amounted to punishment.

The ship ploughed on south into Rhode Island Sound, a stretch of water that edged Narragansett Bay. The wind picked up as the *Florida* ran on, and with the help of a spyglass courtesy of Mr. Fish, Eliza took in some of the new sights. To the east, she saw what she thought was a town, but was merely Gay Head, the desolate and eerily beautiful pastel-colored clay bluffs that formed the western end of Martha's Vineyard. The soft cliffs appeared red, pink, or ocher and a thousand other blended hues, depending on distance, the time of day, the sun, and weather; like all waterside promontories, they were prone to a haunting and otherworldly look, presuming a mariner paused to regard them, for he'd work to do in the Bay. Near Aquinnah, the aboriginal name of the point, survived some of the first whalers of New England—the Wampanoag Indians, who'd inhabited the island for centuries before disease, slavery, and shock had winnowed them to a tiny powerless band hovering near extinction.

Eliza discovered that to the landward side lay Newport, Rhode Island, just now invisible except for a large building called the Ocean House. Newport was a fine and respectable port town, which, like Boston, was once long ago favored by pirates looking to unload their ill-gotten booty. Eliza stayed on deck to watch the tug steamer as it faded from sight on the return voyage to beautiful New Bedford, carrying her brothers and the pilot, as well as a boatsteerer (harpooner), who, "sick of his bargain," was also leaving the ship. She kept staring westward until the last curl of smoke from the tug's stack rose up into the sky and the vessel had disappeared completely. Then she went back down below.

Before catching the first sleep of his voyage, Morgan worked at the ship's log, which it was his legal duty to keep. With a firm, clear, but not overly elegant hand, he noted the lighthouse from Gay Head was sparkling in the night and that the smooth water and the gentle wind had seduced the men into thinking they wouldn't become seasick. He also noted: "Those who have been to sea before knowing the time that must elapse before they return and the hardships they will endure look low spirited and dejected." He wasn't the only log keeper that night, for Eliza began her own diary, recording thoughts she couldn't tell anyone else on the ship. To the blank page she confessed it was too gloomy to recall her home, children, friends, and parents. Having given her last kiss and dropped her final farewell tear, she steeled herself not to despair or even to think of the long voyage ahead. The woman decided, in the face of this awful looming self-exile, to put her trust in the "all wise and good God, and hope for the best."

She also put faith in her tall husband, between whom and God, in her eyes, there probably wasn't too vast a difference. Eliza told herself: "I shall be lonely, though not alone, for I have a kind husband with me." Her day's writing completed, she'd begun what became a sensitive woman's three-year-long running counterpoint to Morgan's blunt and unsentimental log.

> He was a killer, a thing that preyed, living on the things that lived, unaided, alone, by virtue of his own strength and prowess, surviving triumphantly in a hostile environment where only the strong survived. Because of all this he became possessed of a

great pride in himself, which communicated itself like a contagion to his physical being.

— JACK LONDON, *The Call of the Wild*

The first night in the forecastle—or anywhere else on board—was hard on a recruit. Take, for example, the green hand's experience of Jared Jernegan of Martha's Vineyard. In 1839, as a small thirteen-year-old, he signed on all his ninety-two pounds to go whaling on the *Alexander Barclay*. Misery was soon his lot: After the ship left Edgartown, he got seasick and, once asleep, dreamed his father and mother were swimming in the *Barclay*'s wake to return him home—he admitted later he was a "hard looking subject to go to sea." Nevertheless, he refused to ask for discharge. As bad as whaling was, the boy was sure the laughter of the lads on the Vineyard would've been worse. Yet this cabin boy had some spirit, which he soon displayed. While carrying some hot coffee, the ship's steward tried to hurry Jernegan's progress at the point of a carving knife. Young Jared dumped the scalding brew over the man's head, after which "he gave me plenty of room." Instead of punishment, the master sent the "scamp" into the forecastle, possibly realizing such a lad should be put to use in the killing of leviathans.

A whaler's forecastle was a dungeon, school, and refuge all in one. Called the "black hole of Calcutta," this triangular compartment belowdeck in the extreme front of the ship had two-tiered bunks that each carried a straw mattress, called a "donkey's breakfast." Here the men slept as comfortably as they could when off their watches. A drawn curtain was about the only bit of privacy a seaman got, and lacking benches, he resorted to sitting on his sea chest for recreation and dining. The crowded, stifling, and mephitic area wasn't made for comfort: Seawater often leaked in, and it became an oven in hot climes and a freezer in northern ones. Moreover, white men had to submit to the indignity of sharing quarters with Portuguese, Africans, and Hawaiians—whom as often as not they called 'Gees, Niggers, and Kanakas, respectively. (The Yankees pronounced Kanaka "Kanacker"; the word was also applied erroneously to all Polynesians.) Not only were there men of different races, there were Catholics, too, whom most Protestants, those of New Bedford in particular, viewed as followers of a lunatic Roman idolatry that beneficent contact with America might help them outgrow—like a childhood disease.

Whatever their religion, class, or race on land, in the ship's nose these mariners became an uneasy family of men doing everything together. In addition to the human company, there were rats, cockroaches, bedbugs, and fleas that managed to get under the skin and into the mattresses and even the food. If one cried, it was in private—weakness just wouldn't do on a whaler. The singular advantage of the forecastle was that the officers avoided it.

For diversion, when not plotting to kill or maim their officers, or dictating their wills, they told stories, inscribed tattoos, sang, danced, smoked, played cards, fought, or read. Obviously, in that womanless dungeon they had sexual needs that they could satisfy only by resorting to solo pleasures. In maritime parlance, joint indulgence in this practice was known as a "chaw for a chaw." No master is known to have punished a man for it— presumably, if he was caught, it was by accident—although there were cases of attempted rape, which resulted in discharge or flogging—for the perpetrator, at least.

Before he became a master, Williams himself had served his time before the mast. The forecastle became young Thom Williams's lodgings after he'd fled his landlocked home in Wethersfield when he shipped out on the whaler *Albion* two decades earlier. It was that vessel that first provided him with lodgings, a job, and a makeshift family for two years during his initial apprenticeship in the industry. His nostrils had never before inhaled anything like the forecastle's noxious mix of blubber, urine, tobacco, sweat, blood, and, perhaps, fear. The blend of humanity surrounding him was probably similar to that of many other voyages: baby-faced waifs with the "hayseed still in their hair," wharf rats, dispossessed farmers, millworkers, and near criminals, and, perhaps, some able-bodied seamen unable to make officer. The only contact some had ever had with the whaling industry was having been licked with a whip crafted of whalebone. Like them, Williams had to squeeze his bulk into the small bunk space in the forecastle.

Before leaving Wethersfield, he told his mother of his plans to run away and sign on in the whale fishery. Connecticut had its own whaling port, New London, whose fleet traveled to the Arctic and also specialized in hunting whales down in the aptly named Desolation Island chain near Antarctica. Nevertheless, the magical gravity of New Bedford in its proverbial golden age drew Williams in. Whaling then was still in its prime. The prey was more plentiful and, as some of the old-timers later grumbled, the men greater seamen than in later years. Outside of physical strength, young Thom had little in his favor. The blood in his veins wasn't that which ran in those of the lords of New Bedford, such as the Howlands, or the three "R" families, the Russells, Rotches, or Rodmans, and lacking any onboard connections or protectors to look after him, Williams had as much going for him as most of the other recruits who'd voluntarily made themselves virtual orphans. No sailor, his one taste of the sea had been when at age nine he crossed the Atlantic in the steerage compartment of a sailing packet, emigrating from Wales to America with his family.

His people, Welshmen, knew of the whale fishery, except that those who engaged in it frequently returned home missing an arm or a leg. Just why Williams had abandoned home to ship out isn't clear, as he'd just finished his term as an apprentice toolmaker in a blacksmith's shop. Nevertheless, the big, strong teenager chanced to cross paths with one Andrew Potter, a recruiting agent, who signed him on. Perhaps life indoors didn't suit Williams—for example, when younger, while toiling as a weaver, his health had soured. Rather then go west or enter the merchant marine or navy, he went whaling.

Given the fact it was the new center of the whaling industry, New Bedford, like a whirlpool, drew in all types, and young Williams must have gaped at the sights. The city was the sort of place to give any fresh-faced young boy off the farm—arriving by foot, packet, train, or stagecoach—pause, and not just to gag from the exquisitely wretched stench of whale oil. It was a "queer place," claimed Melville, who shipped out on the whaler *Acushnet* at about the same time as Williams launched his career. Men of many complexions and tongues ranged up and down New Bedford's narrow cobblestone lanes. One could see "cannibals stand chatting at street corners" along with "the wild specimens of the whaling-craft which unheeded reel about the streets," as Melville described it.

In the mix were green hands, often brawny sodbusters from New York, New Hampshire, and Vermont—some as "green as the green Mountains from which they had come." One also saw grave Quaker blubber barons, easily recognized by their broad-brimmed hats, dark clothes, and severe gazes; they merited some deference as the most eminent men of the city. Some New Bedford merchants knew how to play the role of men of "great affairs," with beaver hats, gold watch fobs, and the crucial air of self-importance. Such capitalists had a right to be puffed up: They had coolly matched their wits, money, and property—and the lives of men—against the elements in a huge game of chess, and had become wealthy doing so.

The financial rape of the greenhorns (whose services made whaling merchants rich) by shrewd and unscrupulous agents was infamous. When recruiting for the ship, an agent preparing the vessel sometimes handed over a hapless and unsuspecting teenager to "land sharks," or outfitters, who charged too much for gear, and then the agent gave them the most miserable lays possible. Agents would largely tell the rube what he wanted to hear. "Now, Hiram, I'll be honest with yer," said one famous Boston whaling agent to a Maine farm boy. "When yer out in the boats chasin' whales, yer git yer mince pie cold!"

The soon-to-be victim just off the farm put his scrawl or X down on the ship's roster, sometimes demanding the denominator of his lay be as high as possible—not knowing that it translated to the lowest possible profit for himself. Along Water Street, there were rows of dreary inns and rooming houses for recruits and experienced whaling men to waste their last few days on shore; nearby were taverns where they could spend their last few dollars as well. Often, someone kept an eye on the recruit and made sure he found his way to his vessel, keeping him from defrauding the land shark who'd given him an advance on his wages and paid his rooming house and gear costs. The city was also a rough place, housing neighborhoods where "delirium and death were sold," and where "female harpies reigned."

Nevertheless, during this optimistic time, any fool easily could (and many did) believe he just might make a fortune, as unlikely as that was. Marking her rise, New Bedford was about to repay Nantucket, her parent, by wresting the blubber-hunting laurels from the island. In 1839, of 498 ships in the American fishery, 212 were from New Bedford and Fairhaven. On the high end of the seesaw, the small metropolis was becoming the "fishiest" of cities, with riches from every ocean on the globe pouring in. In this town, recounted Melville, fathers gave whales for dowers to their rosy-cheeked daughters, "and portion[ed] off their nieces with a few porpoises a-piece." There, the bright white light of spermaceti candles made for a "brilliant wedding."

At the waterfront, wharf after wharf invaded the river's course, enabling New Bedford to become one of the premier American maritime ports. Among rivals that could be counted on one hand—in terms of shipping volume—New Bedford was port number five, just behind Baltimore. After stealing himself from his master, the onetime slave Frederick Douglass arrived at the Acushnet's west bank in 1837. He was astonished: "Here I found myself surrounded with the strongest proofs of wealth," he later wrote. "Lying at the wharves, and riding in the stream, I saw many ships of the finest model, in the best order, and of the largest size. Upon the right and left, I was walled in by granite warehouses of the widest dimensions, stowed to their utmost capacity with the necessaries and comforts of life."

Muscular workmen supported the industry by forging irons, shaping barrel staves, or stitching sails, working smoothly, quietly, and with dignity, said Douglass. He may have been jaundiced, given his background, but at least he could see these toilers didn't live like slaves. There were also factories, such as the Rodman Candleworks on Water Street, which turned sperm oil into fine tapers. But there was more than just industry, Douglass observed as he walked on: There were churches with fine steeples, plush houses and gardens to admire, and he felt it was a town of comfort, taste, and refinement. "Every thing looked clean, new, and beautiful."

At the dizzying apex of this economic pyramid were the owners of the fleet, who toiled in iron-railed, looming Dickensian countinghouses of stone or brick in which no empty space or clerk escaped use. The first floors of these temples of commerce usually housed chandlery shops; the third floors, rigging and sail lofts; on the second floor the owners' offices. Here the clerks stood or, if their employers were indulgent, sat on high seats behind mahogany desks on which lay ledgers on whose pages they translated a whaling voyage into profits and losses. Sometimes they counted money for sober, thrifty Quaker employers who accumulated more than they could have spent even if they'd indulged in every sensual fantasy known to man—something a Friend was not likely capable of.

Around these clerks were shelves carrying metal or wooden boxes, each one labeled with the name of a ship and stuffed with all that vessel's pertinent documents. Under the watchful eyes of the owners, no one's mind ever strayed far from the task at hand. The diversion of art was just a reminder of their business: Even the walls carried paintings of whaleships. On Merrill's wharf the most successful merchant of them all, Jonathan Bourne, had sealed his prosperity by building a gabled countinghouse of granite that looked as if it could weather the ages—if not the disappearance of the whales themselves. (It remains today, along with the town of Bourne on Cape Cod, in whose environs he was the most eminent citizen.)

A whaler was often the worst possible school for young men, as those attracted to the life were generally not interested in improving their souls. It took a strong will to survive, but some of the men who emerged from the forecastle, like Williams, were among the greatest mariners of their time; possibly ever. By 1851, the keel well laid, ribs and caulking sound, and the last touches to the rigging and canvas in place, his career was fully launched when, not yet thirty and recently married, he took command of the *South Boston*. He was fairly young to be a master—and many whalers never made it out of the forecastle at any age. This first reputation-making voyage netted $140,000, the sort of figure that would make even the most pious Quaker's heart beat in an unspiritual fashion. Williams's own lay allowed him to go home to Connecticut a man of substance—which was just as well, because there was a two-year-old son awaiting him.

With his cash, he acquired a hundred-acre farm, bought cattle in Vermont, and herded them back himself to Wethersfield to graze on the land. There was even money enough left over to buy other businesses—including the old tool shop he'd apprenticed in—although he ran it under the old name. It was common for whaling masters to buy a plot of land where they hoped someday to retire, but if that had been his goal, it appears the gods of the sea had other plans.

This narrative will spend most of its time with this captain from Wethersfield, his wife, and their children. By and large, the story will see the industry reflected through the prism of their point of view. For four decades, from roughly 1840 to 1880, Williams's career itself mirrored the arc of the fishery itself. There were dozens of contemporary shipmasters not wholly unlike Williams, equally successful and colorful, each facing troughs and peaks in their vocations—like a ship plowing through the waters. This one particular whaling family offers a window into the lives of scores of other families living at this time. Because the Williamses were present at the defining and tragic events that finished off the whaling fleet of New England, we can take advantage of their firsthand reports. They are a thread that ties together the final episodes of a grand industry and adventure.

Where thou goest, I will go. —RUTH 1:16

If Thomas William Williams loved anything more than his wife and family, it was whaling. Because of this, Williams was writing a new chapter in the history of his career. Having stolen Eliza away from a quiet, staid existence in Connecticut and having made her part of his crew, he'd become both husband and captain to her. It wasn't a glamorous adventure awaiting her, either. A whaleship was little more than a floating penal colony for prisoners sentenced to years of hard labor, and in constant danger of sinking. If it was of any comfort to her, Eliza wasn't the only woman of the time who'd been dragged into the misery of the whale fishery. Besides whores and promiscuous native females, masters' wives had of late been going on board to keep their husbands company at sea. Their presence might even give a measure of respectability and decency to a voyage, as whalemen putting into port after months, if not years at sea, were notorious for going berserk with liquor and fornication. The temptations—when the men were lucky enough to enjoy them—were considerable.

Take, for example, one Captain Dexter of Connecticut, and master of the whaler *Cavalier*. In 1850, after simultaneously enjoying the favors of two women in his cabin, he passed them to the officers, and then to the crew, not knowing they carried then-incurable syphilis. After this particularly excessive debauch, he complained that "we are half drunk the other half fucked to death."

Into this womanless world Eliza had plunged. Photos of her show a lean face with clean skin under curled hair, with wide, delicate eyes that give a hint of her sensitivity and kindness. Below a long nose is a firm, resolute mouth that carries a serious but gentle expression, a product of her New England reserve and formality, in keeping with being the offspring of a staid old family, the Griswolds. They'd a long time to learn composure, as their roots in Wethersfield had first been sunk in 1645.

Even in her diary, the man with whom she shared her bed, table, and life was almost always "My Husband," never Thomas. Indeed, it had been her almost morbid sensitivity that had pulled her into the midst of the water. Her nature had cringed at engaging in the grubby transactions that were part of conducting her husband's business on shore. This commerce required her to collect money owed and reinvest it, and being shy, she decided to face the monsters of the deep on the *Florida* rather than Wethersfield's debtors.

There were other reasons for her departure. Given his whaling peregrinations, Williams had been away much of the time since their marriage. Three months after they'd exchanged vows in a Congregational Church, in April 1851, he sailed out as master of the *South Boston,* starting a habit of long separation that was just now being broken. Being widowed for years at a time was hard for her, and his letters, arriving months after their writing and telling her of his loneliness, became too painful for her to read. So, unable to hold him back, she'd followed in his wake.

The first morning out, going up on the bustling deck, Eliza found herself surrounded by the strange sight of the "vast deep" with only sky and water visible. Sunrise on the sea, listening to the ripples of the water and watching the foam as the bow parted the waves, was eerie and beautiful. First, a red disc appeared in the east, colored like a wound, and the water changed in color from ink to lead, and then to blood. Finally, daylight illumined all that emptiness, and it seemed as if the entire universe had radically evolved. The ocean sunrise "gives one a feeling of loneliness, of dread, and of melancholy foreboding, which nothing else in nature can give," as writer Charles Henry Dana noted. "This gradually passes away as the light grows brighter, and when the sun comes up, the ordinary monotonous sea day begins."

Eliza soon found the deck hosted in its small area a handful of workshops catering to various craftsmen: sailmaker, blacksmith, carpenter, and cooper included. These busy men made her feel lazy, for she, unlike the crew, had no fixed routine to observe. Such workers were indispensable on board virtually any vessel, but especially a whaler, whose function was unique in maritime commerce. For instance, whalers didn't sail like a cargo ship from port to port to pick up and discharge goods as quickly as possible. They were workhorses built for endurance and strength, designed to wander and hunt over wide areas of ocean and free to take their time about it. Like a cell in a body when injured, such a ship possessed the resources to rebuild herself from the many spare parts she carried. This allowed her to stay at sea for years if need be, should she be unlucky, before returning to home port. Capable of navigation in the unforgiving northern seas, the *Florida* had a sheath of copper or some other metal over her hull below the waterline to help prevent rot and teredo (marine worm) infiltration, to ward off ice floes, and to guard against reefs.

But the ship couldn't shield the distressed stomachs and heads of the greenhorns from the effects of the rise and fall of the ocean. The reaction to the rocking of a ship that is seasickness can be a very subtle thing at first, starting with mild queasiness and a sense of unease. Eventually, it enlarges to become an all-powerful adversary that grips its victim in a torture worthy of Dante's *Inferno*. The second night, whether because of her pregnancy or the *Florida*'s motion, the telltale queasiness of this invisible force gripped Eliza. Nevertheless she braved the sensation to answer her husband's call to come join him up the quarterdeck to watch a "splendid" sun sink into the ocean. Such sunsets, along with the smell and feel of air heavy with salt and the cleansing effect of the ocean on the brain, were among the simple comforts of sea life to offset the many inconveniences.

The other onboard pleasures were precious few, and on the *Florida* they included the occasional fiddle playing of Tim Reed, a "colored" harpooner. One night with the moon reflecting beautifully on the water, she listened to Reed play, while overhead there was the additional spectacle of a streaking comet. Not only did he provide music, Reed was also the best boatsteerer on board—and although African, his high status wasn't unique in the fishery. The Yankee whaling fleet, in part revealing its Quaker roots, was happy to exploit free labor of any color or shape, including African Americans. As whaling was a true meritocracy, blacks rose to the status of mates and even captains. (One such man was Quaker Paul Cuffe, a mixed Native American Wampanoag-black, who became a whaling master and merchant with his own crew of African sailors. There was also the clever African blacksmith Lewis Temple, who, in 1848, first invented the Temple toggle harpoon that was, to a whale stuck with it, an awful torture, but to its hunter a way of more tightly securing himself to

floating wealth. As Temple never patented the invention, he didn't receive a dime from those who copied his design, although it enabled the
moneyed to get a much better return on their investment in whaling gear.)
Career mariner Reed's skill in sticking leviathan was noted and respected
onboard, and first mate Morgan, on whose whaleboat crew he served,
thought highly of him. A cheerful fellow, Reed always had a smile for
Eliza.

The *Florida* was due to sail east through the sperm whale grounds that
lay toward the coast of Africa. From there, she was bound for the Indian
Ocean via the Cape of Good Hope. The presence of whales was highly desirable during the transit. With luck, the monotony would be broken when
the lookouts, standing at their giddy height in the masts' crosstrees, cried
out, "There blows!" with the word "blows" drawn out. Willie Williams,
who once described what a hunt was like on his father's ship, said the cry
electrified the ship, with every hand snapping to attention.

Next, Williams would climb into the rigging carrying a spyglass to confirm the sighting. Asking "Where away?" the lookout gave him the compass
point, and Williams scanned the horizon for the desired prey. If luck was
with the ship and the lookout's eyes hadn't deceived him, he was owed a
reward of extra tobacco, and Williams ordered the boats lowered. If not,
the crew would go back to the usual tedium of waiting.

The actual hunting and full-blown nausea started at about the same
time. On September 9, the *Florida*'s lookouts spotted the dark forms of a
school of blackfish—pilot whales. Rarely longer than twenty feet, these
mammals have the benign-looking snout and eyes of a dolphin, as well as
their long, elegant bodies and scimitar-shaped dorsal fins. While offering
poor oil, the blackfish provided a teaching prop for whaleship officers to
tutor the greenhorns in how to kill his larger and more profitable cetacean
cousins. While Eliza watched the blackfish playing, unconscious of their
danger, the ship's crew went "crazy" and scrambled to drop their whaleboats
from the davits and give chase. Had she enjoyed spectacles of torture and violence, Eliza might have relished having this front-row seat to competitions
not even the spectacle-mad Romans had ever laid eyes on: the grisly and exciting contest between man and the largest beast in the world. Whale killing
was perhaps the most dangerous profession of its time—certainly, at some
moments, it was the most exciting.

Small and squeamish Eliza hated blood—and a slain whale spilled that by the gallon. As much as the hunting and killing made the small Yankee matron squirm, it electrified her husband, the man who commanded the whaleship *Florida* and all on board. Williams dropped his boat to hunt whales whenever he could, unlike some captains, who were content to let the crew handle the most dangerous end of this job.

After the *Florida*'s crewmen harpooned and killed a few of the blackfish, they took the corpses on deck, tore the blubber off for boiling, and threw the carcasses overboard. This seemed "mighty fine sport" to the men, who thought whaling was "all fun," said the mate. That opinion changed the next day as squalls began to blow from the east and rain pelted the decks. The ship rocked violently, the men became "sick as dogs" and unable to eat and said they'd "willingly die if they could get ashore." Some were so ill they lay on the soaking decks with the sea washing over them and offered to forfeit their pay if they could just be left alone. It didn't do any good, as no one died from a little nausea. (A popular treatment, or punishment, for such green hands was to put a piece of raw pork tied to a string down their throats and pull it back up again.)

All the consolation the *Florida*'s mates offered were commands to work: "Come, get up out of that, for it will do you no good to lay there," or "You are not half as sick as you think you are." Those on the deck of a whaleship became targets of plummeting vomit from any seasick men above in the rigging. Old salt Morgan, realizing the magnitude of the voyage he'd set out on, began to feel as if he'd imprisoned himself "for an age." It was also hard on Eliza, who was sick for nine straight days and lay in bed, "perpetual motion" filling her head, and unable to sit or keep food down.

From above, she could hear the mates' bellows, and the rattling of the sails and ropes in the strong wind; in the cabin, about everything was on the move, including dishes, which crashed occasionally. This voyage was already proving very hard on her. Certainly, there was never a less likely candidate for whaling than she. Yet this tiny woman, who probably had never been more than a few miles from her hometown before this trip, flitted all over the Pacific Ocean for three years, from Russia to the Hawaiian Islands to California and Mexico and a dozen places in between. Despite the miles covered, it was still a limited life. Usually a woman never went farther forward than amidships—even as the crew never went rearward past the tryworks. There was very little for her to do, as the ship was solely under the control of men. She kept to her place and didn't interfere with the crew and cause them to resent her. They responded to her kindness, and even brought her flowers or fruit—not every whaling captain's wife was so popular.

By month's end, Eliza got to see her first sperm whale, a dead calf, killed just before dark. For many years, after the depletion of the right whales off New England, the sperm had been the primary target of the Yankee whale fishery. While the cachalot carried excellent and abundant oil, he could be a mean, vicious fighter who might strike even if he wasn't in danger, and was generally afraid of nothing—except possibly a pod of killer whales—or a whale killer like Williams. Generally, he fed on squid, which he caught, reportedly, by just opening his jaws. The squid "walks right into the whale's mouth like a half-drunken boatsteerer going into the bridal suite of a hotel, and there he makes himself comfortable," as one Yankee master observed. By the time the squid realized his predicament it was too late.

A bull sperm was known to "fight at both ends." He could use his tail like a war mace or he might turn on the boat and smash the craft with his head or crush it in his jaws. He had teeth set in his long narrow jaw, unlike a baleen whale, and could bite down, hard, if not evenly, and some whalers trapped in the sperm's mouth had managed to wriggle free. If a sperm was real ornery—and some were—he might try to swallow a man or two, although the story of Jonah had proven such fare went against his digestion. The very worst of these monsters could even attack and sink the mother ship itself, as the unfortunate men of the *Essex* had so famously and miserably discovered forty years before.

Whalemen of the day practiced an ancient art, and key to its prosecution was the harpoon, which consisted of a razor-sharp barbed iron a couple of feet in length, usually of malleable Russian iron, with single or double flues, mounted by a socket into a wooden handle fastened to a line. When sunk into a whale, an "iron," as Yankee whalers generally called it, was unlikely to come free. The single-flue iron had a toggle pin that let the head pivot into a T configuration, and it gripped the tough blubber as

persistently as a shipowner clutched at his profits. Usually before dropping into their boats, whalemen honed their irons and checked their lines
and other gear. The white cedarwood whaleboats, some thirty feet in
length and six feet wide and as streamlined and seaworthy as a dolphin,
dangled over the water and could be dropped quickly. Because of a
whaleboat's relative fragility, a ship would usually carry a spare lashed to
the deck. Inside each whaleboat was a keg of water, a compass, and a
lantern, among other essential items, such as tobacco and pipes. Successfully lowering boats down the falls, the system of tackle and blocks that
held them, was an art. A boatheader, either a mate or the captain, along
with the harpooner, would climb into the craft, which was dropped with
them inside, sometimes with the ship still in motion. Next, the boat crew
clambered down the falls and took their places for the hunt, all the while
trying to keep the boat from crashing into the ship's hull or dunking them.
Only a few men, such as the cook, remained on board the ship to steer her.

Because this was hunting, not fishing, and whales had excellent hearing, the whaleboats on the *Florida* usually stalked them under sail. That
method of powering the boat was even quieter than rowing, although the
crew's oars were specially padded to prevent any telltale noise from escaping. When close enough, at the mate's signal, the harpooner stood up,
turned, and placed his leg in the clumsy cleat, a horizontal half-moon-
shaped recess in the bow thwart, to brace himself. He would take his iron
from the resting place in the bow—often it was a three-pronged wooden
fork called a "crotch." Then he waited for the signal to strike. The preferred moment of attack was just as the leviathan surfaced; a whaler
studied the water for an especially agitated circle of bubbles boiling on
the surface—this was the top of a column made by the whale's great bulk
rising up.

As the quarry roared up into the air, its hearing was next to useless and
it was at its most vulnerable. At the mate's cry of "Give it to him!" the
boatsteerer (harpooner) darted the iron into the dark, slick back as hard as
he could—provided he didn't lose his nerve. Needless to say, this strike
changed the placid whale's demeanor considerably. Anything might happen: It might strike the boat with its head or flukes, "sulk" (slip below and
wait), or run with the iron planted in its back. After the initial fastening,
the harpooner took a second harpoon that was already bent (fastened)

onto the line, and sank it into the whale. If that was impossible, he flung it over the side or untied the weapon and placed it in its resting spot in the bow—a loose iron flying around in the whaleboat was a wicked thing. If the whale ran, as the boat bounced up and down and from left to right, the men "peaked," or raised, their oars from the water, and the harpooner moved to the back to manage the long steering oar. In turn, the boat's mate moved forward to the bow to take the boatsteerer's place.

The harpoon's line was coiled in two tubs inside the whaleboat. As a stricken monster ran, the line, usually tough Manila hemp, might whiz out of the boat at a dangerous speed—in an eyeblink, a kink could grab a man and pull him under, or catch and tear an arm from its socket. Sometimes, when a whale sounded (dove) too quickly for the men to pay out the line, it might pull the boat down if someone didn't cut it fast enough. To regulate the line's speed, it was wrapped around a loggerhead, a small upright post in the back of the boat. Sometimes the line whipped so fast around the loggerhead it began to smoke, and one man's job was to pour water from a bucket (called a piggin) on it to keep it from catching on fire from the friction. After enough line went out, someone snubbed it fast on the loggerhead, and it went fully taut. Then the boat took a rough and wild ride, courtesy of the leviathan—now commonly called a "Nantucket sleigh ride."

To prepare for another attack, the crew pulled the line back into the boat, hand over hand, to close the space between them and the whale. When in striking distance, it would be time for the mate to exercise the responsibility and privilege of making the kill. In his hands he held the lance, a five-foot-long iron shaft, mounted at one end on a hardwood pole; the other end came to an oval razor-sharp point. The mate hurled the weapon at the victim or stabbed down again and again into a spot behind the fin, where he hoped to find a key network of arteries near the lungs known as the "life." If he punctured this with his weapon, the whale's considerable suffering was soon over. Should the leviathan be very spirited and the mate have a fine and steady touch, he might hamstring the victim with a stroke or two of his lance, severing the dorsal muscle that ran along the monster's back so it couldn't swim or smash at the boat with its flukes.

To better the odds for the whalers, some lethally minded inventors had been improving the fleet's killing technology by introducing gunpowder-ignited weapons. Mates of the time like Morgan usually were armed with a bomb gun, a shoulder-mounted, short-barreled smoothbore that fired an explosive feathered projectile, called a bomb lance, into the whale. The fuse on the lance ignited as it left the muzzle of the gun. Accurate to a range of sixty feet, if aimed right, the projectile sank through the blubber near something vital. After a muffled roar, the whale was soon dead. The methods of finishing a monster off were a tad crude, but effective. Accordingly, a competent mate was rewarded when the animal began to spout blood. When the chimney was "afire," as this was called, it meant it was near death, choking on its own blood. The whale also emptied its bodily contents from both ends—half-digested squid or other such fare came from the mouth, excrement from the rear, all becoming ingredients of a bloody sea ragout. When going into its "flurry," or death throes, the whale swam in a circle and flailed wildly. Then the mate cried, "Stern all."

The men rowed backward away from the soon-to-be corpse and waited in safety until the whale at last went still and rolled to one side, "fin out." To ensure it wasn't playing dead, as some whales did, the mate might put his lance into one of the eyes on the side of the head. Proof of demise secured, the boatheader took a spade and cut a hole in the beast, through which was reeved a line. With the huge cargo in tow, it was time to row it, face first, back to the ship, which hopefully wasn't too far away by now. (Whales sometimes towed the boats out of sight of the ship—leaving the crewmen inside to fend for themselves.)

If a crew had to leave its dead whale behind, perhaps to chase another whale, someone prominently planted in it a small flag called a "waif" to establish ownership and to help keep an eye on the carcass. To that same end, irons were often notched with the initials of the ship's name. It was said a ship's master was a regular Argus when it came to claiming rights to a slain whale, and disputes between rival ships over a corpse were heated. Sometimes these differences of opinion even ended up in court on land. The crews rowing back also had to share their booty with the sea scavengers; invariably after the kill, sharks were attracted by the blood in the water. From the air, if the kill was made near shore, gulls swooped down and turned the water around the whale snow-white and deafened the hunters with their cries.

Having made their kill, the *Florida*'s crew tied the whale carcass along the starboard side for the night to await the sunlight to help them try (render) it out. The corpse, particularly if it had been dead for some time and began to putrify, was dubbed a "stinker"— if enough gasses had accumulated inside and it exploded, it was called "blasted." In any case, a slain whale's inimitably vile stench, arguably, was a form of revenge. A whaler was typically steered to windward to ensure the wind and waves kept the carcass as close to the ship as possible. The next morning during a torrential rain, Williams called the anxiously curious Eliza on deck to see this "queer-looking fish." She found the corpse down in the water below a "mass of flesh," and only the elegant "mouse"-colored fins and flukes redeemed its appearance. Eliza didn't find much beautiful about the animal, and after the men raised it out of the water, the more extensive view she had of it didn't improve her opinion. The long shiny whale was more monster than calf, with a flat, formless head and small, unseeing eyes on each side and a great mouth. Williams, who knew his enemy well, told his wife that, instead of having ears, a whale had holes in its head the size of knitting needles but that its hearing was "very acute."

The process of trying out varied, depending on the type of whale, but there was a general set of methods. To start the butchery, the crew lowered from its resting place the rectangular wooden cutting stage, hardly more than a few connected planks that extended out away from the ship's side over the carcass. This contraption provided a crude platform for the mates and harpooners, armed with long, razor-edged spades, fifteen to twenty feet long, to work from while flensing. One of the butchers on the stage cut a hole in the blubber near the head and fin, and a man, usually one of the harpooners (who took the job in turns), climbed on the whale's back, which was generally submerged. Sometimes up to his neck in seawater and tethered to the ship by a "monkey rope," the man fastened into the initial hole a great hundred-pound blubber hook that had a line fixed to it. This line passed between the stage and the ship and ran to a network of blocks that hung from the main mast and from there to the windlass.

With a crew of men working this engine, usually to the rhythm of a boisterous sea-song, the line connected to the corpse went taut. Every board and nail straining and creaking in protest, the vessel listed to the starboard, toward the whale. At last, the ship, weighed down to one side by the carcass's bulk, stopped rolling on her axis. The men on the stage kept slicing away at the most vulnerable spots, and eventually a great "blanket" sheet of blubber, six feet wide, began to tear off the body. With a snapping noise, the first strip of blubber came off the corpse, and with the release in tension, the ship rolled back to an even keel.

Round and round the whale turned, and aided by the cutting tools, strips of bloody, oily blubber peeled off, as if the men were skinning a massive orange. Whale blubber was uncommonly tough, and the mates and harpooners needed their cutting tools constantly re-sharpened as they mined the whale like expert miners extracting minerals from the bowels of the earth. Once freed, the blanket pieces, weighing tons, were raised to the deck very carefully, as these free-swinging slabs could crush a man or knock him overboard. These pieces, which looked to Eliza as if made of white pork fat, were cut in half and then went into the blubber room belowdecks behind the forecastle. There, in this "reception" room, as Morgan called it, men standing up to their waists in blubber cut it down to "horse" pieces, roughly six feet wide by twenty-four inches long, which eventually were pitched back onto the deck.

The crew dragged the horse pieces to a bench called a "mincing horse" where they laid them skin down. One man used a two-handled knife to slice the blubber until it resembled a book with very thick pages called "bible leaves." The *Florida* had a hand-cranked machine on board to speed the mincing process, but this was a fairly rare device in the fishery. It was now time for the tryworks, a sort of rectangular brick oven near the foremast in which a fire was kindled. Whalers had designed this system especially for boiling blubber, after much trial and error. The tryworks held two massive iron pots about four feet in diameter and two and a half feet deep. On top, the pots were protected by a roof called a hurricane house and exposed on the sides from the ship's bulwarks up. To prevent the fire from igniting the ship's deck planks, a waterproof wooden box, called a "duck pen," was built under the tryworks.

Into the pen was laid sand, on top of which were bricks set in mortar that acted as the base of the tryworks. During the boiling of the blubber, the crew poured water into the duck pen, which circulated around the bricks and sand and protected the deck below. The smoke from the oil poured out through two copper chimneys four to six feet high through the hurricane house. Despite the precautions, sometimes the ships caught on fire anyway. (According to custom, at the end of a voyage, the tryworks were disassembled and the bricks tossed overboard.) Fires were lit with scraps of firewood under the cauldrons of the tryworks, and when the fires were hot enough, the men dragged wooden tubs full of bible leaves over and threw these chunks inside for boiling into oil. The flukes and, in the case of a right or bowhead whale, the lips and tongue were boiled as well. There was a lot of animal to process. A single bowhead whale might yield a quivering carpet of fat twenty inches thick for a room sixty-six feet long and twenty-seven feet wide; the tongue alone could weigh five tons. Because the whale might spoil rapidly, once the fires started, the black smoke never stopped rising, day and night—then the ship and its blazing fires looked downright sinister—till the job was finished. It took three hours or three days, depending on the weather, the crew's experience, and the whale's size, to complete the task.

The process had to be nearly perfect: any flesh had to be cut off the blubber before the trying out started, and the blubber itself wasn't allowed to burn or boil over or the final product would bring in less profit at the market. The men made sure all the water had evaporated from the blubber to prevent the oil from spoiling after it was stored in the barrels. They also took care not to let the oil spill from the cauldrons into the blazing fire below or it would ignite. Sometimes the oil sputtered, scalding the men's faces and hands, and the rising smoke burned and reddened their eyes. As the whalers continued, they skimmed "fritters" from the try-pots—pieces of whale blubber that hadn't melted—and fed these into the furnace.

After the crew started cutting in, a mixture of oil, filth, and bits of meat, called "gurry," covered them from crown to heel. "The men are as greasy and smutty as they can be—including the captain, who manages to get into all the dirty work he can," as Eliza once observed. One whaler described being in oil-soaked clothes, eating oily grub with oily hands and drinking from oily pots. On going to the forecastle, he said, you "dream you are under piles of blubber that are heaping & falling on upon you till you wake up with a suffocating sense of fear and agony only to hear the eternal clank of the cutting machine & the roar of the fires under the tryworks—or the wind dismally howling through the rigging—to fall asleep only to dream again till you are called on deck."

Eliza, even if she wasn't directly involved in the rendering, still had to endure the discomforts that were part of it. Nor did the onetime New England matron's nostrils much savor the smell of the smoke that wafted into her cabin from the try-pots as the crew boiled the blubber down. Finally, when the ugly butchery was done, Eliza's unenviable task would be to take the wooden washtub the carpenter had cobbled together for her and clean the blood, oil, and filth from Thomas's clothes. Filth was a useful thing: A good voyage was a greasy and thus successful voyage—on the other hand, a ship that came back clean had wasted time and money and usually, at the very least, a life or two.

In the rectangular sperm's head was an area called the case, filled with oil that had the white color and thick consistency of semen, which thus had given the species its name. The crew used a bucket to draw it out and pour it directly into thirty-gallon casks, and Eliza dipped a jar in one of these barrels to keep as a memento. During trying out, a strong-stomached crewman usually probed the whale's massive network of intestines—if he was lucky, he found a fat lump called ambergris. This was created, presumably, by an indigestible squid beak or some other object stuck in there, and despite its grotesque genesis, the substance was worth more than its weight in gold as a fixative for perfume. After days of backbreaking work, of cutting, snapping, tearing, and boiling, the men had reduced the leviathan largely into his constituent elements. The rest of the carcass—that part of the whale having no cash value—was cut loose or dumped overboard for the sharks, gulls, and other scavengers. This disposal of waste was just part of the job. One year in the Arctic, whalemen dumped a hundred headless bodies to give the polar bears something to feast on. Such was the ignominious end of an animal that, if left unmolested, could live a century. Some of the bowhead whales killed by the *Florida*'s crew were, possibly, older than the Declaration of Independence.

After filling the last thirty-one-gallon barrel, a crew usually cried out "Hurrah for five and forty more!" which was the number of casks the average sperm could fill. Using sand and water, the crew scrubbed the decks of blubber, blood, soot, and grease, and clean and spotless they remained until they processed the next whale and the cycle was repeated. That night, Morgan put a stamp in the logbook—as was his custom, always in the shape of the sort of whale that had been killed. He also noted how many barrels the beast had yielded. This one garnered a mere nine barrels—a steady diet of such fare ensured a ship would be out a long, long time trying to fill her empty hold.

Throughout the voyage, *Florida*'s crew repeated the process again and again, in good weather and in gales alike, allowing Eliza to see firsthand the torture, violence, and suffering, both animal and human, that was the cornerstone of her family's prosperity. Once, presumably just so she could brag about it, Williams had even pushed her into a right (baleen) whale's mouth whose head the crew had detached from the body. As any good whaleman knew, the bone in his mouth could be as valuable as gold—and Williams and his colleagues called it that. When processing a right or bowhead whale, in addition to rendering the blubber, the crew attacked the baleen in its mouth with axes to remove it. (After extraction, the bone was cleaned and stacked below—if onboard rats started nibbling on the precious gold, the belowdecks were sealed off and the crew "smoked ship," lighting fires to asphyxiate the rodents.)

In the universe of oddities through which a whaleman voyaged, a right whale was an especially peculiar constellation. Despite his size, sixty to eighty feet long, weighing a ton per foot, and carrying an amazingly tough thick wrapper of blubber up to eighteen inches deep, this whale's nerves, nevertheless, carry hot vivid sensations very effectively up the long spine to the great brain. Indeed, a bird landing on a sleeping right whale's back will make it start violently. It's fitted with a vast head that constitutes a fourth of its length. This forward section is little more than a massive mouth with a huge lower jaw capped with a smaller curved lid. Although this whale lacks anything like a human face, it sprouts hair on the head that nearly resembles a beard and eyebrows.

Less human-looking are the large rocklike "callosities" or "bonnets" that speckle the right's skin. In shape, each one of these lumps is unique to the individual whale, and through them swarm lice. Rather than slim flippers like other whales, the right has larger flippers on each side that fit, mittenlike, over bones similar to those in a human hand. These water wings look ridiculously small in comparison with the huge body; it's their task to guide the animal through the seas. As nature uses its own private artistry and esthetics in both its design work and final product, the leviathan is elegant and even beautiful in its element—its graceful swimming resembles ballet.

At a distance, surfaced whales, despite their various species, often look similar, resembling in shape the belly of a fat man floating on his back or a dark sleek island or reef. Distinguishing the right whale is a double spout in its head, knit together by skin into something like a pair of nostrils. When it exhales, these holes create a forked spray, or V-shaped fountain, that lets skilled lookouts identify it at a glance. Despite its size, it dines on tiny "feed," usually a shrimplike plankton with minuscule legs radiating from its body that remind some of the snaky-locked Medusa. Moving through a patch of yellow-greenish krill or other brightly colored crustaceans, the right opens its great lips to reveal hairy rows of flexible bone, set a quarter inch apart, resembling black Venetian blinds. Each whale has as many as six hundred of these slats. As it swims leisurely, mouth agape, tons of seawater rush into the cavernous mouth, and with it the feed. The dining sounds like a thresher leveling a wheat field. The great mouth full, the tongue then pushes the water out while the hairy slats retain the krill; after closing the lips, the tongue lifts the food up and sends it down the throat for digestion.

It was, and is, a mighty brute. A surfacing right whale can smash through ice eighteen inches thick; once, thirty hours after being harpooned, one pulled a fully rigged ship behind it against the wind. Moreover, an iron in the back can sour its normally bovine nature and make it dangerous. Enraged, this whale is a fighter, "a most furious and ungoverned character," and prone to swinging its great tail flukes, up to twenty feet long tip to tip, from one side to the other—or from "eye to eye." In one foamy slam, this whale might with his tail reduce a boat to planks and the men to corpses and cripples.

Its arsenal includes tricks of evasion, as well. A right, under attack, can settle in the water, sinking motionlessly without leaving as much as a bubble on the surface. In addition to being able to swim backward, the species also practices the art of back-hollowing, making the insulating blubber there go limp and become as hard as iron so that it bends the shank of a harpoon. The whale also might swim away rapidly. At times, after being struck, he'd dive straight down with the force of a locomotive.

To the diminutive Eliza, the whale's mouth she was trespassing in seemed like a cavern, able to fit six people inside. She might have sat down, but it was wet and dirty from the rain. She wondered how so huge a monster as this could feed on the ever so small crustaceans that passed through its hairy baleen strainer. "These fish are truly one of the wonderful works of God and well may we think that everything in the deep is wonderful," she wrote.

To men like her husband, it was the profitable hunting and killing of the monsters that was "wonderful," and there was nothing abstract about their interest in the whale. The niceties or novelties of its appearance and behavior were lost on a whaling crew. For them, it was just the "right" whale to kill; generally, the corpse stayed afloat and intact long enough to get it to the ship for cutting in, if sharks and weather were cooperative. In pursuing their gritty vocation, whaling men didn't usually give hunting and killing their enormous prey much philosophical reflection. It was a job that, even if at first terrifying and wondrous, became, with repetition, dull. There wasn't much sympathy for the beasts, and a monster that didn't make war on his killers was no candidate for pity.

The difference between Eliza and the hunters on board may have never been clearer when, one day, a pod of playful humpbacks happened to chance upon the *Florida*. This was a species of baleen whales known for aquatic frolics: They are fond of breaching—rising up from the surface of the sea and rolling to one side in a great crash of foam. They are also prone to lob-tailing—hanging head down perpendicular to the water's surface with tails sticking out in the air and smacking the sea with their great flukes to make a sound like thunder. Although humpback oil wasn't worth much, and the baleen unmarketable, the modest take they offered was better than nothing—and it gave the men something to kill. As Eliza watched, the whalemen dropped their sleek boats, crept up on the whales, and the play gave way to murder. Wounded by irons and bomb lances, the monsters quickly were spouting blood into the air and bobbing dead in the red water, awaiting towing back to the *Florida*. "I could not bear the sight, but it was soon over," Eliza said to her diary. It didn't pay to be compassionate in this trade, and Eliza was quick to suffer with those who suffered—whether it was a seasick sailor, a captain's widow, or even a dying whale.

Being a mother herself, she found the killing of the sperm cows and their calves particularly painful. A mother cachalot would fight to the death to protect her young—which sometimes made the calf a very attractive target as bait. That November, Morgan came alongside the *Florida* with his boat's gunwale stove in and minus an iron ring that held the oar. He said he'd attacked a calf—a "poor little thing that could not keep [up] with the rest" as Eliza put it—and the mother, a scarred, tough fighting whale, tried to crush Morgan with her great flukes. The mate dodged the huge tail and finished her off with his lance. (Morgan, apparently a difficult man to kill, had faced this situation before when an ornery sperm whale had capsized his boat. He and his men managed not only to get the boat righted, but killed the monster, too.)

"They exhibit the most affection for their young of any dumb animal I ever saw," he said.

On the other hand, Eliza was also the sort of woman who rooted for her team, and in this contest, that meant her husband and his crewmen, whom she cared for and worried about like her own family. Although class lines were as strong on a whaleship as they were on land, she had an unusual sensitivity to the workers Williams employed in his floating manufactory. A crew was more likely to return to the *Florida* without a whale in tow than with one. Too often she'd seen the men come back from hours of unsuccessful hunting, hands and feet numb, sometimes with their boats stove in, and she pitied them in their discouragement. Poor kindly Eliza didn't win in this game.

As was customary among New Bedford whalers, the *Florida* worked southeastward to the Cape Verde islands off Africa to buy provisions and take on extra hands. Before the *Florida* made the Cape Verdes, however, Eliza and the other green hands got their first taste of real weather, when, on an otherwise idle day, the seas grew rough and the winds started gusting. Some of the greenies were sure if it blew any harder, the ship would capsize, and the hands decided that any man "that has been on one voyage and goes again is a fool," as Morgan noted. Sickly Eliza, lying in the swinging bed in their shared berth, told Williams she thought it was a gale.

With a laugh, he said, "You have not seen a gale yet." Nor did she want to, she decided.

The *Florida* passed in sight of the volcano island of Fogo, just active enough after many years to belch out wisps of smoke. They were now in the Cape Verde island chain, brown, arid, and desperately poor, that had once served as a Portuguese slave settlement. The locals, many of whom were slave offspring themselves, found whaling a welcome escape from a hardscrabble farming life. After the *Florida* was becalmed while approaching another mountain island, Brava, where he wanted to land, Williams with his typical impatience ordered a boat lowered to row ashore. Perhaps hoping to give her a dose of dry solid land as an antidote to her seasickness, he took Eliza with him, which may not have been a prudent choice because of the choppy water. Waves rolled over the boat's sides and splashed on his already nervous wife. Seeing her distress, Williams shielded her with his bulk, allowing himself to be drenched, and comforted her by saying, "Don't be frightened. There is no danger."

There was another adventure for Eliza yet. After they landed on Brava, Williams accepted an invitation to visit the governor's house, which sat high up on a dizzyingly steep mountainside. The couple required asses to transport them to his "Excellency's" domicile, and Eliza could just keep herself from screaming in terror as the animals made their slow way upward. Every time she looked over her shoulder at her giant husband behind her astride his ass, his feet nearly touching the ground, she laughed uncontrollably. The visit concluded, the couple returned to the waterfront for a pull back to the *Florida* with a goat on board, which Williams had procured to provide Eliza with milk for her tea.

Before setting out, Eliza watched as Williams shared his tobacco with some waterfront beggars, but the more he gave, the more they asked, until he became swarmed with supplicants. Not surprisingly, on leaving the dirt-poor island of Brava, Eliza took with her an equally poor opinion of it. At least she had the goat, whose estate was now undoubtedly improved; animals were prone to have a hard time of it in the Cape Verde Islands, as did everyone else who lived there.

At the end of November, the ship made her way through the cold, rugged waters of the Cape of Good Hope and entered the Indian Ocean. New Bedford whalers looking to reach the Pacific usually took the more direct, if more dangerous, Cape Horn route off Patagonia, but Williams went round Africa. He did so, most likely, under orders, or possibly because he had a pregnant wife aboard and was being cautious. The first month of the new year saw a couple of noteworthy events. On January 10, a "green" Portuguese was thrown over the ship's steering wheel and "hurt considerably," but survived. He was fortunate. On shipboard, a simple fall down a hatch could lay a man up for weeks. More significantly, the next day at about noon Eliza presented the captain with "a hearty rugged looking young sailor and an addition to the ship's company," as Morgan noted. The boy was named William Fish. Undoubtedly, Williams acted as midwife. Unlike their English counterparts and rivals, American whalers never shipped doctors, and so by default that job usually fell to the captain.

As an Arctic whaling man, Williams had witnessed his share of frostbite injuries and certainly amputated fingers and toes—without anesthesia—in addition to providing other treatments. Aiding Eliza probably was a more beguiling problem, as midwifery was a mystery to most men, a secretive art usually restricted to women. Nevertheless, either through her coaching or some special skill or intuition or instruction or just plain good luck, he pulled the task off—no small feat given the high mortality rate among birthing women. She must also have been a strong patient. Soon after having successfully piloted Willie into the *Florida*'s cabin, Williams sailed to north New Zealand's Bay of Islands and dropped anchor.

At New Zealand's South Island, an unshaven, motley set of escaped convicts, overboard mariners, and other riffraff (assisted by the natives) had carried on a rough whaling enterprise from shore stations. When not hunting right whales—and any other unfortunate cetacean that chanced to swim by—they mated with the local Maori women and sired children. These whalers toiled not for money, according to one observer, but clothes, liquor, and, of course, tobacco. They weren't a neat lot, and they left the chunks of unused whale meat and bone fragments lying around on the beach by their stations for the cats, pigs, and seagulls to rummage through. With the disappearance of the right whale through overhunting, since 1840 the antipodean fishery had been on the decline.

A convalescing Eliza went on land to rest, and while there, the crewmen brought her fruit and flowers. Additionally, Captain Butler, the local harbormaster who doubled as Episcopal minister (or the other way around), kept her company. In conversation, Butler explained to Eliza that when he'd first arrived there nineteen years earlier, the less than civilized and warlike Maori natives had wanted to kill him, but later decided to spare his life and made him and his wife their father and mother, respectively. He'd seen that since Captain Cook's arrival decades before, there had been a major dislocation of culture. That shouldn't have been much of a surprise: Wherever the peripatetic English explorer arrived, it was just a matter of time before the now-doomed aboriginals lost their religion, customs, land, and pride. Butler said he once witnessed a distressed Maori queen in her throne room, pacing up and down, long black hair streaming down her dark shoulders. "No good has come to us since we left off eating human flesh, and we must commence it again," she said quickly. Then, as Butler recounted to Eliza, she lifted her own arm to her mouth and bit a piece out of it. That made the missionary's "flesh crawl on his bones."

As always, foreign whalers traveling here made a practice of exploiting the generally fearsome face-tattooed Maoris. Among whalers New Zealand had a reputation as a sinkhole of dissipation, violence, and lust. The whites traded their cheap trinkets for rather exotic mementoes such as shark-teeth clubs and human heads they could show off or sell back in New Bedford. (Recall the story of Queequeg out peddling his head in *Moby-Dick*.) The traffic in heads became a regular industry, with whalers purchasing them by commission. The interested buyer would select a given native, place an order with the supplier, and by the time the whaleman docked in New Zealand again, the victim had been dispatched and decapitated and the final product was ready for delivery. So prevalent was this grim industry, it, along with disease, started halving tribal manpower.

One April morning after leaving the Antipodes, a massive whale appeared close enough to the *Florida* to be plainly visible from deck, and an argument broke out among the men over what species it was. Eventually, they agreed it was a sulphur bottom, or blue whale, which at a hundred feet or so in length and at least as many tons in weight, is the largest creature that has ever lived; when spouting, it throws off a plume nine feet long. The monster's volume also meant killing one might provide a jackpot in oil and bone. The whale's amazing swiftness generally made it untouchable, as it could escape before a crew could fasten on to him. But Williams had a secret and (for the American fishery) an unusual weapon: a Greener gun. This was a fifty-two-inch rifle devised by a noted English gunmaker (named Greener) that could fire a ten-foot iron a distance of forty yards, much farther than the strongest arm could hurl it. The weapon, mounted in the front of the whaleboat, could swivel, and because of its range was the boast of successful whaling captains who used it—according to the manufacturer's advertisements, at least.

Williams, armed with his gun, lowered his boat for the attack. Despite the whale's size, he managed to miss, and the leviathan dived and wisely didn't reappear, which was probably for the best, as a slain blue sinks fast and no ship then afloat could lift a hundred-ton monster from the bottom of the ocean. One hears Eliza breathing a sigh of relief: Watching the event from the safety of the ship, she noted: "It made quite a loud noise and looked large in the water."

As conservative as the fleet itself, which rarely embraced new technology, Williams generally eschewed these murderous toys. A red-blooded hunter, he preferred the more intimate if gory practice of lancing the prey, a technique that went back to the days of the hardy and secretive Basques, who'd hunted whales before recorded history. It was the lance, combined with his great strength and long reach, that had made Williams's reputation as a fishy whaleman, and, unlike Morgan, he generally avoided even carrying a bomb gun in his boat.

A bomb gun in any case was not infallible. Take for instance the case of Nathaniel Jernegan—a strict captain who always dropped his boats whenever weather permitted, excepting the Sabbath, which he viewed as a day of rest. During a hunt in March 1864, those blessings might have run out on him permanently when he lowered to chase a quite ornery sperm. After Jernegan and a mate lanced it once apiece, the monster took the master's boat in his jaws and chewed it to fragments while the crew safely made it to another boat. The persistent Jernegan took command of his third mate's boat and once more lanced the sperm, who attacked again. In the ensuing wreck, the master became entangled in a line and even touched the whale's fins. Nevertheless, he had the presence of mind to kick off a boot, free himself from the rope, and commandeer yet a third whaleboat, from which he directed a mate to cut his line and plant five bomb lances into the sperm. The enraged beast thrust its head high above water, then sank forever, denying his killers the profitable oil he carried. By April that year Jernegan, a lucky man, had exited his whaleboat five times and lived to tell the tale.

> The whale is a peculiar animal, never fully understood, and the men who were successful in catching him had to be more or less peculiar too. If they weren't born that way, the life they led would make them so and the worst of them had their good points.
>
> —Whaling captain George Fred Tilton,
> *Cap'n George Fred Himself*

· · ·

Whether Eliza could see it or not, her husband's life was far from a simple or easy one. On Williams's broad back lay the weight of the crew, ship, and mission—which was to fill barrels and holds. Captains had to navigate and find the right grounds at the proper season, the timing of the harpooner's throw had to be perfect, the mate had to kill the whale quickly or know when to cut the line, coopers had to make perfect staves so that one barrel could be disassembled and then put back together with any other staves to prevent leakage, and the shipbuilders had to make tight, perfect vessels to brave all seasons and imaginable dangers. After years of service to the industry, an accumulation of small errors might force a master to return to port in New Bedford broken and poor, facing jeers in the streets from schoolmates or colleagues.

Photos from that time show Williams with a long face and strong eyes (they were blue) under thick lids that looked out directly, almost lazily; the appearance was manly without being handsome, the lips firm and calm, curling up at the edges slightly in an almost half smile that lacked frivolity. He had thick, dark eyebrows, and his abundant hair was parted on one side, covering his forehead. He sported a beard from ear to ear across his jaw but kept the upper lip free of whiskers. Williams owned the inscrutable look of a man who did things rather than think about them— and the expression indicated he could give you a thrashing, if that, indeed, was what he was thinking.

His son Willie described men like his father as plain, rather reticent, serious-minded men devoid of show or swagger. Overall, the Yankee men, formed by a climate with a six-month winter, rocky and often resistant soil, an inhospitable coast, and a harsh religious creed, were not prone to gushing affectionately even over people they liked, and were as stingy with emotion as a shipowner was in sharing out the profits of a voyage. Such a temperament was well-suited for whaling.

For at any time on his rise, Williams might have failed: His aim as boatsteerer could have been off and he'd have been broken and sent back to the forecastle. He might have steered his vessel onto uncharted rocks and lost the trust of the ship's owners, or been killed in a mutiny. But that hadn't occurred: He'd passed through the ranks to the very top, proving his reputation as a lucky captain, the sort of man marked as "fishy" (a compliment) in the private dossiers that the agents back in New Bedford kept for reference when recruiting masters and mates.

As the saying went, Captain Williams had come in through the hawser pipe, the opening on deck through which the anchor chain was drawn; he'd earned his berth. Despite all the challenges, Williams, like all the other masters, had learned the sea life: how to turn the air blue with curses, tie knots, fight, trim sails, and other such necessary nautical skills. Yet he must have sensed he was a bit different than his mates. Unlike almost all other veteran seamen, his arm never bore a tattoo, a form of decoration made so popular by the Tahitians visited by Captain James Cook. While many mariners treated the first whaling voyage as a cautionary lesson, not Williams. He admitted, under oath, he never tried for anything else but this vocation. He loved the life, and stayed ashore only about a month after his first voyage before shipping out again, this time as boatsteerer and blacksmith. Eventually, he made master. Something drove him on, almost demoniacally, forcing him to reach the farthest point north of any whaleman and, eventually, to make his name synonymous with the Arctic whaling fleet itself. He'd become one of that rare order of men who took pride in pitting their abilities and skills against the worst elements in the world.

Being a captain was a complex task for many reasons. He stood between owners and crew and had to negotiate between the two rivals. Owners often tried to stint on food to cut the fitting-out costs; it was up to the master to get as much as he could for his men, because an unhappy crew was less inclined to succeed.

Captains competed against one another to navigate into the most remote and dangerous places in the world. The Cape Cod, Nantucket, and Martha's Vineyard whalers, in particular, were fine sailors. Arctic whaling master John Cook, who hailed from Cape Cod, tried to explain just what made the men of his wind-blasted sandspit of a home excel on the waves. "One of the great reasons is that from boyhood they are accustomed to being in boats and to seeing deeds of valor and heroism performed that have gone with them through life," he wrote in his memoir. Perhaps they'd seen a rescue off Peaked Hills, whose sandbars had taken more lives and ships than any other equal length of shore in the United States, he suggested, or some similar feat.

One English captain who saw Cook pilot his way through the lethal Malacca Strait at night without a pilot said: "There are only two men who would, on the occasion of their first visit here, have taken their ships through the narrows of Malacca Strait in weather like that of last night, one is a Cape Codder, the other a damn fool!" Cook asked: "Then you regard my coming in without a pilot a risky performance?"

In that august company of mariners, Williams held his own and then some. Not that the job ended there. In addition to being a navigator, trader, hunter, and master of men, he was also the ship's doctor. He practiced medicine the only way he knew how, relying on what others had shown or told him. For assistance, a cabin often carried a practical book on surgery and a medicine chest full of elixirs that ranged from the possibly useful to the outright poisonous. He set bones, sewed up wounds, and sometimes performed surgery. Hopefully nothing too elaborate was needed or the patient was doomed. Even on land, the largely ignorant bunglers who conducted Aesculapius's profession were, at best, rolling the dice with the patient's life. (Consider that the doctors attending the mortally wounded president Lincoln prescribed him a mustard plaster.) At sea, with even fewer resources available, it was a practical application of Darwin's principles at work—and only the very strong survived.

Yet some shipmaster doctoring at sea was extraordinary. In 1800, during the taking of a large sperm whale, a hardy Nantucket master named Seth Coffin crushed his leg. Seeing his predicament, he called for one of the sharp instruments used to cut blubber, braced himself on his couch in the cabin, and told the mate to chop off the stricken limb, warning him if he were to "flinch one whit" he would put the cutter through him. The undamaged part of the leg was saved—although after the last bandage had been tightened, both men fainted.

The captain had to rule over other men, often strong ones. Whaling had strict principles enforced even in the smallest matters. During the voyage, for instance, when Williams engaged in a snowball fight, it was with the mates and captains of the other vessels, not the crewmen. There were other dictates, such as that if a man approached an officer, he need not remove his cap, but if his pipe was in his mouth, he might expect to be knocked down.

There were limits to what a master could enforce: One voyage was cut short when the crew dumped all the whaling gear overboard. Given their near godlike power on deck and remoteness from any sort of police force or government that might punish or interfere with them, some captains and officers were able to give vent to their cruelest impulses and frustrations. In the merchant fleet, there were cases of brutal captains working sick or weak men to death. The whale fishery was full of examples of Caligula-like misbehavior. (Right around the time of the *Florida*'s voyage, the master of the whaler *Condor* was accused of forcing two crewmen—one a mere boy in his teens—to box each other on deck, under threat of a lashing. A warrant for his arrest was issued on shore in his absence.)

The master of the *Emigrant* of Rhode Island was so vicious he seized up the ship's tomcat in the rigging for scratching a crewman and nearly whipped the beast to death. Not content with that, he also amused himself by torturing the cook's prize pig. "He was without doubt the most foul mouthed and degraded man I ever knew," as one crewman described him. "He had neither respect for religion, nor morality, nor his own word nor common decency. The names of mother and sister were not sufficiently sacred in his estimation, to prevent his lascivious remarks on them. I have heard him swear one continuous string of oaths, until he was hoarse with speaking; and although he would descend to the lowest blackguardism with the sailors, yet he would treat them like dogs." Those men he deemed not pulling hard enough at the oars, he threatened with a dart through the heart.

Some whaling officers belonged in jail rather than on a ship's deck. The following is a description of a true reprobate, Mr. Chace, the mate on the whaler *Cleone,* bound for the North Pacific: "We had the old Foremast all ready for heaving out when he [the mate] came on bord. we got the mast out after a while, but not without knocking down three or four of the Knackers [Kanakas] not that thay were disobedent or anything of the kind, but because it was customary in Merchant ships when a new Mate first goes on board. Somtimes after knocking one of them down, he would com along with a Smile, and Say to me, if I had only got a fare clip at that Fello I would of fetched him. . . . the Knackers [Kanakas] by this time enterted a complaint to the Ortheriteis against him for ill treatment of them which seamed to check him in a measure whilst lying in port. the next mean action I saw him do was to knock a Sick man over who was about ready to die. This happened in the presence of the Captin. Just to show him that he was a chap to straighten them as he told him when he shipped.

he sayes he told the Capt that no one should loaf about that ship's Decks when he was at work . . . and if there is any loafing to be done after you Comes me, Captin."

There were both good and bad men at sea, as there were on land. One among the ranks of the former, Williams resisted the temptation to abuse his power, especially with Eliza on board. Despite having spent most of his adult life whaling, he hadn't lost his sense of civilized life's finer things. For instance, though he could swear to raise blisters, he was never crude or obscene when his family was nearby. He maintained discipline not just with himself, but also with those on board. He could be stern, which wasn't necessarily a bad thing—strength and courage from a master helped keep order on a whaler, as a crew often challenged their officers or tried to haze them. Some of the more thuggish of the crewmen respected only force, and it took a strong, firm hand, sometimes clenched in a fist, to maintain a semblance of civilization. You ruled the men or they ruled over you. While flogging wasn't prevalent in the whaling fishery (and finally was outlawed in 1866), nevertheless, the punishments available were nothing short of brilliant. One was hanging a man by the thumbs on deck so that just his toes touched the planks. When the ship rocked, he'd hang by his thumbs alone, an unpleasant prospect, or he was triced up in the rigging.

Williams was not a boaster or a bully. If he warned he was going to hit someone, you could bet on it. Nor did he back down. When in his twenties and first mate of the *South Boston,* he once faced down his outgoing and disgruntled crew. The ship had wrapped up a successful voyage in the Bering Strait, where Williams had taken the whale that had filled the last cask on board. When the ship agent Andrew Potter came on board in Buzzards Bay and overheard the crew plotting to give the long-legged mate Williams the beating of his life, the agent advised him to slip over the side and get out of New Bedford. Williams offered his thanks, and told him to stick around and watch. After the ship dropped anchor in the Whaling City's harbor, the crew walked forward and prepared themselves for a gang attack. They clearly didn't know just how powerful an opponent they had. Instead of running, Williams walked toward the forecastle, took off his coat, and faced his crew. In those days, the industry was full of brave, ambitious, and strong men aplenty who settled an argument with fisticuffs as a legitimate method of mediation.

"I understand you feel that I have not treated you fair during the voyage and you now propose to give me a thrashing; very well, I am ready for you," he said. Something in Williams's face and frame cowed the gang. Instead of rushing in, the men, content to mutter threats under their breath, descended into the forecastle to collect their gear.

The *Florida*'s voyage also demanded severity. When the *Florida*'s second mate viciously beat his small nephew, the cabin boy, Williams dismissed the officer from the ship, perhaps at Eliza's urging. She'd been tutoring the lad, after all. This was as extreme a punishment as was generally meted out to an officer. Usually such an infraction, like fighting with another mate, might only result in the offender being forced to leave his whaleboat "on the cranes" during the hunt. The misbehaving third officer wasn't the only man who presented a disciplinary problem on board. The saucy New York City blacksmith was especially troublesome, at times refusing to work; he even sold the ship's bread to natives at Mangonui in New Zealand in exchange for honey. A response was necessary. In this case, Morgan bound the errant smith in double irons on deck, exposing him to the hot sun until he became more agreeable. The sensitive Eliza disliked seeing him manacled, but even she admitted he's "inclined to be a bad Man." The first time the smith had liberty on shore, he ran away to desert, only to be retrieved by Williams. Such a craftsman, even a reprobate like this one, would be hard to replace. Removing the blacksmith from temptation, the master got the ship out to sea.

That May, just before heading north to the Sea of Okhotsk, the *Florida* sailed into the port of Hakodate on the northern Japanese island of Hokkaido. Hakodate had a beautiful (to Morgan), spacious, landlocked harbor, full of exotic junks, foreign and Japanese whalers, and a Russian warship. A snow-capped mountain loomed over the large town, and the harbor's edge was densely studded for two miles with brown and white stone and clay houses with thatched roofs. Land-deprived Eliza found the green grass near the water lovely.

The privacy-loving islands of the Rising Sun had been off-limits to foreigners until the rambunctious young and expanding America sent Commodore Matthew Perry with armed frigates to open the country up to its commercial enterprises—especially the whale fishery. Perry had succeeded in closing a deal in 1854, and as part of the Treaty of Kanagawa, all shipwrecked whalers were guaranteed protection in the city's environs. Enjoying the benefits of this compact between the gunpowder-and-cannon-armed whites and the sword-wielding samurai, the *Florida* dropped anchor safely.

The Japanese, officials and commoners alike, swarmed the ship's decks in their odd-looking kimonos—perhaps to the whalers resembling sails billowing in the wind. The wooden sandals of the commoners made a "good deal of noise" on the *Florida*'s planks, as sound-sensitive Eliza recalled. She and the baby were objects of special interest to the guests. They touched, talked to, and played and laughed with Willie, clearly a charming infant. The officer-samurai class on board ranged from full-grown warriors to toddlers who could barely walk. They were distinguishable by their fine cloth footwear; each one also carried a long sword and a short sword in sheaths on their belt. Professional hunter-killer Williams asked to examine the weapons, but the samurai didn't want the whaler to touch them. After some "coaxing," however, a sword came out, along with a "long sharp dirk knife, very nice and bright." The Japanese interpreter raised the weapons and explained the difference between the samurai method of combat and the American variety. "He said they struck with the sword and we ran it into the body—and they cut off the head with the knife, which it seems they do for a small offence." About this time, Eliza heard the story circulating in the fleet about some unlucky Dutch sailors whom the Japanese—whose ritualistic politeness was matched in its rigidity only by their sense of justice—had mutilated and then executed. The whalers didn't know why.

The Williams family, along with an old whaling-captain friend and his wife and two sons, went ashore and attended a Buddhist funeral ceremony in the local temple. Then there was some shopping in the bazaar—the lacquer work on the various inexpensive glove boxes and workboxes was the most splendid Eliza had ever seen; while there, Williams bought some of these goods to trade. Eliza noted that the polite Japanese, whose English was poor or who spoke through an interpreter, never tired of answering strangers' questions. They weren't the only ones from the *Florida* in Hakodate: The troublesome carpenter and blacksmith also went on liberty and burglarized a store of liquor. Someone saw them committing their larceny and shot at them, and although the duo briefly escaped, they were later arrested. While the *Florida* sailed on, they remained behind in Japan to serve an eighteen-month hard-labor sentence imposed by the U.S consul and commercial agent.

Yankee whalemen in port tended to be ambassadors for the worst elements of their faraway homeland. (It has even been recorded that one nineteenth-century waterfront warning on the isle of Wight stated that no sailors or dogs were allowed there.) While on shore and free from nautical routine, a sailor gorged himself on every pleasure available. His every penny had to be spent while in port, cash being fairly useless on the face of the deep. Added to this, by immemorial custom, was his duty to get drunk—as a part of nautical etiquette, a mariner on shore never refused an offered drink. Thus, hell-raising in any grog shop or tavern from New Bedford to the Azores to Hawaii to New Zealand and Siberia would hardly provoke even a raised eyebrow. At one port, the Bay of Islands in New Zealand, the *Florida* sent a work crew ashore, and "as sailors generally do," noted Morgan, they got drunk and bested the local police in a brawl. Eventually beaten by the natives, they were arrested and paid a fine of twenty dollars.

During the sojourn in Japan, the *Florida* made her way toward a local fishing fleet, whose boats sailed away "with all possible speed," as Morgan logged it. Curious and wanting information about the local whales, the mate lowered his boat and pulled into a group of the fishing craft. Seeing the whalers approach, some of the fishermen threw their nets overboard and pulled away hastily, but Morgan continued on, creeping under the lee of one unsuspecting crew as they hauled in their nets. These Japanese, three men and a woman, were small and stout, bareheaded and barefoot, and looked as rugged and as "tough as knots. " They turned and saw Morgan approaching. The results were unexpected.

The fishermen cried in alarm, dropped their gear, and rushed to the far end of the boat, where they stood in a group, trembling. Gazing at the intruders in terror, they motioned for them to leave. Morgan had never seen people so frightened; one of them even frothed at the mouth. "I made signs to one of them to ask if they caught any fish but he thinking we wanted . . . fish commenced thrusting them into our boat. I stopped him however by making [him] understand we did not want them[,] when he took one and ate it raw to show us they were good to eat." These small fish and a wood dish full of boiled rice were all these mariners in their open boat had for food, Morgan deduced. He and the cooper went on board. The Japanese felt no more at ease, but at least they realized they weren't in danger and pulled in their nets to leave. When the unwanted guests got back into their whaleboat, the Japanese waved adieu, and "were highly pleased to think they had escaped whole." They followed their countrymen, already a mile away to windward.

While sailing through the North Pacific there was another interesting encounter with the locals. Williams had lowered to hunt and was some way from the *Florida* when a Korean junk maneuvered alongside and some of the occupants came aboard. While there, they showed an especial interest in Willie, who was dressed in long clothes that hid his sex; they began to make gestures to each other about him. To Eliza's alarm, the Korean captain even picked Willie up, but when he discovered it was a boy in his arms, he handed him back to his mother with many smiles and indicated approval. The Asians soon left the deck with no harm done, but if Willie had been a girl, the results might have been anyone's guess.

With summer's arrival and the weather turning relatively warm, the *Florida* crept into the Sea of Okhotsk for the real hunting to begin. The shallow sea is an especially problematical finger of the northwest Pacific. It is imprisoned inside of the Asian continent, squeezed on the east and southeast by the Kamchatka Peninsula and Kurile Islands, by Sakhalin Island to the west; and by Siberia to the northwest. What lies inside these boundaries is deadly and inhospitable, and ice and fog are just the greatest of many dangers. The frigid climate requires sailors to wear heavy clothes and gloves even in summer. Whalers, having sailed in just a few weeks' time from the warm and mild South Pacific to the Sea of Okhotsk, found the transition a shock to the system.

To avoid a collision with another whaler likewise blinded when the frequent dense fogs arose there, a ship's crew fired weapons, pounded on empty casks, rang bells, and blew horns. This coast was cold, harsh, and rugged even in summer, and not much more amenable to human life than the sea itself. Serving feebly both for the diversion of sailors and official administration was a miserable settlement at water's edge called Okhotsk City, wherein dwelt some five hundred people "if you counted the dogs." Although the Russian czar had recently decreed that only his subjects were allowed to whale there, the order was enforced with typical Romanov efficiency, and Williams and the other Yankee blubber hunters did pretty much as they liked.

Among the discomforts and dangers faced were meddling officials, man-eating brown bears, and swarms of vicious mosquitoes, so ferocious that at one point they chased Morgan, who was scrounging around on land for drinking water, into his whaleboat. But, by far, ice was the master terror here and a central and undeniable fact of navigation. When the tide was in, the pack ice headed toward shore and threatened to drag the ship with it; then as the tide went out, the ice went out to sea again. The sound of the floes scraping against the ship's copper siding kept Eliza up during three brief evenings, darkness lasting only about three hours. One such sleepless July night, with a heavy swell rocking the *Florida,* the great floes pummeled the ship and made her tremble "as if she would go to pieces."

Luckily, that didn't happen. Whaleships were built for this kind of hard work in dangerous and varied waters. Whalers were uncommon ships, made by uncommon laborers and poets. From dawn till dusk—no work, no pay—expert craftsmen from New Bedford and towns throughout New England took sweet-smelling wood carted in from local forests and with it laid keels, planted masts, and hung rudders until they had a completed craft to float down to the waiting sea. In those days, it was said of such yards that crews needed a quart of rum for every ton of ship built—and even more of the liquor for a proper launching. Apparently, the formula worked—what they made lasted.

Some custom-built whalers were marvels of utility, and if practicality without superfluity is beauty, then they were lovely, indeed. Special woods were selected, cut, treated, and shaped for their particular task in each section of the ship. One plank must bend, another must push back, and so on. Here is a ship's carpenter's description of the New Bedford vessel *Hillman*, named after the family of merchant Zachariah Hillman, an owner who had made the model used to construct her.

"The material for her frame was to be of first quality white oak, this country growth," stated the carpenter in court testimony to settle a claims case. "Her keel was rock maple. Her main transom was live oak. Apron was live oak. Side counter timbers were live oak. Stanchions were locust. Her deck frames were of the first quality Southern yellow pine timber. Her knees [which supported the decks] were first quality juniper. Her plank outside was the first quality white oak and Southern pine. . . . Her fastenings were copper bolts and locust tree nails, these tree nails went through and through and were wedged on both ends, both outside and inside. The workmanship was done in first-rate shape, as well as any ship ever built in New Bedford or anywhere else. . . . All her deck frames and ceiling in between decks was varnished two or three coats. This was done to protect the wood and make it last longer. After the ship was launched she was hove out, and her bottom was graved and covered with tar paper, which helped to preserve the oakum, and the bottom was then sheathed with pine boards put on with composition fastenings, and then coppered as all other whalers are." These are the words of a lover describing his beloved.

Of this class of ship was the *Florida*. At times in the Okhotsk Sea, the ice was like a spreading infection capable of becoming a kind of onboard epidemic; it covered sails and rigging and threatened to make her inoperable just when she needed her greatest nimbleness. When the sun thawed out the ice, it would disintegrate into chunks that crashed to the deck frequently enough to keep the crew busy sweeping it up. These frozen missiles even threatened to smash through the skylight into the captain's cabin, and must have kept the skittish Eliza even more on edge. At one point, the ice pack tightened around the ship and briefly imprisoned her— one of a whaling man's greatest fears—but luckily, with the same arbitrary power that had made the ice contract, it relaxed and released her. Being imprisoned caused a unique sensation: "Then the memories of years go flying through the brain, the cheek turns pale, the heart beats thick and the boldest hold their breath," as whaler Thomas Welcome Roys described it. "In another moment she is free and a shout of joy resounds through the ship."

Because of the ice that hampered the *Florida*'s movement, Williams dropped the whaleboats and let them hunt along the coast independently for days at a time. This was a particularly unpleasant method of stalking leviathans. It required extra work, exposure, and risk as the crews delicately threaded their way between the ice fields and the shore. Navigation had to be closely timed with the ebb and surge of the tide, and at any time the pack could easily tighten and smash a relatively small and fragile whaleboat to pieces.

When time allowed, the exhausted hunters would huddle under a sail or turn their boats over and sleep on shore or on the ice. If they were lucky, there would be fallen trees and driftwood to burn as fuel. If they managed to kill a whale, the crew towed the carcass to shore, and without the ship and its windlass and other tools, they had to do their makeshift flensing there, using jury-rigged block and tackle to turn the whale over, a challenging task. After the tiring butchering was done, the men had the joy of hauling the blubber back to the ship. Such a blanket piece could be anchored temporarily in icy water, then tied on and dragged behind like a raft, with little loss of oil till it was aboard ship for trying out.

The climate made the killing more difficult, too. Sometimes the fastened whale "sulked," sliding down to the bottom in the mistaken hope that men and irons would somehow vanish. But in his haste to escape the pain, a right whale was prone to dive down hard in this shallow sea and hit the bottom, dislocating his head bones. Such a collision between whale and seafloor meant a quick death, and loss, for its pursuers had no means of raising the body. The sulker, scraping the seafloor, could stay under for as long as fifteen minutes, which didn't make setting his chimney afire any easier. In this region a whaleboat crew, biding its time waiting for a wounded leviathan to surface, might get numb fingers and toes or even half freeze to death before the prey emerged again for another round of lancing.

However, at least the right whale and his cousin the bowhead, also native to these waters, were predictable in habit and migration. Hunting them didn't require a maddeningly long search in vast expanses of empty ocean, as the sperm demanded. The bowhead differed very little in appearance from the right whale—most notably, he lacked the bonnet on his head. Rather passive, when struck, the bowhead didn't get violent, or "cross the line" as the saying went, and no self-respecting mate would bother wasting a bomb lance killing one unless he was in danger of losing him in the ice.

From the shores of Asia sprang yet more natives for the whalers to meet, whom Eliza dubbed "Tartars." One party that came on board had never seen a ship like the *Florida* before, and its members found it miraculous that the cabin boy managed to climb into the rigging and come back down again alive. Tartar eating habits were somewhat eyebrow raising to whites, blubber being a popular local staple. It was apparently the greatest of luxuries, as Eliza realized when in disgust she watched some of them devour chunks of otherwise useless humpback blubber raw, the fat dripping from their mouths. Given the toughness of the blubber, it's remarkable they could bite through it. Then again, they were creatures of the region, who drank whale fat and even wore it as apparel.

As always, Eliza continued to tend to her family, especially her son. Like all others aboard, young Willie shared in the *Florida*'s lot, and even showed some promise as a mariner to be. One especially violent storm snapped the bindings that held Eliza's rocking chair steady, and she, baby in her arms, went skidding across the cabin. Although the infant was certainly frightened, to her surprise, he didn't cry, perhaps not so amazing if you knew his father.

As the voyage proceeded, it changed Eliza even as it tried her, and at some point during the cruise, she wasn't so much of a green hand anymore. She'd begun, as if by proxy, to absorb some of the whaleman's habits and lore. She could detect a whale's smell. She knew, when certain birds were flapping nearby, the sperm wasn't far off. She'd learned to read the mate's tone of voice and looks for something amiss. Picking up the habits of a sailor, one moment she'd note in her diary how the baby's teeth were coming in, and in the next jot down the direction of the wind.

Living below, inside the cabin, she got hints, not always pleasant, of the world of action above. Noise permeated her quarters: the pull of ropes; the rattle of sails, rigging, and chains; men driving hoops over staves and the subsequent thunder that shook the ship as they rolled the casks into place. Combined, it was enough to make a nervous person go "distracted," she confessed. In doing so, she may have been revealing a secret to her diary she couldn't share with her reserved husband: The voyage was driving her a little bit mad. She also experienced the way time passed at sea—far more monotonously than it did in Connecticut with its solid, predictable grass, dirt, and stones underfoot. Birthdays and holidays came and went without notice. Homesick, on her son's birthday she wrote: "Words are too feeble to express the great desire of my heart to once more set eyes on those Dear Children, that Dear Home, Parents and Friends, but long and patiently have I got to wait, and as time is ever on the wing, the next three years will fly away like the past, and if God is willing, we will arrive safely at home." The absent and longing mother in Eliza was at least a bit at war with the faithful, husband-following wife.

At times, the boredom could be torturous, with day after day absorbed by a fruitless watch for a spout, all the stories told, every book read, and each quality of any person nearby known with unendurable familiarity. Then, after days or weeks of nothing but dreary routine, a storm might blow in or a reef rudely appear where no one expected it and there was a corresponding excess of excitement. At the bottom of a tedious trough of idleness, the men would spend time remembering life elsewhere, Morgan observed. While cruising in the South Pacific on December 24, 1859, the *Florida*'s men were blue. "This being Christmas Eve all hands are wishing themselves where they have been before and telling what they would do were they there and what they would give to be there," Morgan noted. The next day, which also happened to be a Sunday, when nothing but the most necessary work was done on a whaler, the tedium was near absolute. However, on board was a man named Higgins who was briefly taking passage, along with his dog, which was trained to catch pigs. The only thing to mar the "monotony of the silence" was an ongoing feud between Higgins's dog and any adventurous hogs that came abaft the main mast. Each time a swine made the attempt, the canine bit its ear and held it in place, making it squeal until the noise became unbearable and provoked someone to part them.

Thus could years pile up, making young men old and old men dead. When whaling man Lewis Williams, Thomas's younger brother, chanced to be in the Sea of Okhotsk and came on board, Eliza didn't recognize him anymore. Perhaps it wasn't amazing when you considered a whaler's life. These odd and ornery men were "deprived of Society and Friends, they suffer the hardships of heat, cold and wet, besides the greater dangers they encounter which make the Sailors life a hard one," as she herself noted. (Interestingly, Lewis Williams had attended Boston English High School until he was sixteen. Rather than attend college, he followed brother Thomas into the fishery. His first voyage on the *Florida* in 1854, with Thomas as master, lasted nearly four years.)

To counter the dreariness of the life, the men turned to "gams" (a visitor conversation between whalers), storytelling, crafting scrimshaw, singing, and to competing against one another. Morgan clearly took pleasure when he was able to record any victory over Williams: taking a whale the master had missed, having a better boat or superior harpooner, any petty little thing. (As he was the log keeper, he also had the final say on who'd actually won any contest.) A competitive man, he also bragged about beating the mate of another ship in a sailing race in their whaleboats. (His competitor had claimed his was the fastest in the fleet.) But the best of these whalers' diversions were the highly treasured gams, meetings between ships at sea. In a tricky feat of navigation, the ships would sail close to one another while facing in opposite directions—one's bow lined up with the other's stern—barely avoiding a collision. The masters exchanged greetings, an invitation was offered, and boats from the ship were lowered. Then men from one vessel would go to the other ship's forecastle to swap stories and books with the crew hosting them. The officers and master, along with his wife, if she was with him, went aft to the cabin to meet with their corresponding numbers.

During one such confabulation, Eliza provoked laughter by violating one of the unwritten rules of etiquette. During the gam in question, a crewman visiting from another whaleship proved to be a former lodger of Eliza's from Wethersfield, and she invited him to a sociable tea in the cabin. The sailor then proceeded to overstay his welcome, not discerning the many strong hints to leave, and after he finally went to the forecastle, where he belonged, Morgan confided to his log he'd never laughed so hard in his life.

The *Florida* hosted a rather interesting gam after crossing paths with the *George Howland,* a ship Williams himself had sailed on as a harpooner back in 1843. The *Howland*'s master, Captain George Pomeroy, was, as Eliza vaguely put it, a believer in the "spiritual doctrine," and a mesmerist. While in the *Florida*'s cabin, Pomeroy, by the power of suggestion, put the cabin boy to sleep and asked him some, no doubt, delicate questions—and got some amusing answers. Pomeroy's fleshy good looks and hypnotic powers impressed Eliza. Possibly, spiritualist Pomeroy was in communication with helpful ghosts, as he claimed, because his ship came back to New Bedford in 1861 as one of the greasier in the fleet.

> "Well, Jube, how did you like it down there?" a crewmate asked a man fouled in a line and pulled overboard by a sperm whale of St. Helena, but who had managed to escape and was revived. "O! it is a lonesome road to travel," said Jube. "There are neither mile-stone nor guide-boards that I could see!"
>
> —WHALING STORY TOLD BY NATURALIST AND WHALER
> CHARLES MELVILLE SCAMMON

• • •

The captain's job of filling the holds without losing men to desertion or death and heading back after spending little time and money had rarely been easy, and it was getting even more difficult—and dangerous. During gams, while ships' captains and their wives shared news, the number of catches, and gossip, the subject of death often came up. It was common enough to die in the fishery: Men fell overboard or down hatchways, were attacked by whales, and got lost in thick weather. Eliza heard one dismal story after another—like that of the *Ocean Wave*, lost in October 1858. The masters, discussing her wreck, said they wondered if there would be even one survivor found. Then there was Captain Finton of the Russian bark *Amore*, who, while sailing out of Nagasaki Harbor, collided with another ship, forcing him to return to port, where he jumped overboard and drowned. Another yarn concerned a hapless sailor who'd stepped ashore in Siberia, where a bear killed him and dragged the body off, presumably for dinner. And so on. To Eliza, it seemed burial at sea was the worst thing that could possibly happen.

During the voyage, Eliza saw many a near miss with the Grim Reaper. Whaling was a game of odds; each gamble—that is, each time a man lowered his boat or signed on for another voyage—increased the likelihood of death, and he was the last one to know his luck had run out. A brave man who got excited whenever bone and oil were within reach, Williams did his fair share of life wagering. At the cry of "There blows!" Williams climbed aloft with his glass and trained his experienced eye on the spout and ordered with pleasure his boat lowered. Each of these wagers must've made his wife's heart pound in fear.

In the polar regions, the nearly twenty-four-hour-long day allowed a master to work his crew around the clock, and on July 21, 1859, in Shantar Bay off Siberia, with a thick fog obscuring the water beyond the *Florida*, Williams heard whales spouting and decided to drop his boat. His officers told him to stay on board and let them go. Williams, who had a genuine concern for the well-being of his men, wanted them to have a rest and so went off alone with his own crew. As the right whale threw off a phosphorescent light, night whaling wasn't uncommon, and striking in relative darkness and in a fog gave a whaler his best chance of success—provided he could still see his prey.

Into the mist Williams vanished, and to Eliza's distress, he failed to reemerge from it. In vain, the crew rang the ship's bell for Williams to answer. Eliza passed an agonizing, sleepless night, the time seeming "very, very long." There was reason to worry; she'd heard the stories. Around this time, nearly an entire boat crew from the *Whaling Schooner* had died in Shantar Bay after harpooning a leviathan that had repaid them by stoving their boat in. They'd scrambled on the boat's hull, but as the cold set into their limbs, one after the other, they dropped into the water and died, except the harpooner, who somehow had survived until rescue. Then there was the unlucky Captain Palmer of the *Alice Frazer,* who became fouled in his own line as it ran out of his whaleboat; he was yanked into the deep never to be seen again. His wife wouldn't even know he was dead until word arrived to her that fall in Hilo. With these grisly stories as fodder, Eliza's mind churned out terrible visions—she imagined a monster had stove in Williams's whaleboat and that his men had been unable to help him as they fought to save themselves.

The moment there was a ray of light, Eliza went on deck with a spyglass that was unable to penetrate the fog. It wasn't until eight o'clock that she laid eyes on her husband's familiar boat. It was painted blue and marked with white and black stripes and carried a sail she'd help sew. In more placid times she'd found the craft quite handsome—now it must have been downright beautiful. She was overjoyed. He was accompanied by two other *Florida* crews in their whaleboats, and they towed a sixty-barrel whale behind. As she learned, Williams had killed the whale and, lacking an anchor, tied his boat next to it and lay there mated to the massive corpse all night. This was far from unheard of, as often a stricken whale would pull a boat out beyond the ship's view as night fell. It was virtually invisible on the dark sea, and the men lit a lantern and hoped the ship would find them by morning. Sometimes it worked.

(Waiting in pitch blackness next to a whale corpse could be tough, as evidenced by the experience of William P. Randall. As a young fourth mate on a South Seas voyage, while securing a carcass to his boat he'd accidentally cut his hand to the bone. Forced to tie up next to the dead monster till morning, Randall, his arm numbing, faced an unpleasant prospect: His large Hawaiian harpooner was panicking in the dark. Avoiding disaster, the mate threatened to fire a bomb lance into the Sandwich Islander, which calmed him sufficiently to get them all through the night. Randall later became a Union war hero.)

While the *Florida*'s crew by and large managed to assure that death stayed with the whales, sometimes leviathans evened the score by just a hair. On the morning of August 9, Morgan came down to the cabin to awaken Williams and announce the sighting of a big right, eighty feet long, with flukes that spanned twenty-two feet from tip to tip, a "noble" whale. It was a good sign, Eliza thought, and Williams went up and ordered the boats lowered. A little later, Morgan came downstairs into the cabin, and she saw he was soaked to the skin, a reason to worry.

"Tim is gone," he said.

It turned out harpooner Tim Reed had planted an iron in the whale, which then started running. As Morgan was stabbing at the beast with his lance, it managed to get under the boat, nearly flipping the thousand-pound-plus craft over and half filling it with water. Three terrified men jumped overboard. Despite the confusion, Morgan kept at his bloody task, trying to finish the beast off as quickly as he could. When the overboard trio tried to climb back into the boat all at once on the same side, "Over she went," as Morgan put it. The rest of the crew got dumped into the water.

The line, still attached to the whale, went flying out of the boat, wrapping around Reed who was in the stern at the steering oar. When the monster sounded, the line went taut and dragged the harpooner down. Before tumbling out of the boat, Morgan snatched the knife kept on board for just such a circumstance, and, deep underwater himself, he tried to sever the rope. Someone had neglected to sharpen the blade, and unable to cut the line, the mate gave up and rose to the surface.

Reed, a whale hunter whose aim and arm had never failed, was now experiencing a whaleman's greatest nightmare, entangled underwater by the same tough Manila hemp he himself used to fasten his prey. The five remaining crewmen clambered on the overturned hull to await rescue, and looking down, they saw Reed under the surface of the water, already nearly out of sight and heading down fast. "It was merely a glimpse for he was gone instantly," Morgan said. When the third mate's crew located and hauled in Morgan's line, they discovered both the whale and his victim entangled together, equally dead. During his everlasting and one-way trip down, the rope had wrapped around Reed's bruised torso and arms, and he was "considerably mangled by being dragged along the bottom."

"It was such an awful death to die," as Eliza put it in her diary. She was shocked by what had happened among her extended family. She remembered Reed's pleasant smile, and how he so nicely played the fiddle. Yet, Eliza admitted, at least the troublesome fish had yielded two hundred barrels despite the "awful sacrifice." Morgan kept his entry that day very slender, recording the weather before mentioning that he'd "lost Timothy Reed by the boat getting capsized and he getting foul in the line. Took the whale alongside by 11 o' clock."

The men were upset they'd lost a harpooner who'd taken more whales than anyone else on board, and some said they were certain not a better man was to be found. In the small self-contained universe of a whaleship, a death cast a heavy pall over a crew. The cutting in of the whale was a solemn, quiet event, Morgan noted, reflecting the crew's sadness. The crew wrapped Timothy Reed in canvas, said a prayer, and dropped him into the sea that, along with Groton, Connecticut, had been his home for twenty-seven years. Often on a whaler, as part of the funeral, the captain auctioned off the dead man's clothes and added the money to the slop chest funds. An old whaling custom also required a crewman to dump a bucket of water on the corpse before it went over the side—an insult intended to keep the deceased's ghost from haunting the ship.

The first season north closed out with the *Florida* giving Siberia her back as she headed to more temperate waters for the winter—minus their excellent harpooner. In November 1859, the *Florida* sailed to the South Pacific island of Ponape, a small circular volcano tip about twenty miles across thrusting above a particularly lonely stretch of ocean. Back in 1521, the great, if doomed, explorer Magellan, then on his way to Guam, had sailed by the entire Caroline chain that included Ponape without stumbling on a single one of the islands. Too bad for him, for it was a seductively attractive place. Protecting the island was an encircling reef with six openings to as many harbors. The shoreline inside formed many peninsulas and coves that gave way to an interior studded with vegetation-covered peaks. The island sprouted trees yielding fine fruit, its valleys were lush, and the many rivers teemed with fish. Lea Harbor, where the *Florida* anchored, was lovely; the water was clear, and the tropical fish, sponges, coral, and shells littering the bottom there created a vivid burst of color. The anchorage was also floored with hull-ripping coral that required a pilot's guidance at a ship's helm on entry and exit.

In this paradise lived five clusters of native tribes whose men were physically small, but warlike and tough. As part of a ritual, each male crushed one of his testicles with a rock. In looks, they were black-haired with clean limbs that ended in small hands and feet; their teeth were bright below flat noses. For apparel, they wore only knee-length grass aprons, and tattoos covered them from head to toe, torn into their flesh with bird talons. To repel mosquitoes and make their tattoos more prominent, they rubbed cocoanut oil into their skin until they gleamed. The oil often turned rancid, and its smell offended whites at least as much as the insects.

Before Westerners had arrived, noted Williams, the natives were a generally carefree, good-natured people who'd been vastly more happy without civilization's contamination, something that the whalers brought in abundance. These latter had been guilty of their usual sins; among other transgressions, they were accused of cheating the locals in trade and spreading disease. An 1854 smallpox epidemic caused by the whaleship *Delta* killed two thousand natives in one month alone. Nevertheless, the tribes tolerated the whalers' presence, and there was even a small colony of beachcombers who did their best to marry the chiefs' kin, make babies, and thus become more acceptable to the local royals.

Of course, Ponape wasn't unique in harboring ship jumpers. The shores of the Pacific were dotted with former whalemen who'd jumped ship to avoid the miseries of the forecastle and become half-savage beachcombers. For a while, even author Melville had thus wandered in the Marquesas, where he'd become something of a prized pet among the natives and had to escape from their clutches. While the New Yorker had managed to return to America and become famous after writing up his adventure, these outcasts were sometimes condemned to remain as semibarbaric vagabonds, as captains of other ships found them too untrustworthy to ship again. Bound to a dull life among the locals, without money or property or identity, some became cunning wild men who incited the natives to attack visiting ships.

The Ponapeans also traded for various commodities, including their wives and daughters. This precarious arrangement between whites and natives appears to have been based more on the latters' fear of the formers' weapons than love. Life was cheap, and in the past, the locals had once risen up for a bloody massacre of whalemen.

One item of special interest lay at the island's easternmost point. There, gloomily rotting away, were the ruins of a ten-square-mile city of basalt called Nan Matal, its component slabs weighing as much as fifty tons each. Erecting structures of this magnitude was clearly beyond the current inhabitants' capabilities. The past of this metropolis was mysterious, and no one, certainly not the current islanders, knew its purpose. Visitors from the West hazarded different opinions, some believed it the work of buccaneers or possibly a fort. If it had been a pirate city, then the pirates were of a decidedly different type than was known in the nineteenth century, as Nan Matal was over a millennium old. Whether it was a fort built by a warlike race that had subsequently passed into oblivion or a stronghold for stolen loot, the islanders considered it a place to avoid. (In fact, as we know today, it was built around the twelfth century by the island's Saudeleur Dynasty, which established the first organized rule in Ponape.)

Just as whalers spared no expense to hunt their prey in the farthest corners of the planet, so did missionaries spare nothing to tell the world's innocents their lives were abominable and they were destined for hellfire. While in Ponape, Eliza met a Yale-trained missionary named Albert Sturges, who had labored since 1852 with hardly a single convert to his credit. Missionaries tended not to be popular with whalemen, as they tried to interfere with onshore carousing and the assorted venereal pleasures that could be obtained with any available loose-living natives. One element preached against the fornication and drunkenness that the other found an indispensable relief from the boredom of ship life. Nevertheless, clergy and blubber hunters did form some temporary alliances, and the companionship of a respectable Christian suited Eliza just fine. So there, in the midst of the Pacific, the Williams family and the unsuccessful evangelist formed a long-lasting friendship.

The natives' refusal to enter a "state of conversion" was no mystery to

Morgan. "There are so many temptations placed before the natives there being quite a number of dissipated foreigners living among them and ships visiting the island almost constantly that the missionaries have but little influence over them and are altogether in the most indigent circumstances I ever saw missionaries. But they still persevere and think that the day will come when they can boast of a large number of converts."

This visit to Ponape nearly proved a long one indeed. When the whaler was about to cast off, the pilot came aboard drunk, and Sturges suddenly stood to add to his flock of none the entire crew of the *Florida* (certainly, at least, the pious Eliza). Facing a potential disaster in that dangerous harbor, Williams discharged the pilot, probably none too gently, and managed to get the vessel out on his own safely. (There exists a yarn of an irate whaling master who dumped overboard an incompetent pilot who'd grounded his ship. At least he'd verified first that the wretch could swim before dunking him.)

Sailing on in her solitary pursuit through the Pacific, the *Florida* put in at all sorts of strange and dangerous islands. The ship was following in the wake of Nantucket men, who, a couple of generations before, had in an ever-widening circle discovered these places and spread their religion, diseases, and bad habits. The natives came on board, sometimes buck naked, looking to steal, trade, or even couple with the men, but with Eliza on board, it's not likely the crew had a chance to fornicate openly. (There were even shipping papers carrying verbiage that made a whaler liable to lose his pay if he was caught in the act of love.)

Some natives were quite gracious. At Wellington Island, they decked Eliza's curly hair with flowers and playfully threatened to steal Willie. Such welcomes weren't always the case for whalers. Ironically, some seductively gorgeous and invitingly lush islands were inhabited by hostiles, and God knows how many American men lie in unmarked graves or at the bottom of the ocean after having let their guard down with the wrong tribe.

It wasn't just blind malice on the locals' part: Many whaling skippers had justly earned the hatred of a tribe by kidnapping the native men to serve on board. Sometimes whalers agreed to buy water, fruit, or other goods and then sailed away, in a practice known as "paying with the fore-topsail." Cheating the natives meant the next whaling master dropping anchor at the island, whether he was honest or not, might pay for a colleague's prior transaction with his and his men's lives.

Trading was a big part of the whaling industry. Shipmasters had the absolute trust of the owners, who provided them with letters of credit that, by law, had to be paid. As whaling captain and Yankee trader, Williams did his fair share of commerce, both to supply the ship's needs and to fatten his own purse, by buying tortoiseshells and other goods to sell on the side. That February Williams went ashore at MacAskill Island, where a few years before the natives had killed a whaling master and crew, a fact not lost on the nervous Eliza. As she anxiously watched with a spyglass from the ship, the natives encircled Williams and briefly blocked him from view. It would have been an easy matter for this gang to kill or injure the Wethersfield master, but the intent wasn't bloodshed, and so he survived to trade another day.

Onward the bow cut through the foam of the Pacific to Guam, where on March 6, 1860, Williams lowered a boat and, manning the steering oar himself, headed with Eliza and Willie to shore. The surf near the landing was so rough that earlier that day another whaling master's boat had been capsized by the waves. This dunked captain watched Williams's progress from shore, and the sight of the boat moving through the chop, carrying a woman and an infant, gave him such a fright he nearly passed out. While he and the surprised natives watched, Williams's sure hand successfully guided the craft in. Williams later admitted the water had been rougher than he'd expected. As for his wife, apparently she hadn't worried at all—after all, it was her man at the oar. While on the island, she ventured into a Catholic church, a rather bold and open-minded thing for a Congregationalist to do in those days. Nevertheless, she was offended that the locals profaned the Sabbath with drinking, and even worse, cockfighting; the priests themselves placed bets on these spectacles, and were great card-players to boot.

2

A Lighthouse Keeper

> I will do such things,—
> What they are, yet I know not: but they shall be
> The terrors of the earth.
>
> —*William Shakespeare,* King Lear

It was a cold mid-February afternoon, and although there was snow and frost on the ground, the city, in a political sense, was blisteringly hot and bubbling over with rebellion. Legislators from below the Mason and Dixon Line had in past weeks been leaving their offices almost daily as their states departed from the Union. Perhaps most noteworthy, the prior month an exhausted Senator Jefferson Davis had resigned his office to become president of the Confederacy. Despite the hubbub in the capital, Raphael Semmes, the chief lighthouse keeper of a fracturing nation, had finished a routine day working at his job, and now passed a quiet, if anxious, afternoon with his wife and daughters at his house. Absent was his son, a West Point cadet, soon to be a commander of light artillery in the Confederate Army.

Great things were still unfolding. Semmes's own adopted state of Alabama—by birth he was a Marylander—had voted to leave the Union just ten days before. Yet, even as the grand political drama was being enacted all around him, U.S. Navy Commander Semmes, fifty-one, continued to toil away in his small office in the basement of the Treasury Building, where his mission was to maintain the safety of the Republic's

waterways and shipping. To those around him, he must have appeared a
man uniquely capable of doing nothing when everyone else was rushing
into action. But the stiff and starchy commander had in fact been closely
watching and biding his time with the patience of a hunter.

Semmes was a thin man of average height, with a narrow, plain face
formed into the expression of a simple benign fanatic. He was nondescript,
except perhaps for a long, thick mustache that nearly made him look dashing. An obscure naval officer, Semmes had persevered in a career as un-
noteworthy as his appearance. He was bookish and a devout Catholic, and
according to one colleague, the "mildest mannered man in the navy." No
one expected much of him, and it was unlikely they'd be surprised; those
less than friendly considered him an ambitionless nonentity with too great
a taste for the comfortable life ashore to do great things on the sea. After
serving his years in the navy, Semmes's plan, presumably, had been to retire quietly from federal employment with his brief glory days in the Mexican War, such as they'd been, far behind him.

The resignation speech of former West Pointer and army officer Jefferson Davis moved Semmes powerfully. Because he was a part-time lawyer
accustomed to oratory, the lighthouse keeper had an ear for fine speech,
and Davis had perhaps summarized perfectly the commander's own feelings about the splintering of the country. That included the fact secession
might have a cost: "We will invoke the God of our Fathers," Davis said,
"who delivered them from the power of the Lion, to protect us from the
ravages of the Bear; and thus putting our trust in God, and in our own firm
hearts, and strong arms, we will vindicate the right as best we may." Such
references were easy for Semmes to follow. He was a man of a certain distinctive Southern type who clutched eagerly, and with ease, a Bible in one
hand and a sword in the other. War looked imminent, and in his estimation,
any naval officer from the Confederate states who didn't apply his firm
heart and strong arms against the lion and bear was a sellout or a traitor.

He was not a shirker and he quite possibly suffered from acute boredom, thus Semmes needed little coaxing to abandon his quiet life. So while
he kept up with his less-than-demanding federal job, he was secretly listening "with aching ear and beating heart for the first sounds of the great
disruption," which he now felt was at hand, as he revealed in a letter. His
indolence was rewarded on Valentine's Day at about 4:00 P.M., when his

summons to action arrived in the form of a messenger with a telegram. Taking the document in hand, he scanned it with eyes sharpened by years of staring both at ocean horizons and law books. Geographically, the missive's origin was Montgomery, Alabama, where a capital had been set up to mirror the one in Washington, and to serve a country that didn't yet exist. It was sent by the hand of a naval committee chairman who lacked a single ship to oversee. He instructed Semmes to "repair to this place, at your earliest possible convenience." The chairman had decided the South needed a navy veteran like Semmes, although on the face of it, he was perhaps an odd choice. Semmes hadn't been to battle since the Mexican War, fifteen years earlier, and about the most noteworthy event he'd participated in during that conflict was the loss of his own ship in a gale.

In any case, telegram in hand, secession had come to Semmes, and he was joining it. This was a great leap overboard for a man who'd received his commission from the hand of President John Quincy Adams himself. He knew for certain only that he would be abandoning a stable career in the United States Navy but not what distant point he was heading to. If the South failed, he'd "have thrown away the labor of a lifetime" and the all-important pension that went with it. Nor was leaving the flag he'd saluted for thirty years to rally to a new one an easy choice for so sensitive a man as Semmes. It was also a cause of tears for his wife, whose family was from Ohio and solidly pro-Union, and she was now facing the ruin of her home and future.

Whatever his reservations, that night Semmes wired the committee chairman back. The lawyer and writer, fond of melodrama and long-winded speechifying, gave a reply as terse as the invitation: "Despatch received; I will be with you immediately." The next day, he resigned his commission in a polite letter and removed reference to his naval rank from his stationary, leaving it as just "Esq."

Two days later, Semmes said goodbye to his wife and children, and stepped aboard the train to leave the capital that had been the seat of the power he'd obeyed for three decades. The departure was not, on the face of it, an overwhelmingly portentous event, but it was a pathetic one. The train rolled out of the station, carrying a sad, sleepless middle-aged man without a recognized country, his sword strapped to his luggage, his pocket crammed with notes scrawled for his soon-to-be superiors. As the locomotive thundered south toward the geographical heart of the rebellion, the climate was warming, both politically and in temperature. Rolling through Fredericksburg and Richmond, he knew the citizens were passionately arguing that Virginia should secede, just as gallant, if tempestuous, little South Carolina and his beloved Alabama had already done.

Two days later the train crossed the Alabama state line, and through burning, heavy eyes Semmes saw the night sky illuminated by a blazing pine grove. The scene powerfully moved him as something completely Southern, and he became as one with the flame, trees, and sky. The effect was immediate: His heart started to beat more powerfully, and the blood in his veins seemed a more lively fluid than before. Later, he realized he'd crossed a barrier unworthy of a backward glance. The former man and the former life were something like the ash now dropping from the sky. No longer two souls in conflict but one in pursuit of a goal, Semmes felt relieved and secure, and, at last, sleep ceased to elude him.

Owning a considerable and intimate knowledge of his new enemy, the courtly lighthouse inspector had, even before the war, with great zeal already put much thought into precisely how to dismember the Union's fleets. Just prior to resigning his commission, he'd shared these notions in a letter with a fire-breathing southern congressman. "The ingenuity, enterprise, and natural adaptation of the Northern people to the sea, and seafaring pursuits" had made them second only to Great Britain in ocean commerce. The greatest weapon the North had was its maritime industry—including the great whaling fleet, the envy of the world. "It is at ships and shipping, therefore, that you must strike," he suggested.

He soon was to prove he was no mere amateur military theorist. Given his federal job, he also knew it was the most precious of fuels that kept the nation's lighthouses lit—sperm whale oil.

3

In Wild and Distant Seas

> But ships are but boards, sailors but men: there be land-rats and water-rats, water-thieves and land-thieves, I mean pirates, and then there is the peril of waters, winds, and rocks.
>
> —*William Shakespeare,* The Merchant of Venice

SHIP *FLORIDA*, BANDERAS BAY, BAJA CALIFORNIA, MEXICO, FEBRUARY, 27, 1861

Life aboard obviously was not all work for Williams, for here in this shark-infested dent halfway down Mexico's Pacific coast, Eliza gave birth to a daughter, Mary Watkins. Despite the lateness of her pregnancy, Eliza had ventured aboard another ship for a gam the day before. During the actual delivery back on the *Florida,* as with young Willie, her husband must have played the midwife in the tight confines of the cabin. After liberating the infant from her mother's body, the normally reserved master didn't bother to conceal his pleasure in front of Morgan, who recorded the event and the captain's expression faithfully in his log.

Prior to sailing to Mexico, Williams had wanted to make a stop at San Francisco. To Eliza's disappointment, he thought better of it after discovering some of the crewmen were plotting to jump ship there. Once a hand vanished in that rambunctious hillside town, recovering him was next to impossible. The available sailors, safely in port, were usually not desperate enough to jump shore to replace a lost man. Moreover, San Francisco was also a convenient place for disgruntled seamen to hire lawyers and sue their captains, with virtually all secured damages going to the counselor.

To avoid the Siren of the Golden Gate, Williams had elected to head south and hunt devilfish—gray whales—off Baja California, a dry and deadly wasteland almost as empty and pitted as the surface of the moon. Here in this seaman's "purgatory" only a suicide willingly ventured on shore, and perfect attendance on ship was guaranteed. Whalemen, with their keen eye for the ironic, called service here "liberty." Devilfishing, practiced from San Diego through Monterey to Half Moon Bay, was especially dangerous even by the grim standards of this most perilous of jobs. A gray whale, usually a docile baleen feeder, was a fighter so nasty and full of spite that killing a "Bloody Greek," to use a term of the time, like it was an arduous job, and usually a bomb lance or two was required. A man in a life-or-death struggle with a devilfish soon discovered that the beast had well earned its name. More hunters were killed, crippled, or otherwise injured in this type of whaling than possibly in any other branch of the fishery. A whaler who survived and became successful was known as a "good devilfisherman."

To get an idea of how ornery the gray could be in battle, consider the results of single day's hunting in 1856 in Magdalena Bay, Baja California. The cost included two whaleboats destroyed, while others had been staved in fifteen times; out of eighteen crewmen, six were badly hurt: one with two broken legs; another, three fractured ribs; and a third with innards so damaged he couldn't perform another lick of duty for the rest of the voyage. Not a single whale had been taken. This was just one of many examples that proved this rough customer wasn't worth the effort required to kill him.

The female devilfish were even tougher than the males, the mothers being especially fond of and protective of their young. So violent were the mothers when fighting off a whaleboat, they were prone to accidentally kill their own infants. Often the harpooner would fasten to a calf first to lure the mother to her death, and even when that strategy worked, the boat crews were often exhausted by the tussle. One captain's story, if not exactly true in detail but accurate in spirit, claimed an enraged cow, looking to avenge her slaughtered infant, chased a terrified boat crew to shore, where they beached their craft to gain sanctuary. The master even said the "pow-mucky" whale had them climbing trees.

At Baja California's Turtle Bay, on a small rise just a few feet from the high-tide mark, Eliza saw for herself how dangerous whaling in these waters could be. Here lay a small makeshift graveyard marked by simple headboards that recorded only names and dates. She noted one whale had killed four men just the year before and these unfortunates now reclined together in one common plot. The only vegetation nearby was a few sprouting weeds. This sight gave her pause. "I thought that I would not like to be buried in such a barren spot, far from friends and home—but would, I think, prefer even that spot to the deep," she once wrote.

When the *Florida* dropped anchor at Banderas Bay, the weather was pleasant, and here the shore was green and heavily wooded. The forests swarmed with bandits who tried to make a living stealing where there was precious little to take. For amusement, the locals held weddings—there were four of them while the *Florida* hunted nearby. These festivities consisted of the men getting drunk while the women danced, as one whaling captain told Eliza. Despite the attractive surroundings, the bay was not an ideal place for whaling. Not only was the prey here fickle and hard to catch, but because of the aggressive and plentiful local sharks, towing a dead whale to the ship for trying out was a race against time. Whale fat was an especially attractive treat to the scavenging fish, and the fountains of blood gushing from a dying leviathan often incited whole schools of sharks to a feeding frenzy. Boat crews had to row hard and fast, as each shark's bite took with it a hunk of profit. One ship here, noted Morgan, had taken a whale "but lost nearly all of him by the sharks eating him."

The sharks' constant attention to a carcass also meant those on the cutting stage had to work as quickly and efficiently as possible, or there would be nothing left to try out but the skeleton. The close proximity of so many snapping jaws made it especially dangerous for the men doing the initial cutting-in work, which required them to actually stand on top of the whale after it was secured to the ship. One slip on that slick back and the crewman would be in dangerous soup, although typically he'd have a line tied around him held by some trustworthy shipmate on deck. As whalers didn't like to share their prize, on some ships during the flensing, it would be one man's tiresome job to kill as many sharks as he could by stabbing at their heads with a twenty-foot-long blubber spade. Sharks so brained often became part of the feast themselves. Wounded and disemboweled sharks might even feed on their own entrails, over and over again. During such a commotion, their thumping against the ship gave the crewmen in their bunks something to think about as well.

The *Florida*'s crewmen had to combat an army of these scavengers while flensing a gray whale. Eliza noted how the sharks died. "If they cut them in the back of the neck, they will die instantly. They spun around and around, turned on their backs, and sunk out of sight. They did not get much of the whale, for the Men kept fighting them off." More spectacularly, a spotted leopard shark, large, awful, and beautiful, swam near the ship. Morgan, who had killed as many as seventy sharks in two or three hours while rendering the blubber, tossed a spade into the fish and it bolted. Ominously, the nearby estuary was not only the home of sharks, but also of wicked-looking alligators—a whaling master decapitated one and took the head on board as a memento.

Always the hunter, Williams, son Willie in tow, went on a duck hunt on the mainland, where he bagged twenty fowl, including pheasants, snipe, and curlews. Returning with a limp because his shoes were wet and full of sand, Willie said over and over again: "Papa, bang go the Ducks." He was proving to be a boy's boy, mischievous and requiring constant watching. Eliza noted Willie virtually lived on deck, and was fond of throwing things overboard. During the sojourn off Baja California, one day the crew was both boiling in a whale and caulking the ship. Despite her Wethersfield matron's discipline, Eliza, between the oil and the caulking tar, couldn't keep Willie clean for more than an hour at a time. At this time, he fell while playing and cut his lip on his teeth; his pa stitched it. Although a good patient, he pulled the threads out the next day; Williams sewed the lip up again. Willie didn't like this—but "bore it well."

With the summer approaching, Williams ordered the anchor up and the bow pointed west again, for another trip to the Sea of Okhotsk. He needed some luck up there about now: Correspondence from Fish, Robinson back in Fairhaven indicated things were none too cheery for the firm. According to a letter dated January 3 to Williams, the owners wanted him to get sixty to ninety day terms for his refitting bills, which must be kept "as small as possible," as "we have passed through another squeeze[,] money. . . . more scarce than in [18]57." Other things had transpired, "and we now face a Secession of South Carolina from the Union and probably other Cotton States to follow. . . . political matters in the worst possible state, which frustrates business of every kind." He noted, perhaps with a quiet, dark joy, that a petroleum refinery in New Bedford had blown up the prior night and burned down, killing two men. Perhaps he meant it as encouragement: Whalers didn't care much for the rock oil industry.

On the way to her icy destination, the *Florida* passed the Hawaiian Islands, a lonely string of volcanoes thrusting above the central Pacific's surface, and at all points of the compass nearly three thousand miles distant from any other landfall. Approaching the island of Oahu, Williams sailed to Honolulu, then a small semicivilized port squeezed by vegetationless mountains from behind and the sea before it, but handy for outfitting whaleships or recruiting men. After passing through the narrow coral entrance, the *Florida* anchored in the warm, clear blue water of the harbor, which, though an expensive privilege because of docking fees, ensured the vessel would be well sheltered from the combers that rolled down those many miles from the Arctic. Near this center of Pacific commerce, past the swampy and mosquito-infested Waikiki Beach, was a sight no whaler could mistake: Diamondhead, a small mountain, that in the words of Mark Twain, "loomed high, rugged, useless, barren, black and dreary." Luckily, though, despite its appearance, the promontory's summit was often wreathed in clouds that produced rain that kept the island from dying of thirst.

An arriving ship fired her signal cannon and drew to the wharves an interested crowd from the city's 15,000 mixed inhabitants, including Chinese, whites (known as "haoles"), dark-skinned Hawaiians, and many a mix in between. They babbled in the "chopped language" the inhabitants had cobbled together from all the various tongues spoken on the islands. The native women, often barefoot, wore bright-colored, loose-fitting robes and small hats. A New Englander with lots of time to kill might venture to watch them dance the lengthy and traditional but scandalous hula to the beat of a drum.

As with many of the Polynesian peoples, the Hawaiian men were brown-skinned, large, and powerfully built. The males often covered their great physiques with any discarded clothing they could find, and typically they hid their genitals with an "unnecessarily slender rag" slung between their legs. A warrior might cover his magnificent upper body in a sailor's pea jacket buttoned up to the chin, even on a broiling day, and be all but naked from the waist down. Or, with a loincloth slung about his privates but feet planted in large boots, he might parade about with a dignified scorn that bordered on arrogance. These men were known for their courage, generosity, and good humor. True water dogs and needing little to survive on that temperate isle, they were willing to work for the small wages of a whaler. The *Florida* took a handful of these Kanakas on as crew.

Walking around the city's wide streets a visitor saw its fine buildings were few, and there were no brick houses or yards. For comfort, the houses usually had carpets of grass that yielded easily to the foot. This Yankee outpost of the Far West even had its own seamen's chapel, a white two-story building crowned with a cupola from whose top snapped a bethel flag to welcome ships into port. One seeking an antidote to the island's uncannily bright, clear sunshine and loose ways could go inside the chapel and get a taste of far-off New England's gloomy Calvinist religion. Despite the missionaries, who defined Christianity largely by the pleasures and prizes one couldn't have, catering to the whalers and their wants and vices was a major source of Hawaiian prosperity. The royalty of the islands, when in public, were transported in nothing less than a whaleboat. Refitting and supplying the fleet, along with cattle ranching, was virtually the only source of money. That had been the case since the time of Kamehameha I, the great warlord (and, thanks to western firearms, supreme king), who, decades before, had permitted the large-scale rape of the once plentiful sandalwood forests. These trees, considered by Kamehameha as his private treasure, were much sought after by the Chinese, who transformed them into clouds of incense that pleased both the living and, presumably, their ancestral dead, before whose altars they ignited it. It also served to provide furniture and perfumes. Because of the forty-year obsession with sandalwood harvesting, the natives had neglected their own farms, and the overabundant cattle ate up the natural flora. Both factors had grave environmental consequences. Hawaii's aggressive cows, imported originally from South America, were a nuisance as well, eating the thatch on houses and even attacking people.

Given the necessary presence of the whaling fleet in the harbor, Honolulu could be quite wild. "There is no god this side of Cape Horn" was a saying in the grog shops in the small haole district, and the fines from the blubber hunters' unfailing misconduct was a major source of revenue. Things had gotten considerably out of hand back in 1852 when, after the death of an arrested sailor, some three thousand whalers and other mariners went on a three-day rampage, burning the police station and nearly torching the whale fleet at the docks. However, unlike the more densely settled San Francisco, there were fewer places to hide deserters here, and the police got a bounty for recapturing them—payable of course, from the lay of the caught fugitive.

Commercial growth of any kind, however, always comes at a price. Right from the arrival of Captain Cook, maritime trade had offered mixed blessings at best, and had by innumerable direct and circuitous causes virtually destroyed the Polynesians, whose very remoteness had once been their greatest protection. The diseases (measles, influenza, and recently arrived leprosy, to name a few), not to mention the shock of economic and cultural change that came in the wake of the westerner's ships, slew the Sandwich Islanders by the biblical thousands. Twenty years before, the once-happy and relatively tranquil race had already seemed a doomed people. Moreover, with the introduction of new seaborne invader animals, such as the rat and the cow, and insects, such as those tiny winged vampires called mosquitoes, the ecology of the islands was damaged and thrown out of balance forever.

Religion, whether intentionally or not, had played a role in this slide down. To the loss of their ancestral lands, culture, stories, pride, and health the Hawaiians could add that of their gods. As always, the first arriving whites had the Bible while the natives had the land, and true to form, before a few generations had passed, this arrangement had been reversed. Most natives by 1861 had converted to Christianity, more or less, which had done wonders to hasten their decline; their love of interminable sermons had become a notorious vice. As one observer put it, "Since the missionaries obtained footing upon these islands, there has been so much *praying,* that the natives have been literally *prayed to death.*" The missionaries squandered the brawn of some of the last remaining Hawaiian men, using them as draft horses to pull their go-carts, as a scandalized Melville noted in 1846. These men, treated little better than slaves, had been "evangelized into beasts of burden," he noted with disgust.

Leaving the *Florida* anchored behind, Eliza braved the midday heat to go on shore with her husband for some touring and shopping. She would have attended church had time permitted. She'd heard that once a person could cross Honolulu's harbor over the decks of the anchored ships, and that the wharves had been the scene of great bustle and noise as the whalemen left their vessels and headed to shore. To her, the port seemed in decline. It was relatively quiet and with fewer ships at anchor than the stories of yore indicated. More ominously, perhaps, was the big stir caused by the arrival of the newspapers carrying Lincoln's inaugural address. On that speech, it was expected, hung the fate of the far-off republic of which Hawaii was not yet a part. Being a whale port that served the Yankee fleets, the locals knew the Union's fate most likely would directly affect their own.

SEPTEMBER 23, 1861, SEA OF OKHOTSK,
WHALESHIP *FLORIDA*

As the crew had taken no whales of late, Williams was risking much for nothing. On September 8, the ship had nearly met disaster when the wind filling her sails died, and with a strong ingoing tide, the *Florida* was in danger of running aground in a rocky kink on the desolate Siberian shore. The collision might have staved the ship's side in—and that meant the survivors, if there were any, would be stranded for the winter. To get free, the crew had to kedge off, which required sending a whaleboat out carrying a small anchor attached to a cable running back to the ship. After rowing out a ways, the crew dropped the anchor, and the men at the windlass went to work, taking the cable in. Rather than pulling the anchor up, they pulled the ship out until there was enough wind to sail away from shore.

Then it was time for the *Florida* to cease the hunt. The crew had already started running new ropes through the blocks and bending new sails on the yards, preparing to sail back east toward a troubled country at war. That hazy morning, at about 10:00 A.M., a lone right spouted within sight of the *Florida*. Looking for a late-season prize, the crew took the trouble to scramble and drop two boats from their davits to begin pursuit. Perhaps sensing the danger, the whale sounded, and although a good hunter could usually guess where and when his prey would rise, the victim escaped. At noon, it reappeared, now with fortune's scales about to tip against the whale. For the second time that day, Morgan lowered his boat, but now the harpooner fastened on the whale, and well. Thus stuck, the prey began to move and the boat went flying on a Nantucket sleigh ride through the cold waters of the Okhotsk.

During the hunt, Eliza left the cabin to enjoy the fine weather, a relatively rare treat. With a spyglass to her eye, she looked into the distance at the black form of the whale breaking the surface of the water, something akin to a small dark island, yet capable of an agony whose intensity was perhaps matched only by its vast bulk. It was lying still and showing little fight now, as its type sometimes did with a six-foot harpoon or two planted in its back. Even after three years of whaling, Eliza still couldn't stomach watching the crew kill the monsters. She marveled that she'd been frightened that the crew wouldn't break the weeks-long dry spell to take a prize.

As Eliza watched, Morgan's whale, possibly ill and weak, stopped moving, and just rolled slightly in the water. It was still in sight of the three-masted square-rigged factory that was about to process it into commercially valuable oil and bone. Around the whale were two boats carrying veteran officers and their crews who were ready to close in. They were armed with more than enough lances, bombs, and irons to finish the job of murdering the victim. It was beyond the whale's imagination to know the fate in store for its massive body, or it might have fought harder. On board the *Florida*, waiting to rend its corpse, was an array of virtually unbreakable ropes and chains, cutting spades, oversized stout blocks, pots, axes, and other similar gruesome tools.

Eliza saw the men rewarded by double spouts of dark, glob-filled, tar-thick blood. The gory shower meant something vital in the beast was leaking. Blood was filling the great lungs, and soon it would become still and roll over on its fin in death. She watched as the whale sulked; he broke the surface again, not far from his sounding point, and spouted another clot-filled, V-shaped column of blood and spray. The thickening globs landed in the boats and on the men. By 2:00 P.M., the dead whale was alongside for trying out. Although not particularly fat, he was large, and yielded the crew 125 barrels for their trouble, not so bad a take for the end of the season.

As for Eliza, before the whale was even dead, she had taken the spyglass from her eye and went downstairs to her cabin. There she unburdened herself in her diary, unable to stand the sight of the "poor whale" in its misery.

4

Journey's End

My whaling voyage was over. It was an adventure out of the ordinary,
an experience informing, interesting, health giving, and perhaps worth
while. But I wouldn't do it again for ten thousand dollars.
—*Walter Noble Burns, on arriving at San Francisco,*
in A Year with a Whaler

OCTOBER 26, 1861,
GOLDEN GATE, CALIFORNIA

A pilot guiding her in, the *Florida* left the open Pacific Ocean that had
been her home over the past two meandering years and slipped under the great, rugged, sere cliffs of the Golden Gate. The wind filled the
new sails the crew had bent on the yards in the Sea of Okhotsk the month
before, and the *Florida* ploughed on into the bay. There was a special ur-
gency to reach the city just a few miles beyond the Gate, as infant Mary
Watkins was ill beyond Williams's powers of doctoring and needed a cer-
tified physician.

The Golden Gate, named after a similar portal in the Bosphorus for reasons having nothing to do with its color, was a mile-wide strait of cold,
treacherous water. It was framed on either side by mountainous precipices
whose dizzyingly steep sides plunged hundreds of feet down to the water's
edge. The fog hanging in and near the gut might light up with the setting or
rising sun like a ship's sails, with a wide palette of soft pinks, reds, and oranges. It was a broad-shouldered, hardy region, and vessels sailing into the
Gate had to contend with gusts and fast ship-wrecking currents. The

surrounding region is dotted with roughly cleft brown mountains starkly rising up into the air like broken bones through skin. They are decorated with intimidating bluffs that look like dark olive-brown dents, grooves, and ravines. Despite the Gate's misty, dreamlike beauty, under the mariner's feet and around the hull roiled the always cold and dangerous waters.

Beyond the Gate lies San Francisco Bay, which is, in effect, a vast murky inland sea. It consists of the drowned mouths of two converged rivers, the Sacramento and San Joaquin. In the nineteenth century, through the bay's gray green waters swam sharks, sea lions, and devilfish, among other aquatic denizens. Despite damp, bone-chilling weather and frequent, dangerous, and gloomy fogs, the great and violent bay offered shelter from the winds that battered the California coastline during the rainy season between November and April. After sailing inside the bay, on the starboard a ship would pass the dour Presidio, an antique fortress dating back to the time when California had been an unprofitable Spanish colony. Entering San Francisco harbor proper, a sailor found himself surrounded by vessels from all over the world—including Chinese junks, packet steamers, elegant thousand-ton clipper ships, and, of course, whalers. Standing guard over all this marine wealth was another fort, armed with cannon, sitting on the barren rock-island called Alcatraz. On the shore side, the citizens had wisely decided to improve nature and filled in the extensive tidal flats and added piers to reach deep water.

Only a reckless gambler would have bet that this miserable, isolated, and sand-dune-dotted peninsula could birth the vast, wealthy, and complex city that was San Francisco. The community had started as little more than a handful of beachside tallow and hide warehouses and rookeries. The two institutions of the evangelist and the soldier were the perennial double pillars of Spanish colonization, so there was a mission, around which was clustered a stand of adobe huts, and a fort. First called Yerba Buena, the wretched settlement boasted a population of a few hundred "Greasers, Digger Indians, a few white traders, deserters from whaleships, and adventurers of no nationality." Yerba Buena's estate improved after a young Bostonian named Richard Henry Dana, looking to cure his bad eyesight, dropped out of Harvard in 1834 and shipped out on the brig *Pilgrim,* which was headed west to pick up hides.

In California he found a paradise inhabited by an undeserving "idle, thriftless people." Shrewdly and self-servingly, he decided the land needed the firm and active hand of the Anglo-Saxon to exploit it properly. Dana's hugely famous 1840 book, *Two Years Before the Mast,* planted in the head of presidential "dark horse" James K. Polk the notion it was time to fill out the Louisiana Purchase by laying hold of California's golden sands and all that lay atop them. When the Mexicans refused to sell this coastal prize, there was war. Manifest Destiny prevailed easily in the Mexican War of 1846–1848. Once the clouds of gunpowder cleared, the ownership of California changed, and with it the name of Yerba Buena, which became San Francisco.

Fate intervened further in 1849, when gold—best defined as a yellow metal that makes men go crazy—was discovered at nearby Sutter's Mill. The race to San Francisco was on, and in little more than a generation it miraculously grew into the greatest of Pacific metropolises. While the Gold Rush had spurred the infant city's growth, it had another effect, attracting, according to one purple catalogue of the "hideous brood," Australian convicts, the scum of European cities, eleven "bruisers" from New York, "plug uglies" from Philadelphia, "desperadoes" from Central and South America, Indian pariahs, and outcasts from the South Sea Islands. "Crime of almost every conceivable grade ran riot. Gambling dens monopolized the heart of the town. Murderers walked about the streets unchallenged in midday."

The early 'Frisco felons had operated with little to worry about from the law, until the interestingly named Committee for Public Vigilance started hanging them—the hated Australians in particular—not bothering with the superfluous formalities of a trial. At midcentury, San Francisco was blooming with all the vices and virtues of the restless golden coast itself, taking pride in its luxurious world-class saloons, while frowning on the frequent gang fights and shootings. Physically and spiritually it was as spacious, violently sublime, uncompressed, and oversized as New Bedford on its gentle slopes was small, fixed, and regular.

In addition to crime, sapping manpower from the whaling fleet was another major tradition here. While the sight of deserting Arctic and Baja California blubber hunters walking the city's streets had been common for decades, during the Gold Rush, ship jumping had become a virtual frenzy, with officers and men going overboard by the dozen. Once ashore, these would-be Midases vanished into the tent-and-shanty city that had sprung up to accommodate the flood of Argonauts looking to try their luck panning dirt. The harbor became forested with the masts of derelict whalers lying in the mud, motionless except for the rise and fall of tides. New Bedford alone lost forty of her whale killers.

With their sails removed and strung up to catch the wind in order to power mills, some of these hulks became floating hotels and warehouses. Eventually, they returned to the sea or became literally a part of the city, buried and broken up in the soil beneath San Francisco's thriving, bawdy, and dangerous waterfront. At the time the *Florida*'s voyage wrapped, it was all too tempting and easy to go over the side and vanish among this boisterous city's 55,000 people. A choice between the misery of a voyage and the varied pleasures to be had there—theaters, gambling halls, brothels, and magnificent saloons—was no choice at all, except perhaps for a Quaker. For land-hungry whaling men on board their ships, hearing the midnight bells and seeing the lights on Telegraph Hill twinkling at night made the city beckon like paradise.

While the *Florida* lay in eight fathoms, the crew was treated to the sweet sound of an anchor clinking and splashing in the water. Williams immediately ordered a boat launched and rowed to the bustling wharves just ahead to get a doctor, leaving Eliza behind with the baby. Soon he would be settling the last of the *Florida*'s affairs, having already started the process when he discharged his Hawaiians on the way home. Because the *Florida* had taken in $63,000 in oil and bone, Williams, as a part owner, realized a good profit. The rest of the crew would get their share of the proceeds and leave as well, probably never to whale again—if they were smart, at least.

It was a matter of fact that the masters and owners wanted to squeeze every ounce of oil from the whale and, all too frequently, each cent from the pay owed crews. On some ships, the owners gouged the exhausted and sea-weary survivor of a voyage for the cost of desertion insurance, oil leakage, interest (up to 25 percent) on any cash advances, and other sundry charges—including the cost of recovering him if he'd tried unsuccessfully to jump ship. On a long voyage, a man's gear wore out, so he turned to the ship's slop chest, which often charged rates double or triple the goods' worth. Again, as with the cash advances, the percentage of interest applied might have been the envy of Shylock. Moreover, the lay was usually a portion, not of the actual profit of the cargo, but of a preset figure the owner, in his infinite wisdom, himself had determined. There was often very little left over for the man who'd done the gritty work. Some unfortunate fools returned to New Bedford or San Francisco owing the ship money or getting paid off with one generous dollar.

No matter. At least for a little while, Jack was free on shore. Money in hand, a discharged crew added their cheers to the general din onshore as they ran riot in the 402 or so drinking establishments of the City of St. Francis. It wasn't tough to recognize a freshly disgorged blubber hunter. As one *Harper's* correspondent wrote of a group of mariners just off a New Bedford whaler: "A cart rattles by, loaded with recently discharged whalemen—a motley and a savage looking crew, unkempt and unshaven, capped with the head gear of various foreign climes and people—under the friendly guidance of a land shark, hastening to the sign of the 'Mermaid,' 'the Whale,' or the 'Grampus,' where in drunkenness and debauchery, they may soonest get rid of their hard-earned wages, and in the shortest space of time arrive at that condition of poverty and disgust of shore life that must induce them to ship for another four years' cruise." In one night, by the clear pure light of whale oil lamps, Jack might blow most of his meager wages on whiskey, games of chance—for the participants, not the house—and the sort of women inclined to rent their relevant body parts to sailors. Clearly, just a few too many years at sea might make a man unfit for any other way of life.

For officers, life on shore was a bit more elegant. In San Francisco, a greasy whaling master putting in from a successful voyage stayed on credit in the elegant Russ House or Occidental Hotel; in the register he inked in as the place of origin the "Arctic Ocean" or "Icy Cape."

Crews coming back home after years of whaling were much changed. During the sail, a simple, honest green hand might have been transformed by experience and contact with his colleagues into something probably no longer recognizable. There would be new scars, a sunburned and weathered visage, perhaps a monkey or a parrot on the shoulder, incurable tropical or venereal diseases coursing through the veins, a finger or a toe or more lost to accident or frostbite, and other tokens of a whaling voyage. If a man had been weak, he was now tougher, or he would simply not have made it.

There were many ifs a man had to overcome to survive a first whaling

voyage—let alone, like Williams, to eventually navigate successfully backward to the master's cabin from the forecastle. The inexperienced green
hand had to endure the bad food and the constant dangers of sea and
whale. His constitution faced extreme hot and cold climates, and he risked
the potential brutality of captain or mates, which could tempt him to jump
ship to become a refugee. Some whalemen just stayed wherever the ship
docked—the ports of the Pacific and Atlantic were littered with onetime
whalers. Take, for example, the one-eyed Fall River Yankee who gave up
whaling in Hawaii and made it to San Diego and set up an establishment
where he served out strong drink.

A mariner returning after years of whaling might wonder if the same
family was still living in the ancestral home (if it was still standing), and
who had been added or subtracted from its numbers. One young contemporary of Williams's, Ben-Ezra Stiles Ely, arrived home in East
Greenwich, Rhode Island, more an "amphibious animal" than a boy—as
well as a convert to Methodism. So ragged was his appearance, covered
in stinking tar and rags, that Ely avoided going through the downtown,
"ashamed to be seen by any civilized being." His outfit included a southwester hat of canvas and tar, a woolen jacket darned and patched with
an old blanket, and pantaloons, also crafted of a blanket, which had a
seat, sides, and knees of tarred canvas. The shoes were gone at the toes,
and only the remains of stockings hung over the heels. "I was truly a despicable looking fellow, and should have been a fine figure to sit for a
painting of 'the prodigal son,'" he recalled. Not one article of clothing
had been washed in a month. Clearly, he wasn't someone to be downwind of.

After arriving at the back door of his home, he said "I stood surrounded,
with all eyes turned on me, as if I had been some wild animal, for all were
so lost in amazement, that they never thought of shaking hands; and had
any thing affectionate stirred with them, the scent of tar and bilge water
must have sent the feeling back wence [sic] it came." Even after being
scrubbed down, the stink of the bilge clung to his hair for days, and he
couldn't get rid of his sea legs for weeks. He retired from whaling, noting:
"Generally they who live on the deck have but a short life; and nine hundred and ninety-nine out of a thousand of them are but poor Jack Tars at
last." His and Williams's contemporary, Melville, who required a circuitous

path—to put it mildly—to finally make his way home from the Pacific, also never signed on a whaler again.

Through his own first voyage, Williams had managed to keep something decent alive inside himself, which he proved soon after docking in New Bedford. Agent Potter, as was customary, rowed out to the lower harbor to board the vessel to greet the captain. He saw Williams and remembered the very tall and slender boy he'd signed on, who by now must have hardened into a sunburned, grizzled young man with calloused hands and hard muscles. He'd heard that Williams, while sleeping on deck, had suffered what was called moon blindness, (but was probably a touch of scurvy), and he'd recovered. Desperate, Williams begged Potter a favor: He lacked money, but wanted to return to his mother immediately, before his lay was settled. No doubt he sought to pleasantly surprise her that all his Welsh limbs were intact. In a move of unusual trust, Potter, impressed by his supplicant, forwarded the cash, and Williams returned the loan on the first mail from Connecticut. A friendship had begun.

When a sailor was discharged, if there was a grudge against the officers, this was the best time to settle it. On the sea, insubordination is mutiny, and a successful mutiny is piracy, as onetime mariner and lawyer Dana noted. A wise jack-tar—assuming such a thing existed—waited till safely onshore before applying a blackjack or knife to the object of his hate. No doubt some men had good reason to want to settle scores. Officers and captains could be ingenious masters of hazing, an especially popular diversion at the end of a whaling voyage, particularly if the master wanted a man to desert and forfeit his lay.

(In New York Harbor in 1851, an especially unpopular and sadistic mate named Douglas jumped ship early to get a head start out of port. Looking to set a record voyage from the east to San Francisco, Captain Robert "Bully" Waterman of the clipper *Challenge* took aboard first officer James "Black" Douglas of the *Guy Mannering* before the ship had even docked. Douglas's men so hated him, he feared setting foot on dry land. Over the course of the *Challenge*'s voyage, not only did the duo fail to set a new speed record, they so brutalized their crew that one man died from mistreatment and the others rose up in a failed mutiny. The two officers later were tried and sentenced—lightly—for their crimes.)

It was a different situation with the *Florida*'s docking in 1861, during which first mate Morgan made his last entry in the log, then wrote a poem about the tacking of a ship. Interestingly, the current mix of crewmen was approximately what it had been at the voyage's start. This was rarer than it might, at first, seem. Some ships came home to port without a single member of the original crew. Out of some thirty men who'd shipped on board the *Florida,* six had deserted, another two had been jailed, and one, Tim Reed, had died at the bottom of the sea. There were, and would be, far worse records.

No matter how well Williams and other masters performed, there were, nevertheless, underlying seismic changes on the way that would make success in the fishery, difficult even in good years, frighteningly scarce. That same year Williams dropped sail in Buzzards Bay, forty-eight out of sixty-eight of the ships returning to Fairhaven and New Bedford were unprofitable. Worse, scouring the earth for petroleum was proving a more lucrative and reliable proposition than whaling. During the second year of Williams's voyage, the discovery in Pennsylvania of the cheaper rock oils, as they were called, coupled with a refining process that allowed their ignition without blowing up the user, was set to deliver a death blow to whale oil's value. Kerosene soon was even due to replace whale oil as the illuminant of choice at the Clark's Point lighthouse in New Bedford.

It hadn't improved things that on August 24, 1859, New Bedford had endured its worst holocaust to date, on the order of something from the pages of the book of the Apocalypse. A fire started on the east side of Water Street and leaped to the nearby wharves, stores, shops, and factories. As it progressed, what many held to be the dearest fuel in the world spread over the surface of the harbor and, as it ignited, created a sea of fire.

Still worse in the long run for the city, petroleum was coming in like a slow and steady tide, driving down the price of whale oil. By the time Williams returned to New Bedford, the *Whalemen's Shipping List and Merchants' Transcript*, the weekly industry journal of record, was carrying the depressing news that 1860 was one of the worst years ever. The aggregate value of whaling products had dropped to $6.5 million from $8.5 million. The year 1861 was even worse—twelve months of "unparalleled pecuniary hardship," with overall profits for the industry amounting to only $5.4 million. This was no surprise, given the scarcity of the animal that supported the fishery. One vessel had come back to port after thirty-nine months with the captain claiming he'd seen sperm whales only nine times.

A whaling captain was unable to sail out of New Bedford with much guarantee that he'd come back with a profit. The dangers involved were also increasing so fast that there was less of an assurance he'd make it back at all. All that remained for him was a slow losing struggle. By 1876 the whaling fleet, its glory, tragedies, and the whole grand party, would be largely erased—burned, crushed, or sunk. In far-off and forgotten waters, only a few half-buried old Yankee wood-ship planks, too stubborn to disintegrate, would remain to testify to the fleet's former existence. The savvy capitalists in the City of Light who owned the fleet could see a change in the economic weather, and were beginning to pull their funds out of whaling and invest in petroleum, textiles, and railroads. However, the captains and officers couldn't change tack so easily, and some had to keep working as best they could in the only profession they knew.

The *Merchants' Transcript* also glumly noted that some ships reaching home port would never be fitted out again—at least not until the magic invisible hand of the marketplace intervened and let profits find their proper levels. The industry that had created and defined the community, indeed, the fuel of the City of Light itself, had begun to flicker and was fading. However, some of the sober and steady merchants of Water Street wouldn't go gently. For a time, they indeed hugged the oil cask like a brother, as preacher and lecturer Ralph Waldo Emerson once described the city's philosophy of business. Perhaps they hugged even tighter: They weren't a sentimental bunch in New Bedford. By specialization in one industry, the merchants gave themselves a unique advantage. If they sent out enough whale ships, at least one might come back greasy and make the venture worthwhile.

As for Williams, he had other courses open to him. Given his background and properties, he might have become a merchant master, an industrialist, or a landowner. Nevertheless, the whaling life had fastened to him like an iron, and no matter how much Eliza asked him, he wouldn't leave it. He couldn't be happy back on shore after facing ice packs, whales, savages on the South Seas, and a myriad of other dangers in the worst places on the planet where the foolish, weak, or merely unlucky were quickly disposed of. No matter what the challenges, like the bull sperm, the King of the Ocean, Williams would fight at both ends before rolling over on a fin.

With the war looming, Fish, Robinson & Co. wanted the *Florida* sold, for fear she might be taken by Confederate raiders. However, before Williams could close the transaction, a gale struck San Francisco, whipping the bay's waters up nastily. In the following tumult, the ship dived down into the water and struck bottom, which snapped her jibboom at the bowsprit. Williams later claimed it was the first time he'd ever lost a spar on her. He should have taken it as an omen of worse things to come.

BOOK TWO

The First Iron

5

The Daring Fishermen
of New England

And this Light is within, by which all these things are seen, and you that
love this Light, you will see all these things above mentioned. . . . And
so you all being Enlightened with the Light, receiving it, you receive
Christ; you receive not Darkness nor the Prince of Darkness; And as
many of you as do receive Christ, to them he will give Power to become
the Sons of God . . .

— *George Fox,* Some Principles of the Quakers

WEDNESDAY, NOVEMBER 20, 1861,
NEW BEDFORD HARBOR

It was just past 6:00 A.M., and the sun was still low over the east with a
late fall storm brewing, when the stout form of Rodney French came
over the side of the onetime whaling bark *Garland.* The thickly built sixty-
year-old was one of the commoner sights in New Bedford, he had been,
among other things, a selectman, city mayor, temperance gadfly and advo-
cate, coal and timber merchant, and, up until the past month, an agent
and owner in the "spouter" fleet. Accompanying French was a pilot to
guide the already fitted out *Garland* from the harbor into the bay. Somewhere on his person, he also carried a sealed envelope from the U.S. Navy
holding orders that neither he nor the other fifteen captains he was to command could open, at least until the land had become invisible. Improbable
though it may have been, he was on a secret mission, and to French's existing glories and titles, if he survived, he could add that of Commodore.

The 243-ton *Garland,* like the other fifteen whalers anchored nearby, rode low in the water, and not because she carried supplies for the South Sea or Arctic hunting. Instead, these vessels carried chunks of New England's own backbone: stone. Under her waterline two holes had been drilled whose location only French and his officers knew. In these openings were two plugs that alone kept the Atlantic from gurgling in, and it didn't take a genius to understand, at least vaguely, what the fleet's purpose was. Like French's naval title, the squadron he lorded over was ridiculous— perhaps the most decrepit and ragtag collection of vessels ever to put out from the Whaling City—or anywhere, for that matter. The unopened orders for the captains of the "Stone Fleet" (as the mission was to be named), directed them to sail to Savannah to rendezvous with and report to the blockade commander, J. S. Missroon, who, incidentally, had no idea they were coming. Their purpose: to plug up the ports of the Confederacy using onetime blubber-hunting vessels weighted down with stone.

Such a mission could provide the means for a man, already renowned for dispatching forty pirates, to write his own way into the story of the great Civil War, and add to the repertoire of those stories he was so good at telling. Until this time, about all French and his fellow masters assigned to the operation knew was that their destination was somewhere down south. Their ships were at anchor in the lower harbor by Clark's Point and awaited permission to leave. Each morning for the previous few days they had visited the office of Rudolphus N. Swift, the overseeing agent. Today, during the masters' daily tryst, Swift had presented them with official envelopes from somewhere in South Carolina, and when they rowed back to their vessels, they all took pilots with them. The agent also had given them preliminary orders to protect their ships and notified them that when the mission was discharged, they would be given passage north to New York City.

Predictably, word spread rapidly throughout New Bedford that the fleet was about to drop sail, and a crowd began to assemble along Clark's Point. (This small peninsula was encircled by a boulevard that French had built when he was mayor and even generously allowed the city to name it after him.) This was a chance to see a big event, solve a riddle, break up the monotony, and maybe dispel some of the gloomy clouds that had been lowering over the city. Both the War of 1812 and the American Revolution had been disastrous for New Bedford and Nantucket, and the local blubber lords were hesitant about risking their property in a third conflict. Already the local papers carried news of a raider called the *Sumter,* now roaming the waters somewhere beyond the mouth of the Acushnet. With the Civil War heating up, shipowners were letting their vessels rot at the docks rather than risk them at sea. However, for the past month, those with an eye on the goings-on at the ghost town of a waterfront had noticed that workmen were toiling at a frenzied pace on just four wharves, which were lined end to end with ships, while the rest of the waterfront remained sinfully idle. (The only other hubbub had been the discovery that a former whaling ship, the *Margaret Scott,* had been fitted out for a secret slave-carrying mission. Someone, perhaps a disgruntled hand, tipped the authorities to the *Scott,* and on the evening of November 9, the police carted away Samuel P. Skinner, the agent fitting out the vessel, along with the captain and mates, and shipped them to Boston to be tried for slaving.)

The busy dockworkers were in the employ of the firm of Ivory H. Bartlett & Sons, which was buying up whaleships at bottom dollar. The firm's pockets were clearly deep, and prices ranged from $3,050 for the *Leonidas* to $5,000 for the *Courier.* The agent Bartlett bought one vessel after the other, as if ticking off a list from the pages of the *Whalemen's Shipping List.* After passing papers, he sent the ships to specially leased wharves for what would prove to be a unique refitting.

The odd drama that New Bedford, Rodney French, and the fishery were taking roles in had started playing out some months before in Washington. Although perhaps only a few at first realized it, the U.S. government was picking up and carrying the whaling fleet into national history, like a great breaking wave. Just which bureaucratic impresario had hatched the original idea is hard say. As has been observed, a plan after its success is most likely to have many fathers, yet a failed one often find itself a bastard, and so it was with this Stone Fleet.

We can, ultimately, blame it on General Winfield Scott, commander in chief of the U.S. Army, once dashing and heroic, but by this time so bloated and ailing he was unable even to mount a horse. Before the younger general George McClellan outmaneuvered him, as great commanders do, not in the battlefield but in the planning room, and took his job, Scott

had hatched a plan called rather bluntly Anaconda. It was the Hero of
Chapultepec's idea to strangle the South's commerce through blockade
and thus speed the war's end. With the typical butchery of language that
occurs during wartime, an altruistic federal attorney general even said
starving the southern population was "the cheapest and most humane
method" of ending the Confederacy.

The plan became reality in April 1861 when Abraham Lincoln, reacting
to Jefferson Davis's decision to issue those letters of marque that eventually
were to prove so destructive to the whaling fleet, officially proclaimed the
naval strangulation of the South. Perhaps it was not a bad idea, if it had
been practicable, which it wasn't, as the U.S. Navy soon discovered. There
were far too many ways in and out of the South's ports—river estuaries,
harbors, and inlets—that did little more than make blockade-running a
safe and profitable vocation. Indeed, runners sneaking out of Charleston,
the seat of the rebellion, boasted they piloted their boats at night by the
light of the blockade ships. The vessels slipped out with cotton and exchanged it in Europe for shoes, gunpowder, Napoleon howitzers, Brunswick
rifles, and musket balls. When they returned their lightened vessels floated
over shoals that frightened off the deep-draught navy ships or entered channels protected by the cannon of Confederate forts.

Eventually, some anonymous bureaucrat on a committee took up the
idea of blocking the harbors of Savannah and ever-defiant Charleston by
sinking old ships full of stone in their channels, thus creating a barrier to
navigation. It's known that one capable officer, Charles H. Davis, suggested the plan, only to quickly withdraw it on the sensible (if less than relevant grounds) that it wouldn't work. The soft, muddy bottom of a river's
mouth would shift and just open new channels underwater around the obstruction. For a time, using a stone fleet remained just one of the many
somewhat eccentric ideas to help the Union's cause—there were many
floated during the war—that is, until the Bay State's own Gustavus V.
Fox, the assistant secretary of the navy, began to agitate for it vigorously.

His good advice on scuttling the plan ignored, Charles Davis later noted
the idea was a "maggot" in Fox's brain, and that it gave Fox a chance to indulge a penchant for buying vessels "that amounts almost to a mania." Over
all objections, on October 17 Secretary of the Navy Gideon Welles, a fussy,
wig-wearing Connecticut Yankee, ordered the government's purchasing

firm to start buying, as "secretly as possible," old hulks to sink off Savannah. (The lucky procurement company from New York City was headed by none other than Welles's own brother-in-law, George D. Morgan, who won the sweet deal without even having to go through the formality of submitting a bid. For his services, he was entitled to a 2.5 percent commission on the price of each ship—a healthy incentive from his generous relative.)

Knowing that there were plenty of suitable vessels in the whaling ports of the north, Morgan arranged for agents to start making deals in Sag Harbor on Long Island, in grand but much decayed Salem, and New London, Connecticut. In New Bedford, Bartlett became the government's voracious representative, and in his zealous and constant deal making, virtually no offer was beneath him. It was a buyer's market, and in an unprecedented set of transactions, owners sold their ships off rather than risk them on the seas again. Of course, as those involved were Yankees, there was some arm wrestling over price: On September 17, Bartlett dickered till 2:00 A.M. before closing a deal for the *Frances Henrietta,* the first purchase. Thereafter, the bargaining went on and on. For instance, he bought the *Courier* and the *L. C Richmond* after a dinner.

Eventually, it was French's turn to haggle. Perhaps with an eye to the collapse of the industry, he'd already begun to disentangle himself from whaling, having disposed of four vessels from his five-ship fleet. Now here was Bartlett roaming the waterfront looking for ships to launch against the South. For French, a tireless, persistent, and money-wise Friend, this situation provided a way to serve his glorious cause and mammon both, so he sold his last whaling vessel, the *Garland,* for $3,150 on October 28. To get that sum, he must have bargained shrewdly; one observer called the vessel "crazy" and "rotten." Bartlett was known in New Bedford as a fine Christian philanthropist who dispensed money to the needy and even called in person to minister to the sick and infirm; in French's case, he may have been extending his generosity at Uncle Sam's expense.

By November 18, the government agents had bought twenty-five vessels, sixteen of them hailing from New Bedford and the small towns encircling her. This movable auction drew some questionable commodities, and onlookers may have wondered just how wisely Bartlett had expended his treasure. For example, the *Herald* was past the half-century mark, and may have been whaling before the Declaration of Independence was inked. The *Potomac* was so old and rotted in places that "mere cement" prevented her disintegration. The fast *Corea* of New London, reported *Harper's*, served once as a store ship in the Royal Navy during the American Revolution. That is, until a gang of rebel fisherman led a surprise and successful attack on her off Long Island and sailed the vessel to New Bedford for conversion to Yankee whaling.

For about six weeks there was uninterrupted action on the Whaling City's waterfront, perhaps the most intense ever seen there. The process repeated itself over and over: A ship returning from hunting blubber was sold and tied up at Swift's wharves for workmen to descend on. They took out everything useful—harpoons, barrels, cordage, and chronometers—leaving behind just enough canvas to sail and a single anchor. The loose gear began to pile up in open squares for disposal through auction, and some whaling men found handsome bargains.

There was yet more work to be done. The ships were reshaped to fit as much of the mineral cargo as possible while maintaining the greatest possible sailing speed. As part of the "face lifting," carpenters shrank the crews' living quarters to the smallest possible size, which guaranteed even more space to cram in the stone that was held in place by reinforced bulkheads and hulls. As the duration of the coming trip would be short, no whaling to be performed, and as little money to be expended for preparations as possible, the repairs were sloppy. Workmen sealed open deck seams with tar instead of properly caulking them; they nailed down planks to cover holes; and as for anything else, the hand pumps would address that.

It got odder yet. While some tightfisted whaleship owners might have skimped here and there—especially on food—while outfitting their vessels, they never went so far as to actually drill holes below the waterline—even for the insurance money. Now workmen bored through the hulls, and thrust lead pipes with flanges through the apertures. They sealed the flanges with easy-to-remove wooden plugs connected by a bolt secured with a screw. The location of the openings was secret, perhaps to ensure no one could scuttle these floating barriers before they reached their goal. Given these times, even in New Bedford, one had to be wary.

With the outfitting completed, the ships required freight. On the roads in and around New Bedford and even as far as Cape Cod rattled the wagon wheels of teamster James Duddy, who roamed about buying stone.

He paid fifty cents per ton until he'd procured $7,500 worth—although who bothered to weigh the granite isn't clear. For that kind of money, local farmers—who must've thought he was crazy—parted willingly with their stone. Just as at Jericho, the walls fell and left the land as open to trespass as it had been two centuries before, when the Wampanoags had roamed the woods and marshes unworried about the notion of private property. The collection finished, Duddy carried his treasure back to the Whaling City waterfront for loading on the now empty ships. Apparently no mariner, he and his helpers stored it belowdecks in each ship without any thought to how it would affect the vessel's balance and steering, a potentially lethal handicap for some vessels.

These preparations complete, a signal gun boomed, and the ships were moved to the mouth of Buzzards Bay, dropping anchor on November 15. There their presence was a nautical hazard. As the masters awaited further orders from the government, the fleet's presence in the harbor provided grist for the rumor mills. Predictably, despite the official veil that forbade the newspapers from making any mention of the project, nearly everyone in town had known what was going on, or had guessed at it during discussions over dinner tables and on street corners. Some of the more imaginative wondered whether the Union was reviving the ancient art of the catapult—or using the stone to somehow arm slaves or to build up ripraps.

The ships needed crews, and again Swift had his pick: The port was full of captains, mates, and seamen who'd returned home from their voyages and were "sogering," or hanging back, in bored idleness and needed work and excitement. Thus, men who owned some of the most illustrious names in New Bedford—Tilton, Gifford, even one of the ubiquitous Howlands—signed on. Given the political climate in this Grand Old Party stronghold, if the candidate for the expedition was a Democrat, he might need the endorsement of a radical Republican to get his post. Rodney French himself volunteered, although his ship-commanding days were decades past, and there could've been some peril in this venture, as, presumably, the fleet was heading below the Mason-Dixon Line. Too old for the more bloody action in this great Civil War, he must have decided he could set his hand to the helm of a ship, or at least stand on her quarterdeck while someone else commanded.

With the manpower selected, the masters met one night just prior to sailing and discussed the best way to sail for their presumed destination. They also voted for a commodore. There, veteran campaigner French was able to become first among equals—perhaps first among superiors, in terms of nautical skills—and won the election. "Rodney . . . was a pretty good fellow, told a good story, and was generally liked by the rest of the captains," said J. M. Willis.

There was one holdout against French: a dour, grizzled, white-haired old salt with a sharp beaked nose named William Worth, who claimed he'd served on a warship. Worth was one of the last of the great race of Nantucket whaling men; it wasn't surprising he managed to stand out. True to that island breed's contrary nature, Worth, sure he was better qualified than French (and probably right), found himself a dissenting minority of one. But as Willis later said, "Rodney was good enough for us." They'd elected him to the job, but as anyone knew, there were no democracies on the high seas. Moreover, a whaleship almost always plied her craft alone, and the captains weren't used to taking orders from anyone, excepting maybe the ship's owner, and even then only on the Atlantic side of Cape Horn. To them, military commands and coordination were as alien as Greek. Between them the masters had centuries of pooled whaling experience, while French was merely a long-retired merchant mariner who clearly had used diplomacy and perhaps a bit of political influence to win his post. Consequently, the result was that Old Rodney pretended to lead, and the men under his nominal command pretended, badly, to follow. Nevertheless, the masters took the job itself seriously, and they posed for a self-flattering photograph portrait, with the intent of creating a historical event. The resulting image captured a glimpse of a universe fated for obsolescence.

At last, after taking the spacious harbor of Port Royal, Admiral and Flag Officer S. F. DuPont sent up word he could accommodate Welles's secret weapon. Agent Swift in turn got his orders from the secretary and passed them on to the Stone Fleet commanders at their morning meeting. Sometime around 7:30 A.M., on board his pretend flagship *Garland*, Commodore French, more *opera bouffe* actor than real brass, ordered his signal gun fired. This was a rare call to battle to come from the Quaker side of the Acushnet, and surely pleased the crowd. Anchors wet with the Acushnet brine were hauled up, sails set, and under overcast skies with a snowstorm in pursuit, the fleet began to sail out of the harbor. One captain on shore watching this junk armada of broken-down, cast-aside, and leaky vessels setting out said it was the "roughest-looking fleet he ever saw."

Although New Bedford frowned on that temple of sin known as a theater, this scene was proving to be like a great dark comedy orchestrated by a master impresario, with bright absurdity glaring out from under the pomp. No great hardship was this voyage. On board the vessels were plump Thanksgiving turkeys for the captains and officers, courtesy of Bartlett. Not that there was much for these career whalers to be thankful for, as they were sinking their livelihood, some in ships they'd taken around the world and on whose decks they'd risked their lives again and again during their voyages. To top the farce off, French had run out amidships his own "Quaker gun," a section of spar painted black to look like a cannon, with his signal gun mounted on top. Such deception was customary for whalers, who also often painted black squares on the sides of their ships to look as if they had gun ports, to frighten off pirates or hostile natives. Now they hoped they would warn off privateers.

By the time of departure, a crowd of thousands had gathered on Clark's Point to cheer and wave handkerchiefs. As the vessels sailed on, the harbor became a confusion of explosions, perhaps as if all the frustrations over the war and the idleness of the waterfront were finally venting themselves in noise. From off the starboard side came a thirty-four cannon salute from Fort Taber—one of the few occasions the garrison had a chance to fire its guns; the *Varina,* the U.S. revenue cutter escorting them out, fired her gun as well. Even the lighthouse keeper at Dumpling Rock shot his pistol, and to these booms, the fleet responded with its signal guns. By 8:15 A.M., the small flotilla was outward bound, standing south, and going off "in fine style"—or at least as fine as could've been expected, given it was "to be put to the inglorious use of stopping rat-holes." Although the local journalists had held their tongues and avoided publicizing the Stone Fleet, the New York press soon after trumpeted the departure.

Predictably, given the preparations, there were problems from the start. Duddy and his helpers had so awkwardly arranged the stone be-lowdecks it threw the balance of the vessels off, and made navigation dif-ficult for their masters. With the drunken response some helmsmen got from the wheel, it's surprising none of the vessels collided, were sunk, or dropped cargo prematurely in Buzzards Bay. Nor had the workers sealed all the leaks adequately: The crew on board the *Richmond* carefully looked to their pumps. Despite these problems, by around 10:30, the fleet had cleared the outer harbor and the pilots were going overboard to return to New Bedford.

By 11:00, buffeted by light squalls that covered the decks with snow, the vessels were passing the Sow and Pigs Reef. Through the squalls, the Stone Fleet crews busied themselves for the voyage down to somewhere southern; no one would know until the next day, when the masters opened their secret orders. However, over their protests, French had instructed his captains to stay to the west of Long Island. But being deep-sea whalers, they'd no interest in hugging the shoreline, especially when they might be driven into shallow, rocky water carrying all that stone and be smashed. "We were not coasters and didn't want to get in too near the coast," as Captain Willis said.

In a moment of high comedy, French tried to signal the fleet to follow his instructions, but the other masters ignored him. At about 4:00 P.M., as noted by Joseph Howland in the log of the *Leonidas*, the commodore made some "strange maneuvers" and tried to call out to the nearby ships. Briefly, several of the fleet hove to, but soon left him in their wake without changing course. A breeze wafted down from the north, meaning the wind ran around the ships' quarter, or sternwards, sections—a good point for a square-rigger—and carried them at about six knots and gave them some headway as they passed Gay Head. Just as if they were chasing a whale, the masters turned this gloomy expedition into a yachting race, each man looking for the right to boast he'd delivered his ship for sinking before his colleagues. French, in the slowest vessel, was left limping behind.

The sailing of this flotilla was yet another sign of the time. Not that anyone necessarily knew it yet, but the crowd that'd lined the water-front earlier that day had said its goodbye to more than the fleet. Be-cause the city had for so long prosecuted whaling with the guts of its mariners and cleverness of its money men without cash infusions from outsiders or subsidies from the government, none believed the industry's days were numbered—even after a spectacle like this. As an editorial the next week in the local paper claimed: "Very few men in New Bedford really believe that the whale fishery will ever cease to be carried on from this port."

The outfitters were aware of the dangers faced by the fleet, and did not want the government's investment lost before its time, so in his instructions, Welles's brother-in-law Morgan stated: "The only service required of you, is the safe delivery of your vessel, and as she is old and heavily laden, you will use special care that she sustains no damage for unskillful seamanship or want of prudence." To that end, he advised them for safety "to keep in company of your consorts" and show lights at night and in case of coastal fog, to sound horns or bells, as well as check the pipes in the hull daily.

With no naval officer to oversee them, the masters raced on to Savannah as they saw fit on a trip that was neither exactly a military operation nor a whaling voyage. For one thing, there was plenty of fairly decent food for everyone, crews included, courtesy of the government. As there were no whales for them to hunt, discipline was fairly lax, and there was little for the crews to do except avoid sinking or hitting another stone-laden vessel. There was an exception to the general rule that prevailed in the fleet, however. Captain Worth, who'd wanted to be the commodore himself, apparently so hated the idea of an idle crew he made his men take some of the ship's granite, pulverize it, and use the smaller bits to holystone the very uneven decks. Although the decks had been sloppily sealed by tar and pitch during the hasty preparations, by the time the leaky *Archer* reached Savannah, they were smooth. And while some captains had allowed their crews to live so well that they ate their way through their provisions before arriving in Savannah, he kept his men on a stingy sea-ration diet.

Initially the fleet's luck held, and the weather was fine, with a fair wind for three days, and the masters staying as close as possible. Although the line of ships began to stretch out, usually a master could look out from deck and typically see two or three ships nearby and enjoy a daily exchange of news on latitude, longitude, and soundings. The *Garland*, as always, kept sogering (hanging back) in the rear as the other captains continued to play their little joke on Old Rodney. With the *Sumter* and God knew who else roaming the seas, there was obviously some concern, and French noted in his diary, quite possibly with a grin: "Passed a schooner which eyed our big gun attentively and kept off."

The season's own mood was another threat, and after several days, the weather became heavy. The winter storms set in, pummeling the whalers and "obliging us to part company," as the captain of the New Bedford bark *Cossack* put it. The Stone Fleet, running this seasonal gauntlet, responded by taking in sails and manning pumps. The rough wind and seas demonstrated the biggest danger wasn't privateers, but rather the bad condition of the ships and the haphazard way the stone had been piled inside. The rough ride threatened to break the few boards in the forward storage areas that held the stone—the potential redistribution of the cargo could throw off the ship's balance in the sea, and after that happened, what came next was anyone's guess.

The outfitters however knew, or hoped with a reasonable certainty, the whalers' skills and expertise handling stricken or damaged vessels in all climes and seas would compensate for the fleet's wretched condition. And wretched the ships were: The *Courier* leaked so badly her captain asked master Joseph Howland, who was sailing under his stern, to steer his *Leonidas* nearby just in case he needed help. Howland had his own problems. The wind gusted so hard the bolt that held the *Leonidas*'s mainstay (a line that secured the mainmast), broke, and the crew hastily replaced it with "four fold takle [sic]," which took till sunrise to rig.

As it was, not liking the *Leonidas*'s attitude in the sea, Howland "throwed overboard" about several tons (worth $2.25) of stone from the bow. Some other masters who disliked the sluggish feel of their bows also executed deep-sea ocean dumps, and the consensus was that had less experienced men been in charge, most of the government's property would've wound up at the bottom of the Atlantic prematurely.

Not a lot went right for Old Rodney French or the armada he pretended to command after passing through Buzzards Bay. On the evening of November 25, the *Leonidas* entered the Gulf Stream, the current of warm northern-moving water that had been known to Yankee whalers since the days when Nantucket was the bull sperm whale of the industry. The next day was "laborious" as "tremendous squalls of wind and rain" struck. Howland claimed that his bark was a "bonney sea boat and easy ship at sea" that kept the water out during this rough spell. When the heavy weather finally eased, some of the captains held a gam on the *Herald* and dined on the fine government fare.

As the New Bedford men worked their way to their rendezvous point, they caught sight of other sails on the horizon belonging to a half dozen New London whalers. The *Fortune* was the flagship of this fleet, and on her quarterdeck walked one of the greatest masters of the city, John "Bony" Rice. He was a ripe old salt who'd led his contingent—which, with typical Yankee subtlety, he called a "frowsy lot of old tubs"—out from New London simultaneously with the New Bedford squadron. As in the City of Light, hundreds of curious onlookers with nothing better to do came to the harbor there to cheer as the vessels put out to "choke up some rebel harbor," as some of the local sailors put it—one adding "that's about all they're good for."

Born in 1798, Old Bony had won his nickname by his admiration of the French emperor and general Napoleon Bonaparte. He was something of a great field marshal himself in the endless war of Yankee versus leviathan, and his success in those combats made his services highly desirable to the merchants of New London. Fittingly, this was going to be the last voyage of his successful whaling career, and as the New London fleet had sailed down to Long Island Sound, Bony told the ill-named *Fortune*'s crew: "Boys, it is forty years since I sailed down this harbor as master of the *Pizarro* and it seems to me that I don't feel a day older than I did then. We shall probably meet rebel craft before we get rid of this cargo and they may blow us galley west." He also noted, prophetically, "We can't get on an even keel with those rebs."

As he explained: "I was never afraid of a whale even when he riz up in the water and was likely to send our boat's crew into kingdom-come for there was one chance in a hundred to galley [frighten] him. It's different with rebs' ships of war. They won't be gallied and you can't heave an iron into 'em, while on the other hand they can sink you with a single shot."

Appropriately, the bark *Fortune* was, like Bony, a weathered old sea dog and monster hunter, with yellow sails "innocent" of a coat of tar, having been whaling from Plymouth, New Bedford, and New London for forty-one years. As the New London ships wove their way among New

Bedford vessels, it was a combined if ramshackle Stone Fleet that headed down south. A *New York Times* reporter described the ships, calling them the "queerest quaintest specimens of ship building afloat" over the bar (sandbar). He detailed their whalers' appearance: the tall spars that tapered like "whip handles," the weathered sides that were sheeted over with pine planks to cover the gaps in the rotted wood below, and the painted Fiji ports that stared out to frighten off any would-be attackers.

Regrettably the secrecy Welles had hoped to maintain over the project was soon gone: The New York newspapers covered the armada's progress widely enough to unite both those above and below the Mason-Dixon Line in making it a widespread topic of conversation. As the ships progressed, their condition became more dangerous. The seasonal gales tore the Sag Harbor ship *Timor*'s sails to rags, and she was leaking badly. Her crew tried straggling back to port, but the vessel's wretched condition prevented them from holding a course. She overshot, not just her home port, but the entire state of New York. By the time she could navigate again, it was December and she was off Gloucester, the Bay State's leading fishing town, on rocky and rugged Cape Ann, forty miles north of Boston.

6

⚬⚬⚬

Old Rodney

As this instrument is purposely made and used for the destruction of mankind, I can put no weapon into a man's hand to destroy another, that I cannot use myself in the same way.

—Nantucket Quaker William Rotch, on being asked to sell bayonets on the eve of the Revolutionary War. He later threw them into the sea.

Rodney French, the nominal commodore of the Stone Fleet, deserves some consideration, as he was an example of the owning and ruling class in New Bedford at the twilight of the whaling industry's eminence. Energetic and ambitious, he was the sort of man every small city has—always connected to some office or political group, constantly in the view of the public as he expanded his connections and influence. Building a bridge, enforcing killjoy liquor statutes, giving a speech, laying down a street—the tedious business of his metropolis was never beneath him.

Perhaps as much as anyone else in New Bedford, he'd lived by the Latin phrase *Lucem diffundo*, or "I spread light." Ever since its incorporation, this had been New Bedford's motto: It provided the oils that fed the flames that pushed back the dark all over the world. But there was another dimension to the phrase that the first mayor, Abraham Howland, or someone near him, almost certainly had in mind. Howland was a Quaker—though members of the movement referred to the sect as the "Children of the Light," and to one another as "Friends."

The Friends sought to kindle moral illumination in the world, and opposed with considerable vigor and little but much deserved success slavery, war, and conspicuous consumption. There were wealthy Quakers who lived in virtuous penury, sobriety, and chastity by choice. In Nantucket, where the Friends had ruled with near tyranny for a hundred years, they even buried their dead in a common graveyard without the luxury of headstones, bedeviling later generations looking for their ancestors' eternal spots of repose. Such observances applied to their whalemen, and it was common for Nantucket mates on whaleships filling in their logs to end the day's event's by saying "by the grace of God."

The story of the City of Light's whaling days is inseparable from that of its Quaker founders. Their ability to hate pleasure and ostentation and sustain an iron creed of self-denial helped them succeed in the masochistic and sadistic industry of whaling. Some of the early inhabitants of New Bedford were rigid to the point of eccentricity, which may also have been a source of their success. In 1759, Jonathan Hathaway, father of a great shipbuilding merchant, Thomas Hathaway, wrote the following as part of his will:

> I give my soul to God, my body to the dust, and order that my
> funeral expenses shall be paid out of my live stock. I bequeath
> to my beloved wife, Abigail, as long as she remains my widow,
> the use of one-half of the lower rooms of my dwelling house, the
> use of the little pantry closet and the use of one-half of what is
> called the big closet, the use of the two drawers in the big chest
> in the kitchen, the use of one-third of the pewter dishes, the
> wool from six sheep every year, half the apples of the orchard
> every year and two pairs of stout leather shoes every year.
> I also will that my son, Thomas, shall live with and be clever
> [good] to his mother, keep a horse and pillion and see that his
> mother goes to meeting.

Prosperity was a just pursuit for the Friends: abundance was a sign of divine favor, and wealthiness was next to godliness. (It didn't matter that the treasure had been stolen forcibly from the whales.) In New Bedford, money had a certain sanctity, in the sense of an absolute certainty. The Merchants Bank and Mechanics Bank on the corner of Water and William Street even had the exterior of a temple, and given the region's proclivity to sectarianism, this mock-church, in one building, had managed to host some dissent. Because the two banks had each hired separate builders and hadn't exactly agreed on how to erect the Greek Revival building, the slope of the four columns on the left didn't match their mates on the right. The merchants high up on County Street at the peak of the city skyline lived in oversized mansions fit more to hide the spirits of Greek gods or house the debating chambers of great statesmen.

Of old, the Quaker whale-oil barons' strict religion forbade most pleasures: music, cards, liquor, and loose women. One of the eminent fathers of the town, Gideon Howland, was reputed to have caused a scandal when he snuck a piano into his house. As the religion evolved with changing prosperity, some of these otherworldly millionaires expressed their carnality in their lodgings, which included fine three-story mansions in walking distance of their offices. No simple saltbox cottages or clapboard Georgian houses for them. The Elect of God were in favor of overstated grandeur and pomp: the staid and stable lines of Federalism, the tortured elegance of Gothic, and the frighteningly clean symmetry and order of the Greek Revival temple—although the last connoted paganism and freethinking. From the roofs and cupolas of these houses, owners of the whaling fleet, in their city on a hill, or hills, could look over the harbor and literally watch their ships come in, with a full cargo in the hold and riding low in the water, they hoped.

Divine intervention aside, New Bedford's success had been by no means assured. Originally, it was just one of many New England ports competing for the same fat, dangerous aquatic resource. Fairhaven was similarly situated on the river, but it never rose as high in the firmament of whaling. According to sailing prodigy Joshua Slocum, who was from Nova Scotia, the denizens of Fairhaven were "thrifty and observant." This was perhaps the kindest thing ever said about them. To some degree, being located on the economically accursed eastern shore, they'd been forced to be mean. The problems were both natural and manmade. A bridge built in 1798 to link New Bedford (then called just Bedford) to the villages of Fairhaven and Oxford (just to Fairhaven's north) had changed the Acushnet's currents. The span caused so much sediment to be dumped at Oxford's waterfront, just to the structure's north, that the village was unable to expand as a port. To the south, Fairhaven Village was squeezed in without room to expand its wharves, until in the 1830s a stubborn farmer finally relented and sold off a piece of choice riverfront property adjacent to the bridge for development.

The circumstances had meant that, in Biblical terms, the west bank had been the Jacob of the river, the east bank its Esau. As for the bridge, as if in some sort of divine judgment, it was destroyed in the "Great Gale of September" 1815. The replacement span that was erected in its place was something of an eyesore, and "thought by many to be a great public damage," according to historian Daniel Ricketson, writing in 1858. And just a few miles offshore lay once-great Nantucket, which New Bedford had also eclipsed. Nantucket, Fairhaven, Sag Harbor, to name just a few— the merchants of the City of Light had stepped over many rivals to become preeminently rich.

But there was more to the Quakers than accumulating money. Man's fallen nature being what it is, the Children of the Light had to be persistent to fight off the darkness faithfully. This was a port where many not of the elect gathered together to serve the whaling industry that made the elect so wealthy—with limited success. The growing city faced growing pains. Promoting virtue was a full-time job in the workers' precincts, geographically mere blocks from where the wealthy lived in cozy rectitude, but miles away in mind, spirit, and style. Among the toilers persisted the sort of desperate poverty that breeds crime, and children went about "begging pig's livers at the expense of their integrity," according to one account. Naturally, rough diversions were the order here, with rowdy dances and dog and rooster fights blocking sidewalks in Precinct Four. In 1852, there were seventy-eight liquor shops and fifty-six houses of ill repute in town. Four years later reformers launched an assault on the Arctic Saloon on First Street, on the waterfront, to make dancing, fiddling, and "high times generally" a thing of the past.

At times, mere anarchy threatened to dominate. In 1826, some of the more criminal element tried to "run the town." A chief headquarters of this group was a whaleship, which, lying in the shallows of the harbor, had been converted into a brothel. This Ark, as it was called, being conveniently in the African and colored section of town, was allowed to operate until the body of a ship's carpenter turned up nearby, and the clergy, in its reliable role as occasional rabble-rouser, incited a crowd to take action. The Ark's defenders fought with boiling water and stones, but after the righteous mob leveled a Quaker gun at them the battle ceased. The ruse worked like a charm, and the waterside Gomorrah went up in smoke.

In 1829, in what appeared to be an act of revenge by the Ark crowd, the Elm Street Methodist Episcopal Church in turn was torched. Another brothel arose, just west of the original, called the Hard Dig, and became the headquarters of the "bully" and "desparado" (not to mention African) Titus Peck. He didn't last long. The following August, a twenty-five-strong crowd of dangerous rabble, on word that a colored assailant had maimed a white man on the road from Dartmouth, attacked Hard Dig with crowbars and burned it down, along with some nearby houses. Later, a Committee of Vigilance formed to oversee the town's rectitude.

So, right was right, in the Friends' eyes. George Howland Sr., one of the city's most eminent Quakers, whose son became mayor, was outraged that he couldn't change the name of the *Rousseau,* one of his ships. Howland considered the Swiss philosopher who'd bequeathed his name to the vessel a freethinking atheist, and he wanted to sever any connection with the rascal and Howland's property. He satisfied himself with chopping the obscene bare-breasted figurehead off and mispronouncing the name as "Russ-o." She proved a great earner for his firm.

New Bedford was moral on another level; at times it was even decent. Although fanatics, the Quakers expressly valued compassion to all mankind. Thus, like the Baptist/Seeker (a proto-Quaker group) Roger Williams, by necessity, they fled the harsh Puritan colonies in Plymouth and Massachusetts Bay to follow their inner light. Contrary to the agreed-upon fables, the Puritans founded their plantations, not for the freedom to pursue their religion, but for the right to suppress with brutal efficiency everyone else's. They reserved a special hate for Quakers, whom they whipped from town to town, mutilated, banished, and murdered. Facing this treatment, the Children of the Light made their way out from among the Separatists to hack from the rocky soil and dense forests their own towns and livings. One such settlement was Old Dartmouth, whose borders included what became New Bedford, Fairhaven, Dartmouth, and other surrounding towns. The Friends didn't forget their independent ways, and three different times the Puritan fathers ordered the imprisonment of the selectmen in Old Dartmouth for refusing to pay the taxes to support the state church.

Yet New Bedford's inhabitants were able to treat other races as remotely human, even if decidedly inferior. The Friends frowned on slavery and even had adopted the novel idea that blacks had been crafted after the image of God, and permitted them to worship with them at their meetings. With this influence, New Bedford and Nantucket became a refuge for Africans. One census revealed that 1,000 of the city's 12,000 inhabitants were black, and were enslaved only to their wages—which they earned in the fleet and as laborers—rather than to masters. A paper called the Boston *Pilot,* disgusted by a day of revelry in which blacks and whites mingled freely, called New Bedford the "very Sebastopol of Niggerdom."

Comfort had always been a formidable temptation to the severe but prosperous Friends, and by the mid-nineteenth century, their purifying instincts lost, many of them were tacking course and embracing Unitarianism and Congregationalism. The sect of George Fox embraced these looser creeds in part because they offered softer rules of conduct—most important, one could enjoy earthly treasures more openly. A Congregationalist didn't have to fret about justifying the erection of a fine mansion high up on the hill that crowned New Bedford. One could even indulge in a large green and tended lawn and garden—protected by a stylish iron fence, each post topped by a harpoon tip. Without guilt, one enjoyed the luxury of chatting in a silk wallpaper drawing room, reading from a private library stocked with many books, or reclining on fine English or French furniture. When eating, domestics served meals on china that cooks had prepared from an excellent larder. More freely, feet tread on soft carpets and bodies were warmed at marble fireplaces, and one passed the summer in a fine seaside cottage with a refreshing ocean breeze, outside the oppressive heat and stench of the city. Succumbing to the dangerously soft, seductive life of wealth, the New Bedford Quakers were largely a spent force, akin to a squad of vessels in the doldrums.

Unsurprisingly, the group of trimmers who turned from the strict tenets of Quakerism didn't include French, who'd kept his childhood faith, despite his prosperity. He was as stubborn and tough as the pasture oak that grew around the tiny village of Berkley where he was born, just a few miles inland, northwest of New Bedford. Next to the town, through marsh flats and thick woods, wound the lazy, dark, and brackish water of the Taunton River, on its way toward windy Narragansett

Bay. The sea was not far off, either geographically or in the mind, and at the water's edge in Berkley was the Dighton Rock, a massive boulder scarred like an old bull sperm whale's back, with inscriptions carved in it three hundred years before by a hapless Miguel Cortoreal, a Portuguese mariner, who, needless to say, was very far from home, stranded on this alien shore.

Also across the narrow river in nearby Dighton, by one account, was one of the many great shipyards that dotted the Bay State. So it was no surprise that French, still in his twenties, took to the sea, eventually rising from sailor to master in the merchant service. Around 1830, he came to expanding New Bedford and set up shop as a whaleship owner and agent, building up a small fleet of vessels, as well as dealing in coal and timber— including live oak. Live oak trees grew in primeval Georgia and North Carolina forests, and their wood was harder than iron; the branches also grew out at right angles, which made them desirable for reinforcing key stress points on hulls—particularly at the ship's knees—that had to contend with reefs or ice. (French wasn't the first merchant to import these trees north: Since 1791, the venerable firm of William Rotch and Sons itself had sent men down to Savannah and Charleston to engage in the difficult and dangerous process of cutting and moving this prized timber.) It was a gritty business. The loggers left huge empty swaths of dead forest behind them, and a single mistake during the harvest could kill or cripple a man easily. In pursuing his enterprises, French became tightly linked to the South, a connection that led to rumors of his ships carrying more than lumber and shingles in their holds.

In his political battles, French attacked with ferocity. He'd the endurance of a verbal Hercules, producing when needed a "windy and forceless" speech that wore down an opponent—and even tried a Friend's patience. Some claimed he was tough to worst in a debate, always cool, smiling, and certain of his facts, keeping documents and papers in reserve to buttress his arguments. Critics believed French a mere opportunist who happened to serve a high-minded cause. Certainly one's stance on the slavery issue counted for something in the City of Light's small political circles. When the not-a-little-demented abolitionist and would-be revolutionary John Brown was hanged, the city's church bells tolled in sorrow, and black ribbons were the decoration of the day.

While rising higher up in the city's affairs, French, one morning in 1853, according to a rather colorful account, stood on a cistern cover in front of the Custom House, and accepted the nomination to the recently created office of mayor. After a tough race against patrician William Rotch, he won. (According to one story, French's supporters lifted a house on the border of neighboring Dartmouth and turned it to face New Bedford so its inhabitants could vote in the election.)

It was also at about this midcentury mark that he rose to his highest moral platform. As a matter of course, any Friend was duty bound to oppose on principle war and slavery, but it was at this time that French's fiery devotion began in earnest. His true conversion occurred when, on business down in Raleigh, North Carolina, he "saw men and women going to the auction block to be sold like horses, their teeth examined and their bodies prodded." French found the spectacle so ugly, any mental obstruction holding him back from complete devotion to abolition was dislodged, and his energy was freed like water from a broken dam.

One of French's protégés was a runaway slave, who eventually won a great measure of fame that eclipsed that of Old Rodney himself—Frederick Douglass. After taking a job as a caulker at his boatyard, the future agitator called French a "distinguished antislavery man." Such a job was an honor for the ever-ambitious Douglass: A caulker held one of the most eminent jobs a New Bedford craftsman could have, as it required a man to take his live oak mallet and drive a twisted tarred yarn called oakum between the seams of the ship's planks to keep them tight. Depending on his tempo and the force of his blow, each caulker added his own dinging music to the symphony of the waterfront; the ringing of the hammer could even deafen him. Caulkers earned two dollars a day, double the wages of a common laborer, and so trusted were their skills that no one checked their work.

Unfortunately, as was typical in the city, French's caulkers didn't feel quite the way their Quaker employer did about Africans. Douglass was unable to fill one seam before the entire work crew of white men walked off the job, threatening to quit rather than toil beside a black. French was stymied and to avert a shutdown of his shipyard, he gave Douglass another job, hauling heavy fittings. Eventually, the fugitive's path led him to another eminent Quaker's wharf—that of George Howland—a "hard driver, but a good paymaster," as Douglass noted. There he worked on fitting out the whaler *Golconda,* destined, like the Confederacy that destroyed her, not to outlast the Civil War.

Even his critics had to admit French took risks for his adopted cause. After hearing from an express rider that a ship was sailing up the harbor with a company of U.S. Marines to recover escaped slaves destined for Canada, French ordered the city's so-called Liberty Bell rung. Its ringing served as warning to any escaped, not to mention highly nervous, slaves to scurry into hiding. While the threat turned out to be bogus, one chronicler later said the city was ready to offer the marshals a "warm reception." The act took on the status of the legendary, and when a fire destroyed the hall and melted the Liberty Bell, French, then mayor, had small handbells cast from its remnants, and gave them away as gifts.

Just a decade before his election as the Stone Fleet commodore, he'd had a rift with the burghers of the city of New Bern, North Carolina. Here in this port, the seat of Craven County, he'd a joint business venture in timber, until its citizens accused him of being so "liberal in his abuse" they passed a resolution to eject him. So incensed were the men of politics and commerce in New Bern, they told the abolitionist's partner, a merchant captain: "Dissolve with French and we will extend the hand of fellowship. But if you do not, we will give you no support, no aid, no employment," as French later recalled it. He also overheard rumors that the prickly New Bernites were thinking of burning one of his ships right where she lay in their harbor.

The partner, presumably seeing a business opportunity, was for splitting the firm; it took ten minutes for French to sell out to him at a loss. It was perhaps a wonder the Quaker been able to conduct what he claimed was an honest business for thirty years in the South. Instead of apologizing to New Bern, in October 1851, French chastised it in a long, windy letter as if it were Sodom. In the epistle he declared slavery "the most disgraceful, atrocious, unjust, detestable, heathenish, barbarous, diabolical, tyrannical, man-degrading, woman-murdering, demon-pleasing, Heaven-defying act, ever perpetrated in any age of the world, by persons claiming to have consciences and a belief in a just God. In one word, it is the sum of all Villainies."

But he later recalled philosophically: "I am getting accustomed to these things. As the boy said of his eels, 'It don't hurt them at all to skin them after they got used to it.' So it is with me. Being so accustomed to such treatment, it produces no pain whatever."

So while French counted among his enemies the powerful, his friends included the Africans of New Bedford. Aware of his deeds, they even reached into their pockets and, at the behest of their ministers, collected enough silver to have a Boston artisan cast French an elegant pitcher and salver, which they presented to him in gratitude for his "great antislavery service." But even then, the shadow was present, as some preachers refused to ask their congregations to assist, for they felt French was not all he claimed to be. Perhaps things had happened on French's ships that he was not aware of, or pretended he was unaware of, went the libels.

In any case, with the great war for freedom having arrived, French and the other Friends saw their labors against slavery begin to succeed, even if in the process it was seizing up the gears of commerce. Although one of Quakerism's most strongly held beliefs was pacifism, that least popular of Christ's teachings, they accepted this conflict as necessary. This was a new tack for them, as shown by a Revolutionary War incident that involved some Fairhaven men taking a group of British prisoners. The men on the eastern bank were known as Congregationalists; they could stomach war, as opposed to the Quaker men of the west bank, who were useless in a fight, unless it was with a whale. So, a delegation of New Bedford Friends crossed the shared harbor to demand the Englishmen's release; the gesture didn't help either the prisoners, who'd been moved, or the New Bedford men, whose wharves and ships went up in smoke anyway when Crown forces had attacked.

In the minds of the Quakers, if not of the pragmatist Lincoln himself, the war's underlying purpose was to destroy slavery. This allowed them to overcome their sect's aversion to bloodshed to offer their support. Three days after the attack on Fort Sumter, the city sent out a regiment of militia, and behind came their mariners, among the best and boldest in the world, to join the Union Navy. The war had other effects. After becoming mayor in 1862, handsome and charming George Howland Jr., fearing draft riots (if the state militia did not have enough volunteers, they were ordered by the War Department to draft soldiers), ordered troops into the stately granite city hall (now the library) and mounted patrols to guard the roads leading into New Bedford.

He stated: "There will be no blank cartridges fired." Strong words for a Friend. In May 1861, at Clark's Point the city dedicated an earthwork fortification, which at some point took the name of Fort Taber, after the mayor who sponsored it. The redoubt was equipped with cannon and manned by undertrained home guardsmen carrying out one of the more pointless tasks of the war. (The former U.S. army officer and engineer Robert E. Lee himself had been on the committee that drew up the first plans for the fortification, but these documents had been misfiled, and it would've been a bit difficult then to ask for his advice.) Some citizens resented the cost of maintaining the fort, as it meant the community had to cut the wages of its teachers and the number of streets it lit by half.

As noted before, the November after the war started, in the midst of the transformation of this large section of New Bedford's shipping assets into rock-carrying hulks, virtually escaping notice, there had been another former whaling vessel fitting out, the *Margaret Scott*. Her preparations, however, were not typical of whalers but rather of transporters of human cargo—presumably, workmen had been storing many casks of water and cracker barrels on board. Eventually, as the slaving trial would reveal, there was a connection here with a New York slave network. The Empire State was long a hub of traffic in black ivory, and stories of whalers turning slavers weren't exactly new. (There were rumors of formerly poor masters of Sag Harbor who'd suddenly acquired great wealth through the trade.) After the *Margaret Scott*'s guilty were convicted, a Boston judge, apparently unaware of the irony, doled them out sentences of hard labor in the Taunton city jail.

Slaving was the sort of thing to create quite a bit of indignation in town—even if New Bedford's Quaker patricians' fortunes had been built on driving men to the worst places in the world to murder whales and recompensing them with a pittance. The case of the *Margaret Scott*, however, had other consequences. Until the August before, she'd carried the initials RF on the ensign—signifying none other than Rodney French. In one of history's jokes, the name of a fanatical abolitionist and Quaker had become forever spliced to slaving. His trip south, therefore, may also have been a way to expunge any blot connected with the *Scott*'s slaving enterprise. If so, it lent him no actual authority. Few, if any, of the masters obeyed French's order—or to put it more accurately, suggestion—to hug the coast. Plowing through the wake of the vessels he was ostensibly commanding, the unlikely Quaker warrior French had lost whatever semblance of authority he claimed to possess.

7

—oxxo—

An Indifferent Screw Steamer

It is to me a painful sight to see a fine vessel wantonly destroyed, but I
hope to witness an immense number of painful sights of the same kind.
—*William Whittle, Jr., executive officer*
of the Confederate warship Shenandoah

DECEMBER 8, 1861,
NORTH ATLANTIC

Despite the war and the sinking market for her goods, New Bedford
launched more than the Stone Fleet that fall. While Commodore
French's "Rat Hole Squadron" worked its way down the eastern shore, the
crew of the badly leaking and imperiled whaler *Eben Dodge,* only twelve
days out of the City of Light, was also plying her way through the North
Atlantic. However, her task was not to lug hunks of New England's backbone, but to hunt monsters in the Pacific.

For whatever reason, the *Dodge* had evaded agent Bartlett. Apparently
her owners, of whom the most prominent was Benjamin Franklin Howland, must've felt that the fine bark was worth more blubber hunting than
as a submarine wall down south. Whaling wasn't the Howland family's
only venture, and in keeping with the changing times, they co-owned a
kerosene refinery in the city. Nevertheless, Benjamin Franklin Howland
was one of the thinning number of gamblers with faith that a whaling voyage was worth risking his precious capital on.

When casting off on November 25, Captain Gideon C. Hoxie's intention had been to take the bark round stormy Cape Horn and roam the

South Pacific for three years. Sailing southwest till he was midway between Africa and North America, he met a gale that battered the *Dodge* savagely enough to stave in most of the whaleboats, spring the spars, and open leaks through which the Atlantic poured. Luckily for Hoxie, earlier that morning the wind had moderated and it appeared the weather might even break and become tolerable. He'd kept the bark, which carried an exceptionally tall mast, running cautiously under light sail. For a voyage that would last several years, it wasn't a good start, and as whalemen were a superstitious lot, some of the twenty-two on board must've wondered why they'd picked this unlucky vessel.

About 10:00 A.M., from out of the foggy weather abruptly appeared a bark-rigged steamer, about a mile and a half distant. Almost immediately, a boom rang out over the water, a cannonball passed by the *Dodge*'s bow, and Hoxie gave the order to heave to. Seeing the stranger carried the Union flag, he ordered the Stars and Stripes run up in answer. Despite this, the steamer kept a cautious distance, running between the *Dodge* and the wind, giving her the weather gauge in case the whaler tried to run. The mystery of the steamer's presence was solved when she came round to the *Dodge*'s stern and the Union flag came down and up went a curious sight—the Stars and Bars of the Confederacy.

When in hailing distance, a voice called out across the water: "Come on board with your papers, this is the Confederate war vessel the *Sumter*."

Hoxie dropped a whaleboat from its davits and rowed out to the steamer, a less than an impressive vessel, he decided. That wasn't surprising given that the *Sumpter*'s original purpose had been only to convey passengers on short trips rather than cruising on the open seas. On coming aboard, he was shown into the captain's cabin, where awaiting him sat a slender man with a large, almost theatrical mustache: Raphael Semmes, the former U.S. Navy career man, who since June had been roving in this vessel, the *Sumter,* taking prizes. Apparently, in keeping with his new status as a raider, he'd allowed the mustache to grow out dramatically so that the tips extended past his cheekbones, and that—along with a tiny goatee—gave him the appearance of a stage Mephistopheles. Those of his colleagues who'd considered him too soft for a hard job were much mistaken, having only seen the mask that hid another much different man. Indeed, the lighthouse keeper's departure from the Union was proving one of the worst catastrophes to befall

American maritime enterprise, the Yankee whaling fleet in particular. In northern eyes, Semmes's scrawny neck would become one of the foremost of any Confederate's as a target for the noose.

Since receiving that summoning telegram in Washington the prior February, Semmes had enjoyed quite an odyssey. After arriving by train in Montgomery, the commander's first mission as a Confederate fighting man was to procure armaments from Yankee merchants in preparation for the coming war. These northerners owned factories in Massachusetts, New York, and Connecticut—all states with whaling ports the South would soon terrorize. Although they knew where their supplies were headed, Semmes found them not only willing, but anxious to contract with him, he claimed. He cut deals for a stream of supplies—percussion caps, light artillery, powder, and other munitions—some of which shipped. After war broke out, the flow of hardware, powder, and other goods headed below the Mason-Dixon Line stopped, and having become decidedly Union-leaning, the same manufacturers began to sell their wares to the U.S. government.

Toward the end of March, Semmes headed back to Montgomery. He still held the rank of mere commander, and was once again condemned to an unglamorous and tedious role as lighthouse board chief, albeit for the Confederacy. This was not the ideal job for a man who felt that when facing the "swarming hordes of the North" anyone who could wield a sword had to draw it in defense of his country. However, at his age and rank, Semmes was not the most likely candidate for an active naval wartime command. He evaded the dreary fate the Rebel government had consigned him to only after reading a report about a five-hundred-ton passenger ship called the *Habana*. Confederate agents had bought the vessel only to condemn her at the dock in New Orleans because she could only carry five days' worth of coal. Something about the not so promising steamer appealed to Semmes, and he said to Secretary of the Navy Stephen Mallory: "Give me that ship; I think I can make her answer the purpose."

Arriving in New Orleans in April, Semmes noted the Union blockade had managed to make desolate the once bustling and prosperous levee that had handled so much cotton and other goods, including live African cargo. Gloom hung over the once gay and reckless—not to mention highly dangerous and gang-ridden—port. Nevertheless, when Semmes laid eyes on the blatantly unwarlike-looking *Habana* moored across the brown, lazy Mississippi in the town of Algiers, he decided with his typical gallantry he liked her "easy and graceful lines" and "saucy air." With a work party under him, Semmes braved the intense heat, enervating humidity, and the assaults of the ferocious Louisiana mosquitoes to convert the former passenger vessel into something approximating a warship, which he dubbed the C.S.S. *Sumter*.

Among the armaments he installed were a 68-pound pivot gun and four rifled cannons that could lob 32-pound shells at their victims. While she was by no means a ship of the line, the *Sumter* was adequate for preying on unarmed merchant vessels. The painstaking labor completed, Semmes's only problem now was getting past the mouth of the Mississippi, guarded by Union men of war that easily could've sent the makeshift cruiser and her crew to the river's muddy bottom. Attempting to skirt the blockade was so undesirable a proposition that Semmes threatened with arrest any pilot who refused to guide him out.

He bided his time in the sweltering heat until June 30, when he steamed down the Father of Waters. On the banks of the river stood a handful of local women who waved their handkerchiefs in salute; the courtly Semmes uncovered his head in respect for the "fair" young wife of the daring pilot navigating the *Sumter* out. Soon after, there followed a dramatic race between the ragtag steamer and the more heavily armed and faster U.S.S. *Brooklyn*. At one point, the chase was so close, Semmes ordered his paymaster to prepare to heave the ship's papers overboard in case of capture. Nevertheless, in a bold and skillful piece of seamanship, Semmes had outrun his hunter and escaped with the first Confederate warship to ply her trade on the open sea.

The former lighthouse commissioner, now escaped from his prison, carried a letter from Secretary of the Navy Mallory authorizing him to "do the enemy's commerce the greatest injury, in the shortest time," but to stay, somewhat ambiguously, "within the limits prescribed by the laws of nations, and with due attention to the laws of humanity." To communicate with Richmond, he coded his dispatches using as a cipher key Reid's *English Dictionary*.

As night fell, at last breathing in air that carried neither malaria nor mosquitoes, Semmes stood on the deck of his bark, plowing quietly through the Gulf of Mexico. He watched a blazing comet with a massive tail streak through the sky, its light reflected on the surface of the Caribbean just one hundred feet from the *Sumter,* adding its image to that of a thousand other stars whose faces also sparkled on the sea. Semmes might have taken it as a propitious sign, for whether he then knew it, he'd launched what would prove to be one of the most successful sea-raiding careers ever—and one of the greatest blows to ever fall on the whaling fleet.

The bold commander next plied the Atlantic around Cuba and South America, taking a dozen prizes, but no whalers. Then, by sheer chance, the *Eben Dodge* had conveniently appeared about five miles off, and the chase was on. Yet, either because of the weather or the preoccupation of the crew of the whaler with staying afloat, it wasn't until Semmes had closed the gap by three and a half miles that the men of the *Dodge* noticed the *Sumter* in pursuit. The raider originally suspected the *Dodge* was a cruiser because of her tall mast and skysail—a square-shaped piece of canvas that hung over the main royal sail on the mainmast—but was soon disabused of that notion.

Unfortunately for the men of the whaling fleet, the sort of vessel they sailed on was all too easy to make out. She had the telltale signs of her vocation: a bluff bow, brick tryworks amidships, whaleboats hanging over the sides on cranes, and double hoops in the crosstrees at the tops of the masts that supported the lookouts in their dreary and tedious, if essential, task. As soon as Semmes realized he had a slow-moving, toothless blubber hunter in his clutches, he ordered the engineer to cease firing up the boilers and collapse the funnel.

For the commander, this was a special day, and not just because he was taking a whaling ship. Exactly fifteen years prior, when in the service of the U.S. Navy during the Mexican War and commanding the U.S.S. *Somers* in the waters near Vera Cruz, a ferocious storm rose up suddenly. The tempest engulfed the warship, and in minutes she capsized and sank, taking to the bottom sixty men, half the crew. Semmes himself just escaped drowning and after rescue had to exonerate himself at a court-martial. Now today it was for him to decide another captain's fate.

With Hoxie before him, he read the *Dodge*'s papers over. The unlucky master must have been incredulous that his was the first whaler since the

War of 1812 to be taken by an enemy power on the seas. He'd probably heard of the *Sumter* or saw mention of her in the New Bedford papers, one of which compared the elusive Confederate to the *Flying Dutchman.* After examining the official documents, Semmes said: "Oh yes, it's all right. She is a lawful prize of the Confederate States, and I shall burn the ship. We are short of water and you have plenty; I must have some of that."

Apparently, starting a trend almost universally imitated by his colleagues, Hoxie offered no resistance to the power of Semmes and his junk vessel. While a whaler was an excellent fighting ship if your enemy was a cetacean, carrying no weapons except small firearms, lances, harpoons, and bomb guns, she made a poor man-of-war, and a battle against a warship armed with rows of cannon would be something of a one-sided exchange. Certainly whalemen were no shirkers when it came to offering up physical violence where they felt it appropriate—as proven not only by their willingness to hunt whales, but also by their innumerable tavern brawls. (There is even a story of a Nantucket captain who accepted an Englishman's challenge to a duel. However, when the two men from their respective islands arrived to fight, the whaler's weapon of choice was a harpoon, with which he was clearly an expert. The prudent Englishman settled the quarrel as gracefully as he could without combat.)

But such courage was useless during war. Whalers couldn't even run with much hope of success. They were built for hunting, processing, and carrying the finished goods back to port; they "sailed about as fast as you can whip a toad through tar." No doubt with that in mind, Hoxie submitted to his fate supinely, as so many other masters did, men who'd fought warlike natives, pirates, mutiny, enraged whales, and every type of storm and even dangers no one had ever dreamed about, and who were not inclined to submit to anything they could beat.

Firmly in control, Semmes ordered Hoxie back under armed guard to the stricken *Dodge* on what surely was an unpleasant trip for the luckless master, who'd passed through terrible weather only to be bagged abruptly by a Confederate. Contrariwise, it was as if, through the dark weather, the sun was smiling on the cash-strapped Confederacy that day, for Semmes, with his characteristically devilish good luck, was in need of the same supplies that the whaling bark carried. Despite the rough, wild seas and lowering clouds that portended an oncoming storm, Semmes was able to take from his prize a thousand gallons of much-needed water. Without paying the slop chest's outrageous fees, he also secured for his crew gear to keep them warm and dry while sailing the North Atlantic this nasty season: short, heavy, wool pea jackets, boots, and flannel overshirts.

As the day continued, the man who'd once devoted his career to protecting the nation's shipping now helped himself freely to the *Dodge*'s tobacco, charts, carpenter's tools, sextant, and, of course, the precious chronometer. Knowing their value, the crew also took two of the undamaged whaleboats and placed them on the deck beside the *Sumter*'s own launch. As for Hoxie, Semmes restricted him to one bed and trunk for his clothing; the mates and crew got one bag each. Later, Semmes complained about crowding on board and then took away everything from them but the clothes on their backs. It was not going to be a good voyage for these monster hunters who'd turned into the hunted.

Among his other treasures, Semmes also found some Boston and New Bedford newspapers, and read of the celebrations of the recent Union naval victory in Beaufort, North Carolina. He also laid eyes on copy about Thanksgiving, which New England had observed with "more than usual piety and pomp." He noted with typical spleen: "The pulpit thundered war and glory, the press dilated upon the wealth and resources of the Universal Yankee Nation, and hecatombs of fat pigs and turkeys fed the hungry multitudes—pulpit, press, pig, and turkey, all thanking God, that the Puritan is 'not like unto other men.' "

Luckily for the whalers, his eyes scanned no word of the Stone Fleet, or his treatment of them might have been more unpleasant—or rather as unpleasant as it later became. Yet, the commander also had a grudging respect for the blubber hunters. During his career, he overhauled just one whaler not flying the American flag, a Portuguese brig. He believed the New England whaling supremacy was not "derived from any sovereign grant, but...from the superior skill, energy, industry, courage, and perseverance of the Yankee whaler, who is, perhaps, the best specimen of a sailor, the world over." Friends may flatter, but an enemy almost never does.

His opinion of whalers may have been the reason Semmes acted so cautiously with the twenty-two men of the *Dodge*'s former crew, even if they probably were mostly greenhorns. As they swelled the ranks of captive passengers on the *Sumter* to forty-three, as a precaution he ordered half of them to be kept in wrist manacles for twenty-four hours at a time, one group alternating with the other. Semmes claimed later, perhaps exaggerating, the prisoners "submitted cheerfully to the restraint." An easterly gale blowing up, the wind howled through the rigging, and with the weather turning worse, the crew of the *Sumter* fired the *Dodge* at half past six and sailed away. A ship soaked with precious sperm oil made quite a bonfire, as the *Sumter*'s crew discovered. Through the murk sitting on the North Atlantic, Semmes watched the *Dodge* bobbing up and down on the swelling waves, appearing and then disappearing, as the flames ate her stem to stern. The burning whaler reminded Semmes of a jack-o'-lantern. These blazing prizes invariably brought out the poetry in the heart of these Southern raiders.

Watching one's own ship and aquatic home going up in flames is unpleasant, as indicated by this description of the burning of another of Semmes's later victims, the whaler *Virginia*. Her provisions taken, the last boat off, the Confederates torched the *Virginia* in three places. A New Bedford chronicler claimed the flames burned at first "with all fury, as if battling with the raging winds, emblematic of Semmes' barbarity." As night fell, the winds dropped and the fires shrank, but she was still visible, a "disheartening sight" for the whalers, burning alone on the ocean till midnight—twelve hours in all. At 12:00 A.M., there was only a "spark" left, "the last bright symbol of what their noble ship had been to them, now only a phantom in imagination. Oh, that day's experience, what a thought! so weird, so terrible in their overwrought and excited brains." The loss of the ship, to a whaler, was an inexpressible experience.

Now, there was yet another humiliation for the captive Yankee master. Semmes, desiring good solid Yankee dollars, asked if Hoxie had money. "It would be as well to be candid for if I have reason to doubt what you say, I'll have you searched," he said. Hoxie admitted he carried $150, which he turned over to the ship's purser, who kept it under the rather imaginative title of "contraband of war." However, outside of losing his steward—an ailing man doomed to die while a Confederate guest—along with his money, vessel, personal belongings, and liberty, Hoxie later noted with magnanimity Semmes's treatment gave him nothing more to complain of. Ordered to share a "very small noisome berth" with the petty officers of the *Sumter*, Hoxie found his floating prison an "indifferent screw steamer" in "very dirty" condition. The bark kept leaking, and Semmes, who believed in the innate laziness of blacks, decided to break up the idleness of ten of the imprisoned Africans on board by forcing them to man the *Sumter*'s two pumps. However, if the vessel was a poor specimen of ship, she was well matched by the crew, made up mostly of rough, discontented Irishmen who appeared ready to desert, said Hoxie.

The onetime whaling crew had it worse than their master, for besides their manacles, Semmes ordered them into the narrow berth deck in a situation "greatly to their discomfort." But the confinement was the least of their worries. Semmes was now steering them in his unseaworthy craft into an even more severe example of the North Atlantic's legendary seasonal gales.

8

⸲⸲⸲

A Pirate Deed

When it was announced that the operations of the great naval expedition were to be directed against Port Royal and Savannah, considerable disappointment was expressed that Charleston was not to come in for the first share of its attentions. It is better as it is. It would have given too much importance and gratification to the cocks of the little dunghill State. They will feel more keenly the fact of their city being wiped forever out of the list of commercial ports by a simple stroke of Secretary Welles' pen, and that without the chance of their firing a single shot in its defence.

—New York Herald

The cause of Charleston is the cause of the South.
—*Robert A. Toombs*

SOUTHEASTERN COAST OF NORTH AMERICA, DECEMBER 1861

Even as the bobbing timbers of the *Eben Dodge* became soggy ash and dispersed over the water and air of the Atlantic, the constituent parts of the ramshackle Stone Fleet sailed on to Savannah. The trip was proving to be quite an adventure. The ship *Corea,* for instance, had met some inhospitable southern weather, and her captain found himself fighting one gale after another. By December 2, she was off Charleston and heading out to sea when an ever-growing dark spot in the sky bore down on her to the sound of "tremendous roaring." It became evident that riding over the water's surface and headed right at the ship was a waterspout, a funnel-shaped tornado, potentially hundreds of feet wide, typical of the region.

With the ferocity of an enraged sperm with a harpoon in its back, this violent child of the South Carolina's spinning air tore at the ship with a "clap of thunder" for about thirty seconds—long enough to split nearly every sail—while "fire flew through the shieve [pulley] holes in the yards." Within ten minutes, the water was two feet deep on deck, leaving her master with a bad mess to sort out. Sometimes the dangers were more comic than tragic. When Bony Rice reached Savannah, the approach of a federal gunboat was enough to confirm his worst fears about Confederate raiders. He hurried to his cabin, fetched his best clothes, and reaching the deck tossed them into the Savannah estuary, proclaiming no rebel would ever cover their hides with his possessions. His crew imitated the venerable master, and by the time they all realized the stranger was a Union ship, their garments were already flotsam in the Atlantic.

Regrettably, despite the considerable risks involved, the voyage was shaping into a fool's errand. The majority of the fleet reached Savannah only to discover the rebel forces had bottled up the harbor with their own hulks and the Stone Fleet's presence was no longer required. The frustrated and mystified blockade commander J. S. Missroon sat idle as one rebel hulk after another destroyed itself trying to cross over the Savannah bar. The orders were then changed for the granite fleet. Instead of Savannah, their new rendezvous was Port Royal, South Carolina, and thereafter the destination for the ships still afloat was Charleston.

At last, the *Garland* straggled into Port Royal, solidly in last place in the race down. French, being in the rear, had been intercepted by a messenger and given the new orders with the altered destination. With his late arrival, he'd achieved the status of worst among equals, quite a feat, given the wretched condition of his rivals. We'll never know if the slowness of his 243-ton bark was from poor sailing or her general unseaworthiness, in which case, he'd undoubtedly taken the government for more than the vessel was worth. Certainly all the other masters had a chuckle at Old Rodney's tardiness, although the unflappable Friend didn't seem to mind. With the politician's sense of the dramatic, French was flying all his pennants, including a commodore's flag at the mainmast, which he had no right to display.

Although the vessel was the property of Lincoln's Navy, from the foremast fluttered his own soon-to-be-retired house flag—the black initials RF

centered and edged by two narrow horizontal red bands. As the ship came
to anchor, he announced his arrival by firing the signal gun on the Quaker
cannon that had thus far protected the *Garland* on her perilous journey.
The report of the explosion caught the attention of no less than DuPont
himself, who sent a boat over to find out why someone had broken the
peace.

The officer in charge of the investigation saw the make-believe cannon
and reported it back to DuPont, who just smiled and passed it off as a
joke. Some in the fleet, however, began to tell a story (if not necessarily accurate in fact, yet containing the best truth of fiction) that French, when
asked who'd fired the signal gun, replied: "The commodore of the Stone
Fleet." The rejoinder: "I know of but one commodore in these waters, and
that's DuPont. Haul in your colors and never fire the gun again."

The whalers wasted another week awaiting the final orders commanding them to sail for Charleston. During the hiatus, one newspaper in New
Bedford reported during his stay, the "Hon. Mr. French" had been observed at a "religious meeting of the Negroes."

PORT ROYAL, SOUTH CAROLINA, DECEMBER 16

On board his temporary flagship *Cahawba,* Captain Charles Henry Davis
choked down any spleen afflicting him and dispatched a boat to go from
one soon-to-be whaling hulk to the next to alert those on board to prepare
to sail. He had orders and would obey them, even if he was facing one of
the more distasteful tasks in his long and solid career as a navy man. He
was well qualified. A decade prior, C. H. Davis had been dispatched to
Charleston to find a way to deepen and improve its narrow and unreliable
outlets.

Now in one of fate's many little jokes, as lead shepherd of the Stone
Fleet, his goal was to destroy the commercial utility of that same piece of
aquatic real estate he'd sought to better. This "pirate deed," as Melville
would later call it in a rhyming lament for the Stone Fleet (he pitied the
vessels, not the city), didn't sit well with Davis for a number of reasons. For
one, he wisely doubted it would work, and if it did, all it would do was hamper the Union fleet's operations after the city eventually fell. Presumably,

he kept that gloomy tidbit hidden from the blubber hunters under his command. His point was sound, and in perspective, the foolhardiness of the
scheme stands out, but it was no less odd, perhaps, when compared with all
the other innovations the Union and the Confederacy would devise to win
the contest for Charleston. (Some of the others employed in that long fight
would eventually function as the prototypes of weapons that kill, maim,
and cripple men and boats to this day—including the submarine, the floating mine, the ironclad, and the torpedo boat. One couldn't patent an idea
like the Stone Fleet, however.)

Davis was also sensitive to the operation's unsavory nature, viewing it
with a "special disgust," and saying that this disagreeable duty was one of
the last he should have selected for himself. A photo of him shows a face
with a pure fixed and abstracted expression more suited to a scholar, almost out of place on an officer who conducted war against a civilian population. Nor was there the solace that the operation would ever translate
into glory. Despite the gushing of the war correspondents sailing with
him—they were busy portraying the voyage as a grand adventure—there
was never any truly great danger involved. Davis's ships at all times were
considerably beyond the range of enemy cannon, and the greatest menace
to the fleet was its own wretched condition. The one advantage for Davis
was his resources, more then he'd a right to expect, which included
five war and three transport steamers. Even better, on hand were those
New York City newspaper reporters who would give the event the best
possible attitude in the seas of public opinion and win the ultimate war—
of propaganda.

Davis's job might've been easier if the enthusiasm of these scribblers
was shared by the hard-bitten and still sleepy masters of "his fleet," as he
called it with not so disguised contempt. The whalers had about the same
reluctance to obey the orders to make ready to sail as Davis had in giving
them. The captains offered a variety of excuses for not leaving the expan-
sive and safe Port Royal, most of which were valid. One blubber hunter
claimed his vessel had lost her main rigging; another had an unsafe rudder; a third was stuck "milking"—or pumping out water. This reluctance
to participate, apparently, even spread to the Union officers, as shown by
the captain on the steamer *Daniel Webster.* After receiving a polite request to help tow the Stone Fleet outside the bar, he said: "I'll see you

damned first. I'm going to New York. Anything I can do for you there?"

Even the mild weather prevailing off the coast was an impediment. With the breeze so slight, the desperate whalemen might as well have gone on deck and tried to move their ships by blowing into their sails. No matter: Davis had as escort federal steamers with real cannons (as opposed to French's fake one) to discourage any interference from the Confederates— to the degree they could interfere at all. It took till evening to remove the whalers outside the bar, and the next day, Davis sailed on in the *Cahawba* with his bastard fleet. Some of the worse-off ships required towing, while the remainder dropped their sails and used the wind. The fleet of old square-riggers with their great expanse of canvas turgid with wind, plowing through the sea on their ultimate voyage, made a beautiful sight. Even if in the service of the Union, it seemed to a correspondent a sad thing that these ships, some of which had been lucky in their day and had brought so much money to the various Coffins, Starbucks, Howlands, and other blubber barons, were to be cast aside like this. But their time had come.

By five that night, Davis had dropped anchor into the relatively soft ocean floor that edged the Charleston bar. He was in sight of Fort Sumter's outline; although four miles away, the haze made the onetime Federal stronghold loom massively. After spotting a couple of whalers on their slow way to the bar, the city's defenders fired off cannon and raised signal flags in expectation of attack, thinking mistakenly first-class frigates might be about to attack. As the night wore on, the straggling whalers from Port Royal arrived one after the other, joined by the *William Lee* and *America,* the swiftest of yet a second Stone Fleet, cobbled together in the same way as the one preceding it. Another arrival from this bunch was Rodney French's onetime vessel, the scandal-ridden *Margaret Scott,* following her former owner like a nasty reputation. After her seizure for slaving, a federal marshal had auctioned her to the ship-hungry Ivory Bartlett or one of his agents, who sent her south for scuttling. (Some navy man looked her over and decided she would be better as a store ship and spared the *Scott*—at least for a little while longer.)

After dark the Union men heard a loud explosion. The next morning, they discovered the jittery Confederates had blown up the tall white light-house on Morris Island, which lay in front of the main channel. To the Yankees it was no matter—at least as the newspaper reporter propagandists saw it—the Confederates were going to be possessors of an inland city shortly, their harbor paved over with New Bedford and New London cobblestone, and a lighthouse was redundant. In any case, enough of the structure's foundation remained there for use as a landmark by which Charleston's hated enemies could navigate. It certainly didn't interfere with the fleet's main task. Under a bright, illuminating moon, Davis sent out a pilot who knew every drop and swell in the bar to ferret out the precise spots to sink the vessels. The scout also discovered the wily Rebels had moved the channel buoys to confuse just such an operation, and to overcome this new obstacle, he sounded the channel through that night and into the next morning.

The operation was about to start, and it was something for the whalers to relish. They showed about as much pity for Charleston as they might have for a hated and vicious whale. It wasn't surprising. For some New Englanders, this city was the symbol of all they hated about the Confederacy. Although the tiniest of secessionist states, what South Carolina lacked in size, it more than made up for in pride and ferocity. It was easy for Charleston to strut like a prize cock: Its founders had selected for their community a choice location on a peninsula bordered by two converging rivers, the Cooper and the Ashley, whose two flows united to form a large harbor. From there, the combined rivers flowed down as one estuary to the Atlantic, making a fine gateway for shipping, whose architect was nature herself. Surrounding the city was a low swampy coastline dotted with beaches and harbors, and forests full of mossy live oak and palmetto trees.

Although it had fewer than 50,000 dwellers, Charleston always managed to seem larger. In fact, the inhabitants liked to style this metropolis the Athens of the South, an apt comparison, as the city of great statesman Pericles had swelled with slaves toiling for men of leisure and conversation. Charleston had a ruling class of uncommonly rich denizens, whose slaves underwrote lifestyles of lavish idleness. Certainly these lords had style, living in fine houses that ranged in style from Georgian to Palladian to Federal to Greek Revival, many with fine gardens, set in rows on cobblestone streets. Those inhabitants near the waterfront could turn from fine portraits hanging from their walls and look out through silk curtains over rows of fine-gabled and hip-roofed houses, and toward the wide harbor. There visible was the eternal give-and-take of a port that had the regularity of the tide. On the one hand, stevedores loaded the most profitable export, the rice grown in the surrounding plantations; while from other ships they unloaded imports. (The city also had a slave market.)

The hand of nature had blessed Charleston, but it had also stinted it a bit, too. The very forces that had created the harbor also had cursed it with a weakness, similar to the vulnerable spot behind a sperm whale's flippers that hid his life and lungs. This flaw was a dangerous and ever-shifting sandbar at the harbor's entrance, formed by the tides and the flow of the two rivers. The ceaseless flow of the sea kindly kept four channels scoured for ships to sail through the bar. Yet the frequent and violent tropical storms often reshaped these four openings and ensured the navigator earned his money when discharging what there was a difficult task. Thus did the Achilles of the South offer up to the Union Navy a weak heel as a target.

Now with Anaconda's coils tightening and the blockade taking effect, the prior year's initial secession joy had begun to dim. By the time the anniversary of the fall of Fort Sumter was rolling around, the city's fortunes had plummeted drastically. On December 11 and 12, 1861, Charleston, no stranger to diseases or other kinks of fate, found an especially trying disaster to contend with: a huge fire. The flames devoured a large swath of its environs and even sent the beautiful spire of the Cathedral of St. John and St. Finbar, tall enough to serve as a landmark to mariners, loudly crashing down in what must've seemed one of the Great Good God's darker acts. The smoke rose high enough to be visible to the Union sailors blockading the city, and some optimistic Northerners decided prematurely the holocaust had "wiped out that rebellious city almost as effectually the wrath of God did Sodom."

For the citizens of now gloomy Charleston, there was little else to occupy the time except to discuss the conflagration. Food was expensive, and the poor, as always, bore the worst of the hardships and shortages. The locals also had begun to turn a mistrustful eye at the many slaves surrounding them, fearing they would take advantage of the city's vulnerability to rise in a rebellion. All in all, proud ash-covered Charleston was at a low point in a long career, and now the Stone Fleet had arrived to make its condition even worse. A successful attack on the fragile harbor which connected the life-sustaining ports of Europe and the Caribbean to Charleston and the Confederate military, would be a potential death blow to the city. Not that the whalers or many among the north were anything less than happy to lend a hand in the Siege of Charleston, the war's longest and most bitter campaign.

At sometime around 3:00 P.M., the 245-ton New London bark and former whaler *Tenedos* became the first of the Stone Fleet to actually serve the purpose the government had contracted her for. Named after an island in the far-off Aegean Sea, according to the poem by Melville (not at the high point of his literary career), she was an India ship that had carried spices and other cargoes from the east, and "a glorious / Good old craft as ever run." She was so old, said one navy mate, her keel had been laid when Adam was a boy, which according to one sharp-eyed correspondent, dated some of the other ships as hailing from the days of the mastodon.

Despite her grand past, the bark was doomed. Running out a hawser cable, the gunboat *Ottawa* towed her to the northeast end of the main channel, where the water was eighteen feet deep at full tide. A small boat lay at anchor there to mark the position where she'd be sunk. When ready, the *Ottawa*'s captain yelled through his trumpet for the *Tenedos* to ease off the hawser. Immediately the line flew back in, and still in motion, the whaler struck the bar where intended, trembling as she hit the soft bottom, perhaps something like a dying whale going into a flurry. Her crew gave the anchor its ultimate drop with the cable "rattling out as cheerfully as any chain might which had made its last run."

As would be repeated again and again over the course of the operation, the men on the discarded whalers removed the bolts from the plugs belowdecks, knocked them out (presumably with mallets), and let the gurgling seawater rush inside in a flow the "size of a man's leg." In case the plugs refused to budge, there were two augurs on board to do a drilling job on the fly, but they proved unnecessary. The Atlantic complied nicely with the intentions of the scuttlers, and the *Tenedos* went down according to plan, dropping into the shallows as the sun correspondingly dropped into the west. Anchored with her cargo, she now marked one end of the channel as firmly as her namesake island, claimed *The New York Times* reporter.

The crew dropped their whaleboats from their davits and rowed away from the sinking vessel, carrying with them their baggage, sails, and anything else worth keeping, while the *Ottawa* went back to the line of awaiting ships to fetch the next victim.

The *Leonidas,* commanded by Captain Howland, had the dubious honor to be the second sacrifice, marking the southwest border of the channel, about one-eighth of a mile from the *Tenedos.* The 231-ton New Bedford bark appropriately bore the name of an especially brave Spartan captain who'd died blocking a strategic pass during one of the Greek wars against Persia. The sinking of the two ships only marked the beginning of the operation, and while the high tide and the moonlight lasted, Davis added six more vessels to his submarine wall. Again and again, mariners who'd spent their careers fighting to keep the water out of their ships now willfully let it in before abandoning them.

As the vessels continued to slip under the waves, Davis's scheme became evident. Although he didn't like the assigned task, he'd nevertheless applied all his analytical powers to overcoming the formidable enemy he'd faced a decade before. He knew that short of forever draining the Cooper and Ashley Rivers, it would be impossible to cork the Charleston harbor up like a wine bottle. Moreover, he feared replicating the Union's failed attempt at sealing up the Ocracoke Inlet, where sunken hulks had actually deepened the channel. And besides the all-powerful flow of the twin rivers, beneath shallow, opaque waters, the harbor's bottom was covered in a thin layer of sediments, including sand, clay, shell, and bits of coral. Such a soft, gentle, absorbent bed was as unreliable as a politician's vow, and the hulks laid to rest there would be prone to sink deeper or slide out of position. As Davis must've been aware, there were prevailing strong east winds here, capable of smashing the upper works of an exposed ship to pieces. To counter these challenges, the scientist of the water had devised an elegant plan to drop the hulks at regular intervals in several succeeding columns, with the final configuration arranged something like the dark squares on a checkerboard. The hulks would cling to the sandbar like barnacles to a ship and create a "combination of artificial interruptions and irregularities." The tides could run in and out freely, with the flows and currents that had formed and preserved the sandbar working to naturally maintain Davis's artificial barrier.

The characteristically bad luck of the expedition managed to hold out even now. As the tide ebbed, the weight of some vessels exceeded the power of the water to buoy them up in the shallows and they had to be dragged on to the bar. After placement, some vessels sank slowly, rolling over like whales on their flippers until the stone, with that native love of an object for earth that is gravity, guided them into their graves. Some listed on their beam ends, their yards tangled in a last embrace with those of the ships adjacent to them. Other whalers went stern first or down by the bow; some rested on their keels. As they sank, the sea began to sweep over them, washing the decks; sometimes fountains of water spouted from the open hatches.

The Navy Department had expected it would take only fifteen minutes to sink any given vessel, but in practice, it usually took an hour for a thorough scuttling. None disappeared completely, and heavy swells raised the less steady ships up and dropped them again. Some vessels so resurrected stayed afloat so long the waves began to swing them out of position, requiring the intervention of a steamer to replace the hulk as closely as possible to its original spot. The reporters, even though presumably sober, couldn't help but get maudlin. One writer described a whaler that went "down with every rope and spar in place as a brave man falls in battle with his harness on." At 9:45 P.M. master Willis repaid the *Rebecca Sims,* whose performance had gotten him to Savannah first, by knocking the plug out of her side and abandoning her to the sea. With about half the fleet sunk, the low tide ended the operation at around ten P.M. The scuttled vessels settled "comfortably" between the *Tenedos* and *Leonidas* and the harbor full of whaleboats heading to the *Cahawba.*

The next morning, the balance of the Stone Fleet, eight vessels strong, was planted in the channel to keep their sister ships company. Yet as if to frustrate the mariners who'd taken so much care to make the port unusable, at about noon the *Pocahontas* was able to run the gauntlet of masts and jib booms successfully. In tow behind the steamer was Nantucket Captain Worth's vessel, the *Archer,* and the Nantucketer, odd man out again, was the last to have his ship sunk. The men of the fleet watched with admiration as the master of the *Pocahontas* deposited the vessel in her place. Any mistake here would have meant a collision and possible damage, and whether he succeeded through the excellence of the pilot or by the sloppy arrangement of the vessels was impossible to tell.

The task finally completed, the junk fleet of sixteen ships lay across the channel, each vessel in her position as if in a line of battlefield fortifications. There probably hadn't been so many whalers thus disposed of at once since the San Francisco gold rush. Their presence created a desolate appearance, resembling a fleet at anchor run aground after the tide has run out. As a final touch, the water ebbing, Davis gave the order for whaling crews, armed with axes, to row back and strip their vessels of any remaining spars, sails, cordage, or other equipment that might be useful to any daring Rebel trying to scavenge.

The sound of axes chopping rang out as men went to work to sever the braces and shrouds that supported those masts whose sails had caught the wind in a thousand waters throughout the globe. It only took a few blows to part the rigging, and with the balanced system of ropes suddenly gone, the masts swung for a moment, then snapped, sounding like "brittle pipe stems" cracking. One after another, each spar hit the water with a loud, protesting crash and throwing spray and water into the air before floating by the board and out to sea with the current. For two hours the explosions of the distant Confederate guns seemed to keep time with the sound of the tumbling masts. A *New York Herald* reporter managed to find "unalloyed pleasure" on seeing the masts, the engine of the ships' motion, fade into the distance, as he knew their disappearance was vital to this operation's success.

Although by now the ships had been mostly picked clean of anything valuable, there were fittings and other bric-a-brac enough left behind to drive a junk man insane with desire, noted the *Times*. The navy had seen to this as well, awarding stripping rights to private wreckers to retrieve the anchor chains, rigging, and spars that couldn't be carted back on a whaleboat. These salvors had sailed down with the fleet, like pilot fish in a school of sharks. One skipper on a New Bedford schooner carrying out his scavenging claimed the sunken vessels were too far apart and it "was very easy to sail between" them: He concluded the venture wouldn't do the Union much good.

Naturally, the Confederates watched closely the goings on in their harbor, but outside of a few perfunctory approaches from a Rebel steamer that cautiously kept two miles of sea between herself and the Yankee fleet, they did nothing. As the thick weather that had prevailed 'on the harbor cleared, residents with spyglasses could see the parts of the ships that stood out of the water. Though something of a mystery, clearly the presence of the old whalers didn't bode well for the city. "The Charlestonians must have felt themselves chagrined beyond measure at the mischief which had been done them," said the *Times*.

Out in the harbor, destiny had yet to rule on a single remaining ship: the former Mystic whaler *Robin Hood*, called "the wonder of her day." During operations, the 395-ton New London ship had collided with the U.S.S. *Alabama*, and though damaged, she had remained afloat till now. A navy steamer approached her and an officer ordered the captain to take aboard all the sails and cordage salvaged from the other vessels, after which "you will then sink your ship!"

After her immersion, at 6:00 P.M. the *Hood*'s crew torched her, partly in celebration, partly to give the Confederates a "grand sight of a bonfire." To make the pyrotechnic display more memorable, the crew had "frapped" the ship, cutting the rigging and tying it to the masts. After this effort, she burned brightly but slowly, with "more smoke than flames," taking till 8:00 P.M. for her mizzenmast to collapse. The watching Yankees found it a "novel and beautiful sight." Soon after midnight, she slipped to the bottom and little remained of her except one of the four placards that had carried her name—oddly abbreviated in gold lettering as *R.Hood*. (One eventually became a memento for Barnum to display in his famous circus.)

If one believed the newspaper reporters, the sinking of the whalers was a great victory, in horror, eclipsing in magnitude even the recent Charleston fire. One writer claimed, "The bar is paved with granite, and the harbor a thing of the past." The sea dogs had taken their just revenge for the many wrongs South Carolina had inflicted on the long-suffering Bay State. At least on the battlefield of newsprint, the event might offset the humiliation the Rebels had inflicted in their defeat of the Union army at First Bull Run. Their relatively brief, for a whaling man, task completed, most of the officers and crews from the Stone Fleet took the Federal steamers *Empire State* and *Ocean Queen* to New York City. From there they sailed on the Fall River steamship line back home, arriving just after the New Year. Old Captain Worth, who'd put his men on sea rations, took back more than stories to Nantucket: In his bag was a full unsliced ham salvaged, or possibly hoarded, from the *Archer.*

It didn't take long for the navy to discover the expenditure of the sixteen whalers on the main channel was too stingy an offering to the gods of the sea. The recently discovered Maffit's Channel was still open, as the blockade-running steamer *Isabel* demonstrated by slipping through it successfully. That was no great matter, as there were still more whalers available. Intending to bottle up Charleston more thoroughly, on January 26 the navy turned the second bungling Stone Fleet loose. Commander E. G. Parrott, head of the blockading force of Charleston, took command of the new fleet of some fourteen to twenty ships. (There are no reliable numbers.) The second squadron proved to be not only far less famous than its predecessor, but also less lucky weatherwise. During a gale on January 24, three of the vessels parted their chains, and the wind and waves pushed the helpless bark *Peri* out to sea, where she drifted for three days. Despite the "pretty hard time," as Parrott put it, he managed to get half the fleet sunk the first day at the Rattlesnake Shoal. One vessel, anchor gone and plug already loose, took on water as she drifted northeast and sank in some shallows before a steamer could rescue her.

This gesture at Maffit's channel proved to be the final contribution of the Yankee whaling fleet to the graveyard of ships known as Charleston Harbor. Returning home that February, Captain Hinckley of the *Sea Ranger,* a salvage vessel from New London that carried spars, rigging, chains, and anchors from the sunken vessels of the second fleet, believed the operation had been a complete waste. The ships of the Stone Fleet were sunk both too far apart and in water too deep to keep out any self-respecting blockade runner, and not even the Union operations in the channel were stopped.

The adventure did little for whaling in anything like the long term. Although the men could bask in a little glory and tell their stories to listeners eager for war news, it didn't much fatten their purses. Most of the remaining whalers remained tied up at dock, the industry was still in decline, and now Confederate warships were striking as they soon found out when a local newspaper published an account of the unlucky *Eben Dodge*'s demise.

Although acknowledging the Second Stone Fleet lacked the more precise placement of the first, the ever-cheery DuPont was confident it would do the job. Wisely, he'd entertained low enough expectations to be satisfied with the results he got, and even told Fox he thought the task was worth it even if the obstructions lasted only till March or April. The remaining open channels, the Swash and North, weren't deep enough to pass heavy draught vessels, so whatever whaling vessels tied up at the docks north of Sag Harbor could swing easy at their cables, free of worry from predatory government agents.

On the Union side that December, the Stone Fleet earned the status of an object of ridicule by a wit in *Vanity Fair*. On the other hand, the fleet didn't exactly provoke an outpouring of love from the Mosquito Republics, as Seward called them. None other than the South's own marble man, Confederate States general Robert E. Lee, lost his composure. "This achievement, so unworthy any nation, is the abortive expression of the malice and revenge of a people which it wishes to perpetuate by rendering more memorable a day [secession] hateful in their calendar," wrote Lee in a letter to the secretary of war, in a moment when his potent temper apparently exceeded his considerable self-control. It's hard to blame him for such an outburst. He was at a low point in his career, stuck in a fool's errand of protecting what he knew to be a vast and indefensible coast against a formidable navy. Lee also neglected to mention that he himself had ordered the placement of such obstructions to frustrate any attempted assault.

As for the prickly Charlestonians, they needed little goading to hate their perceived oppressors even more. When the truth dawned on them in all its unpleasant details (via a reprinted *New York Times* article), they assumed this "piece of barbarism" wouldn't provide any long-lasting exultation. They were certain that the great powers of England and France would intervene on their behalf in this mess. Indeed, the Anglo-Saxons on the other side of the ocean, who depended on Southern cotton to keep busy the looms of their dark satanic textile mills, were angry enough to enter the war. In the inimitably British way, they raised voices of protest.

This vandalism from the Dark Ages, "an infernal revenge which only the brains of Northern Yankees could hatch out," would shame even Attila the Hun, claimed the ever and always hypocritical and aggrieved English. (They omitted the fact that they'd used this very method of blockade again and again themselves.) Moreover, they were hardly being Olympian in perspective, being rivals of the Union in every sort of sea commerce, which included their relatively feeble attempts at whaling. "People who would do an act like this would pluck the sun out of the heavens to put their enemies in darkness; or dry up the rivers, that no grass might forever grow," claimed a London *Times* editorial.

It was left to Secretary of State William Seward to pour some diplomatic oil on the choppy seas of English anger and so smooth them. According to a report, on January 14, 1862, Seward attempted to defend the "barbarous attempt" on Charleston by explaining to Her Majesty that the Union was attempting to block three thousand miles of coast with a fleet unprepared for such an operation. "The Secretary of the Navy had reported that he could stop up the 'large holes' by means of his ships, but that he could not stop up the 'small ones.' It had been found necessary, therefore, to close some of the numerous small inlets by sinking vessels in the channel." Also, he explained to the Crown, the just and wise Union's desire wasn't to seal the harbor in perpetuity, just long enough to starve Charleston out. The apology seems to have assuaged the aggrieved island empire.

Even before the diplomatic waves had subsided, both of the Stone Fleet's incarnations slipped underneath the waves of Charleston Harbor, a victim of the local currents, tides, and storms, all of which appeared to have taken up the Southern cause. By February 12, Major T. M. Wagner, commander of Fort Sumter, reported the hulks of the first fleet had vanished from view within a week of their sinking and eventually disappeared completely. As the ships disintegrated, their constituent parts washed ashore. By May 1862, the last view of any ship was the end of a yard attached to the southernmost wreck. A usable opening had formed to the north of the channel. By the next year, the Stone Fleet had disappeared completely into the soft bottom of the harbor, spreading all that New England granite in Rebel territory (and reportedly being found on occasion by those delving there till this day). The reluctant Captain Davis had accidentally fulfilled his old commission of improving the harbor, as the old whalers had left behind a deeper channel than the one they had originally found. At a cost of about a quarter of a million federal dollars, blockade running was a relatively easier task at the war's end than it had been at its beginning.

The government's money, expended on the thirty-six junk vessels, was

pretty much a waste. As Melville's poem put it: "A failure and complete /
Was your Old Stone Fleet." The project's two primary fathers, Fox and
Welles, skirted public acknowledgement of their bastard son, and in his
year-end summary, the latter didn't even bother to refer to it. The only
demonstrable value to the U.S. government was the profit gained by the
resale of a few of the vessels that had been spared from scuttling. Some of
the others, including the *Garland,* became store ships and survived until
Appomattox and beyond. Ultimately, the Stone Fleet became a puny if
odd footnote to the history of the Civil War, if not that of Yankee whaling,
of which it is a milestone.

Interestingly, at about the time the Stone Fleet set out on its quest, the
city journals were also carrying the story of an explorer, Dr. Isaac Hayes,
who'd recently completed an Arctic expedition in Greenland, where he'd
managed to get an unfortunate carpenter killed. Presumably, this was a
cheap price to pay for such an explorer. Indeed, it was almost niggardly in
a line of work that apparently esteemed, even demanded, the spending of
lives. Simultaneously, two whaling ships wintering over in the same region
had returned home profitably with oil and bone, and had gained as much
scientific knowledge as Dr. Hayes, while having an exciting trip, to boot.

A New York writer said he believed that paying whaling ventures rendered these suicidal and profitless scientific ventures superfluous. Probing
the underbelly of the Arctic should be left to blubber hunters. After all,
whaling as practiced by "the daring fishermen of New England" was the
"Jove of enterprise." Yet, these brave fishers had turned their skills to an
enterprise of doubtful purpose, whose mission, as one journalist put it,
was as pitiless as the granite their ships freighted. It had also been aimed
at a civilian foe that had been unable to fight back.

Yet, not surprisingly, back in New Bedford the much exalted memories
of the junk fleet persisted long after its physical artifacts had vanished.
Some of those masters who'd been captains in the operation were rewarded by having streets in New Bedford and nearby towns named after
them. They never received government pensions, which Captain Willis
felt they merited for the dangers the fleet had survived. So proud were
many of the denizens of the City of Light, they decorated their walls with
a lithographic reproduction of the first Stone Fleet putting out to sea under
full sail, each vessel depicted above her name. This artistically rendered

fleet was serene, grand, and undoubtedly more majestic than the real one had appeared when it sailed out that snowy November day, given that some of its ships had concealed holes with planks that couldn't keep out the sunlight. When the century turned and many of the older houses in New Bedford were torn down, with them went the popular lithograph that had hung on their walls. The amiable Friend Rodney French had earned the right to be called commodore to the end of his long life while cementing his personal history with that of the war for emancipation. From this disposal of a large portion of the whaling fleet did the abolitionist emerge from the great sea of obscurity, clinging as if to a raft one of the great conflict's footnotes, if not the main narrative.

While he must have been exultant to be able to strike a blow for a (if not *the*) just cause, if by doing this he was looking to blot out any connection between him and slaving, he was wrong. All he'd secured was a hollow title that he kept till his death, and being one of the Children of the Light, a chance to flail in the gloom of man's condition. Yet it was his duty to do so—to act as the conscience of the world and push back man's night, as the light of a candle would. But as French must have known, even the best sperm lamp could keep the dark away only for a while before sputtering out.

In the long run, as for the intended victim, Charleston, ultimately it wasn't an action to "point a moral or adorn a tale," as one observer predicted. There was nevertheless a series of consequences that at the time no one in the whaling fleet foresaw. It was apparent to the Southerners just who'd been responsible for the temporary bottling up of their crucial waterway. Even if Lincoln had been the brains of the act, it was the Yankee whalers who'd been the arms and legs that set this maneuver in motion. With every succeeding newspaper article printed and piece of junk that washed ashore from the harbor, the Confederates had a fresh reminder of the northern whale hunters and their role in the assault. The blocks and spars the wind and tides kept pushing ashore raised eyebrows in the city, and not just those of the local wreckers who profited on the betterpreserved flotsam. It was said that on a clear day, Charlestonians could make out the name of New Bedford painted on some of the wrecks that closed off the outside world—at least until the ships sank below the water.

A Southern observer of the time soon proved prescient. One Saturday night, a piece of a New London ship (gone to the bottom as part of the Second Stone Fleet) thumped up against a Charleston wharf. After retrieval, the Charlestonians recognized this piece of flotsam as part of the "submarine investment" of the Lincoln-ites, a journalist recorded. He claimed the Federals had conducted this operation mostly to enrich the Yankee owners of the useless old hulks. He concluded: "The drifting ashore of such a piece of a wreck or hulk, with the name of *New England,* may be taken as an omen by some."

9

Like Pursuing a Coy Maiden

The fellows seemed to be so well pleased, that I believe, with a little coaxing, they would have been willing to give three cheers for the *Alabama*.

—*Raphael Semmes*

AUGUST 24, 1862, AZORES, SHIP *290*

Although this bright shining day was the Sabbath and usually a day of rest, it had been a busy morning on board. The vessel had been a dirty, chaotic mess for the past two days as the crew prepared her, but she now looked ready for action. Her awnings were spread, the yards squared parallel with the horizon; her decks were holystoned to be white, clean, and fragrant; and the brass was bright. The Union Jack at the peak fluttered in a gentle southeast breeze while a pennant carrying the number *290* flew from the main royal masthead. To the trained naval eye of her commander, Raphael Semmes, the handsome barkentine-rigged cruiser, on whose now-quiet deck he stood, was like "a bride with the orange wreath about her brows, ready to be led to the altar." The twenty-four officers on board shared their captain's belief: She was a thing of beauty. However, her eight newly mounted guns marked her as something else, besides.

The vessel about to become the South's first active response to the Stone Fleet was in sight of the blunt verdure-covered humps of the mountain island of Terceira. She was at the outside edge of the marine league, that imaginary line three miles from shore that defined a nation's maritime boundary. She was also just under the prows of a pod of whalers, all of which had been spared from disintegration in the muck of Charleston

Harbor. These whalers were prowling the local grounds before sailing on to the Arctic and other regions. This proximity to the Spouter Fleet had nearly been the *290*'s undoing. While offshore awaiting a rendezvous with Semmes and a provisioning vessel, a whaling schooner from Provincetown had dropped anchor nearby her. To make matters worse, when onshore, the *290*'s purser had foolishly revealed the vessel's identity, and the Confederates feared the whole game lost. Nevertheless, with fortune on their side, they'd sailed on without Uncle Sam's interference, in a preview of what was to be a long run of devilish good luck.

On board, a harsh-looking ragtag crew now shared space on the quarterdeck with a small military band. For the past days, it had been these roughneck mariners, faces smeared with dark streaks of coal, sleeves rolled up and lapels opened to reveal brawny chests, who had toiled under a hot sun moving cannon and stores on board. A few of them were brave, perhaps even decent seamen, but the majority were a "precious lot of rascals," said Semmes. The roster included liars, thieves, and drunks culled from the waterfront dives of Liverpool. Although mostly Irish, Welsh, and English, the crew had a smattering of Portuguese, Spanish, and other nations present, including an Italian steward of reputedly genteel blood that too often had been diluted with spirits. This collection of international riffraff ill understood and cared little, if it all, about the war that had divided the United States—a conflict in which it was so famously about to intervene.

In honor of the commissioning about to unfold, the officers had managed somewhat to clean and neaten the crew. For the occasion, Semmes wore a gray uniform—a break with the blue of naval tradition—that displayed plenty of gold braid to impress the assembled "waifs of the ocean." As the ceremony began, both the leaders and the led removed their headgear—the latter's a mix of hats and scotch caps—as if the Queen herself was on deck. Carrying two documents, the not-so-tall Semmes mounted a gun carriage to gain some elevation and began to read his new commission as captain of the Confederate Navy. He also recited his order to take command of this warship, which would bear the name of his adopted home state, Alabama. Looking over the verdant patches on the humps of Terceira rising up from the ocean into a cloudless sky, Semmes felt the smile of nature itself on him.

And perhaps it was. He'd already been extraordinarily fortunate, having managed to get the less than seaworthy *Sumter* through the foul North Atlantic weather—along with the hapless as well as helpless crew of the *Eben Dodge*—to Cadiz, Spain. There he'd landed these destitute wretches and left them to find their own way back to New Bedford. Later, in Gibraltar and dogged by Federal warships he couldn't outfight and unable to buy coal, he'd sold the steamer. Nursing a frenzied hatred for Uncle Sam, he slipped out of Spain and again presented himself in England for service to the Confederacy.

While dwelling in that small and foggy if royal womb of kings, he learned of a mysterious vessel whose keel had been laid in Liverpool, known only as *290*, her number in the sequence of ships launched by the capable Laird firm on the River Mersey. This new vessel was no *Sumter*, a refurbished passenger carrier, but a craft lovingly constructed as a formidable hunter of merchant ships, perhaps the best cruiser of her class in the world. In this 235-by-32 feet of floating Confederate property, purpose and design matched beautifully, and she was, as Semmes noted, capable of riding the waves with the lightness and grace of a swan. Larger than most whalers, she was well equipped. Her masts were of the best Georgia pine and could bend to the roughest wind, and from her yards hung the best Swedish wire.

For auxiliary power, the *Alabama* had an engine that delivered 300 horsepower, and she could run unusually fast under either steam or sail. Combining the power of the two, she made 15 knots, and when under canvas alone, the propeller could be hoisted into a well to keep it from dragging and reducing her speed. Though built more for swiftness than combat, she carried eight guns, and rounding out the armaments was pettifogger Semmes's library of law books. These furnished him with ammunition to blast away at any legal bulwarks that a clever ship's master with an eye to technicalities might try to erect to protect himself and his vessel.

Also present that day on the deck for the christening (and perhaps concealing what must've been considerable disappointment) was Semmes's friend and onetime colleague in the U.S. Navy, James Bulloch. Bulloch was in his late thirties and easily recognizable by his great forehead, from which the hair was receding like an ebb tide on a mud flat. The *Alabama* was his daughter: He'd supervised her construction from planning to launching in expectation of being rewarded with her quarterdeck. Just prior to this project, he'd outfitted and launched another vessel, the *Florida,* under James Maffit, and now felt he was due a command. Nevertheless, the latest prize of the Confederate Navy had gone to Semmes; apparently Bulloch's task was limited to providing the cruisers and leaving to others the danger and glory that commanding them offered.

Certainly Bulloch was clever, and he'd taken unusual precautions during the *290*'s launching from Liverpool. To avoid the vigilant eyes of the Federal spies that plied the waterfront, the *290,* minus armaments, had cast off, as if on a pleasure cruise, carrying a "large party of ladies and gentlemen," on the Mersey. To avoid violating at least the letter if not the intent of England's neutrality laws, the revelers soon took their party to the deck of a tug, allowing the *290* to plough south through a protecting squall to the Azores to await her transformation. Bulloch, who'd been aboard the cruiser during the merriment, went ashore and spent the night in a small hotel sipping a toddy of the best Coleraine malt, listening to the wind and rain pelting the gables and fretting over his little ship buffeting her way around the rugged north coast of Ireland. Later, with Semmes and his officers, he'd sailed out of England on the *Bahama* to give away the *Alabama* like a father bestowing the bride at a wedding.

As Semmes pronounced the words of his commission, two balls of fabric slowly rose up the lines to replace those that had been fluttering there, while a gunner was at the ready on the weather-bow cannon. His speech finished, Semmes waved his hand, and the gunner fired. Simultaneously, with a jerk of the halyards that'd sent them up, the two balls of fabric unfolded, revealing the Stars and Bars and the ship's new pennant. The quartermaster struck the English colors and the *290* flag came down. As the men and officers cheered deafeningly, the band played "Dixie," that "soul-stirring national anthem of the new-born government," as Semmes deemed it, inaugurating what became a daily tradition on the ship. A gun boomed from the nearby *Bahama* and her crew cheered what had become under their eyes a Confederate warship.

Even before the commissioning was done, Semmes had formed a plan of attack. At some point, he'd learned of the pernicious Stone Fleet and had a particular distaste for the New Bedford species of Yankee; on board were pilots from Charleston and Savannah, to boot. To aid him in avenging the wrongs to the South, during his days as a federal employee he'd learned much about the habits of the whalers. The former navy professional realized hunting the hunters was an easy task. Although they might sail tens of thousands of miles in their travels, the whalers, generation after generation, always congregated at the same grounds to kill the leviathans who went there to feed and breed—just as their ancestors had since a time farther back than human memory. Semmes had a second advantage in his favor. Because he was hunting over such a wide area (i.e. the oceans of the world), once he struck, word of his prowling would spread very slowly among the fleet. Additionally, as he was aware, now was the height of the sperm-hunting season in the Azores. Fate having placed his ship right in his hated enemy's lap, he planned to start his reign of terror by, as he later put it, spilling a little "ile." (The Yankee pronunciation of oil.)

However, the raider had a slight problem: His fine ship had no crew. The men who'd served on the *290*, the *Bahama,* and a supply ship hadn't signed on for a Confederate war cruise, such an act being illegal, and they were now contractually free. So, with the effects of the ceremony still strong, and in international waters and free from the neutrality law that barred enlisting Englishmen, Semmes made an appeal to the assembled men to join him.

The field had already been sown, as the shrewd Bulloch had ordered the paymaster, Southern born, to be friendly and propagandize the men with stories of how his country was fighting to uphold the English concept of liberty—and ignore the little technicality of slaving. Bulloch hoped to sweeten them on the notion of being killed or killing in a cause in which they had no direct interest.

"I want you all to join me and I am going to burn, sink and destroy all the enemy's property and any that goes with me will be entitled to two-twentieths prize money," Semmes declared. "There are only four or five northern ships I am afraid of. I do not want any to go with me that is not willing to fight and there is a steamer alongside us to take them back if they are not willing."

Working like a skillful New Bedford land shark, Semmes persuaded eighty men to fill his roster. That he was able to convince so rough-hewn and motley a crew, not particularly susceptible to idealism, to follow him, trusting in the generosity of a year-old far-off government and facing a considerable naval power as enemy, testifies to something—possibly even Semmes's leadership. Even with these warm bodies at his disposal, Semmes still hardly had a crew worthy of the name, and discipline proved to be a shaky, uneven affair at best. Through the liberal application of punishment, along with soap and water, at least the officers of the *Alabama* made them resemble military sailing men. While none ever saw a penny of the pledged money and some never returned to their homelands again, at least they could boast they made New England, New Bedford especially, yelp, and loudly.

The day after commissioning, as Bulloch returned on the *Bahama,* Semmes ordered the *Alabama* to begin the hunt "on the bosom of the trackless deep" and repay a debt of honor to those who'd so rudely bottled up his harbor.

NEW BEDFORD HARBOR,
SEPTEMBER 2, 1862, BARK *JIREH SWIFT*

The pilot not even off his vessel, ship's master Thomas Williams, homesick and blue about embarking on yet another voyage, was already penning a letter addressed to his wife, to whom he confessed: "I can not bare the Idea of bein from you all so long." His letter lacked punctuation—possibly he was ignorant of those stops and starts of language that guide the course of ideas. Or, perhaps as always, he was barreling ahead as fast as possible and couldn't bother with any of the reefing or steering niceties of grammar.

From his cabin, heartbroken, Williams justified his departure to Eliza:

> I supose you will say I had no reason to go I cofes that I might
> have lived at Home but when I thought of raising so many chil-
> dren I wanted to have them brought up in the best way and
> with a good education[.] I know the want of it[. . . .] I want you
> to put Stancel to a good school where he will have a man over
> him never mind consulting him to much[.] Harry I think will do
> to go to a common school for a year or 2 yet[.] Kiss Little Mary

for me also Little Wille and the others and your self escept all
the Love a man can send on a pias of paper be sure and write
me often and *Long Letters*[.] I can not say any thing more I
hope you have got a long letter for me in some of my close that
I shall find byanby[.] the wind is fare and the pilot is soon to
leve and I am lift alone I shall think of you a great many times
on this voyag[.] except a kiss from me So give my Love to all
Brothers and sisters and mothur Fathur[.] I remain yours affectionate Husband Thos W Williams"

But as miserable as the master from Wethersfield was, at least he had a
command now. Old whalers and greenies from the farm and countinghouse alike were eager to sign on the few available ships and take advantage
of the rising oil prices caused by the war. Breaking from the gentlemanly
custom then prevalent in the industry that permanently bound a master to a
given firm, Williams had tacked sharply and made an alliance with the venerable house of Swift & Allen in New Bedford.

Williams had been sogering along with the other whaling captains since
arriving in San Francisco with the *Florida*. As evidence of the gloomy situation he had been facing, a June 28, 1862, letter from Fish, Robinson & Co.
to Williams, then residing in Wethersfield, indicated how grim things had
become. "With regard to another vessil for right whaling we do not [hear]
much encouraging," he wrote. "We note in your letter to Mr. Potter [an
agent and friend] that you do not seem fully persuaded about what course
you will pursue." Mr. Morgan [first mate of the *Florida*] had an offer for another ship, which they felt he should probably take while he had the
chance. Williams apparently had proposed to launch a small vessel, and
the firm was willing to help him buy one and fit it out. "We are not making
a red cent this year and must hold back for emergencies or whatever comes
up. . . . Best regards to Mrs Williams and the small fry—"

Apparently his former associates were not calling out the tune Williams
wanted to hear, and he changed allegiance. This must have been an op-
portune move, for as a result he was entrusted with one of the city's largest
and possibly her fastest whaler, the bark *Jireh Swift,* whose combined
122 feet and 428 tons comprised a "sharp ship." Williams called her
"Mrs. Swift"; others called her *"Jerry."* Her keel had been laid in Dartmouth

in 1853. Although originally ship-rigged, she'd been reregistered in New Bedford as a bark, and on her in that form, Williams was sailing.

Eliza herself was in New Bedford, baby Mary in tow, to see her husband off. She was as racked with guilt and sorrow as her husband, but for the reverse reason. She was ready to go back to sea with him, and regretted she wasn't. Rather, she was due to head back to Wethersfield and mark the time away from Williams with his parents; her own mother and father were dead. She was more than willing to brave the sea again, if just to be with him. At least then she'd be happy.

"I have suffered a good deal in my mind, I have felt ugly, and wicked, about it, which I know is not right, but I feel that you are the only sincere Friend that I have in the world, and I cant bear to part with you," as she herself put it to him in a letter she had sat down and penned two days before her husband's departure. She had a foreboding about the torture she'd endure, until in "due time" her man returned home. "I fear that you will spend many lonely hours, and knowing much about whaling life, your every care will be my care, and you will be often, very often, in my thoughts, I shall imagine many things, and think that you are in trouble many times." At some point, she'd be reconciled to sharing Williams once again with the ocean—but not now. When, she didn't know. She knew, lacking an alternative, she could only trust in God, despite her weak faith. Poor Eliza admitted she wasn't as good as she hoped to be.

After the *Swift* set sail, that expected letter from Eliza appeared, hidden in Williams's clothes. With so many conflicting emotions, her ideas on paper flowed out choppy and wild like the waters of Buzzards Bay in a rough wind. Yet she urged him not to worry and pledged that she planned to do well and obey his instructions and teach the children to "reverence, respect, and love" their father. She admitted her tortured feelings to Williams:

> no one knows but myself how bad I feel to have you go, but [I]
> have got to give you up[.] I have liked going to Sea so well with
> you, that I have even wished at times, that you might go to Sea
> again some day, if I could only go with you. . . . I feel now that I
> would go willingly, and patiently, bear with you, any privation
> at Sea, if I could only go, and be with you, but I cannot. . . . it is
> the wish of my heart, that you shall be happy.

Seemingly reconciled, she commended him to God's hands, "knowing that he is on the Sea as well as the land. . . . I remain now, and ever, your true and affectionate Wife, Eliza A. Williams."

If it was any consolation to Williams, he had a fine ship under him, as he soon discovered while sailing to the Azores to pick up some recruits. Williams described the *Swift* as "splendid for the business, she was built for it." Of her unique speed, he claimed, "I always had four hours a day more [extra] than any other ship her class." In one of the letters he wrote Eliza each Sunday, he bragged that, when passing another ship, "we calculate that [stretch] we beat her 24 miles in a Seven Hours [when passing another ship]." Also, luckily, he had a good steward on board, who served him the best bread and duffs he'd enjoyed in a long while; he ate mince pies and corn cakes every morning. He declared to Eliza he liked the officers "first rate," but that "I would like if you ware here with me I do miss you so much." He might have thought twice about that sentiment if he'd known the "here" he was discussing was aimed in the general direction of one Raphael Semmes.

SEPTEMBER 5, 1862, NORTH ATLANTIC,
WHALING BARK *OCMULGEE*

This was a big strike, and fortune seemed good, decided Abraham Osborn Jr., a long, lean master who'd put out of Edgartown on Martha's Vineyard just two months before on his way to the Arctic. Soon the winter gales would strike the Azores, the whale feed become scarce, and the hunting shift to other regions. Luckily, earlier that day, his crew had killed a noble sperm whale, the jaw a whopping twenty-eight feet long, and now the stinker's carcass was tied up next to the whaler and making her list to one side. Captain Osborn wasn't afraid to lend a hand, even if his father was the majority owner in the ship. Osborn, who hailed from the Vineyard, was an example—not universal—of a captain who had been conceived something like a mile from the water's edge of the port from which he sailed.

Never as eminent in blubber hunting as Nantucket or New Bedford, the small, sandy, and generally none-too-fertile island of Martha's Vineyard nevertheless grew fine whaling captains, who, it was said, could make the very air salty when they met to swap tales. Even though the ports of Cape Cod, Nantucket, and Martha's Vineyard were in decline, they still berthed mariners of legendary proportions.

Of this sort was young Osborn. His father and fellow owners had entrusted him with this fine vessel, matched in tonnage by only four others in the fleet. Outfitted in the best condition, with a new copper bottom, there was quite an investment at stake.

In any case, she was proving lucky with this early-season strike, and her crew had torn off most of the whale's blubber. It was just after a light wind from the east died when a fine-looking ship flying the U.S. flag came across the horizon. The whaling master assumed Gideon Welles had dispatched a new gunboat to protect the local whaling grounds. The stranger dropped sail and became larger, yet Osborn and his crew, processing the rich prize, continued to ignore her. In the middle of the toil, an explosion rang out over the water as the stranger fired a cannon. She sailed to within hailing distance, and Osborn, at last turning away from his work, saw a frightening change occur in her appearance. Down came the Stars and Stripes (the "flaunting lie" as Semmes called it) and up went the Stars and Bars. It might as well have been the pirate's Jolly Roger, and the Vineyarder's lean face became a "blank stare of astonishment."

A boat soon came alongside carrying an officer in a gray uniform. He delivered a message soon to become familiar throughout the fleet: "You are a prize of the steamer *Alabama.*"

The officer told the stricken master to fetch the ship's papers and report to the nearby cruiser, and soon Osborn was looking into the sun-burned visage of Semmes. Looking over his tall, rangy prisoner, Semmes decided Osborn was a genuine specimen of the Yankee whaling skipper, as "elastic as the whalebone he dealt in." Semmes explained with his typical restraint: "You are my prize. I am going to burn the *Ocmulgee,* and every other vessel bearing the American flag I can catch. I will have the whole fleet of whalers."

Like the Yankee trader and master he was, Osborn fought back to save his vessel, although he would've had better luck arguing with a typhoon as trading arguments with Semmes. The Yankee's blank expression may have made the Confederates want to grin, but they couldn't help but admire his stoic demeanor. He bore this fate as "philosophically as a true sailor could, and that is saying a great deal," noted the *Alabama*'s executive officer Kell. Semmes sent Osborn back to his bark to retrieve some of his finer clothes, while the *Alabama*'s crew helped themselves to sails, ropes, beef, pork, and other provisions. The crowning prize, of course, was the chronometer, which Semmes added to what would be his second burgeoning assemblage. With a hunter's luck a whaler could only envy, Semmes had picked the best ship to capture—not just any whaler, but one outfitted to spend years on the seas.

Along with thirty-seven men, limited to a bag of clothes each, Osborn returned to the *Alabama*, leaving the *Ocmulgee* with her wheel lashed in place and a light shining from the mast to mark her position. Semmes ordered the prisoners into irons above deck, under guard, and exposed to whatever moods the often-surly Atlantic chose to vent. With the last provisions hauled aboard, around 9:00 P.M., Semmes, who delighted in igniting vessels almost to the point of pyromania, had to deny himself the pleasure of making the *Ocmulgee* a nighttime torch for fear of tipping off any other nearby whalers to his presence. "I had now become too old a hunter to commit such an indiscretion," as he put it, refusing to uncover the birds faster than they could be bagged. Instead, he'd await the morning, when the dense smoke billowing from the whaler would appear to be that of a passing steamer.

Visible by the light at her peak, the *Ocmulgee* lay overnight near the *Alabama*, the large sperm corpse still attached to the cutting stage awaiting a final trying out never to come. Only two dogs remained on board, destined to be shot after what must have been a confusing night. The next morning on board the *Alabama*, Osborn saw something especially galling. Two whales surfaced near the ship, and bound in his manacles, all he could do was look as all that precious lard swam nearby with impunity. At midmorning, Semmes ordered the *Ocmulgee* burned, a fairly easy task; her decks were so covered with oil, the boarding party didn't have to bother vandalizing the vessel and soaking her with fat for ignition.

To the boarding party handling this first of so many torchings, the task seemed unpleasant. After all, they were sailors. Just as it was for whalers killing their great mammalian prey, war among men "soon blunts the sentimental impulses, and what seemed at first sheer ruthlessness became in time a matter of course," noted one Confederate officer. It proved quite a spectacle. As one *Alabama* man pointed out: "The whaler makes a grand blaze."

Filling the sky with smoke, the *Ocmulgee* seemed to one young midshipman "as though she was calling down curses on the head of Abe Lincoln and his Cabinet. May he live long enough to be crushed to death under the Government which he now rules, and his fate be such as he merits." This was the first prize taken since the Confederates had christened the *Alabama* eleven days prior, just a hundred miles away. Although denied the thrill of the chase, it was a beginning. Even though he was not forced to go down with his ship, life was less than pleasant for Osborn. He'd lost one of the best ships from tiny Edgartown, a blow that hurt what was already a fading whaling center. Worse, the insurance underwriters hadn't included roving Confederate cruisers in her policy. The shining white-clapboard island town was not a great city like New Bedford, with considerable amounts of capital to draw from to rebuild a lost vessel. As the crew brought no cargo home with them, their lay would be a percentage of zero, slightly less than if the voyage had been greasy.

Osborn and his men remained the passengers of the *Alabama* as she sailed the next day to the western tip of the Azores, where a familiar sight loomed into view as night fell. It was the mountain island of Flores, whose green-festooned peak thrust up one thousand feet from the ocean into the darkening sky. Whaling captains often used the mount as a landmark to check their chronometers. (Masters knew the latitude and longitude of certain points, and often matched a known figure with the one they were calculating. If the two were not the same, they knew either their calculations or the chronometer was faulty.)

The next day, with the brass work glittering in the sun, Semmes read the Articles of War to his green and rough crew. Ignorant of their sea duties, they took as long as an hour to set two sails, and they advertised their misery by the expressions on their faces.

The poor morale was matched by indiscipline. Already some men had been called to the mast to answer for their infractions. There was one particularly rough spot needing holystoning. A Liverpool gamin named Egan had, a few days after putting out, sealed the ship's cat in the pivot gun with a tampion. The men were fond of the animal and, wanting it returned, soon fingered the culprit, whom they hung spread-eagle in the mizzen rigging in the vain hope he'd confess. Showing criminal promise, young Egan kept the cat's fate a secret until the first sail came into sight and the gun crew pulled the tampion out of the pivot gun in preparation for firing. Out jumped the fortunate feline—down at least one life—and at last Egan confessed his guilt and gave an explanation of his deed: "Oh, to see what effect the firing would have on the cat!"

Overseeing this untidy, undisciplined mess of a crew was First Officer Kell, a six-foot-tall, hulking, broad-shouldered, middle-aged, red-bearded, blue-blooded Georgian with a "refined sense of gentlemanly propriety." Despite Semmes's harsh measures, the *Alabama*'s polyglot crew began to take to the aloof and dictatorial, not to mention pious, Roman Catholic skipper, who faithfully bowed down before the makeshift shrine in his cabin to observe his matins and evening prayers. They were amused to see Semmes's gray eyes glint blue when the chase was afoot, and began to call him "Old Beeswax," in honor of his great mustache, kept presentable by steward Bartelli's preening.

On the eighth, the second day after the *Ocmulgee*'s capture, while sailing toward a small seaside village on the south shore of Flores, Semmes paroled Osborn and his crew and put them overboard in their whaleboats, which had been towed behind. This way Semmes was able to dispose of his prisoners without putting into port, and was back out to sea to prowl without having risked notice. After landing, Osborn was left to fend for himself with only his boats and provisions to his name. He managed to write to the consul in Fayal and warn of Semmes's plans for the whaling fleet. He also asked the warship U.S.S. *Tuscarora* be recalled from Cadiz, where it was bottling up the long since abandoned *Sumter*. In this matter, the Portuguese government of the Azores was of little help. Its once great navy had shrunk to insignificance, and most of its vessels were back in the mother country to celebrate the king's wedding.

The spreading news of the raider caused distress both to the whalers in the Azores and the owners back home. Five masters who put in to Flores to recruit the desperately poor locals or land oil now refused to sail out, and as provisions ran short, the welcome among the Western Islanders also wore thin.

As the sun was setting on September 9, Semmes took the becalmed whaler *Ocean Rover*. She had been out three years, four months. Her captain, James Clark, had already shipped home two cargoes of oil, with another 1,100 casks in the hold. He also had another freight of a more sentimental type: an uneaten cake in a huge tin, the last of four his wife had baked for him to celebrate their wedding anniversary at sea. Although he wanted to see his spouse and his baby—in fact, not quite a baby anymore—he couldn't resist slowing down to take another monster or two in the Azores before pointing his bow to New Bedford.

New England whaling men tended to put their vocation over all other considerations: family, friends, and politics alike, as shown during the American Revolution and the War of 1812. (During the latter, Nantucket, aware of the vulnerability of its far-flung ships, had actually wanted to secede to protect the whaling fleet.) In spirit, it appears master Clark was no different, and he "abused Abe Lincoln for everything that he could think," and given his profession, that must have meant he invoked a considerable range of profanity. He ended his peroration wishing Secretary of State William Seward be hung on the nearest tree. On board the *Alabama,* knowing Clark faced the not inconsiderable prospect of losing the *Rover,* Semmes felt pity, but just for a moment. Remembering what these diabolical New England men were doing to his country, he began "out-Heroding Herod," and the milk of human kindness curdled in his veins.

He also had his cause to sustain his cruelty. A devout Catholic, Semmes believed in the divine ordination of slavery; that it was an institution clearly worthy of defense. To fuel his passion to resist even more, he'd also adopted the creed that the northern hordes didn't just want to merely put the slave's foot on the neck of the master. The Yankees also wanted to allow the slave to afterward invade his master's wife's bed to bastardize his posterity. Such an atrocity, he was certain, "nothing but the brain of a demon could have engendered."

Facing such a fanatic, tears would've met only contempt, but Clark showed he was tough as knots when he offered his captors his wife's cake. "Well, the wedding day is not at hand yet, but you had as well enjoy the cake, gentlemen," he said, in a day when they made men who knew how to lose like men. Exactly what happened next could be—and was—debated. According to Semmes, Clark asked for permission to take his whaleboats and make his way to shore about five miles away. When the raider pointed out it was some distance to pull, Clark said: "Oh! that is nothing, We whalers sometimes chase a whale, on the broad sea, until our ships are hull-down, and think nothing of it. It will relieve you of us the sooner, and be of some service to us besides."

The sea was smooth, and Semmes said he believed a whaleboat could ride "an ordinary gale of wind." So, Clark headed back to the *Rover* and for the next two hours worked as intently as a Yankee beaver, loading six whaleboats to the gunwales with provisions. Among the inventory were seamen's chests, bedding, pork and beef, and even the ship's tabby and a parrot. Clark, with a mind to a "main chance," had also brought along the cabin's fare for his own consumption; he'd land a richer man than the governor of Flores—which may not have been saying much. The task complete, the *Rover*'s crew pulled alongside the *Alabama*. "Captain, your boats appear to me to be rather deeply laden; are you not afraid to trust them?" asked Semmes.

"Oh! no, they are as buoyant as ducks, and we shall not ship a drop of water," said Clark.

Parole granted, Semmes gave them his permission—or order—to leave. Under a bright moon whose light was broken only by a few occasional high-flying clouds, the long, sleek boats shoved off one by one from the side of the *Alabama,* and forming a line, headed for shore. Remaining on the deck, Semmes watched the whaleboats fade into the night, the boats' peaked bows and sterns reminding him of Venetian gondolas. To fill out the scene, the splashing noise of the oars was soon joined by a strong musical voice rising from somewhere in the little flotilla. The men pulling echoed it in a chorus—in the whaleman's customary way of making a tedious and dangerous burden a little lighter. The raider found himself much moved by the beautiful spectacle of the boats moving "swiftly and mysteriously" to shore and he claimed the "echo of that night song lingered long in my memory."

Rowing past rocky barren islets and greeted by the smell of flowers and shrubs that wafted from shore, Clark and his men landed on the cloud-covered mountain by 10:00 P.M. Later, the master accused Semmes of casting him and his men adrift on a stormy ocean in unsound and leaky boats, something the Confederate denied, claiming he'd set the whalers up as "nabobs" on the island. Whatever the exact story, after disposing of Clark, Semmes pushed on through the North Atlantic, proving himself the greatest threat to the whaling fleet in decades. As men often excel at what they love, so it was with Semmes. "Chasing a sail is very much like pursuing a coy maiden, the very coyness sharpening the pursuit."

The *Alert,* sixteen days out of New London and headed south to the whaling and sealing station on stormy Hurd's Island, was no common spouter ship. She was glamorous. When she'd been a noted Indiaman, Dana had served on her during the voyage he later made famous with his memoir, *Two Years Before the Mast.* After his book appeared, anyone seeing her name would always ask if indeed she was that *Alert.* Later, after she'd been reincarnated as an oil processor, she seemed to have carried her good luck along. At least until just before midnight on September 9 as she was drawing toward Flores and crossed paths with the *Alabama.* Her master, Captain Edwin Church, looking to preserve her, ordered every rag of sail spread in a bid to outmaneuver her pursuer. Sailing on the starboard tack as close to the wind as possible without luffing sails, he managed to put some distance between the *Alert* and the cruiser. Excited, Semmes looked on his prey with her square yards and white canvas with every sheet home and leach taut, and was moved. "I could but admire her," he admitted. Although the *Alert* was to the windward of the *Alabama,* the cruiser began to gain after a four-hour race, and finally caught the famous whaler.

Church was hoisted to the *Alabama*'s deck, where Semmes—fresh and clean from a bath prepared during the chase by his forlorn steward Bartelli—greeted him. The raider announced that her crew had the privilege of signing on with the steamer or taking a parole. A skilled Yankee whaling man who knew the intricacies of the trade was a prize indeed, but "thank God no one accepted the former of these offers," read the *Alert*'s final log entry. As for Church and his men, they hurriedly piled their goods into four boats and headed for the green hills of Flores, fourteen miles away. At 6:00 P.M., soon after reaching shore, they saw the flames of the *Alert* blazing in the distance, and knew a pro-slavery "gang of miscreants" had ended their voyage on a foreign shore. Indeed, so bright was the funeral pyre of the *Alert* and two other prizes taken that day it made the heights of Flores and even nearby Corvo glow. Semmes decided the surrounding whalers must have thought there were a good number of steamers crisscrossing the sea-lanes that day.

Semmes sailed on, taking whalers, the volume of the ticking from the chronometers on board was swelling. No master fought back or resisted, although some tried to talk their way out of their predicament after capture. "Why, captain, it is hard that I should have my ship burned" was a common refrain. Semmes, who never doubted once the rightness of his cause (and therefore isn't always trustworthy), claimed that most of the masters he captured, between pleas to save their ships, revealed they'd been good Democrats and were at sea only to avoid the draft. They also took pains to explain they'd no great love of the Africans; some even told him niggers were but the pets of ancient Yankee spinsters, akin to lapdogs. The Negro's back was a type of ladder, some said, the "means of some cunning political rascals, who expect to rise to fame and fortune"; the New England people really cared nothing for him. During his two weeks' captivity, the master of the whaling schooner *Kingfisher*, Thomas Lambert, confessed to Semmes that in 1860 he was one of three people in Fairhaven who had voted Democrat.

They might as well as have saved their breath to blow into their sails. Lawyer Semmes had an irrefutable reason for what he did: "Every whale you strike will put money into the Federal treasury, and strengthen the hands of your people to carry on the war. I am afraid I must burn your ship." On they argued asking to ransom their ships by means of a bond, until Semmes cut the badinage short and ordered their vessels burned. Increasing their humiliation and anger, Semmes always made a point of putting the whaling masters in irons, feeling this random act of disregard would even the balance for what the Spanish authorities, at the behest of long-armed Uncle Sam, had done to the *Sumter*'s paymaster, who'd handled the ship's wages. The Spaniards had arrested him, shaved his head, and tossed him in jail. If a captured spouter-captain remonstrated, Semmes just replied his own paymaster had "held a high position also, and was a gentleman, an officer of unblemished character and great worth, and should not have been treated like a felon."

At times, the Rebels wondered why they captured with so little effort the men reputed to be the most enterprising and toughest mariners in the world. "Nothing was more practical than to refuse our commands, [and] take our desultory uncertain fire," speculated one Confederate officer. In any case, as the unlucky whalers were rescued from the Azores, they let the world know of Semmes. In all fish tales, there's exaggeration, but these stories grew in size and force like a rising gale. Rumors began to circulate that the privateer had blown up the one ship that had attempted to fight back, sending everyone in her to the bottom, and these yarns stirred the more violent emotions of the Union Navy. On the gunboat *Kearsarge,* destined to joust with the *Alabama* in the Confederate cruiser's one true battle, the stories of the Yankees' suffering had a strong effect, and got the boys "highly indignant," as one correspondent noted.

While hunting the whale hunters, Semmes picked up a compliant and very faithful teenage slave named Dave White, who stayed on board till the end of the *Alabama*'s cruise. He earned a wage, and the crew treated him with all the kindness they might've shown to a ship's cat. Dave wasn't the only captive taken aboard in this interval: Among his other prizes, Semmes also liberated a whaler's canary to the Confederate cause, and in his cabin it sang to him from a gilded cage.

On Semmes went, divorcing whaling captains and crews from their vessels and livelihoods. Approaching the cone-shaped columns of smoke that once had been ships, and with a rakish-looking steamer only a league away, Captain Samuel C. Small, master and part owner of the whaler *Weather Gauge,* had the sense to decide something smelt worse than a stinker. The vessel hailed from the village of Provincetown, a town nestled on the barren, wind-blasted tip of Cape Cod; metaphorically speaking, if the cape was a long curved arm rising into the exposed gut of the open Atlantic, Provincetown was the fist, complete with two sets of knuckles. To compensate for the infertility of the sandy, overfarmed land there, the inhabitants had turned to their fine harbor, which still fielded a modest fleet of whaling schooners. These relatively small vessels took short "plum pudding" cruises of a mere six months, hardly enough to even get one's feet wet in a New Bedford man's estimation. (Already Provincetown had seen its small fleet whittled down by the Confederate privateer *Calhoun*—previously the New York tugboat *W. H. Webb*—which had taken the schooners *John Adams* and *Mermaid* and the brig *Parana.* The privateer's captain, armed with letters of marque, had in a two-hour stretch captured the vessels and their cargoes, about 215 barrels of sperm oil in all, along with sixty-three crewmen, about ninety miles south of British Honduras [Belize]. The *Calhoun* towed her prizes to New Orleans and auctioned them off, dumping the crewmen at the dock. These vagabond whalers included eight "negro sailors" whose exact status was problematical as they, presumably, could have been sold off as slaves. The Confederate marshal refused to accept the Africans into custody, and eventually, all of them, white and black, were deported by the government.) Now another member of the fleet faced his doom. Coming on the scene of destruction Semmes had scripted, Small had the sense to turn and run, but it was too late and he was taken.

On the morning of September 13, Captain Rufus Gray of the hermaphrodite brig *Altamaha,* deceived by the *Alabama*'s American flag, didn't run until it was too late. When the boarding party came on deck, he carried his bungling to a level of perfection, emerging from his cabin with a sword. In a bizarre gesture, he offered it to the boarding officer in charge, saying: "Sir, I surrender up all my arms to you." That night under the light of the moon, Semmes took the New Bedford whaler *Benjamin Tucker,* whose captain, William Childs, being quite the Yankee, didn't blink an eye when he learned of his fate. The next morning, the fine-looking Provincetown whaling schooner *Courser* was at the receiving end of Neptune's trident after a morning fog burned off to reveal her position near the *Alabama*. So impressed was Semmes by the gallant master's sea skills, he wished by any means to separate him from the "Universal Yankee Nation" and spare the pretty little craft—but he couldn't. As he said: "There were too many white-cravatted, long-haired fellows, bawling from the New-England pulpits, and too many house-burners and pilferers inundating our Southern land, to permit me to be generous, and so I steeled my heart, as I had done on a former occasion, and executed the laws of war." After using her for target practice, he gave the *Courser* to the fire.

Semmes now carried seventy unwanted prisoners, and the crowding both hindered the ship's routine and was a source of discomfort for the whalers. After sailing back within four miles of Flores, he cast off the crews of his three prizes in eight whaleboats, deluging the island with yet more vagabond sailors, whose number pehaps equaled that of the natives. To improve their lot, the whalers took with them a Mississippi of prizes: fine whaleboats, sperm teeth, harpoons, cordage, baleen, and jackknives—this in a place where one was wealthy if he possessed a canoe and drift net. Semmes was aware what these whalers might do once stranded. "Jack, suddenly released from the labors and confinement of his ship, must have run riot in this verdant little paradise, where the law was too weak to restrain him." He decided the history of his little colony of men would make quite a read, the police reports being of "especial interest."

In their loaded boats, the whalemen couldn't help but turn the tedious row ashore to Ponta Delgado into a race, just as if they were trying to reach a whale's back to plant an iron as quickly as possible. It was quite a regatta in the lee of Flores, observed the literary-leaning Semmes. "The fellows seemed to be so well pleased, that I believe, with a little coaxing, they would have been willing to give three cheers for the *Alabama*.".

With the time left to prosecute his war against the whalers shortening, Semmes headed northwest. On the seventeenth, he took the New Bedford whaler *Virginia*, whose illustrious name gave the Rebels pause as they burned her. The whaling crew showed consternation but no objections to the Confederates—except the ship's large Newfoundland dog, which became enraged when the "pirates" came on board. He rushed to the highest spot on the stern and growled and barked fiercely. "He seemed to know they [the Confederates] were disturbing the peace," claimed a Yankee chronicler. Although it probably never occurred to them, the whaling masters might have been better off throwing their New Bedford newspapers overboard once the *Alabama* loomed into view. The more Semmes read the broadsheet screeds against the South, the more his anger flamed. Being a self-proclaimed follower of the Good Book—or at least its somewhat more violent first half, vengeance was Semmes's, as the *Virginia*'s Captain Shadrach Tilton soon realized.

"Am I to be put in irons?" he asked Semmes.

The reply: "You Northerners are destroying our property, and New Bedford people are having their war meetings, offering a $200 bounty for volunteers and send out their stone fleets to block our harbors, and I am going to retaliate." Semmes admitted his "particular antipathy to New Bedford people."

Watching the vessel go up in flames, Tilton, a part owner, wept; his son shared his grief. After the *Virginia* was burned, the ship's dog, who was allowed to join the crew on the *Alabama,* seemed "sorrowful and full of compassion for their ill fate." When the ship was torched, he even shared the crew's "distracted" feelings.

For the next seventeen days, Semmes kept Tilton and most of his crew manacled and under guard in the lee waist, where they had a miserable time of it. They were on deck in rain and shine and constantly tired from exposure. There were only a few planks to lie on, and just an old sail separated them and the seawater that ran in through the open gun ports whenever the ship rolled or the weather grew rough. At night, sometimes Tilton woke up almost completely submerged. When the Atlantic weather tossed them about the waist, they tried to steady themselves by holding on to the ship's rail, but were hobbled by their manacles, which chafed their wrists, causing an extreme pain that added to the sum total of their torture. The handcuffs cut so deeply into Tilton's wrists they left deep scars. For bathing, there was only saltwater; for dining, the officers ate the same fare as the crew.

At night while on deck, the prisoners were forced observers of the entertainments of the *Alabama,* for wise old Semmes allowed his seamen to gather on the forecastle to sing and dance. During these festivities, one half of the crew, pretending to be the fairer sex, was led on the makeshift ballroom floor by the other half of the crew, which played suitor. During the dancing, when the suitors stepped on the feet of their partners, the latter spouted curses, dispelling any illusion of femininity. As a frequent finale for the nightly entertainment, as many as a hundred voices joined loosely in what must've been an execrable version of "Dixie." The unenthusiastic Englishman, the stolid Dutchman, the mercurial Frenchman, the grave Spaniard, and even the serious Malaysian, as Semmes recounted, all vowed to live and die in Dixie—where they likely had never been and would probably never go.

To endure this daily spectacle was the fate of the whalemen in their manacles. Although he hanged no one and was about as fair as circumstances allowed, the New Bedford-ites considered Semmes a Lafitte or a Kidd, a corsair among the worst pirates who'd ever lived. They resented his habit of lingering by a condemned ship while she burned, believing this to be a technique to lure in and capture any would-be rescuer. The whalers also noted the Rebel officers were "very dainty gentlemen," who only stole the finest personal items. If they took kid gloves, they had to be white; if sugar, it also was white (clearly not brown), and so on. Tilton and others brought back stories about how "Semmes does all in white kid gloves," and that the sad-eyed Bartelli waxed his mustache every morning. One can only imagine the reaction back in New England.

FLORES, SEPTEMBER 17, BARK *JIREH SWIFT*

The same day Semmes took the *Virginia,* at 3:00 P.M., Williams reached the island of Flores. So far, he'd managed to avoid the cruiser. Once on shore, he discovered just how lucky he'd been, having seen Captain Clark of the *Ocean Rover* himself and "learned a Privateer was about the island." As he described it to Eliza, Clark was already saying Semmes had forced him overboard ten miles offshore. It didn't take long for Williams to decide he wanted neither to sulk in port nor return to New Bedford. Not daring to remain at Flores to recruit, he returned to his bark, dropped canvas, and headed toward Cape Verde.

Almost immediately, Williams had his first close call with the Confederacy. At midnight, as he described it, "We saw a ship or a sail of [on] some kind of corse we thought it must be Jeff Davis so we gave her all the room she wanted[.] we made Mrs. Swift do all she could that 24 hours [.] we made 200 miles by the wind [.] I suppose you are sailor enough to explain to your friends [.] at any rate you can call it good going." If it was the *Alabama,* he either evaded or outraced her.

Indeed, so fast was the bark, he even overtook a large clipper ship (a type of vessel whose sailing capabilities were legendary), sailing from Cardiff. To the clipper, he entrusted some mail; the master sent Williams back six bottles of ale, and the praise that *Mrs. Swift* sailed like a dolphin. "I thought he sent me quite a compliment," Williams admitted in a letter to Eliza, dated September 21.

Despite the week's excitement, as he told Eliza, "we live first rate and get along all rite, only you are not here this is all I want to make thing just right[.] I suppose I ought not excite your curiosity on this matter[.]" The chronometer ticking nine, it was time to wind it up. He promised he'd write again—"if Old Jeff don't get us." Pledging his love to her and the children, he said: "I am going to bed and dream of you."

There was no more sight of the *Alabama* from the decks of the *Swift*. In any case, Williams could've just awaited his fate in the Azores without all the trouble.

On the morning of the eighteenth, Semmes caught and burned the New Bedford bark *Elisha Dunbar,* although the whaler probably could've escaped in the rough weather then prevailing. As she burned, torrents of rain poured down and veins of lightning jumping from cloud to cloud gave spectators glimpses of the flaming *Dunbar,* tossed by gusting wind and waves. The fire burned on, catching the sails. Blazing, they flew off the wildly swinging yards, which eventually crashed into the sea. As a finale, the masts snapped, collapsed, and went by the board, leaving the powerless hulk to rock until the Atlantic poured inside her, quenching the flames. Not surprisingly, the Rebels thrilled to the show they had stage managed. She finally sank, "a victim to the passions of man, and the fury of the elements," as Semmes in his characteristically purple language put it.

In early October, Semmes discharged Tilton and the other prisoners on the neutral ship *Emily Farnum,* along with the Newfoundland dog. The *Farnum* dumped them all in Liverpool. As word of the Rebel pirate found its way to New Bedford that October, there was panic among the bankers and insurers on Water Street. The fleet's owners met and issued letters to Washington requesting assistance that, by and large, was unavailable, as Welles planned to keep his blockade intact and was willing to sacrifice the entire Union merchant marine to do it. Better to make the South starve than protect Yankee property. Nevertheless, on October 10, the New Bedford moneymen issued a telegraph to Welles to tell him "the rebel steamer *290* has seized and burned five of our whaleships off the Western Islands about the 5th September. There is a large fleet of whalers requiring the protection of the Government; an armed steamer or steamers should be sent at once." The Federals, usually happy to do the bidding of the blubber barons of the Northeast, were suddenly recalcitrant. Clearly the secretary wasn't going to let a handful of Quaker merchants tell him how to run his war.

With the vagabond whalemen beaching in New Bedford, the city inhabitants weren't exactly surprised. One story reprinted on the front page of the local paper read: "It is piracy without either the profit or romance of piracy. There are neither doubloons nor damsels to be got. This is the petty larceny of the seas and maybe the only excuse is the Stone Fleet in Charleston."

After his successes in the Azores, Semmes didn't allow his ship to remain idle. He ranged far, sailing to Newfoundland and then down to George's Bank, the abundant if perilous fishing grounds off the New England coast. Heading south to Martinique for some much-needed coal, it was about 8:30 A.M. on November 2 when eyes on the *Alabama* caught sight of prey, the New Bedford ship *Levi Starbuck,* about four miles away. The *Starbuck* was captured and burned, but Thomas Mellen, her captain, later boasted that he had refused to strike his colors. His reasoning was that he hadn't surrendered; he'd been captured. He even threatened to shoot any man on the *Starbuck* who tried to strike the ensign, forcing two of the *Alabama*'s raiding party to take the flag. His stubbornness incensed the boarding party officer. "He was the maddest Reb I had ever seen," Mellen recalled. (Born in Holmes Hole, Mellen had a bit of a temper himself. During one voyage he knocked a man down for claiming his sweetheart "looked like an Irish girl.") While a captive on the *Alabama,* he was reduced to berthing in a boat hanging from the ship's cranes.

The capitalists of New Bedford didn't need word of the *Starbuck*'s demise to attempt to block the "extreme peril" their fleet was in. On November 6, the Pacific Mutual Insurance Company met and addressed the president, giving him a reminder of how their fleets had provided thousands of sailors for the Union Navy. Apparently, they wanted a return on that investment of human wealth. They told the Great Emancipator of the "magnitude of our whaling fleet, immense amount of property invested in the whaling business, the thousands of American citizens actively engaged in its prosecution on the ocean, merit and demand some attention from the government."

Unvexed by these fulminations, Semmes headed toward Venezuela, off whose coast lay the island of Blanquilla, a lonely rock whose soil and brackish water produced virtually nothing. Largely ignored by the world, it drew only tough, ornery inhabitants: turtles, goats, and, just then, the enterprising Yankee whaling crew of the schooner *Northern Light.* The master had anchored his vessel off the beach on Blanquilla's west side and pitched a tent, sheltered from the buffetings of the local trade winds. On Friday, November 21, he was trying out oil from a recent kill when he saw a steamer flying the U.S. flag approaching the shore. Pleased to see the reassuring presence of the Union Navy, the master himself rowed out to pilot the vessel into the harbor. After boarding the warship, he said he'd heard about the *Alabama,* and marveled at this ship's batteries and speed, claiming she'd give the freebooting pirate Semmes "fits." Plied with questions about the anchorage, he obliged with answers.

After the anchor dropped, the steamer's captain, who wore a very large gray mustache, invited the master into his cabin and gave him some unexpected news: This ship was the *Alabama.* The unsuspecting blubber hunter realized he was looking into the face of the notorious pirate himself. The Stars and Bars went up the mainmast and the whaler collapsed to his knees. "Spare my life," he begged.

"You are perfectly safe on board the *Alabama,* and that out of respect for Venezuela, I will not even burn your ship," said Semmes.

To prevent the men from gallying the rest of the nearby whaling pod, he extended the hospitality of the *Alabama,* insisting the master and mate stay on board nightly. The Yankee wisely agreed, becoming a familiar sight on the raider over the next five days as she recoaled.

"Say, Cap, did Old Beeswax really tell you he should not burn your schooner?" asked a young officer of the Yankee.

"Why, yes; of course he said so."

"It may all be in good faith, Cap"—he sighed, shaking his head—"but it's very like a joke of the old man."

The gloomy look that appeared on the master's face made the prankster happy.

Despite the captivity, when the mate sighted a whale outside the harbor, the schooner's boats were permitted to immediately launch in pursuit. In a few hours, the whale was dead and the crew towed it to shore for trying out. Before Semmes left, the Yankee master thanked him for not destroying his schooner. "Do not thank for me it. If you had been three miles from shore, I would have burned you as quick as any vessel. Now go and tell the truth. Do not tell a damn lie as the rest of you have done."

The attacks on blubber hunters continued. On March 23, Semmes took the Fairhaven schooner *Kingfisher,* after which *Alabama*'s Executive Officer

Kell forced the all-Portuguese crew to load their own provisions onto the *Alabama.* The transfer complete, the schooner's oil-soaked decks went up in "fits and starts" during an equatorial thunderstorm. The image was weird and powerful, one of a number that the raiders witnessed fit for re-creation with an artist's brush. Even after the schooner's hulk had gone under, the oil continued burning on the water's surface.

On April 15, 1863, the whaling bark *Lafayette* of New Bedford and the Fairhaven-based hermaphrodite brig *Kate Cory* dropped anchor about four miles offshore yet another small desolate island, the dead volcano of Fernando de Noronha. One of twenty-one members of an archipelago two hundred miles off the east coast of Brazil, among the few noteworthy distinctions of the island was a solid peak of granite rising "up heavenward like a giant cloud." Sharks and dolphins teamed in the clear waters around the island, and a nasty surf often pounded its shores; when it did, boats trying to land were prone to capsizing.

Because of a narrow entrance, the inland lake that served as harbor was known as the "Hole in the Wall," and its complicated tides and currents made navigation dangerous. Although desirable enough for Dutch, English, French, and Portuguese governments to successively invade Fernando de Noronha (the last nation even erected a fort), it never had much success in attracting permanent residents to brave its year-round heat. That is, except the convicts serving out sentences in its penal colony, and the soldiers whose fate was bound with them as their overseers. There was one advantage to being imprisoned here, so to speak: As it was impossible to escape to the far-off Brazilian mainland, the convicts were free to leave their huts or caves and wander the onetime volcano at will.

Lacking grog shops or brothels, mariners had little more use for Fernando de Noronha than to use it as a landmark to check their chronometers or, if they were Brazilian, see if there'd been a convict uprising. However, given its position near the migratory paths of the sperm whale, sometimes whalers— who would probably have put ashore in hell had it been necessary to get what they needed to continue to hunt and kill leviathans—landed there to trade for fresh water and other provisions. Like others of their profession, these two whaling masters, William Lewis of the *Lafayette,* and a Captain Stephen Flanders of the *Cory,* were pulling toward the harbor. As scurvy was spreading among his men, Lewis urgently needed to land and trade with the locals for antiscorbutic provisions. Usually, they would have sailed their vessels into the anchorage, except there was a shoal that made navigation inside the harbor tricky, and so they had dropped boats to land.

Two vessels lay about a mile offshore, a rakish-looking steamer with no flag, and a tall, fine cargo ship. As was the custom here, the whaleboats drew up to the cargo ship, called the *Louisa Hatch,* and the masters called out and asked to barter some of their whale oil for provisions and for news of the *Alabama.* A broad-shouldered man, about five foot eight, with brown hair and blue eyes, came up on the deck, went to the gangway, and tossed the whalers a rope. However, the masters were in too much of a hurry to come aboard.

"What are you doing here?" one asked.

"We sprang a pretty bad leak, in a late gale, and have come in to see if we can repair damages," was the reply. The brown-haired man, who claimed to be a Yankee captain but whose native accent was Yorkshire, explained the ship next to his was a Brazilian steamer carrying fresh convicts for the colony. He told the masters he thought the pirate was in Jamaica, and although he urged them repeatedly to come on board, the invitation remained unaccepted. During the tense conversation, a gust blew across the ship's deck. There was a start in both whaleboat crews and the nautical chat ended abruptly.

"Starn all!" bawled out a voice from among the whalers, as if they were in danger of an enraged whale's fluke coming down on their heads. The rowers backed out double-quick and went at their oars as if they "were pulling for their lives" toward shore.

Their would-be host—George Townley "Hell-fire Jack" Fullam, who was not a Yankee but rather the prize master of the *Hatch,* the *Alabama*'s supply vessel—was shocked at the sudden departure of his guests. However, looking around the deck, he soon discovered the cause—a boat's coxswain had draped a small wet ensign carrying the Stars and Bars over the spanker boom of the vessel to dry, and with some help from the wind, it had unfurled. The whalers realized they had indeed stumbled on the re-coaling *Alabama* and her prize ship. Still on board were prisoners of the most recent strike, and it had been an incarcerated whaling captain who'd acted as pilot into the dangerous harbor when the *Alabama* arrived there.

Now looking to continue his lucky streak on Fernando de Noronha,

Semmes got the *Alabama* under steam and started after his prey, anchored conveniently just outside of the protective marine league. There was no occasion for "guile or coquetry," Semmes flew the Stars and Bars. Flanders signaled his vessel to turn and head into the marine league, but without a breeze, it was too late to escape. Thus, the "*Alabama* throws 'three sixes' with fortune's dice and closes with the vessels about five miles from the land," as one *Alabama*-er put it.

Master Lewis of the *Lafayette* had taken the ship's papers on the whaleboat with him; without them, the whaler was a legal nonentity, giving Semmes the pretext to burn her on the spot. She made a fire bright enough to throw a glow over the entire island and light the *Alabama*'s way as she towed the *Cory* back to the harbor, Semmes noted with some satisfaction. He wasn't alone to enjoy the sight. The convict inhabitants were excited as they watched what must've been a refreshing spectacle from the shore. The two unfortunate masters, whose crews had done perhaps the "tallest pulling" in these waters, landed on shore, to learn from the governor they'd indeed crossed paths with the dreaded raider.

The *Lafayette* was still burning and had by the next morning drifted so far out that only a column of smoke was visible. Master Lewis, who wore clothing into which a "considerable" amount of money was sewed, vowed Semmes would never take his now useless papers while he was alive. While hiding among the convicts, he managed to write to the owner of the bark, Ivory Bartlett, back in New Bedford. Clearly this was not a name to provoke much pleasure among the Rebels.

"Capt. Semmes says he wants to get hold of all your ships that he can, and their Captains as hostages, because you fitted out the stone fleet," wrote Lewis. "He will keep the Captains as hostages, that you will not fit any more stone ships." He hoped Bartlett had insured what had become a total loss.

Semmes deposited 130 prisoners on the island, whose sympathetic governor, for the price of some provisions taken from the Rebel prizes, gave permission for a Brazilian schooner to land some whalers at Pernambuco on the mainland to notify the U.S. consul. Forty days later, an English brig, the *Mary Garland,* set out with the whalers for New York. The whaling men, knowing more about navigation than the *Garland*'s Captain James, and in a hurry to reach home, effectively took over the ship.

Over James's wishes, they crowded the brig with canvas. When the "heartsick" James said he thought there was too much sail, the Americans responded by rigging up an extra spar to carry even more of it. Next, the unruly whalers assaulted the *Garland*'s master with a batch of badly cooked plum duff, prepared incompetently from a barrel of flour on board by the ship's cook. The former prisoners hurled the lumps of "soggy dough" into James's ears and mouth. Unable to order the whalers into irons, James's remained a virtual prisoner belowdecks for two days until the duff finally ran out. Interestingly, with her decks crowded with men, no other ship came near the *Garland* for fear she was a privateer. Landing in New York, the whalemen took their mattresses off the ship with them. James attempted to stop this looting, but after a detail was formed to pitch him overboard, he relented. "When the men were well away from the brig, they could still hear Captain James venting his opinion of American whalers," according to Ulysses Mayhew, cabin boy of the *Lafayette*. No matter, the whaling captains had enjoyed some "fun" despite their bad predicament.

The *Alabama* continued on. She had shown Fernando de Noronha her stern just twenty-four hours before when, in the early hours of Friday, April 24, someone cried, "Sail ho!" Another whaler had appeared. Even Semmes was amazed at his continued luck. However, as all good things and bad must at last draw to an end, this was to be Semmes's final battle in his war on the blubber hunters. The victim was the bark *Nye,* sailing home to New Bedford after twenty-one months in the Pacific, the last eleven without a touch on land.

At around 2:00 P.M. the cruiser fired a blank, and the *Nye* halted. The Rebels went on board and gave the captain, Joseph Barker, and his twenty-four men five minutes to get off the vessel. At about daylight, she was ablaze. The *Nye* was carrying 425 barrels and "being greased to saturation, it made a splendid conflagration." Semmes noted that with this, his sixteenth whaler, he had exceeded the famous record of the feisty Yankee commodore, David Porter, who, while commanding the frigate *Essex* in the War of 1812, had accomplished the twin feats of rounding the Horn and making England's Pacific whaling fleet suffer. Semmes's last prize convinced him that indeed Fate had a grudge against "these New England fisherman" and would persist in throwing members of this ubiquitous race of Yankees in his path even when he wasn't on the whaling grounds. If indeed Fate was responsible, she was hardly even half finished. (That same day, one of the tireless Bulloch's other inventions struck in the same stretch of ocean, when the cruiser *Florida* overtook and burned the one-time whaler *Oneida* of New Bedford.)

If it was any consolation to the idling Yankees back in New Bedford and other places who'd lost property, time, or profit, the charmed *Alabama* had considerably less luck in sinking ships that could fight back. On June 19, 1863, she put out of Cherbourg Harbor into the English Channel, where Semmes's former friend and roommate, Captain John A. Winslow, was waiting for him. His command was the U.S.S. *Kearsarge,* named after a triangular knuckle of rock protruding from the New Hampshire landscape. Her crew had been longing to get their clutches on the Rebel ever since her first strikes off the Azores.

Here was a very public venue for the showy Confederate master to perform his act: the English Channel, "theater of so much of the naval glory of our race," in Semmes's own words. Thousands of spectators from the Continent gathered to watch the spectacle. Anyone of importance was at the water's edge—including, reputedly, the painter Edouard Manet—to behold what was essentially a joust between two warring countries on the deep. For about an hour, the two warships pounded away at each other in a nautical ballet, describing great circles on the water and firing as their courses converged. The brief, bloody fight ended with the results unevenly in favor of the better armored and maintained *Kearsarge*. The gore was so thick on the *Alabama*'s decks, it had to be shoveled off and thrown overboard so those crewmen still able to fight wouldn't slip on it.

The *Alabama* must've resembled a whaleship in the midst of butchering a whale. At last, the cruiser, following in the wake of her numerous victims, went to the bottom, agonizingly sinking into a whirlpool. As if in consolation, Edouard Manet in 1864 unveiled a canvas that recreated the sinking of the *Alabama* beautifully, in a voluptuous Impressionist style that made the blood and death seem gently sublime—which gives credence to the story that he hadn't been there, after all.

Among those who drowned were the gentle steward Bartelli and the likable slave, Dave, a fate they both might've easily avoided if they'd bothered to share with their fellow crewmen the fact that they couldn't swim. Although wounded, Semmes, with his typical near-satanic luck, escaped. Hurling his sword into the channel, he went overboard with Kell, swimming in the cold water. An English nobleman sympathetic to the "cause," who happened to be yachting nearby, plucked them up. Squirreled away safe from the *Kearsarge,* Semmes survived both his wound and the loss of his ship with all his fury at his former employer in Washington still intact. A hero in his soon to be extinguished country's eyes, he was later appointed a Confederate admiral, despite the fact there wasn't much of a navy left to lord over. He even started a precedent, never to be repeated, by adding the title "general" to his naval rank. Doomed to not long outlive the cause he'd toiled for, in 1877, Semmes died an unrepentant—or unreconstructed—rebel, leaving behind a lengthy tome to present his side of the story to the eternal court. (Among his many admirers was Hohenzollern prince Kaiser Wilhelm II, who adopted Semmes's blockading techniques during the First World War. In place of cruisers, he used a submarine fleet, however.)

New Englanders were not exactly sad to hear the news of the raider's demise. "The pirate *Alabama* has at last met the fate she deserves," a U.S. consul wrote to Washington on June 21, summing up New England's feelings as succinctly as possible. The New Bedford *Republican Standard,* quoting the *Kearsarge*'s engineer, said the battle was over before the men had hardly got warmed up and that the *Alabama* sank "beautifully."

As for the raider's survivors, none of the wealth they had so callously turned to ash ever found its way back into their pockets. By war's end, there was no Confederate Congress to vote them the promised prize money for the whalers and oil they had destroyed. Only one young officer, in fact, ever saw a shilling for his toil, having sold his claim for 5 percent of its face value to a "speculative London Hebrew." He went down to his grave soon after the *Alabama*'s sinking, presumably after having spent some of the money.

During the peaceful interlude the *Kearsarge* provided from Rebel deprivations, the whalers went out in relative safety. While Semmes may have turned flukes, so to speak, the whalers still faced their typical dangers, which of course, given the profession, were never exactly typical. The threads of the *Alabama*'s story were still destined to entangle the spouter fleet ever so gently again, however. Arthur Sinclair, one of Semmes's officers, made his way to Paris, where he continued his work for what was left of the Confederate Navy. While there engaged, he found himself quartered with a six-foot, limping, mustachioed North Carolinian named James Waddell, an ex-Union Navy man awaiting a vessel under preparation to replace the *Alabama*. Not surprisingly, Waddell was willing to take some advice from a member of the illustrious raider's crew, and the two discussed where the new vessel might do the Union the most damage.

Viewing the sea charts, they realized they faced a problem. The Shark of the Confederacy had taken a considerable bite out of the Atlantic whaling and merchant marine fleets. The sea-lanes there were now cleared of potential prey. But it wasn't all despair. The maps spoke to the duo, describing what the next course of action should be. They indicated there was one great region that remained to be harvested, fertile with Union ships that sailed in deadly waters, and where there would be no interference from the U.S. Navy. There sailed the great Yankee whaling fleet of the North Pacific, among whose august members was one William Thomas Williams.

James Waddell's duties weren't purely theoretical for long. A very capable man—James Dunwoody Bulloch—was seeing to his command. It was indeed a sad day for the whaling fleets of New England when Bulloch decided to cast his lot in with the Confederacy. The inventor of the *Alabama* and other similar devices to injure Yankee whaling and sea commerce had enjoyed a remarkable run of success. His endeavors had taken their toll on the whalers in both lost ships and lost time spent profitably hunting.

A letter to Thomas William Williams from Swift & Allen's office in New Bedford, dated January 21, 1863, notes the relief of the owners after they'd heard from the ship's cooper that the *Jireh Swift* had arrived safely in the Cape Verdes, having escaped the *Alabama*.

Nevertheless, they were disappointed that Williams's cruise had taken him away from areas where other ships that season had sighted whales eighteen times before October 27. The vessel *Hercules,* in which they possessed an interest, had only harvested seventy-five barrels from so plentiful a crop of monsters. Wistfully, Swift & Allen told Williams they were certain that under "any circumstances you would have rather exceeded that quantity with the same opportunity. However, in consideration of the depredations of the *Alabama* you took the best course by working South on the 'Double Quick.' "

With the war on, outfitting costs had "materially advanced," they explained. Prices were going up like mercury on a hot day: The cost of cordage had risen 50 percent, and cotton goods and tobacco had risen 25 percent since Williams had sailed. "And from present appearances you can hardly ask too-high a price for the goods you have for sale—" presumably, the writer was referring to the slop chest. The outfitters also had to pony up the cash for war risk insurance—an additional 3 percent for the *Camilla*—meaning it would "require great energy and perseverance to make a successful voyage. These qualities we think are in an eminent manner possessed by Capt Thomas [of the *Camilla*] and yourself, and should you be blessed with health we have great hopes, (should the present high prices of our staples continue) you both will bring your voyages to a profitable termination—"

Williams and his partners had Bulloch to thank for this. The Georgian was a rare man, indeed. Even a critic would have to admit this former U.S. Naval officer was energetic, thorough, and persistently, even disturbingly honest—at least in regard to his sponsors. Although entrusted with vast amounts of money from the Confederate states thousands of miles away, he managed to live modestly in England, as Semmes observed.

Along with honor, Bulloch had backbone as well, as he demonstrated after war had broken out while he was in New Orleans commanding the New York packet vessel *Bienville*. The Confederate authorities in the Crescent City decided they wanted to add the ship to the roster of the Rebel navy, as yet a-borning, and let the Georgian know it. Although Bulloch's loyalty was clearly with the South, he said: "I have no authority to sell the ship, and therefore cannot fix a price, nor can I make arrangements for transferring her to the Confederate states."

Although, skirting a direct fight, Bulloch also avoided handing the prize over by steaming out of New Orleans—grieved and annoyed at having to run from friends to save the property of his soon to be enemies. Later, he showed courage and ability while captaining a blockade runner called the *Fingal*, which he'd loaded with guns and other supplies. During that voyage, he also proved how lucky he could be. Stuck in a thick fog off Savannah in a dead silence broken only by the swish of the water on the hull and the throb of the engine, Bulloch and the crew looked for signs of land and Union warships. Just then, a cock in a cage on deck began shrieking as loudly as a steam whistle with an unearthly noise audible to any "blockader" within five miles, as he put it.

An officer tried imposing silence by reaching into the coop on deck to kill the offending bird—but managed only to twist the wrong rooster's neck. This set all the other birds off, while the real culprit "crowed and croaked, and fairly chuckled over the fuss of feathers, the cackling and the distracting strife he had aroused." It required a number of dead fowl to make it through that day, but the Georgian entered Savannah in December 1861. He was in time to act as a military observer just as "the much talked about" Stone Fleet appeared. It may have been while observing that futile endeavor of the U.S. Navy and Yankee whaling fleet that Bulloch's mind received the seed that blossomed into an ambitious plan.

Secretary of the Confederate Navy Stephen Mallory was well aware Bulloch could do great things—such as build a navy—and he sent him to England to do just that. After five months back South, he departed again for Great Britain, leaving everything behind, including his young nephew Theodore Roosevelt, and became a political exile. Although Mallory had promised him a command in one of the vessels, he never delivered, as he knew Bulloch was virtually unreplaceable. It was an odd fate for a fighter at heart to be transformed into a slippery bookkeeper, diplomat, and contractor who waged his war through back alley commerce, diplomacy, and law. Still, he prosecuted his fight with as much courage and determination as any Rebel sea captain ever did. Through the war, the persistent agent stayed in the shadow of men such as Semmes who held the coveted postings and took the risks and the headlines. The dogged Bulloch ever remained the stage manager who made it possible for the active officers to act out their epic roles.

To give him his due, although he never faced great personal danger, there were easier tasks than Bulloch's. He was matched in wits against a formidable opponent—the U.S. Ambassador to the Court of St. James, Charles Adams, son and grandson of presidents, a true Yankee, appropriately dubbed the "cold codfish." In the person of the ambassador, New England's various sea-faring enterprises had a tireless defender—and perhaps no other could have been so close to being Bulloch's equal. (Charles wasn't the first Adams to serve the fishermen of New England—his grandfather John Adams had negotiated the Grand Banks fishing rights as part of the legal settlement of the Revolution, and also had fought English tariffs on newly born America's whaling goods.)

Now Charles Adams of New England, the scion of an eminent family, perhaps the most eminent, was fulfilling his duty to protect its fishermen. Under the sharp-eyed Bay Statesman were vigorous consuls in cities such as Liverpool, along with a network of spies, which Bulloch attempted to subvert with his own double agents. Despite the Union arsenal arrayed against him, with England's implicit tolerance of the Confederacy, Bulloch had nevertheless managed to launch no mean number of vessels to hamper Yankee marine enterprise. With almost admirable cynicism, he navigated through the English bureaucracy, honoring the letter of the nation's neutrality laws while outrageously flouting their intention. While the *Alabama*—which put out to sea because an English clerk had gone insane and unable to stop her—was the most prominent example of his handiwork, but she was far from alone. Indeed, the prior July another of his raiders, the *Florida,* had taken the whaler *Golconda* (the property of New Bedford mayor George Howland), a mere forty-eight hours sail from her wharf, 160 miles south of Long Island.

(The *Florida's* story, unlike the *Alabama's*, had initially been an unlucky one. After leaving port in Nassau in the Bahamas where she'd been commissioned, it became apparent there was an unwanted guest on board—yellow fever. The disease spread through the vessel, decimating the crew and nearly killing the captain, James Maffit. In wretched condition, Maffit steered a course to Mobile, Alabama, where, after a pummeling by Union guns, he anchored safely. The second time out, she had a fine run of it, and was finally taken prize by the U.S.S. *Wachusett* in October 1864, and later sunk under mysterious circumstances.)

Despite what he'd already achieved, Bulloch wanted to finish the job he'd started on Yankee whaling. Now it was time to execute the South's and his latest and last plan. A number of factors seemed to converge around the North Pacific whaling fleet, leaving it exposed as if a fog had suddenly lifted. Mallory's office had decided it was time to balance out the destruction between the Pacific and the Atlantic by aiming its remaining cannons at the bowhead whaling fleet. Not that it was going to make much difference to the war effort, given the rise of petroleum, which had bestrode the world like a colossus, leaving spermaceti and other oils to seek a dishonorable grave.

At least such a feat would hurt the pride and purses of some of the South's most prominent and hated opponents. There was hope that New Bedford, Boston, New York, and Washington would howl when their citizens discovered the whaling fleet had been wiped out by a Rebel raider. So with the *Alabama* embedded in the mud of the English Channel and the Confederacy itself slipping away, Bulloch set to work to quickly overcome an unusually formidable challenge: Semmes's own excessive success.

Not only were there fewer shipping lanes to raid, there was no place left where Bulloch could build cruisers, because spies had infested the English shipyards like marine worms in a rotten hulk. A detective working for the U.S. consul had even infiltrated the Laird works. Bulloch couldn't be brazen enough to commission another warship, so he decided this time to buy an existing vessel outright and outfit her as needed before launching. There was just such a prize available to suit this purpose, he recalled—the *Sea King*—a beauty, with spacious tween decks and large air ports, ripe for conversion to war cruiser without too much fuss. Initially, her owners hadn't been interested in selling her, but eventually Bulloch managed to close a deal on September 20, 1864. As a buffer, the wily Georgian used as an agent a British subject to prevent anyone with even the faintest odor of rebellion from getting near the vessel.

The *Sea King* was quite a catch for Bulloch. A three-masted ship weighing 1,100 tons, 222 feet long and 35 wide, with fine lines and a long rakish hull, she was the daughter of a celebrated father, shipbuilder Stevens and Son on the River Clyde in Scotland. Although only a year old, she had already proved herself worthy of her name during a single voyage to New Zealand, where she made 320 miles in twenty-four hours under sail. For power, belowdecks she had 850 horsepower engines with 47-inch diameter cylinders with a 2-feet 9-inch stroke that let her steam along at 10 knots. Like the *Alabama*, to save coal, she could raise her propeller up into a well to keep it from dragging as she ran under the "cloud of canvas" whose outfit included state-of-the-art roller reefing sails and wire rigging.

Not merely one of the fastest vessels afloat, she was solid as well, with an iron frame supporting six inches of hard East India teak planking. Insurer Lloyds, not much given to exaggeration, had even rated her "A1," showing the man who had bought her—none other than the exiled Bulloch—knew something of his craft, and he would soon justify his opinion that she "was well suited for conversion into a vessel of war."

10

The Other *Alabama*

You are to proceed upon a cruise in the far-distant Pacific, into seas and among the islands frequented by the great American whaling fleet, a source of abundant wealth to our enemies and a nursery for their seamen. It is hoped that you may be able to greatly damage and disperse that fleet, even if you do not succeed in utterly destroying it.
—*Official orders to the* Shenandoah

The 5:00 P.M. train from Liverpool deposited at the London station the unlikely harbinger of the worst disaster to cross the bow of the Yankee whaling fleet in its long history—at least thus far. Onto the dock stepped a slender, baby-faced twenty-four-year-old man who proceeded, as instructed, to the Wood's Hotel, Furnival Inn, where he spent the night under the fictional name of Mr. W. C. Brown. As there were spies working for the Union, secrecy was important for the young Confederate naval officer, whose name at birth had been William Whittle Jr. The next morning at breakfast, Whittle sat down at the restaurant reading a morning paper, a napkin peering out through a buttonhole in his coat. If the journal's news was of the far-off Civil War, it would have been gloomy fare for the exiled Virginian, because his cause was clearly a doomed one.

Noticing the napkin, which was a prearranged signal, a stranger walked over to him, and said: "Is this Mr. Brown?"

"Is this Mr.—?" Whittle omitted in his memoir to list the contact's name, but he was indeed his man. For his part, Whittle also confirmed he was, at least for the moment, Mr. Brown. Breakfast completed, the two then went to Whittle's room to prepare for a voyage he was to make on the waiting East Indiaman the *Sea King*.

Whittle and his new companion later went to the waterfront and at "an unsuspicious distance" viewed the ship—not that Whittle had shown himself to be a man of caution, already having proved to be a brave, if not reckless young man. Earlier in the war, he had, against orders to the contrary, successfully taken the Confederate vessel *Nashville* from Beaufort through a Union blockade and delivered her to Georgetown, South Carolina. Later, he had been captured, and spent time as the Union's guest at Fort Warren, Boston, until exchanged. Now, he was willingly about to enter the bloody mess again.

Early on October 8, Whittle crawled over the black side of the vessel at the forerigging and she quietly left her moorings and headed down the filthy Thames estuary to the sea. Detectives working for the U.S. consul watched her with spyglasses, but despite her true purpose, nothing was amiss. She carried no turret mounts or railroad iron or anything particularly suspicious—only two standard eight-pound guns, nothing "to excite even passing attention." Because of the vigilance of Uncle Sam, particularly on the waterfront, Bulloch was not present for the *Sea King*'s departure. Soon at a "safe rendezvous" point, Whittle met the vessel's master, an Englishman and former Union blockade-runner named Corbett, who'd already cleared her for a voyage to Bombay. As there were legal niceties to be observed, with him were also written instructions from the owner to sell her at any time for 45,000 pounds.

Despite Bulloch's absence at the *Sea King*'s departure, his quiet, skillful hand was very much evident. On board, Whittle maintained his fictional role of "Mr. Brown," supercargo, to everyone except the captain. But as he was the future executive officer of the ship, his task was to study her closely and learn the details of such things as her outfitting and the arrangements of space—facts useful for the successful pursuit of the Yankee whalers. The subtle Bulloch had also sent secret instructions to Whittle that orders were to be given to Captain Corbett as if they were requests. Intending to leave no telltale wake behind the *Sea King* once she sailed, Bulloch planned to reprise the routine he'd used for the launching of the *Alabama* and the *Florida*. First, his orders sent her hopping between several ports to deceive anyone about her mission. He had also forbidden Whittle to signal any passing ships if it was avoidable, as Bulloch wanted to keep secret the real destination of the ship, the small island of Madeira, where there was a planned rendezvous with another vessel. In this way, with Whittle aboard and observing the technical legalities, the *Sea King* would soon be able to creep up on the North Pacific whaling fleet like a whaleboat sneaking up on an unsuspecting leviathan.

The elegant bow of the *Sea King* was hardly clear of land when electrical signals were flying over the telegraph wires from London to Liverpool, carrying a special message intended for very special ears. By 8:00 P.M. that dingy night, a messenger was flitting about the Liverpool waterfront, that fertile if somewhat polluted field for Confederate recruiters to harvest men for their cruisers. The messenger went from hotel to boardinghouse to apartment, in each delivering orders to young men with Southern accents, a score in all, who had been awaiting him in their quarters. One at a time, they began to trudge through the chilly night air to the water's edge over wet, slippery streets in a fog so thick anything only a dozen steps away was nearly invisible.

Although clueless about their ultimate destination, if anyone asked, their response was to be "home." Orders were explicit, and while they may have known each other, if they crossed paths in the foggy night, greetings were forbidden, as the "Lynx-eyed" spies of the enemy were all about. Eventually, they made their way to a waiting vessel, the *Laurel,* where each presented a special receipt for admittance that said: "Received from Mr. Elias Smith, thirty-two pounds, for his passage in the cabin of Steamer *Laurel,* from this port to Havana."

By midnight, the Liverpool waterfront had emptied itself of every man assigned to the *Laurel*, and each had been shown to his stateroom and berth. Already on board was their gear, stored in trunks in dry-goods boxes marked with a diamond under a special number designating the owner. Sharing space with the Confederates' gear were other crates, looking innocent enough and marked "Machinery," but they held guns and carriages: 6 large 8-inch 68 pounders and 2 small 32 pounders. Although destined shortly for use against Northern shipping, the *Laurel* flew an English flag, and this was certainly a violation of the country's neutrality laws, in spirit if not by the exact letter. However, by the time anyone who counted found out, all they could do about it was complain.

By 4:00 A.M. on the ninth, the legal if not actual master of the *Laurel* put out to sea under steam with passengers no longer obliged to pretend that they didn't know one another. These men were officers of the Confederate Navy, and had put their faith, as one of them put it, "in Providence, Neptune, and the Southern Confederacy."

Just before noon on October 16, seven days after sailing from Liverpool, the *Laurel* dropped anchor in the harbor of Funchal on the southern side of Madeira. This rocky island just off Morocco's coast was the property of Portugal, and site of a great fort commanding the picturesque harbor. Since Elizabeth's reign, Madeira was a source of a popular fortified wine that bore the island's name. Also here was an asylum for the blind, where sightless girls wove artificial flowers out of feathers to earn their keep. The most spectacular landmark was a 3,000-foot bluff on which rested a church surmounted by a white tower. Despite the port's attractions, the *Laurel*'s crew remained under strict orders to stay on board, and they had to content themselves with a spyglass view. Enclosed in their uncomfortable, cramped lodgings the officers remained in "tedious suspense" until early in the morning of the eighteenth, when, under a bright moon, a mysterious black, ship-rigged steamer slowly approached Funchal and began signaling.

One of the passengers on the *Laurel*'s deck, watching the black form, was the limping Lieutenant James Iredell Waddell, soon to be commanding officer. He would also be known by the whalers as "His Satanic Majesty" and the "pirate chief," among other choice titles. Like the other men on board, the identity of the steamer was of some interest to him.

"That's her," exclaimed someone, meaning the *Sea King*. Her arrival was a relief and an excitement: The time had come to transform the new vessel into a weapon. Later that morning, while under a fiery sun, the men prepared the *Laurel* to leave, when the steamer came into view once more. Fishermen, in bumboats around the anchored steamer trying to beg or trade for goods, immediately exclaimed something the whalemen of New Bedford would have cringed to hear: "*Otro Alabama.*" The "other *Alabama*" followed the *Laurel* around the island shore.

If the black ship was a reprise of the much celebrated *Alabama,* her commander wasn't quite another Semmes. Although forty-one, Waddell had never before held a command, and his sometimes harsh and uneven treatment of his officers soon made enemies of them, along with the Union's whaling fleet. He was generally honest and courteous and, although at times uncertain of himself, was also able to demonstrate the fanatic's ability to ignore any fact that collided with faith. A photo shows the dour and especially humorless face of a man attempting to create a forbidding expression; perhaps he was steeling himself for his voyage. In the portrait, a fierce Waddell appears to be trying to create distance, possibly to hide his diffidence. Under a head of dark hair, parted to one side, is a pinched mahogany-colored face with hollow cheeks framed by thick sideburns. The eyes over the large nose are cold, almost vulturelike, and above the thin, humorless mouth is a sweeping walrus mustache. Although there is something ornery about his look in the photo, he isn't wholly unattractive.

He'd acquired his telltale limp while attending the U.S. Naval Academy. During a duel, a fellow student fired into his hip a pistol ball that was still with him these many years later. After taking his commission, Waddell had married a wealthy wife and passed a relatively obscure career in the navy, rising to become assistant professor at Annapolis. Like Semmes, he might have floated through history unknown, had not war plucked him from obscurity. The November after hostilities began and still in the East India service, he tendered his resignation, for no more profound reason than his home happened to be on the southern side of the Mason-Dixon Line. He was no abstract thinker, had spent little time on shore, and politics appears to have interested him little. Although he took up arms against the "capitalists of the North," his loyalty was perhaps more to the fleet of the Confederate Navy than the country it represented. The separation from Uncle Sam—at Lincoln's command his name was "stricken from the rolls"—was not cordial. After resigning his commission on the U.S.S. *John Adams,* he refused to swear not to take up arms against his onetime government, and so the Navy Department denied him three months' back pay.

The following March, Waddell took a new commission in the Confederate Navy. Active commands were hard to come by, and those who received them were subject to the envy and resentment of their less fortunate peers. Thus it was that Waddell's career was as lackluster while he was wearing a gray uniform as it had been when he wore blue. His one notable act was the destruction of a ram at New Orleans, accomplished just before the once gay Crescent City fell to the Union. Later, entering the longest-running fight of the war, he took command of Charleston Harbor, where he could study firsthand the results of the Stone Fleet's perfidious mission. Looking for more challenging work, he volunteered to capture a Union monitor expected to cross the Charleston bar, although he'd no idea just how one could accomplish such a task. In any case, the project ended when the warship inconveniently failed to appear.

In May 1863, he was ordered to Europe for foreign service. In France, the less than sociable Waddell reliably managed to hold off success, fame, and popularity, leading a nondescript and unremarkable life. It was here, however, that Waddell's luck began to change. Although having little faith in Waddell's abilities and knowing his lack of personal skills, Bulloch decided to bestow the last plum he had to disburse—the orders for war against the Yankee blubber fleet.

Burning to enter the war actively, Waddell accepted with delight the orders Bulloch, with misgivings, issued him. He was in the hunt at last. "You are to proceed upon a cruise in the far-distant Pacific," it read, "into seas and among the islands frequented by the great American whaling fleet, a source of abundant wealth to our enemies and a nursery for their seamen. It is hoped that you may be able to greatly damage and disperse that fleet, even if you do not succeed in utterly destroying it." Bulloch wasn't exaggerating about how the fishery was a nursery for Yankee mariners, but whether he was looking to punish it or disable it isn't clear.

To fulfill his mission of destruction, Waddell's means were left open— "always tempering justice with humane and kind treatment." To fulfill his broad task, he took a set of sea charts made by Matthew Fontaine Maury, an accomplished cartographer dubbed "the pathfinder of the oceans," who, when working for the Federals, had studied and mapped out the grounds of the whales—and hence, the American whaling fleet.

On October 19, anchored in nineteen lonely fathoms of smooth water on the north side of the barren rock of Las Desertas, the work to create a cruiser began. For the next thirteen hours, using tackles strung between the two vessels, the crew moved heavy guns, clothing, and munitions from the *Laurel* and laid them helter-skelter on the *Sea King*'s decks. Despite this mess of goods and gear that needed to be ordered into something capable of war, Waddell was confident he'd a good, fast ship under him. He also felt the promise of success. Not that he knew what he was doing, for as he noted, "Now I was to sail and fight and to decide questions of international law that lawyers had quarreled over with all their books before them." Nor had Waddell ever been in anything but a fully equipped man-of-war.

Under him there were, at least, some proven men from the *Alabama* and other cruisers, including Irvine Bulloch, James Bulloch's brother; also on board was Robert E. Lee's own nephew. Nevertheless, Waddell still faced the thorny problems of filling out the ranks, and so he summoned both vessels' crews to the *Sea King*'s quarterdeck. Armed and dressed in his Paris-made gold-braided gray uniform, Waddell stepped forward and notified the assembled men they were now on a southern ship of war called the *Shenandoah*.

"Men, I am an officer in the Confederate Navy, authorized to take command of this ship."

He offered to read the commission, but his would-be recruits told him not to bother. Knowledge of the *Alabama*'s fate must have dimmed this latest prospect in their eyes, and, besides, the South's war was all but lost. Desperate, Waddell showed he was willing to buy with a handsome wage those not tempted by adventure or a cause, offering fifteen pounds a bounty and four to seven pounds per month. For those who feared for their skins, he said: "I do not intend to fight. . . . I intend to run away rather than fight, unless in a very urgent case."

To his dismay, the invitation attracted a contingent of only twenty-three out of eighty men, most of whom enlisted for a mere six months. Among the feeble group there weren't even enough hands to raise the anchor, so the officers, mainly Southern gentlemen, some of whom had never done a day's manual work before, removed their fine French-made jackets and put their own shoulders into it. Even the embarrassed commander had to lend a hand to fulfill his commission to do the enemy the greatest amount of damage in the shortest time. His only hope now was to assemble a crew as he went along, plucking them from the ships he hoped the raider would soon be destroying, that is, if the vessel didn't happen to cross paths with a Union warship.

To make the transaction legal, or at least give it the appearance thereof, Corbett handed Waddell a bill of sale for the ship. Completing the conversion, the steamer's Union Jack came down, and the Confederate flag went up to catch the rays of the warm sun, transforming the *Sea King* into the C.S.S. *Shenandoah*. Woes mounting, Waddell conferred with the two English captains, who said going to sea under these circumstances was "impracticable." Waddell also sought out young Whittle, who assured him he knew all the officers personally and that they were all "to the manor born." Showing his youth and pluck, he reprimanded his commanding officer for his chat with the Englishmen. "Don't confer, sir, with parties who are not going with us. Call your young officers together and learn from their assurances what they can and will do."

One shot in the *Shenandoah*'s stern would have ignited the magazine and blown her up, but realizing they were undermanned, underequipped, and in danger, Waddell's men still were all for going to sea. If fact, they didn't see why they remained under light canvas even during this fine weather. This was just the beginning of a set of queries and complaints from subordinates Waddell would face about his conduct through the trip.

The men homeward bound boarded the *Laurel,* cheered the new warship, and headed back to England, where Corbett would cancel the *Sea King*'s now outdated register, and be arrested for deceiving his men about their true mission. The situation they left behind on the *Shenandoah* was worse than difficult, it was ridiculous. On the starboard side, in Waddell's cabin—"as cheerless a spot as ever the sun shone on"—powder kegs shared space with a broken armchair. On deck, as there were no blocks to run the gun tackles through, the recoil from a firing cannon would have sent it flying across the deck into the rail on the opposite side. Adding to the confusion, someone had mistakenly placed the fighting bolts in a barrel of beef. Some officers slept on the leaky deck, while seams in the hull let in the ocean in the form of a fine mist.

Things might have gone very badly for Waddell had this trend continued, but on October 30, his luck changed slightly for the better when the *Shenandoah* crossed paths with the bark *Alina* of Searsport, Maine, also on her maiden voyage. Even though his cannons were inoperable, Waddell managed to bluff her captain into surrendering, and before scuttling the prize, he obtained a mattress for his own comfort, as well as the indispensable gun tackles. However, the chief gunner warned that while any two cannon could fire simultaneously, a full broadside might break the fine ship apart.

Despite the challenges, the middle-aged raider was more or less ready for his mission, and another of the great pivotal events in Yankee whaling history could be marked as having begun.

SUNDAY, NOVEMBER 12,
ATLANTIC OCEAN

Loaded with barrel staves and other supplies needed by the whaling fleet, the small schooner *Lizzie M. Stacey* was not the sort of vessel a mariner expected to see in the rough waters of 1 degree 43 minutes north latitude. A new, fast craft, she had put out of Boston for Hawaii with the intention of doubling the Cape of Good Hope, a transit that gave captains of even full-size whalers pause. Yet Captain William Archer, her master, thought nothing of it. In fact, just two days before, he'd passed an English ship bound for Australia, and the hands on board found his presence there so remarkable they rushed forward to get a look at the *Stacey,* and stared at him as if he were a "Sea Serpent or some other almighty curiosity," as Archer later noted.

He repaid their amazement with contempt, and sailed on without so much as a courtesy visit. With a good stiff breeze powering him, he'd "no notion of losing a good run for the sake of showing off a little before a lot of chaps who seem to think nothing less than a seventy-four is safe to cross the ocean in." This sentiment also suited his Irish first mate just fine, who decided the "dirthy blackguards" wouldn't have appreciated the compliment, anyway.

On November 12 at 1:45 P.M., Archer discovered an unknown cruiser was dogging him; he decided to run. The *Shenandoah* got up steam, lowered her propeller, and took up the chase in earnest. Despite this, so fine a sailer was the *Stacey* that the hunter needed three hours to capture her victim. When escape became impossible, Archer raised the federal flag. A boom rang across the water from a blank fired on the *Shenandoah,* and Archer brought her to. When Archer was on the cruiser's deck, one of Waddell's officers noted: "No one but a Yankee skipper would thus venture half way round the world in such a vessel, but the old sea-dog did not appear to think such a trip anything worth mentioning."

When the officer did in fact make mention of it, the old man, who was the worst, most untalkative curmudgeon he had ever seen, laughed. "Shiver my timbers!" he said, mentioning the reaction he had gotten from the English transport ship, "If there ain't the most lubberly set of sailors afloat in these latitudes that I ever fell in with."

The Irish mate chimed in, saying, "What's more my hearty, if we'd had ten guns aboard there you wouldn't have got us without a bit of a shindy, or if the breeze had been a bit stiffer, we'd given her the square sail, and all hell couldn't have caught her."

Waddell asked Archer if he had gold, jewels, or other valuables. "None that I am aware of," he replied. He went back on board to retrieve his clothes, only to discover a boarding party had been through his stateroom and, to borrow a whaling term, flensed it, stripping everything of worth and tearing what wasn't to pieces. "I took a suit of clothes from the vessel and that was all I could get," he recalled later.

After pilfering her stores, at 6:00 P.M., with regret, the Confederates put the *Stacey* to the torch, destroying about $15,000 in maritime wealth and ensuring the barrel staves never reached the whaling fleet. Waddell wanted to outfit her as a "capital" cruiser, but he couldn't even spare the necessary ten men from the *Shenandoah* to man her. Thereafter, the *Shenandoah*'s officers found it impossible get a civil word from Archer, although his Irish mate loosened up and in days "could spin a kuffer with any one on board." Clearly, the lack of manpower was pressing. One of the *Stacey*'s crewmen, a Swede, was hung up by his thumbs on deck, forcing him to stand on his toes until he switched loyalty.

The *Shenandoah* pressed on through the Atlantic whaling grounds, although her real prey lay far to the west. While the luck aboard the New Bedford whaling bark *Edward,* out four months by December 4, had been nothing to brag about, it was shortly much worse. Her captain, named Worth, had spent twenty-five years making a good reputation among the fleet. The crew, mostly Kanakas, were cutting in a good-sized right whale, despite the heavy weather coming off the island of Tristan da Cunha, which lay about fifty miles northwest.

The *Edward*'s crew was too busy getting the big horse pieces of blubber on deck to notice the ship that appeared suddenly, flying the English flag. Worth raised the federal ensign, and soon there was a prize crew aboard his ship. Taken prisoner, after going over the side of the *Shenandoah,* Worth said, "Good afternoon, gentlemen. You have a fine ship here for a cruiser."

"Yes, sir, and that vessel of yours looks as if she was familiar with traveling saltwater," said the officer of the deck.

"Yes, she was laid on the stocks before you and I were thought of," he said, leaning with ease against the bulwarks and continuing to chat as if this were a gam.

The bark had been so well fitted out—among the prizes were several thousand pounds of excellent ship's biscuit and two new boats to replace the *Shenandoah*'s old and worthless ones—it took two days for the *Edward*'s crew to transfer its own flour and bread to the *Shenandoah.* During the transaction, the Confederate officers examined the whale, still tied up alongside. To penetrate even further into the mystery of blubber hunting, they even braved the "horribly offensive" stench below decks. Waddell said the bone room carrying the baleen stank beyond his ability to describe it.

As so many other whalers had before and after, Worth had to endure the firing of his ship. He was so clearly a brave, generous, and openhearted man that one green Confederate master's mate named Cornelius Hunt regretted the act. He wasn't alone in his admiration of Worth. Whittle described him as the "most manly looking Yankee" he'd ever seen; he also considered the *Edward,* when on fire, a "grand sight."

The *Shenandoah* crew's method of ignition was first to remove all live animals, kegs of gunpowder, and anything they found usable. The men then located any "combustibles" in the hold, such as turpentine, and poured it through the vessel to be burned. They opened the hatches and tore down bulkheads and piled them into the cabins and forecastle. The halyards were let go, making the sails hang loose, slowing the ship down, and then someone visited the galley to start a torch and complete the "painful duty." If they were lucky and the ship was very old, she burned like tinder. To finish the job, they usually smashed the whale boats with spades making them useless to anyone else.

The captured men, including the whalers, totaled twenty-nine, equal in number to the *Shenandoah*'s own crew. Deeming it less than desirable to try to stretch his own manpower thin watching prisoners, Waddell steamed to Tristan da Cunha to strand them. This ocean dot was the crown of a volcano that accommodated about forty (Europeans and Americans mostly) full-time residents, but it also took sporadic visits from whalers looking for provisions. The waters around were deep but populated by bottom-growing seaweed whose tendrils might hinder a vessel's progress. They were even capable of grasping and disabling a steamer's propeller. Among the scanty facts in its history was that, in 1810, one Jonathan Lambert of Salem, Massachusetts, had gone ashore there and proclaimed himself king. His "absolute possession" lasted about eighteen months, until on May 7, 1812, he and his only two subjects went fishing in a boat and never returned. While under British "protection," it once had hosted a garrison to prevent Napoleon, then in permanent exile on nearby St. Helena, from using it as a base to launch another of his eponymous eras.

Here on the northwest side of the island, Waddell deposited his prisoners with their clothes and six weeks' worth of rations. However, a New York carpenter, much needed on the cruiser, switched allegiance to the South and remained on board. The natives were a bit curious; one said he didn't think the United States would put up with this sort of activity. However, the governor, like all unprejudiced minds, sympathized with the South, Waddell observed. Rumor maintained that the local women were in dire need of mates, and to assist them, a Connecticut Yankee, the oldest resident of the island, and a dealer of poultry and beef, tied the knots of marriage as well as served as "surpliced priest before the chancel rails." The Confederates thought it would probably be a good place for a stranded whaler, even if no one had a clue just when the mast of a rescue ship might poke into the horizon.

The *Shenandoah*'s officers pitied their victim. As the ship's doctor wrote: "We all felt sorry for Captain Worth. There was a frankness and freedom from all meanness which made us respect him." The officers gave the unfortunate master a quadrant, medicine, fishing hooks, and a book on navigation. After three weeks, the less than outstanding vessel U.S.S.

Iroquois found and rescued the stranded whalers, only to transport them to a life of dire poverty in Cape Town in South Africa. While there, Captains Worth and Archer of the *Stacey* passed some time by re-creating from memory for the U.S. consul a description of the *Shenandoah* that proved surprisingly accurate.

Leaving Tristan da Cunha in her wake, the *Shenandoah* pointed her bow to the Cape of Good Hope for a swing round the tip of Africa into the Indian Ocean. As this leg of the voyage began, Waddell noted there was a grating noise coming from below his cabin. During a routine check the day after departure, the engineer discovered two cracks in the brass band in the assembly that connected the engine to the propeller, making the screw useless. Rather than put into port for repair, Waddell decided to sail on under canvas. Things were not going according to plan.

MARCH 21, 1865, SOUTH PACIFIC

At about 6:00 P.M. near the equator, with the sun about to drop below the horizon, the Honolulu trading schooner *Pelin*'s five-month cruise was interrupted by an English cruiser that fired a blank from a 12-pounder. The schooner hove to, and a party armed with cutlasses boarded her, behaving arrogantly until its officer had closely examined the master's papers. The *Pelin*'s Hawaiian provenance established, the boarders now became polite. The Sandwich Islands then were their own independent if feeble republic, currently in transition between being owned by one or another of the European nations, and therefore the *Pelin* was off limits as a prize to either Yankee or Confederate vessels. The boarders learned the schooner's task was to search for precious tortoiseshells and cocoanut oil for winter trading among the nearby Cannibal Islands; summers, she roved north, swapping whiskey for furs and ivory.

After enquiring about the whale fleet, the party returned to their waiting ship, which bore the name *Shenandoah*. In the addendum to the boarding officer's report presented to Captain Waddell was something of great interest. The unsuspecting master of the *Pelin* had revealed there were five whalers at Ascension Island in the Eastern Carolines chain. Here was a chance to break an unlucky streak, as the rebels hadn't viewed a sail since February, which they took as evidence the fleet had scattered before them.

After leaving Tristan da Cunha, fearing capture by the Union Navy at Cape Town in South Africa, Waddell had decided to sail on to Australia for repairs. The *Shenandoah* doubled the Cape of Good Hope, where the crew passed a miserable Christmas pummeled by damaging storms that opened up seams on deck and doused the crewmen below with cold seawater. Under these less than joyous circumstances, Waddell marked his New Year's celebration by pondering the South's agonies.

He didn't know it, but the *Shenandoah*'s sister cruiser *Florida* had just received her ticket to the bottom on November 28, 1864, punched by the Union cruiser U.S.S. *Wachusett*. (Appropriately, she was named after a mountainous piece of New England's granite vertebrae that rose starkly out from the low rolling green hills in the center of the Bay State.) Nevertheless, the last of the Confederate cruisers survived her trip, and on January 25, Waddell dropped anchor in Hobson Bay, near Melbourne, carrying a penguin as a gift, the damaged propeller band, and "big ugly guns." The authorities there nervously granted Waddell permission to make his repairs, while the vigorous U.S. consul promptly denounced him as a pirate.

While anchored off the Fatal Shore, Waddell and his crew found themselves surrounded by sympathizers in the sons and grandsons of convict Englishmen and Irishmen who had been transported here in years past and were now in the process of subduing—if not outright exterminating—the dark-skinned aboriginal population. So it was therefore unsurprising many of them found the Southern cause appealing. It was also in Australia that the *Shenandoah*'s men saw their only fight. A Union sympathizer crashed a dinner in their honor in Melbourne and denounced the Confederates. The hotheaded Irish assistant surgeon McNulty punched the malcontent between the eyes, knocking him down. Subsequent mayhem broke out as glasses and decanters flew, knives left their sheaves, and pistols went off. Despite the fracas, no one was hurt.

The U.S. consul made Waddell's already troubled command even more difficult. He accused him of recruiting men on the street and forced the commander to answer charges about allegedly hiding Australians on board, including an infamous "Charley the Cook." Employing Waddell's own tactic of buying loyalty outright, he even bribed a black crewman with $100 to defect to the Union. Nevertheless, despite persistent lobbying, he was unable to get the *Shenandoah* seized by the Australian authorities. In the end, his efforts were overcome by red tape and the intemperately long bureaucrats' dinner hours that prevented anything like real action.

His wasn't the only assault launched against the warship. Sharing an anchorage with her was the coal transport bark *Mustang,* and her pro-Union captain, named Sears, defiantly flew the American flag at his mast. Not content with symbolic resistance, Sears and five of his men hatched a plan that perhaps required a greater proportion of courage than intelligence to execute. They first devised a makeshift torpedo composed of a 250-pound barrel of gunpowder rigged with a cocked revolver, a line attached to its trigger. Under the cover of night, the conspirators rowed over to the *Shenandoah* as she lay at anchor and successfully planted the jury-rigged contraption under her stern, hoping it might break her back and give the "skulking freebooter a slight surprise." However, the swing of the *Mustang* at anchor snapped the cable attached to the weapon, preventing the "blow out" from coming off as desired, and the men abandoned their, no doubt, worthy enterprise. As planned, the *Mustang* sailed back to San Francisco, but in a way unplanned. Sears died of a bowel inflammation before reaching port, his exploit duly recorded by the Californian press.

Repairs completed, at the urging of the Crown's representatives the *Shenandoah* left Australia on February 17, carrying fresh provisions and forty-five stowaways, the latter quite as illegal as they were unwanted. The fugitives emerged from hiding claiming to be Confederates, and while the excuse was feeble, the *Shenandoah* at last had enough crewmen to properly man a ship of her size. Also, as shown by the example of the *Alabama,* the Federals had little aptitude for stumbling over Rebel cruisers in the vastness of the sea, thus Waddell was free to ply his task largely without fear. Looking to catch their prey toiling away in the blubber fields of the Pacific, the Confederates headed north with plans to first touch at New Zealand. Because of rough weather, Waddell bypassed the intended landfall in an act of caution his officers blamed on weakness. From there, the ship headed to the New Hebrides [Vanuatu] and Fiji, but to the crew's discouragement, no bluff-bow, square-stern vessels had accommodated them.

During her wanderings, the ship had visited Strong Island and ran close enough to see Chabrol Harbor, where whalemen often dropped anchor. Still nothing. Waddell ordered the propeller lifted and sailed toward Ascension, where the raider chanced at last to cross paths with the *Pelin*. Some members of the fleet would soon have good cause to curse the captain of the *Pelin* and his big mouth.

APRIL 1, PONAPE,
SOUTH PACIFIC

The sun had already burned off the morning mist hours before when George Baker, master of the whaleship *Edward Carey* of San Francisco, looked into the horizon. He was in a whaleboat pulling away from the sheltered Lea Harbor, and with three other masters whose vessels, like his, swung placidly at anchor about as safely as if they'd been in the embrace of the twin arms of Boston Harbor. Baker's veteran eyes caught a steamer under sail, about fifteen miles away, moving slowly out on the weather side of the island. There was a fine offshore trade wind to carry her to shore.

The *Carey*'s mates included the *Hector* of New Bedford, the *Pearl* of New London, and the *Harvest,* originally a New Bedford vessel but whose ownership had been hastily transferred, it appears, to shield her from Confederate attack. The captains were capable men. Born in Dartmouth in 1837, Baker been out to sea since age eleven. After joining the blubber trade in 1848, he'd managed to work his way backward from the forecastle to the master's cabin. However, since leaving San Francisco the prior June to hunt sperm, his crew had yet to see so much as a spout, and so he'd dropped anchor here three days before to recruit some men, presumably from the beachcomber colony that dwelt here in half-savage, half-civilized twilight.

Also in the boat was Amos Chase, who for seventeen years had been the master of the *Harvest*. Of her he said, she was the "fastest whaleship in light winds I ever saw." She was also tough: After leaving the Arctic whaling grounds the prior year, she'd struck a cake of ice that spun her around. Expecting her bow stove in, the crew immediately sounded pumps. Chase recalled, they found no leaks and "never after did we find the ship suffered any injury from that collision in the ice."

Baker and his fellow masters were on an eight-mile trip to Hadley Harbor to visit a friend, Massachusetts missionary Edward T. Doane. This apostle, who along with Reverend Sturges had cofounded the Ponape mission in 1855, was apparently not content to lay up only spiritual treasures in heaven. Reputedly, he also dealt in turtleshells for the needs of this present life. In any case, he'd apparently planted one lasting seed of faith with the copper-hued natives—that he was untrustworthy.

Now there was this steamer offshore. They didn't know who she was, but there was no reason to fear molestation from any Confederates this morning. The masters, intent on their "jollification" that day, decided she was a merchantman, and apparently gave her no more thought as they rowed on, leaving their ships bottled up in a harbor that one could argue was as much of a prison as it was a fortress against the wind and waves. It would be an April Fool's Day to remember. However, as is often the case, the fools were the last ones to realize their folly.

The wind dying, the crew on board the *Shenandoah* furled sails and raised steam for the approach into Ponape. At about 11:30 A.M., steaming parallel to the mouth of the harbor, she came into view of the anchorage. In need of a pilot to enter safely inside, the whalers dispatched a heavily tattooed, semiwild Yorkshire-born beachcomber in a canoe. He was taken aboard, and in what was hardly English he asked the ship's nationality; not knowing where the pilot's sympathies lay, someone on board said an American man-of-war. This beachcomber, whose name was Thomas Harrocke, agreed to lead the vessel in for thirty dollars in tobacco and other goods, and along with an armed Waddell, he went ahead in his canoe. The captain let the beachcomber know it would cost him his life to lead the vessel into any harm, a prospect that frightened the "poor pilot out of his wits," noted midshipman Francis Chew. During the hour it took to get the steamer inside the harbor's mouth, neither the terrified pilot nor menacing commander volunteered much information, but as Waddell eventually discovered, Harrocke was one of the odder specimens of the Pacific.

He'd originally been convicted of some crime in England—there were many to choose from: for instance, one could be put to death for impersonating an Egyptian—and then had been transported to Australia. Against all odds, thirteen years before, he'd managed to escape and survived long enough to become shipwrecked on Ponape. The natives, after initially menacing him, opened their arms to Harrocke, if not in complete adoption, then at least in toleration. As he claimed, he took a native wife who'd born him a brood of two children, one of which had survived. To the men of the *Shenandoah,* his physique gave hint of a diet that was less than healthy, and he appeared to be "descending by slow but sure stages to the grave." Barely able to speak his mother tongue, he'd covered his once robust but decaying body with tattoos. He'd gone native, and it was unlikely anything could have persuaded him to try his hand at civilized life again. (It may be that he was also the same drunken pilot who had six years before tried to steer the *Florida* out of the harbor before master Williams took over the helm.)

Before leading the *Shenandoah* to her anchorage spot, a useful Harrocke started to tell Waddell about the whaleships and the harbor. At last, the *Shenandoah* dropped two anchors just inside the channel in fifteen fathoms, effectively sealing the whaleships in. Because of a large water-lapped and potentially hazardous reef in the middle of the harbor, the crew secured the cruiser with hawsers run out to thick trees on shore. Seeing the *Shenandoah* about a mile away, three whalers raised the American flag, while the *Harvest* hoisted the ensign of Hawaii. The raider's deck became busy with crewmen arming themselves with revolvers and other small weapons as they prepared to board the awaiting prey.

The show began when a signal cannon boomed over the harbor, catching everyone's attention, including that of the natives watching from shore and already in terror of the sight of the steamer. The *Shenandoah* was a type of vessel they were unfamiliar with, seemingly using magic as her motivating power; after the explosion, the Ponapeans scurried away to hide in the bushes that edged the harbor. Ready for their task, the Confederate sailors climbed over the cruiser's side in four boats—two of them whaleboats kindly provided by the now defunct *Edward,* and her true colors—to the degree she had any—went up the spanker gaff, the latest designed white Confederate flag with the Battle Flag canton of thirteen stars. The whalers, who could never have seen this ensign before, nevertheless picked up its meaning and struck their flags, far too late.

On the deck of the cruiser, Harrocke watched in confusion as the

boats with the boarding parties faded into the distance. One of the officers pointed out the strange flag flying in the *Shenandoah*'s rigging and
asked if he had ever seen it before. "No," was the reply, and he asked one
of the officers what was happening.

"Those four ships are prizes to the Confederate government," said an
officer.

"And what the hell is the Confederate government?" Harrocke had
gleaned some information from the newspapers that had fallen into his
grasp that told about the far-off Civil War. He'd even relayed something
about the conflict to the local native king, but clearly his knowledge of the
war wasn't very intimate.

"The best and biggest half of what was the United States of America,"
said someone. "The Yankees didn't sail the government ship to suit us, so
we cut adrift and started on our own hook."

"The devil ! What are you going to do with your prizes?"

"Set them on fire bye and bye, after we have taken what we want out of
them."

"Well, you and the Yankees must settle that business to suit yourselves.
If I had known what you were up to, maybe I should not have piloted you
in, for I don't like to see a bonfire made of a good ship." He added, "Well,
well, I never thought I would live to see Jeff Davis's flag." He also admitted: "It is pretty, and looks like the English white flag."

Within an hour, the seven-man boat crews drew up to their targets, captured the ships' mates, the relevant papers, and, most important, the whaling maps. "With such charts in my possession I not only held a key to the
navigation of all the Pacific Islands, the Okhotsk and Bering seas, and the
Arctic Ocean, but the most probable localities for finding the great Arctic
whaling fleet of New England without a tiresome search," Waddell said.

At sunset around 4:00 P.M., the whaling captains were pulling back in a
single boat toward their ships, oblivious to the transfer in ownership happening on their decks. Finally, they saw to their surprise the steamer that
had appeared that morning, now close to the *Harvest*. No flag fluttered,
and her identity was a mystery. Paddling closer, their astonishment got the
better of them, and they rested on their oars to watch. "What is she?"
asked one master, referring to the cruiser.

"Russian, I guess," said Baker, and a boat that had been detailed just for them drew near. In the craft was a "fine and determined looking set of fellows" wearing their Paris-made yellow gray uniforms. Each bore a shoulder strap of blue silk, decorated with a single star surrounded by thin gold cording. A gold band circled each gray cap.

"Boat ahoy! Halloo, go alongside of that ship," ordered the Confederate officer, named Grimball.

"We don't belong there," a whaler replied.

"I don't care. Go alongside." They were armed.

"Chase, you're a goner," said Baker with Yankee subtlety to the master of the *Harvest*. "That's the Confederate steamer *Shenandoah*."

The masters claimed they made a brief run for it, but the boarding party gave chase and soon caught and arrested them. Although a short man, Captain Chase showed plenty of fight, claiming he'd resist. Fortunately, his companions successfully convinced him that course was unwise, and after capture, the whalers bore the situation with "as good grace as could be expected."

Over the gangway came the whaling masters, who, on learning it was the *Shenandoah*, were astounded. "What a perfectly April-fooled party," noted Whittle, delighted that all the monotony was repaid with a fine catch of whale ships, the cargo of one alone was worth $40,000. "The Yanks were certainly caught napping this time." He only wished it had been fifty and not four prizes he was bagging. The whalers repaid him by giving him some "very very bad news": Confederate General Hood was beaten at Nashville, and Savannah was in Yankee General Sherman's none too delicate hands. Charleston was sure to fall as well.

Chew observed the masters sitting on the cruiser's poop, and trying to speak of their misfortunes with "saddened expressions." While on board the *Shenandoah*, Waddell said to Baker: "Your ship is confiscated to the Confederate government." Ordered into irons, before execution of sentence, he was allowed to observe Waddell enacting the same ritual with his whaling colleagues. One after the other, Waddell examined each ship's papers, condemning them all, including the *Harvest*, which he concluded was Hawaiian in name only. Although there was a bill of sale which an officer had accepted as legal, there were American flags on board, as well as a U.S. register; she also carried the same mates and master as she had when a New Bedford ship. Waddell declared her a prize of war.

Portrait of the Captain Thomas
William Williams. (*Courtesy of the New
Bedford Whaling Museum*)

Matching portrait of Eliza Azelia
Williams, wearing a pendant.
(*Courtesy of the New Bedford
Whaling Museum*)

Wharf scene of New Bedford, showing ship hove down for repairs and casks. (*George
Brown Goode, from* The Fisheries and Fishery Industries of the United States, Volume 5: Plates;
Washington: Government Printing Office, 1887)

LEFT: Port view of a whaler at sea, the vessel recognizable by the whaleboats hanging from the ship's davits. *(Courtesy of* The Century Magazine *and courtesy of Cornell University Library, Making of America Digital Collection)*

BELOW: Top view and side view of the New Bedford whaler *Alice Knowles*. *(George Brown Goode, from* The Fisheries and Fishery Industries of the United States, Volume 5: Plates; *Washington: Government Printing Office, 1887)*

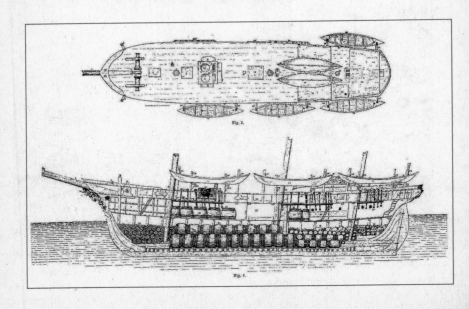

Fig. 1.

Fig. 2.

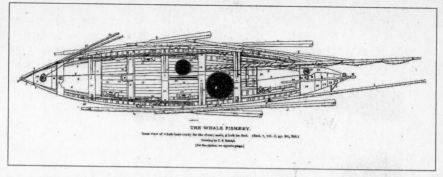

Whaleboat ready for the hunt, top view. *(George Brown Goode, from* The Fisheries and Fishery Industries of the United States, Volume 5: Plates; *Washington: Government Printing Office, 1887)*

The mate/boat header lances a sperm whale in the life—the network of arteries near the lungs. The sperm whale's chimney is a afire— that is, it's spouting blood, indicating it's near death. *(Courtesy of* The Century Magazine *and courtesy of Cornell University Library, Making of America Digital Collection)*

Three whaleboat crews pull to their quarry, whose dark back is visible in the distance. *(Courtesy of* The Century Magazine *and courtesy of Cornell University Library, Making of America Digital Collection)*

Two whalers trying out—in the foreground, the ship is lifting the blanket piece off the stinker; the dark smoke rising up indicates the trying works are already in use. *(Courtesy of* The Century Magazine *and courtesy of Cornell University Library, Making of America Digital Collection)*

Rodney French's Stone Fleet at sea. *(Courtesy of* New England Magazine *and courtesy of Cornell University Library, Making of America Digital Collection)*

Portrait of the Stone Fleet captains just prior to their departure. Rodney French is in the center holding the spyglass; seated just to his right, Captain Worth looks at the map; Captain Willis stands second from right. *(Courtesy of the New Bedford Whaling Museum)*

The Shenandoah's Lieutenant Commander James Iredell Waddell, who chased and burned the *Jireh Swift* along with thirty-three other ships. *(Courtesy of the U.S. Naval Historical Center)*

Raphael Semmes, the onetime lighthouse keeper turned Confederate raider. Although he failed to capture the *Jireh Swift*, his war on the whaling fleet was exceeded only by that of his colleague James Waddell, who did burn the bark. *(Courtesy of the U.S. Naval Historical Center)*

The sleek, rakish *Shenandoah*, among the ice, on the prowl for whalers. *(Courtesy of the U.S. Naval Historical Center)*

The *Shenandoah* burning the ships off Cape Thaddeus on June 23, 1865. From left to right: the *Susan Abigail*, foreground; the *Euphrates*, in the distance; the *Shenandoah*, foreground, is third from left; the *Jireh Swift*, burning, in the distance; the *William Thompson*, in the distance; the *Sophia Thornton*, dismasted, in the foreground; the *Milo*, crowded with men, is in the foreground. Between the *Thornton* and the *Milo* is a whaleboat containing *Ebenezer Nye*. *(Courtesy of the U.S. Naval Historical Center)*

Captains of five whalers burned by the *Shenandoah* in San Francisco. From left to right, Captain Smith of the *William Thompson*, Captain Tucker of the *Sophia Thornton*, Captain Hawes of the *Milo*, Captain Hathaway of the *Euphrates*, and Thomas Williams of the *Jireh Swift*. The caption reads "the last act of expiring insolence." *(Courtesy of the New Bedford Whaling Museum)*

ABOVE: The Arctic whaling fleet caught in the ice off Point Belcher during the winter freeze of 1871 *(Courtesy of New England Magazine and courtesy of Cornell University Library, Making of America Digital Collection)*

LEFT: Abandoning the barks: *George, Gay Head,* and *Concordia* off Point Belcher September 14. *(Courtesy of New England Magazine and courtesy of Cornell University Library, Making of America Digital Collection)*

LEFT: The whaleboats fleeing to Icy Cape to rendezvous with the southern fleet. *(Courtesy of* New England Magazine *and courtesy of Cornell University Library, Making of America Digital Collection)*

BELOW: Lewis Williams's bark *Florence* making good her escape from the Arctic freeze-in of 1876. (Harper's Weekly, *from a sketch by Captain Kelley)*

New Bedford Wharves, probably from the turn of the century. In the foreground, second ship, is a whaler, apparently decrepit, with snapped masts. *(Courtesy of* New England Magazine *and courtesy of Cornell University Library, Making of America Digital Collection)*

When hearing his pronouncements, the responses of the masters varied, as Waddell recounted. One captain claimed he'd been birthed by a Virginia mother, although was passing himself off as a New Englander. The master, whom Waddell didn't identify, even yielded (presumably in private) some good tips on where to find other whalers. It was for Chase, "boiling with indignation and full of grit," to offer the closest thing to a fight after Waddell ordered his ship burned. "Well, that's pretty quick done," he said.

"None of your impertinence to an officer of the Confederate navy," said the normally courteous Waddell.

"I'm not impertinent, but it's pretty quick done." That reply won him double irons and an order he be gagged, although the officer assigned to muzzling him held off from that humiliation. For some reason, Waddell took it into his head that Chase had been involved in "the infamous blocking of the Charleston channel with stone," and so punishing him thus must have given him some pleasure. No matter how intensely Chase's passions had blazed, Waddell later noted that "a pair of irons cooled him down," and the diminutive whaler went to the topgallant forecastle—a mere hole—to keep company with seventeen other captains and mates.

After condemning the vessels, Waddell now had to cope with a problem of his own making: He'd 130 men on his hands as prisoners, mostly "Honolutians," whom he described as "a timid, mongrel race, easily imposed upon and cheated, but suiting the purpose of such men as command whalers." They weren't the only sailors of color on those whalers. In fact, one black blubber hunter had an odd reunion when he recognized a black crewman from the *Shenandoah* whom he'd met before sailing from New York. Despite his low opinion of the dark-skinned Sandwich Islanders, they inspired enough fear for Waddell to keep them in irons for nearly two weeks.

Because he was violating the marine league, at least to the degree such a law existed in a place like Ponape, the next day Waddell decided he needed to affix the mask of diplomatic legitimacy on the affair. So before proceeding with the destruction of the little fleet, he decided to approach the natives, although it seems this charade was purely for the benefit of white scruples, as the islanders had little idea of maritime law or the means to lodge a complaint. As Harrocke explained, "No principle of honor controlled them in their intercourse, but fear of injury made them respect whatever they solemnly entered upon." The pilot also explained that the cocoanut was the medium of exchange here, rather than metal, but they liked nice clothes, tobacco, liquor, and gunpowder and shot. While they had no knowledge of the Creator as he was defined in the American South, at least they did admire Jeff Davis as a king, or at least as a successful, if distant, warlord, which perhaps in Waddell's mind was just about as good, if not better.

There was some apprehension, when, at 10:00 A.M. on the third, he sent Master's Mate Cornelius Hunt as his representative, along with Harrocke, to invite the king of the local tribe on board for what might pass as negotiation. When young Hunt arrived at the king's camp, he found a crude bamboo shelter with high peaks and eaves that nearly reached the ground, as well as three hundred "of the most hideous human beings it was ever my fortune to behold." He claimed they were a frightening bunch, not only ugly, but armed with rocks they could throw with riflelike accuracy, and clubs bristling with shark's teeth dipped in an infallible poison. He was certain they viewed him as a potential barbecue or roast.

The Confederate met the king of this so-called weather tribe, Ish-y-paw, a "miserable little savage" whose five feet of copper-colored flesh was smeared in rancid cocoanut oil. A tobacco pipe peered through a hole in his ear lobe, a common local decoration. Avoiding as best as he could getting downwind of the king, Hunt delivered the captain's salutations, then partook of the court's hospitality, sipping from a cocoanut cup an elixir called *gorwa*, "the vilest smelling, most nauseous compound upon which a man ever attempted to get salubrious." The liquor had the unique property of making its consumer drunk enough to trip over his own legs, while leaving the head clear.

Before departing, the king, "to effectually guard himself against any machinations that might be meditated against his peace and dignity," was anointed with a fresh coat of cocoanut oil. Then Ish-y-Paw, Hunt, the pilot, a "hereditary prince," and three chiefs put out from shore toward the cruiser in the captain's gig, followed cautiously by a swarm of seventy war canoes festooned with faded bunting and cotton. Waddell was, like his officers, attired in full uniform and wearing his sword as he limped to the gangway to meet the glistening chief. Once on board, the pilot, without fanfare, jerked his head back and said: "That's the king, sir."

As Waddell later guessed, Ish-y-Paw was more an object of adoration than of respect to his people. Although the retinue was at first nervous, the officers assured and relaxed them and Waddell even managed to coax the king, in his "state of nature," down to his cabin for some hospitality. He also apparently wanted to give his men something to chuckle at. After arriving in the now rather luxurious captain's quarters, through Harrocke, the king told Waddell: "I wish to spit, but don't like to spit on the carpet."

A spittoon was provided, along with some tobacco and a couple of bumpers of schnapps to help the severely dignified Ish-y-Paw forget his aloofness and to express friendly sentiments. Getting to business, Waddell told him the vessels in the harbor belonged to his enemy, who'd been hostile to his people "for forty years and will be always so until the end of time."

"Then," said the king, "you don't like one another."

"No, it is incompatible with virtue that the South should ever be reconciled to the North again," he said, cataloguing the spilled blood, lost lives, and the outrage of the South's women. Through gulps of liquor, of which he was the foremost consumer, Ish-y-Paw grunted in acknowledgment. Apparently the story translated well, because the king offered Waddell anything he wanted. The Confederate explained that he wanted to destroy the whaling vessels, provided it didn't violate the "laws of neutrality." That abstraction, not surprisingly, drew a confused look from Ish-y-Paw.

Plowing ahead, the commander sweetened the deal in language more concrete and easy to understand: He would let the king take what he wanted from the ships—after the Confederates had plundered them— before putting them to the torch. This was a once-in-a-lifetime proposition to take all the whalers' rich prizes without having to give something in exchange. When Waddell finished, the king consulted briefly with the chiefs—the hereditary prince being excluded—then announced: "We find nothing conflicting with our laws in what you say. There are shoals in the harbor on which the vessels can be run and there destroyed."

Fearing a stray shot would injure one of his people, Ish-y-Paw stipulated the Confederates not open fire on the vessels. Waddell agreed, but asked the king to provide warriors to guard the onshore stays holding the cruiser in place inside the reef. As a few whaling men had made it to shore and hid when the *Shenandoah* had run her flag up, he feared a "wicked person" might slash these ropes and send the vessel on the rocks. When the king said he lacked weapons, Waddell gave him seventy-seven prized muskets and ammunition, liberated from the trading reserves of one of the whalers, and as a further sweetener, two boxes of tobacco. Although he also had some infantry coats and pants, Waddell wanted to keep those for his marine guard, as yet nonexistent. Even Waddell had to admit he'd no idea if the natives knew anything about how to use the weapons or what risk they now posed.

Business concluded, Ish-y-Paw told Waddell he wanted to tour the warship with his retinue, a request the commander granted. Pursuing diplomacy, Waddell even offered him a sword taken from the *Stacey*. Having never seen such a weapon, the king looked at it suspiciously, and when he questioned the propriety of having it so near the royal person, Waddell couldn't resist laughing. Ish-y-Paw didn't take offense. Indeed, by this time, he was on such friendly terms that the captain had become his "dear brother." Apparently successful as a diplomat, his new sibling from North Carolina felt free to make suggestions and jokes without incurring his highness's wrath.

Although the king tried to unbuckle the weapon, Waddell insisted he keep it around his naked waist during the tour. It entangled in his legs as he descended the ladder into the engine room, requiring the assistance of the prince to free him. Thereafter Ish-y-Paw entrusted his son with it. On inspecting the engines, whose purpose must have been a mystery, the king clucked with interest, and the royal party echoed him. The inspection finished, the natives left the ship, having contributed a residue on the deck that remained until the crew holystoned it off the next morning. Keeping his bargain, Waddell commanded the officers on the prize vessels to run them on the shoals at places the king had condescended to say he wished them sunk.

The Confederates begin liberating the Yankee goods first. "It would be almost impossible to give an idea of the various articles onboard in the way of plunder," wrote Chew in his diary. A rather luckless twenty-four-year-old virtually without nautical experience—and held in a kind of contempt by Waddell—he was nevertheless a serving officer on that desperately undermanned cruiser. Whittle noted that "Chew the Unfortunate," in fine weather, was capable of making clouds materialize and pour torrents. It had been the Unfortunate one's assignment to take the *Pearl* and to that ship he returned, finding at least a half dozen boats already there, loaded to the water's edge with the whaler's goods. He boasted in his diary of the "plunder" he took: a collection of shells, a "curious" Fiji spear, a whale's tooth, and some beads.

Picked clean of everything the *Shenandoah*'s crew wanted, the whaleships were soon swarming with natives who covered their decks, presumably, like vigorous ants on a carcass. Back and forth went canoes from shore to ship, as the natives ferried bread and harpoons, whaling lines and tobacco, a mermaid figurehead and medicines "for illnesses contracted in a sailor's youth." During the pillage, they handled their canoes "more beautifully and skillfully than I had ever seen man handle boats," Waddell noted. Not all that was performed was done so skillfully. When stripping the *Harvest,* the Ponapeans were unable to rig a block and tackle to hoist out the barrels of flour and meat, so they broke them open in the hold, making a mess as they disgorged their contents. One plucky islander climbed up to the royal yard to get the sail down, but "in his passion for cutting, cut away the royal lift, which of course cockbilled the yard and left him swinging about between wind and water much to his astonishment and discomfiture."

On went the plunder, with the vandals tearing off planks, spars, and sails, ripping bulkheads from the decks, and even divorcing the copper sheaths from the hulls they protected, for use in crafting spears and breastplates. About noon on the third, flames enveloped the bark *Pearl;* the next day, the *Carey* and the *Hector* joined her in destruction. In what was an amazing spectacle for the Confederates, the *Hector,* named after a doomed hero from the *Iliad,* slipped her cable, drifted into a reef, and burned to the water's edge before sinking. Hunt noted the ships sent up a lurid glow like an exploding volcano on the normally smooth waters of the bay, while on shore, scattered groups of natives, examples of "grotesque humanity," watched in amazement or made wild gestures. Apparently they were puzzled over the destruction of such wealth, which was completed on the tenth, when the last vessel, the onetime Honolulu property, the *Harvest,* joined her mates and became ash.

Before leaving, Waddell paid a visit to the royal residence, a location coinciding with any spot where there was good fishing. While at the exalted retreat, Ish-y-Paw told Waddell he expected him to kill the whaling men, a charge the Confederate denied. The king, worried he'd be sharing the island with these vagabonds whose ships his tribe had plundered, said through Harrocke: "But war cannot be considered civilized, and those who make war on an unoffending people are a bad people and do not deserve to live." Although confronted by such irrefutable logic, Waddell took the civilized course of action, according to Waddell's own account.

The cultures clashed again when Waddell rudely declined the gift of a royal princess, hiding behind the excuse that he was already married, although it's not clear the native had anything like an American marriage compact in mind when he made the offer. In any case, the would-be bride—to put her title politely—according to the normally gallant Waddell, was the first woman he'd seen who was "downright ugly." The captain was lucky the king accepted his apology, as the Ponapean women became old-looking while still in their teens and, despite their gracefulness, were "decidedly homely." (Local rumor then circulating stated Ish-y-Paw had just recently poisoned his own wife in order to remarry.)

The odd duo parted amiably, the Confederate taking a pair of slain chickens earmarked for Jeff Davis's table, a man the king considered no less than a brother and a great warrior. Ish-y-Paw didn't realize that such an honor was misplaced or at least mistimed, as Davis was soon after deposed of both government, position, and country, and eventually even his freedom. The commander had less than a favorable view of Ish-y-Paw, a "selfish old beggar until the schnapps and pipe warmed him, and he did not consider it undignified or selfish to ask for whatever he fancied and show displeasure if refused." Yet, the not overly philosophical Waddell said: "He is, however, not unlike his brother sovereigns of this world in that particular."

He still had the prisoners to dispose of. Captain Baker, who'd maintained a cheerful front for a week of imprisonment, received an invitation by the master-at-arms to the wardroom. Waddell was there, waiting, and after the whaler's manacles were removed, he said: "Baker, this is no place for you—aboard here and in irons."

"That's true enough, captain, but I have been unable to avoid the situation."

"Take a drink and join the ship."

To sweeten the proposed treachery, Waddell offered him a place in the wardroom and the not despicable sum of $125 a month. He clearly knew Yankee. Baker later claimed he was within an ace of becoming an admiral of the Confederacy when he replied: "I'll sleep on that proposition a few weeks."

After enduring a curse, Baker returned to the forecastle in irons. Although the *Shenandoah* shipped a handful of whalers as crewmen, most of the former chose to stay on Ponape and trust in fortune rather than try their luck as raiders. After seventeen days of imprisonment, it was time for parole. Baker, along with the other masters, was forced to kiss the Bible and swear never to take arms against the South if he wanted to be freed. Of course, even if they had wanted to make war, that feat would have been a tad difficult, as the political arrangement called the Confederate States of America had all but ceased. Chase swore more oaths than demanded, and had to kiss the Bible a second time.

On the thirteenth, the crew of the *Shenandoah* undid the fasts binding the vessel to Ponape, and Harrocke guided her out of the harbor, leaving behind more than a hundred vagabond men. The sum total of their wealth amounted to a few provisions, two whaleboats and the missionary—not to mention the goodwill of the less than loving natives. Waddell, whose malice was considerable, had the satisfaction of knowing his enemies were now trapped and under the tender care of a king secure in his weapons, whose people they'd mistreated, cheated, and "given loathsome diseases."

Waddell headed north, and as Ponape faded behind the middle-aged commander's stern, he was confident he'd achieved something noteworthy. "That harbor will always be one of interest to the Yankee whaler, and tradition will point out the exact shoals on which the prizes were burned, the management of the affair, and where the *Shenandoah* lay calmly at anchor amid that scene of vengeance and destruction."

As for the castaways, the next five months involved "supporting and protecting ourselves with great difficulty from the savage inhabitants," as Baker later claimed in court. Nevertheless, while stranded, he "happened to make a hit with the king" when there was an uprising among the Kanakas (as he termed the natives) that threatened to engulf the stranded colony. During the uprising, the Ponape rebels stole whatever they wanted from the whalers without any intervention from the king.

Overcoming his democratic tendencies, as he explained, Baker tied a sword around his waist with rope yarn and fought against the "common people" on behalf of one of the local royals—possibly Ish-y-Paw—whom he called "King Bambazoo, or whatever his name was." With eight men, he defeated twenty-eight of the small rebel warriors who were attempting to rob the castaway whalers, making him a "mighty general," something of a Grant, he later said. His army killed two natives, wounded three, and sank one of the marauding band's two war canoes. The whalemen's fighting prowess was so great, the king feared for the throne, but, as Baker claimed, he and his soldiers weren't "imperialists," so the worry was vain. Eventually the king, too fat to walk and needing passage on the back of one of his subjects, paid a visit to Baker. In addition to offering him fifteen wives, he tried to adopt the whaling master as his son. However, "I rejected adoption and crown alike," he explained.

On September 5, after enduring nearly a half year of yam eating and the rough ministrations of the natives, the Hawaiian bark *Kamehameha V* rescued the stranded men. The arrival was perhaps not exactly joyous: The whaling industry was suffering badly, and Baker was unable to get another steady job for three years.

The *Shenandoah* ploughed on to pursue whalers and prize money, and by May 20, the snowy peaks of the Kurile Islands came into view. The Kuriles were a chain of volcanoes that ran from northern Japan to the Kamchatka Peninsula, marking the boundary of the Sea of Okhotsk, and in a sense, the wretched tip of the biggest and perhaps worst-managed empire in the world. Passing through the Amphitrite Strait, the gateway to the historic whale hunting grounds, the cruiser also slipped into one of the region's cold fogs. This matched Waddell's own personal confusion. The great martial events back home had closed, the second nation he'd served was gone, and his mission was worse than pointless. Nevertheless, he was oblivious to his situation and acted accordingly, in what was to be the last semiofficial gesture of an already dead Confederacy.

11

Come on My Deck and Fight Me

An erratic ship, without country or destination.
—*Gideon Welles, Secretary of the Navy,*
on the Shenandoah

MAY 29, 1865,
SEA OF OKHOTSK

Luck was just not on the side of Ebenezer Nye this season, unless it was of the bad variety, yet it was going to get far worse. The whaling master had put out of New Bedford on a three years' voyage in the half-century-old *Abigail,* known as a regular old tub, and he wasn't seeing much action by way of any leviathans. It was the sort of situation, in that God-intoxicated time, that might be credited to the state of a man's soul, and indeed, it appears the betterment of his fellow men may not have exactly been the whaling master's most pressing concern in life.

Not that it was that he killed whales, which no one then faulted anyone for, unless they killed too few. Rather it was the side business he carried out that some might have looked at askance. Like many a whaling master, in the best and worst of the Yankee maritime tradition, Nye was also a trader, and not just in overpriced second-hand dresses. Inside the *Abigail*'s hold was something very dangerous—and very desirable—to the tribes of Siberia: alcohol. One could buy an entire village with it. It was recorded one Aleut offered to swap five bottles of whiskey for his $800 bank account.

The region had little pity for vice, and drinking was a major one along the edges of the Arctic. In the hands of the local Eskimos and other peoples, alcohol, especially the sort of poison that then passed for whiskey or rum, could be downright lethal, and not just in the near term. "New Bedford never made any money out of that stuff [rum]," explained the whaler, James Henry Sherman. Whalers handed the rum out to the children of the north, whose ignorance in this matter was anything but blissful. "It was a miserable low grade of liquor, unfit for pigs," said Sherman. "Ships carried it up there to the Arctic and traded it to the natives for valuable walrus ivory and whale-bone. . . . it blasted the life out of 'em."

The stories of mishaps caused by firewater among the natives on either side of the strait were legion. One whaler witnessed a drunken Eskimo kick his wife to death, to cite one example. "To the Eskimo it is misery and oftentimes quick death," wrote naturalist John Muir, noting no ban on it could be too harsh. He'd personally known of several hundred natives who'd starved because drinking rum had proven more interesting than acquiring enough food for the winter. After eating their dogs, they lay down and died in their huts, their bodies remaining untouched.

This happened over and over again, said Sherman. The trade in liquor "was the blackest mark on the whalin' industry," he noted, believing it was also bad business, as it brought God's judgment down on the fleet. "New Bedford paid dearly losin' so many ships and cargoes." To their credit, many whalers frowned on distributing the stuff. When stranded in the Arctic, they were at the mercy of the natives, and it was "prudent to keep them as simple in their habits as possible," they reasoned. Dealing in it was denounced by missionaries, too, not that this stopped whaler Nye, who carried cordials, bottled ale, and liquor from his brother William's distillery on Middle Street back in New Bedford. Indeed, down belowdecks in the *Abigail* was a cargo that any dipsomaniac looking to warm his innards in that icy clime might envy: 462 gallons of gin, 736 gallons of whiskey, eight barrels of rum, one barrel of pure alcohol, and even a barrel of Indian Antidote, "a fine beverage that I had been some years manufacturing." To round it off, the vessel held cases of port and other wines whose aggregate volume exceeded the amount of whale oil she carried, not exactly any great feat.

On May 29, Nye watched as a black ship from the west skirted an ice field that stood between the two vessels and then rounded its northern point. As she showed the flag of Russia, Nye took her to be one of the czar's two annual supply ships headed to the miserable settlement at Okhotsk City, laden with official cargo.

His assumption soon proved a bad one when a cannon boomed and someone from the steamer called out to "heave to on the starboard tack, damn quick." To Nye's shock, the Russian flag changed to something very different: the great white flag of the Confederacy. Soon after, eyeing the gray-clad officers who came on board to make him a prisoner, Nye said with Yankee stoicism: "Well, I s'pose I'm taken! But who on earth would have thought of seeing one of your Southern privateers up here in the Okhotsk Sea. I have heard of some of the pranks you fellows have been playing, but I supposed I was out of your reach."

Master's Mate Cornelius Hunt gave a response he must have been rehearsing: "Why, the fact of the business is, Captain, we have entered into a treaty offensive and defensive with the whales, and are up here by special agreement to disperse their mortal enemies."

This made the Yankee laugh. "All right! My friend. I never grumble at anything I can't help, but the whales needn't owe me much of a grudge, for the Lord knows I haven't disturbed them this voyage, though I've done my part at blubber-hunting in years gone by."

The second mate, Thomas Manning, (who soon proved to have fewer scruples than his master, if that was possible) claimed falsely that Nye had already lost a vessel to the *Alabama* and said: "You are more fortunate in picking up Confederate cruisers than whales. I will never again go with you, for if there is a cruiser out, you will find her. You have caught a whaler this time."

Keeping a poker face, Nye invited the officer below and offered him a warm drink as he fetched his papers. At last, he nonchalantly announced his readiness to go on board for a perfunctory visit to the *Shenandoah*. When he was before Waddell, Nye was hardly able to digest what was happening and appeared "frightfully astonished" at his predicament. He showed the presence of mind to try fast talking and even bribery to escape and have his notions spared. For response, Waddell sent him back to his vessel to order his men off onto the cruiser, where they would be received with single irons in the forecastle. Despite their treatment, this crew was perhaps the pluckiest the *Shenandoah* ever deprived of liberty and ship, with one man saying as he came over the side that he "had not expected to take steam home, and to tell the truth would just as lief trust to sail."

Through the night, the two vessels stayed close as the Confederates lightened the load of the *Abigail*. Here fate, the great comedian, launched perhaps the greatest challenge to the cruise's success yet. It began when some of the forecastle "gentry" who were helping themselves to Nye's silk dresses and workboxes, stumbled across boxes containing corn whiskey marked "In Case of Sickness"—that is, of course, only if sobriety is an illness. Before the officers knew about it, most of the watch was as "gloriously drunk as men well can be." No other prize taken, Hunt noted, created so much excitement for so little gain, as three successive waves of crewmen, along with petty officers and marines, went to the ship and partook of the elixir, until there weren't a dozen sober men. Some officers had to be locked in the wardroom, a situation that must have amused Nye and his men. An English carpenter called "Old Chips" burst out of his room twice, and for his pains was awarded a pair of bracelets, then tied to his bunk, dunked with water, and eventually gagged for insolence.

Wisely, the few sober officers took out twenty-five barrels of corn extract, then fired the rest of the liquor, and thereafter the vessel itself, which was worth $18,000. Nevertheless, John Barleycorn proved an elusive opponent, for, over orders, some of the grumbling crewmen hid private stocks of the liquor, from which they got drunk over the next four days. Facing these cracks in discipline, Waddell suspended one officer, forced a clerk into steerage, and derated the boatswain's mate. Threatened with imprisonment for fourteen months—perhaps not that frightening a prospect to a veteran blubber man—and forced to work round the clock, the crew nevertheless held nightly dances or singsongs before going into their prison in the forecastle, which served as their jail.

Nye had similar grit, always displaying good humor, shrewdness, and tact, showing some new eccentricity every day, going about repeating: "In New England we can make a substitute for ile, but we must 'ave bone." He was fond of telling "fish" stories. One portrayed him as a castaway in a whaleboat with six other men near the Galapagos Islands, and covering 1,700 miles in thirteen days with only six biscuits and half a beaker of water. While the Rebels listened to him politely, they didn't bother to believe him. With glee, he explained: "I guess, after all, the loss of the old ship won't swamp me. There is another ready for me at San Francisco as soon I get off your hands, and another cruise would set me all right." Hunt decided that didn't matter, either, as Nye was a part owner of the *Abigail,* which was insured, and he was guaranteed free passage home, in any case. To Waddell, Nye boasted: "You have not ruined me yet; I have ten thousand dollars at home, and before I left I lent it to the government to help fight such fellows as you."

Indeed, Hunt was amused by the Yankee's general lack of scruples, and dubbed him a "thorough bred speculator." He noted Nye's habit of selling cheap whiskey and secondhand clothing to the savages of the north or his own crew was done "at such an advance on the first cost as would have frightened a Chatham Street Jew into serious apprehensions for the future well being of his soul." If Nye's demeanor failed to capture the respect or trust of his captors, at least it won their goodwill.

Although the whaleship hunting was poor here, in any case the crew could enjoy the lovely illusions. The atmosphere was like a mirror that revealed the mountains of Kamchatka seventy miles away; the snow-clad summits reflected directly above the real promontories. The illusory mountains touched peak to peak, "with perfect delineation," with the actual ones. Similarly, real ship and ghost ship touched masthead to masthead, "Just as if you put your finger to a mirror you would see the finger and reflection, point to point," as Whittle said. If it was a place of desolate beauty, with the perennial fog and ice conspiring against them, it was also a place of terror, particularly for mariners unused to the harsher climes. The frequent and swift summer gales tested the "forbearance of every object" within their paths," said Waddell, who survived several of them in his brief sojourn.

And, of course, there was the ice. Continuing the pursuit, Waddell made his way up to Ghinkisk Bay, but found it too full of ice to pass inside. When the ice pushed him from the shores of Siberia, he made for Shantarski Island, but again was forced south after reaching 150 degrees east longitude. Regarding the gloomy horizon of the coast of Siberia, Hunt contemplated how the political exiles there toiled in misery collecting furs for the greater profit of the corrupt government in St. Petersburg that had banished them.

The conditions that were accepted by whalers as part of their everyday lives weren't much to the Confederates' liking: By the first of June, the thermometer was still fifteen degrees below freezing, and as Waddell prowled the shallow waters of the Okhotsk, he cautiously left the cruiser running under light sail to let the crew stay belowdecks and avoid exposure. Nevertheless, having gone from tropical to subarctic weather in just twenty days, the men developed colds. The surgeon insisted they stay warm and dry and doled out extra grog and hot coffee. A stove liberated from the *Abigail* kept Waddell's own cabin warm.

Unaware that Jefferson Davis was now a prisoner in a Union jail, on June 3, the usually aloof Waddell, champagne in hand, took the unusual step of mingling with his officers to celebrate the Confederate president's birthday. After that brief respite, on June 4, he was caught in a nine-hour gale, twenty miles to windward of an ice floe. Had she been too leeward, the cruiser would have been smashed. During the storm, and needing protection, Waddell ran the cruiser along the ice sheets until an open passage appeared through which the *Shenandoah* steered to the safe water beyond. Now the ice was to windward and a good friend and protector, and the waves broke over it in swells as tall as twenty feet that looked like banks of fog.

Yet the *Shenandoah* and its men weren't safe. The bitterly cold wind froze the falling rain over the ship, forming stalactites everywhere. To the crew's dismay, the running rigging, braces, blocks, yards, and sails became encrusted in ice two inches thick, creating an exterior skeleton that left the vessel inoperable. She was then imprisoned by floes that stood a quarter mile wide on each side, and her braces were useless. Yet when the storm ceased, some of the men coming on deck couldn't restrain letting loose yells of delight as the sunlight burst on the "fairy ship" and made her sparkle and glitter as if coated in diamonds. Not blinded to their task, they went to work with mallets to pound themselves free, and lovely chunks of ice crashed to the decks, making them slippery and dangerous. Much of the ice was sealed in casks for drinking.

The ice of the floes was as high as five feet over the port sides, and to starboard it rose threateningly to the sails. With a viselike grip it forced the *Shenandoah* on in a dangerous waltz. With no way out, and unsure how the teak sides would stand up, for diversion, the crew watched as the ice floes smashed together like rams butting heads, creating blocks of crystal rubble as "immovable and imperishable" as shore bluffs. These imprisoned the cruiser, rounding the scene out, a group of walruses played nearby. Because few, if any, on board realized before how fickle the ice could be, the men's spirits dropped. "But a woman's temper is not more capricious than the movements of the ice in these Northern Seas," as Hunt put it. The next day the wind broke up the floes, and the crew ran out warps and grapnels and worked to open water.

The cruiser headed west to Jonas Island, some two hundred miles distant, hoping to find a whalers' "caravanserie" (a meeting place for caravans) where a squadron of the ships might be taken without too much effort. Neptune apparently had other ideas, for in eight hours, the ice again caught the *Shenandoah* and thundered against her sides and terrified the crew. In some places the hard ice even bit through the siding. Fear openly appeared on the mariners' faces. "Lips unused to prayer, now sent up a supplication," said assistant surgeon McNulty.

Luck turned after the sun rose into the "low mocking noon" and its warmth softened and bent the rigid sails. After the ice loosened, the vessel moved ahead, the crew lowered the propeller, and the vessel went stern-out from her prison. "We had now enough of floe ice; our errand was not that of a Franklin or a Kane, but to follow wherever the hardy whaler went," as McNulty, with Celtic flourish, described the retreat.

The notion of a trip to Jonas Island was now out of favor, and the *Shenandoah* sailed back toward Amphitrite Strait. Some of the men must have breathed a little easier. As Hunt well described Okhotsk, it "may be a most desirable locality for whalemen and other amphibious animals who enjoy a temperature below zero and have an affinity for ice fields and fogs; but for my part, I would not spend six months thereabouts for all the leviathans that ever poured their oily treasures into the coffers of New Bedford." They learned later that, had they proceeded to the Island, they could indeed have had a "splendid haul." No matter, they could do fine enough without the risk, Hunt concluded, preciently.

The officers wanted very much to sign on the onboard captive blubber hunters, with Waddell talking about arming a whaleship to hunt her mates. Frustrating them was Captain Nye, who had been using every argument in his power to keep the non-Yankee "dagoes" (presumably Hawaiians) in his crew from joining the *Shenandoah*. The master warned that the cruiser would be caught by a federal warship and any traitors hanged. However,

Whittle wanted these men to pull ropes and feared that the weak-nerved already serving in *Shenandoah*'s crew might become discouraged by Nye's pronouncements. The youthful officer sent for the captive captain and explained to him that if he continued in his particular line of conversation, he'd be put in double irons.

Lacking a traitor as of yet, Hunt kept plying the *Abigail*'s first mate, a burly and bearded septuagenarian, as "true as steel to his own government," with nautical questions as the voyage continued. Hunt's queries were not exactly abstract: He was fishing for information to feed Waddell and perhaps improve his own station on the *Shenandoah*'s list. No matter, with pleasure—and perhaps with an eye to self-preservation—the "staunch old sailor" pointed to the places on the charts that were the most dangerous and what to expect. Although Hunt relayed these facts to the captain, they still needed a competent pilot with experience in these waters.

As if in answer to the commander's prayers, Nye's second mate, thirty-three-year old Thomas Manning, decided his Baltimore birth qualified him as a southerner obliged to step forward for service to his country. One wonders how such a patriot had managed to stay out of the conflict until now—his homeport had been under occupation by the Federals since the war's outbreak. Then again, he had a wife in New York and had spent years in the New Bedford whaling fleet. Manning's politics were suspect—there was a rumor that while in San Francisco he had voted for Lincoln in exchange for a drink of whiskey. Just why he converted is unclear, but certainly switching allegiance was better than being a prisoner. So, on the tenth, he approached Waddell and said: "I am acquainted with the seas in the neighborhood, and will pilot the vessel *Shenandoah* to a place where we would find fourteen and fifteen United States whaling vessels together."

Waddell had a lofty opinion of the character of those fighting with him, believing it was the "principles of honor and patriotism which animated every southern gentleman." Now here was a veritable Judas offering his services—"a Baltimorean by birth, anything by profession, and a reprobate by nature," whose transfer of loyalty was a peculiar matter for so high-minded an officer. Nevertheless, he overcame his distaste for Manning and even elevated him to the rank of corporal in a Confederate Navy that was all but defunct. In return, he "not only steered the pilot towards our whaling fleet, but gave the rebel commander the first information as to where it lay," according to one account.

Manning decided to be a devout traitor and even helped get several whalers to sign on along with him, although it's unlikely they knew their task was to hunt down boyhood friends on other whalers. However, the fourth mate, John Dowden, a native of New Bedford, not only shipped before the mast but said, "I am now a Southern man, and would cut my own brother's throat if he was opposed to me." This decision was final, for reputedly he never courted the society of the whalemen thereafter.

Between dollops of liquor and Manning's persuasion, the Confederacy also managed to snag a Prussian, a Portuguese, and an Englishman, along with a handful of Kanakas, although the ship's surgeon rather happily disqualified two of the Hawaiians as unfit for duty. "I do hate to see our ship's company filled up with men such as these," the surgeon said. "Won't we look beautiful while going into port with such men as these."

Whittle admitted he'd never seen the sort of names that twelve Hawaiians gave out when they signed on: Jim California, John Boy, and Long Joe. Mr. Joe had acquired his moniker from his height; someone told him to reverse it, possibly to give him the anonymity of an alias, so he signed as Joe Long. "They are a poor looking set but they can haul on the ropes," observed Whittle.

Not surprisingly, some among the Confederates decided they liked the cheerful and loyal holdouts of the *Abigail* more than Manning. When in sight of the Kamchatka Peninsula some of the whaler's crew asked to be stranded ashore, hoping to be found by a Russian whaler and continue their craft legally—at last—under the czar's flag. Given that it was fifteen degrees Fahrenheit out, Waddell refused with an eye to his reputation: He feared being accused of inhumanity. On the fourteenth, after twenty-one days in the deadly Okhotsk with only one prize taken, the cruiser passed on a reverse course through the Amphitrite Strait and reentered the North Pacific. Waddell had risked much, and gotten very little for his troubles. A few hours after the passage, a "cracking southwester" storm kept at the cruiser's heels.

Almost exactly seventeen years after the invisible barrier of the Bering Strait had first been crossed by Sag Harbor's Thomas Roys, on June 13, the morally guideless Manning proved a competent navigator as he laid a course toward the whaling grounds Roys had discovered. With the Kamchatkan coast fading to the stern, a good breeze rose up, pushing them into a particularly nasty region of the North Pacific. Here, the Kuro Siwo, the warm North Pacific current, mated with the icy blasts of the Bering Sea, birthing thick fogs, a condition lasting through June.

The cruiser reached two island chains: the Aleutians, which define the edge of the Bering Sea, and the twin Komandorskies, which lie offshore of Siberia. Manning steered the cruiser through the gap between Attu, the westernmost island of the Aleutian chain, and the easternmost of the two Komandorskies. The Bering Sea and Strait, as well as the Komandorskie—"Commander"—chain, were all named after Vitus Bering, the Danish explorer who had discovered the region while in the employ of the czar of Russia. (Not surprisingly, the Dane paid for the privilege of this fame with his life. After discovering the strait—a fifty-three-mile-wide tunnel that required only the slightest error to sink and kill a ship's crew—he'd been caught in a forty-day gale on a barren, rocky Aleutian outcrop and died of cold and scurvy.)

The waters near shore were irregular in direction and force, as well as powerful. At Fox Island in the center of the Aleutians, whaling master Roys once saw waves reaching one hundred feet, rising up to the top of a cliff. So Waddell aimed for the middle of the channel between the twin chains. It only took a few hours for a thick black fog to envelop the cruiser, making celestial observations impossible and forcing Waddell to rely on dead reckoning. First he kept running her north for twenty-four hours, a potentially dangerous mode of navigation. When the fog broke slightly, someone cried "Land ho!" as four miles away lurked the hull-wrecking shores of Copper Island. The wind dying and with just enough power to fill her sails, Waddell ordered the ship tacked, and turned the bow away as the fog renewed its assault and left the cruiser in even greater obscurity.

On June 16, they entered the Bering Sea, the northern extremity of the Pacific, where the cruising, as Waddell noted, was not of a "very delightful character." The weather changes were more abrupt and the fogs were even more frequent, even if not as dense as those in the Sea of Okhotsk. At one point, fog covered the *Shenandoah* so thickly it was impossible to see the ship's length looking in either direction, and through the obscurity the crew heard the thunder of ice floes colliding. This was not a desirable place to be.

As Hunt put it, "It is a region of terrors, which start up grim and formidable on every side. And absolutely without an attractive feature save the wealth borne on the backs of the great right whales, or worn in the shape of choice furs by the seals that inhabit its waters, and the foxes and sables that abound upon its icy shores: and for wealth, man will dare any peril, face any danger." Not to mention for military glory, for Hunt knew the waters here and at other nearby places such as Indian Point and the Bering Strait yielded whales, and so they also offered unsuspecting whalers.

The sterile promontory of Cape Thaddeus, whose best use was to correct an errant chronometer, came into view. At the 180 meridian, it was the exact counterpart to the distant point on the map called Greenwich, half a world away. The raiders had heard many blubber hunters were sailing there, but the only ship they saw—and chased for two hours—turned out to be a rock. Working as the whalers did from eastward to the westward, they lost a day crossing the International Date Line, which they regained next morning. After a five-day fog, the landmark of Cape Navarin became visible, as well as a telltale and promising sign, heading northeast in the water's current: discarded whale meat and blubber. Waddell knew they were approaching prey and brought up steam. The prize of fifty-eight whalers beckoned to the obscure middle-aged commander who was about to write a page in history.

On the morning of the twenty-second, in waters about eighteen miles south of Cape Thaddeus, dense choking smoke rose up from the trypots of the *William Thompson* of New Bedford. Reputed the biggest ship in the fleet, already she carried 250 barrels of oil and 3,000 pounds of bone, to which she was added the fruits of this day's work. Nearby was another whaler, the *Euphrates,* with whom she shared the same home port. Fears of Southern raiders were a thing of the past, for it was commonly known Lincoln had woken, as he himself put it, from his four-year nightmare, and the war was concluded.

However, the peaceable pursuit of the war on whales was due for a rude interruption. The *Shenandoah,* flying a Russian flag, steamed into cannon range and, soon after, the *Thompson*'s master, Francis Smith, met a prize crew at the rail. When he went to his cabin for the ship's papers, the first mate said to the prize officer:

"My God, man, don't you know the war has ended?"

"Did Grant surrender?"

"No, the army of Virginia is surrendered. The war is over."

"Sir, the war will not be over until the South is free."

The master and mates went to the *Shenandoah,* where Waddell asked Smith: "Well, Captain, what's the news?"

He said Lincoln had been assassinated on April 14.

"I was prepared to hear that!" he said.

"And General Lee has surrendered with 30,000 men."

"That I was not prepared to hear, and I don't believe it." There was emphasis in the voice, and Smith offered to bring him the papers. "It is a damned Northern lie, anyhow, and I wouldn't believe it if I saw it," said the commander.

With a prize crew left behind to keep him company, Smith now had the pleasure to be on board as the *Shenandoah* went in pursuit of the *Euphrates*. Her master, Thomas Hathaway, had noticed the cruiser at about 6:00 A.M., ten miles off under short sail, but decided the wisp of smoke coming from her decks meant she was a whaler trying out. His men went on with their business, not realizing just what was approaching, until the cruiser was a mere ship's length away and the "piratical Confederate flag" replaced the Russian ensign. Although he lacked a breeze, Hathaway tried to run, but by noon, the cruiser had overhauled her about ten miles from shore and the crew, mostly Azoreans, received a one-way ticket to the *Shenandoah*. After the prize crew took away no less than three chronometers to tick away in captivity, along with other stores, the destruction began. For some reason, every whaler with more than $25 lost his entire sum, or so the crew claimed.

After her previous frugality, fate now appeared rather frivolous in her treatment of the *Shenandoah,* for during the plunder of the *Thompson,* yet another sail came into view. However, after overhauling her firing a blank, this whaler proved to be Her Britannic Majesty's *Robert Towns.* The luck was doubly bad for the Rebels, as the whaling master was Yankee Frederick Barker, who asked the steamer's name. The *Petropavlarski,* a Russian ship, was the reply, delivered by trumpet via the boatswain—"a broad Milesian, with a touch of Sclay upon his tongue." The cruiser looked familiar—like the *Shenandoah,* which he'd seen back in the Antipodes, and so, not surprisingly, the ruse failed.

Waddell returned empty-handed to the *Thompson,* passing the *Euphrates,* now transformed into "one sheet of flame fore and aft." The *Thompson*'s master, trying to save his ship, told him the war was over, but the commander had only a weak syllogism as refutation, that "unless the Confederacy had gained its independence there was no end to the war." So, he proceeded in the destruction of a North-based whaling fleet that the South had been unwilling or incapable of duplicating itself.

The *Shenandoah*'s three captive masters remained in a coal pen between decks till the following day. At 3:00 A.M., despite Hathaway's protests, the Confederates burned the *Thompson,* then steamed north through fog, ice, and flurries in search of more Yankees. That day, the cruiser also crossed paths with the Honolulu-based whaler the *Hae Hawaii,* commanded by master John Heppingstone. Captain Hathaway, then on board, told Waddell they "were a Kanaka ship and he could not touch that fellow." "We will see," he replied, apparently considering it in the same light as the *Harvest.* "I'll attend to him when I have more time." Heppingstone wisely decided he had business elsewhere and to find it up through the Bering Strait in the Arctic Ocean, warning everyone he met.

As the raider entered the higher latitudes, the crew had to contend with the oddities of the region, such as the near absence of night. Sleep was elusive for those unused to having noon and midnight appear to be almost the same thing. By four, the weather clear, the crew made out five whalers separated from the cruiser by a field of ice. Not surprisingly, only two of them were foreign, while the others flew the guidon of Uncle Sam, that "enterprising and wide-awake old gentleman," as Hunt put it.

To the starboard was a vast sea of ice glittering with a beauty almost beyond words; to port, as if in contrast, lay the forbidding and less than attractive shores of Asia. Before them was a stereopticon of whaling, and the Confederates found it well worth a view. To seaward was a whaleboat, powered by a harpooned bowhead, gliding swiftly through the cold, shallow water. Other ships were trying out the blubber of the "ponderous animals which they pursue with such consummate courage and skill," as Hunt said. Seals by the dozens swam around the cruiser or sunned themselves lazily on the ice.

The first victim came into the *Shenandoah*'s view. She had a white hull, and seeing her, it was evident by her staunch shape and bluff bow, she was outfitted for this rough line of work and could resist the bites of the ice. On this stage the great tragicomedy of the *Shenandoah* began in earnest.

Jonathan Hawes's crew was cutting in a slain whale and the decks were covered in slippery and potentially dangerous gurry. He was master of the whaler *Milo* and had the assassination of Lincoln on his mind. Hailing from the small town of Acushnet near the City of Light, Hawes carried his half century of age well, being noted as a tall, fine-looking veteran, six foot two and standing straight as a harpoon. Just the night before, he'd learned of the Great Emancipator's own emancipation from life itself, and wanted more details. Back in his home port of New Bedford, a world or so away, the city had already gone into mourning, and a handful of notables, no doubt highly aware of the significance of the event, had summoned their oratorical skills to deliver speeches in honor of the event.

The Arctic whaler Hawes was about to get his wish—and something more as well. At about 11:00 A.M., a large steamer flying the American flag approached. He assumed it was a telegraph vessel from San Francisco engaged in the difficult and expensive process of laying wire to connect Siberia to North America. The steamer came close up under the *Milo*'s stern and dropped a boat, and when in hailing distance, a man in a "sharp peremptory manner" called out from on deck, "Ship ahoy! Come aboard and bring your papers."

"What ship is that?" asked Hawes.

"Never mind. Come aboard and bring your papers and bear a hand about it, too." Although surprised, to say the least, about the identity of the steamer, the tall Hawes came over the side with the dignity of an admiral, as one observer noted. An officer met him at the after gangway, took his papers, and politely showed him to the captain's cabin, where Waddell motioned him to sit and informed him of the new, rather unpleasant situation. During the ensuing chat, the typically courteous (to captives) Waddell, proved himself to be pleasant spoken, polite, and gentlemanly. He said: "This is a deplorable war."

"Yes, and no one deplores it more than I do."

"I suppose, of course, you look upon this matter as the fortune of war, and understand I have no personal feeling?"

Hawes didn't reply, but when he mentioned he'd thought the cruiser a telegraph vessel, Waddell said: "Yes, I am a telegraph."

"I had heard of her [the *Shenandoah*] being in Australia, but did not expect to see her in the Arctic Ocean," observed Hawes. When the whaler at last got to discuss the assassination, Waddell said: "I am sorry it has been done, not but that I believe he deserved to die, but I like not the manner of his taking off. I hope his murderer will be captured."

After Waddell asked for news, Hawes told him the war was over, but the commander wanted proof by way of "documentary evidence," and there was none to give him. That wasn't satisfactory, Waddell declared.

However, luck was with the Yankee. Instead of burning the *Milo*, Waddell, realizing he must do something with the burgeoning number of castaways he was manufacturing, said: "I shall put on board your ship ninety paroled prisoners of war."

Hawes didn't think he could house so many men, but Waddell wasn't interested in the objection. "You had better send your boats for the prisoners as quick as you can, as I shall detain your clearance until it is done. Come, come!" He was insistent. "Bear a hand about it, as I have other work to do."

"I see how it is," said Hawes, closing a transaction that back in New Bedford would later be described as a compromise. "I will give bond and receive all prisoners."

After ransoming the vessel for $46,000, Waddell dismissed Hawes with instructions to keep his fore-topsail aback and follow in the wake of the *Shenandoah*, on pain of being blown out of the water. The *Milo*'s crew soon busied themselves cleaning off the decks to receive their guests.

Business concluded, Waddell ordered steam up to chase the next two vessels, the *Sophia Thornton* and the pretty bark *Jireh Swift*, whose Old Man was Thomas William Williams.

. . .

Williams's career had taken some precarious twists and turns after he'd put out from the Cape Verdes. Somewhat embarrassingly, on November 12, 1863, while off the Sandwich Islands, the *Swift* had collided with the whaler *Mount Wollaston* and a "fine time we had," as Williams observed in a letter to Eliza. The subsequent thumping resulted in the bark losing her foremast, ship rails, bulwarks, boats, and davits. The next thing that went was the main-topgallant mast—all the while a gale blowing in the "bargin."

He admitted: "If you had seen us I think you would have pitted [pitied] us[.]" It took a day to clear the mess enough to command the ship. With no way to control the head of the vessel, Williams sailed back to port, eventually making his way to Honolulu for repairs. While anchored off the reef there, a pilot came on board to tell Williams "all the ships from the artic have all don first rate this is to bad[.] I felt bad enough before but this put the finishing tuch on[.]"

He estimated the cost for repair would run to $12,000. Although he thought that insurance covered two-thirds of this, he admitted, "Swift and Allen will wish me to the devil I suppose." Nevertheless, Williams sailed onward and arrived in San Francisco on December 9, 1864, with a catch of whalebone and oil worth more than $100,000. That year was not all success for Williams—while at sea, his nine-year-old son, Henry, died of scarlet fever. Unable to return home to comfort Eliza—whaling had to continue—he sailed on to Honolulu, and on April 11, 1865, had voyaged from there on to the Arctic.

It was a fine day with the ice scattering to the eastward, the forbidding Siberian coast about twenty-five miles off and not a cloud to trouble the horizon. It seemed a very good time for Williams. He and Moses Tucker had taken four whales each; he'd evaded the *Alabama* in the Azores, and avoided the *Shenandoah* at Ponape (where he'd procured fifty pounds of tortoiseshells worth $400). There were four hundred barrels of oil in the hold, and a freshly killed whale with blubber enough for another hundred barrels yet to be tried out. "I had done well and my prospects never looked better," Williams later claimed. He'd been writing copiously to Eliza that he felt well, was flushed with success, was boiling-in that large whale, and had more prey all around.

Just prior to the appearance of the raider, Williams went on board the *Sophia Thornton* to see Tucker and enjoy "some fresh eatables and the latest news," according to one eyewitness. From his perch on the *Thornton*'s crow's nest, a lookout scoured the sea, but rather than spouts, he caught sight of clouds of smoke. A ship was approaching leisurely from leeward looking like a "blubber logged"—or overloaded—whaler moving so slowly from the south she appeared to be trying out a blanket-sized piece of blubber. By about 1:00 P.M., it was clear she was under steam.

"It must be the *Shenandoah*," someone joked, but the quip ceased to be funny as the whalers watched the steamer approach the *Milo* and boats began passing back and forth between them. One boat visited the whaler, and four came back—and that satisfied even the skeptical on board about just what sort of transaction was unfolding. Whether it was just a lucky guess, or perhaps the same instinct that signals a man to duck when the business end of a whale fluke is about to descend on him—both Williams and Tucker decided something was not exactly right. Both decided to flee, heading in separate directions to make pursuit more difficult. Back on the *Swift*, at first, luck seemed with Williams, because a breeze sprang up as he and Tucker raised anchors, dropped sails, and took to their heels. With the vagaries of the Arctic, the chances were excellent an intervening fog or ice field might ensure at least one might make it away.

Naturally, Waddell was aware what the masters were up to, noting that if he didn't take them quickly, "the rascals would have a good joke on me." The fleeing vessels parted ways until a mile was between them, with Tucker headed into the ice. To bag both his quarry, Waddell first ran between them, then tacked toward the *Thornton,* which was also the farthest away of the two. Engines chugging, he came in range and fired a live shell that passed by the whaleship's figurehead and splashed harmlessly in the water. Clearly a cool head, the master kept up his flight until another shell went through his main-topsail. On board the cruiser, the order came to put the next ball directly in her hull. Tucker, knowing the *Shenandoah* could easily riddle his vessel with lead, decided the game was up. He turned his course away from the ice to meet with a prize boat that had been dispatched to him.

The officer of the prize crew greeted the whaler: "How are you, Captain.

You are a prize of the Confederate steamer *Shenandoah*. Get yourselves ready to go on board the steamer as quick as you can."

While *Thornton*'s officers prepared to switch vessels, the Confederate went into the cabin and generously helped himself to the eyes of the ship, her chronometers, spyglass, and quadrant, and everything else that struck his fancy, including clothing, some of which he took from the officers' drawers, as noted by the first mate, J. W. Thompson. (Presumably his garments were among them.) A boat took Tucker and his mates on board the *Shenandoah,* while a prize officer stayed behind to guide the whaler in the cruiser's path. The *Thornton*'s officers had the privilege of watching the spectacle from the deck, while a coal hold, usually reserved for hogs, was cleaned out for their berth.

Under steam and staysails, Waddell started the pursuit of the forty-five-year-old Williams, who had unfurled all his canvas to save his bark. The whaling master had two choices, either push into the protective bowels of the ice where his skill might allow him to elude his pursuer, or head toward Siberia and the magic protection of the marine league. (This was assuming that Waddell intended to observe such niceties. He hadn't bothered doing so at Ponape.)

The breeze filling all his sails, he tacked west to the shore of Asia. For two hours, in what Francis Chew claimed was an "exciting chase," the *Swift* kept the warship behind her, and might have escaped had it not been for the region's unreliable weather. To Williams's dismay, the wind dropped, and with it, the bark's speed.

The *Shenandoah* loomed ever larger on the horizon, until by 6:00 P.M., a shell passed close to the *Swift*'s stern and Williams hove to about twenty miles from Cape Thaddeus. Despite Williams's "obstinate effort," Waddell believed if the whaler had stayed in the ice, he would have made good his flight. Instead, he was about to lose his first ship. Chew praised the bark as the "fastest fastest ship in the whaling fleet. There was a light breeze or I fear she would have eluded us."

Once the *Shenandoah* was in hearing distance, Williams, "not in his best mood," turned to her and called out over the water: "A lo there, you are a coward. Why don't you go down south and fight our men of war instead of coming up here and taking a defenseless whaler? Or come on my quarterdeck and fight me? If you thrash me, burn my vessel—but if I thrash you, let me go in peace." There was no response.

However, when a prize crew drew near and found that Williams had yielded to "his misfortune with a manly and becoming dignity." He and his crew were already packed and ready to leave in their whaleboats. Realizing he was taken, and worried about what the letters to Eliza might reveal, he threw them overboard. For the trip off *Mrs. Swift,* the master wore a big monkey jacket, a thick sack coat, and even managed to take a few white shirts and a mattress. Among the things left behind in his cabin was a *Webster's Dictionary,* expensive charts, and the $250 chronometer from the *Florida.* Gone also were two suits—a light one he wore in Hawaii and an unused broadcloth suit, together worth $500, indicating he liked to dress well.

The boarding party stove in a barrel of oil, poured it around in the cabin, and ignited a fire, which took only minutes to become a blaze. Just thirty minutes after her master surrendered to his fate, the lovely *Swift* was a torch. The crew of the *Shenandoah* may have been middling sailors, but they certainly were excellent arsonists.

Also in obedience to an ancient law of war, the whalers had to forfeit their money to their captors. Captain Tucker lost all of the $90 he carried, but not wanting to be a beggar when he landed, he asked for some of the money back. "No, sir," said Waddell, "your people have beggared me and my family and taken away all our property, and I can't see any good reason for accommodating you."

When on board the cruiser, perhaps looking to even some old score, Manning claimed Williams had disposed of some oil and had $15,000 on board. Williams swore he carried only $150, and as the newly minted corporal's word was less than sterling in the eyes of the Confederates, after a quick search, they decided Williams's oath was enough. However, the Connecticut master had the proverbial last laugh, having cleverly secreted whatever money he carried in his coat collar and other places. His natural reserve apparently did him well here, for had his interrogators discovered the loot, the outcome would certainly have been the same as Captain Tucker's.

The captured officers of the *Swift* were crowded into the cruiser's former pigpen along with their colleagues from the *Thornton.* Later, they were moved to a small berth walled off from the forecastle where the raider's own crew slept. While the men weren't put in irons "or otherwise ill used," contrary to assurances, their money was taken, and the Confederates ransacked whatever they wanted and the losers took back what was left. Williams was put in the coal hold, possibly to set an example for his defiance. Nevertheless, during his few hours on board the *Shenandoah,* Williams did meet with Waddell for a conversation.

"I do not believe the war is over," said the whaler, "but am certain the South will yield eventually." He added that the Confederacy had erred in not sending a cruiser to the Arctic Ocean two years ago, for the destruction of that whaling fleet, from which New England gathered her wealth, might have more seriously affected the Northern mind than a dozen battles in Virginia.

To the Marylander, the idea that money and the war were intimately connected north of the Mason-Dixon Line was gospel: "The Yankee captain spoke the genuine philosophy and morality of his countrymen." (Waddell duly recorded the aggregate value of the *Thornton* and the *Swift* as being $132,000.) However, Williams's efforts paid off for other whalers in the area. Before the cruiser could return from chasing the *Swift* to get at them, they managed to get safely behind a field of ice. After a thick fog rose, they escaped; two other vessels, a French and a Hawaiian one, were foreign and therefore inviolate.

Waddell spoke to the *Milo* again and asked Hawes politely if he "would be kind enough" to come on board. The raider was certain Hawes, safely obeying his orders, "rather enjoyed the sport" that day with the other whalers, he having only lost a voyage, while his associates also lost their vessels and cargoes to boot. The Confederate delivered yet more unpleasant news to Hawes: Williams wanted to see him about booking a trip to the Golden Gate. Again, Hawes asked just how he and his men would survive. "If you want provisions you must take them from the *Sophia Thornton,* and you must take her crew also," said Waddell. He returned Hawes's papers, and generously let the vagabond crews take whatever they wanted from the *Thornton,* with the proviso they burn her afterward. As an observer noted later, Waddell still "pretended to disbelieve" in the South's capitulation, acted as though the "Confederacy" was still a power in the earth, and that he was one of its "gallant" naval heroes.

During the *Shenandoah*'s pursuit of the *Swift,* former master Nye got an idea. On the night of the twenty-second, with a thick concealing fog on the water and a crew still loading the *Milo* with stores from the *Thornton,* Nye manned two boats. He set sail for Cape Bering, 185 long and potentially lethal miles away, where he hoped to warn off any whalers he met. He may have been trying to compensate for the treachery of his mates. Possibly he wanted in some way to even the score with Waddell. In any case, he willingly risked stoving in his fragile whaleboat among the great ice floes or being swamped in a swell or freezing to death; he also faced being recaptured and hanged for parole violation. However impractical the attempt, the cutthroat bargain maker was to show both grit and uncommon navigational skill in executing his mission.

By nine, the *Shenandoah* was back by the *Milo* and the *Thornton.* The latter's crew, along with some of Waddell's own carpenters, pulled to her for the less than pleasant task of cutting away the spars. In case any of the more adventuresome mariners entertained thought of flight, the *Shenandoah* kept her guns trained on the prize. When the now-paroled whalers began to go over the side for the pull to the *Milo* and the long, uncomfortable voyage home, an odd thing happened: Some of them shook hands with their captors. Hunt noted that among the whalers were some of the "noblest, most high-minded and generous men belonging to the great brotherhood of seamen. A kindness they seldom forget—to a friend, their hand is ever open...." An enemy was someone who might have been friend except for "some political accident which it is out of their line of business to examine into very closely."

Hawes, armed with a certificate that explained his missing register, set out for San Francisco under pain of "being blown out of water." On board the *Milo*—named, appropriately after a legendary Greek strongman—was a human cargo with no market value: one hundred and ninety-four luckless whalers. Although the crew used every nail, pike, and bit of canvas to make extra berths, in the midst of this "terrible havoc" there was never enough room for all the men to sleep at once. As Waddell believed, the overcrowded ship's arrival in port would alert his government in Richmond to his activities and location. He didn't really know the Confederate government no longer existed in Richmond, or anywhere else, for that matter.

Gliding northward in the direction of the Arctic Circle, the men on the

The Lost Fleet

Shenandoah could see the completely helpless *Thornton:* her masts, with sails set, dragged behind her as the crew transferred stores in whaleboats over to the *Milo*. Helpless, she was like a whale with a severed fluke muscle waiting for the final lance thrust. Before the sun made its brief disappearance for the day, a bright tongue of flame shot up in the air signaling the task of destroying her was done—and that the whalers on board the *Thornton* had earned the right to complain they'd done about the most unpleasant task available to a sailor.

After the cruiser pushed on, an odd thing happened. One of the neutral vessels, the gray-hulled French whaler *Gustave,* had been visible two miles away from the action, but safely out of Waddell's clutches, although he had signaled her. After the *Shenandoah*'s departure, the one ship became two. Waddell hadn't been able to guess it, but the *Gustave* had warped together with the American bark *William Gifford,* and from a distance, the two whalers looked like one vessel. It appears the Gallic master had been lending his aid out of gratitude to an American who, during the Crimean War, had tipped him off that a Russian ship was stalking him. After separation, the American headed south, the *Gustave* north, to alarm the other whalers.

The forlorn whalers on the deck of the *Milo* watched the *Shenandoah* shrink on the horizon as she crept up on the brigantine *Susan Abigail,* a fur and whalebone trader out of San Francisco. The master, arrayed in a grand fur coat procured during his prior voyage, begged the captain not to burn his ship, as this was going to be his last trip and he expected to make $30,000. Waddell—given these reasons—of course paid no heed. A fog rolled in, and by the time it lifted, the *Abigail* was no more. From her, however, Waddell confiscated some newspapers with the dismaying news that Lee had surrendered and the government had removed to Danville. However, a greater part of the Army of Northern Virginia fought on. The *Abigail*'s master claimed ignorance of the far-off war's outcome: "Opinion is divided. . . . how it will end no one can know, as to the newspapers, they are not reliable."

All Waddell needed to read was that President Davis had announced the losing struggle would be carried on with "renewed vigor." While this sounds like a convenient excuse, it was certainly true the crew found it hard to swallow that Robert E. Lee had actually surrendered. As McNulty put it, the men "set it down as a smart Yankee trick, thought of to save his ship." Not that the imagined ruse worked. Waddell burned the vessel that brought him the news, anyway, which at least offered some consolation.

Farther west near the Gulf of Anadyr, the whaler *Mercury* was contending both with the leviathan and gale winds when a whaleboat appeared from the ocean side. Soon on board was none other than master Nye, who explained his *Abigail* had been burned by a Confederate pirate. "The ship is in a few miles of you and if you go any farther east you will be in danger," said Nye.

The master hauled his wind, and passed the warning on to the whalers *Florida, Corinthian*, and *Peru* before heading west. On board the *Minerva*, master Edward Penniman faced a thorny problem. Hearing the warning delivered by the French *Gustave*, he decided immediately to recall his whaleboats, already out hunting, but there was no wind to unfurl a signal flag. However, the master did recall there was an old cannon stored below, which might answer his purpose, and he brought the weapon on deck and lashed it to the gangway for firing.

"When the gun went off it rose right up in the air and, coming down on deck, made a great hole on the planking. Everybody was scared half out of their wits, while the concussion was so great it broke all the glass in the skylight to the cabin," Penniman said. It must also have been a shock to his wife, who was below at breakfast.

There was skepticism over the threat. When E. R. Ashley, master of the *Governor Troup*, heard Penniman's news, he said: "I don't believe a damned word of it. It is a damned French trick to get north of us and best us in whaling." On leaving, he said he was going up the strait. Luck watched over this fool and he evaded Waddell. Ebenezer Nye remained with the fleet until he arrived at San Francisco on November 1, 1865, as a guest on the *Mercury*.

The master of the *General Williams* of New London may have been the only master to conclude he was the personal target of the war against the Arctic whaling fleet, or so Hunt decided after getting an earful of the Yankee's complaints. After being overhauled on the twenty-fifth and taken on the deck of the *Shenandoah*, the whaler openly blustered with displeasure, asking "what injury he had ever done us, that we should hunt him like a wild animal, and destroy his property?"

An officer explained that it was not him, but his government that the *Shenandoah* was striking against. Nevertheless, hearing his vessel was to become a fire in the Arctic wastes, he did something that sparked no pity in the hearts of his captors and would have been disastrous in the fore-castle: He cried openly. One officer called him a "miserable old whine of a Yankee." Waddell, who concluded he was "certainly a Jew and the second of the kind I have seen," as well as a "dirty old dog," took from his care thirty-four prisoners, three hogs, and $405 in cash—the whalers claimed it was $600. In either case, it was the heftiest purse yet, indicative of the great wealth of New London, noted Hunt with some amusement.

While she was lying next to the whaler, about thirty umiaks, the light, walrus-hide-covered boats used by the Eskimos to hunt bowheads, pulled toward the *Shenandoah* to bargain for goods. The animal-skin-clad na-tives were from St. Lawrence Island, and Whittle found them "a miserable looking race of people of a light copper color. . . . They live on fish & whale blubber and are known to be no more choice in their diet than are buz-zards." Despite the lack of a common tongue, the Rebels conducted a bit of trade, after which they took the whaling crew aboard, leaving them with one hundred prisoners in all. Three more sails lay to northward. After the firing of the *Williams,* during the late evening Manning piloted the cruiser through a field of drift ice to creep up on the *William C. Nye* of San Fran-cisco. By about one o'clock in the morning, with "not a breath of air stir-ring," they reached her.

The *Nye* had been out since December, and after cruising off Califor-nia, presumably chasing devilfish, had gone north for bowheads. The men on the whaler's deck had seen the steamer coming up to Indian Point and St. Lawrence Island. This dismal-looking mass of lava, locked in ice half a year at a time, was one hundred miles long and fifteen miles wide and studded with snow-covered volcanoes. The whalers had given the steamer no thought, at least until she was on them and it was too late to do any-thing about her. So far the crew had taken 240 barrels of oil, and one of her boats was even then on the water trying to increase that amount, when the obligatory statement rang out: You must consider yourself a prize to the Confederate man-of-war *Shenandoah.*

S. M. Cootey, her master, later said the master-at-arms treated him with every indignity he could invent, allowing him and his men only their wretched bedding and ordering them to turn their pockets inside out to display any potential loot. The whalemen's clothing was "rudely examined," and they were ordered to sit down on the floor with "some Chinamen." The Confederates even broke open Cootey's trunk for plunder, but the *Nye*'s steward had wisely taken the precaution of removing the money. When the fourth mate refused to sign parole, he won a choice spot in irons. Waddell briefly forbore from the joy of arson to avoid tipping his hand to the next victim, the *Catherine* of New London. The crew was already cutting into a bowhead when the *Shenandoah* came along and interrupted the process, and instead of whale blubber, a mere half hour later it was the timbers of the *Catherine* herself rising into the polar sky in the form of ash.

Despite his setback with the *Alabama,* whaling master James Clark, formerly of the *Ocean Rover,* had decided to go back to sea again. His quarterdeck was now on the *Nimrod,* also of New Bedford. Apparently she was a good choice, as he'd already taken seven whales—according to one source, something of a record so early in the season. At 1:00 P.M. on June 26, he was off Indian Point on the eastern side of the strait, where there was a settlement of Siberian natives who made it a popular stop off for whalers. The officer of the watch informed Clark that a steamer was coming their way. Unsurprisingly, Clark became apprehensive as his ship, named after a great hunter from the Bible, turned into the hunted. Soon Clark was looking into the face of an officer, possibly Irvine Bulloch, whom he'd first met on the deck of the *Rover*. The reunion wasn't a pleasant one for the "indignant" whaler, finding himself cast once again into the same role he'd played with Raphael Semmes. Nevertheless, the Confederate officer, treating the scene as a joke, smiled, and extended his hand as if to an old acquaintance. Clark didn't think the meeting was half such a joke as the lieutenant.

Clark requested bond, and while Waddell certainly could have used the *Nimrod* to carry some of the unemployed mariners he was accumulating, he refused the offer. There was perhaps just too much whale oil and bone in the great hunter's hold for Waddell to show Clark mercy. It was his job, after all, to keep the precious stuff from enriching the pockets of the capitalists of the North whom he so detested. When the unfortunate master told Waddell the war was over, the reply was: It has just begun. Clark pointed out that the great Lee had capitulated; Waddell agreed, but refused to accept that General Joseph E. Johnston had done likewise. Clark and the other masters and mates were put in isolation in a coal hold, where the mood must have been glum.

By 4:00 A.M., the freshly captured trio was afire. (We don't know if Clark had any wedding cakes with him this trip, but among the *Nimrod*'s losses were a panama hat, a sable coat, and a teak and ivory fiddle belonging to a mate.) Now with 250 men as part of the "Yankee delegation" plotting mischief, and three more sails on the horizon awaiting chase, Waddell decided to just tow the prisoners behind in whaleboats, as many as twenty-four of them at once. The *Shenandoah,* whaleboats in tow, entered an ice field through which she could make only a tortuous six knots as she described a serpentine course. It was an amazing scene, at least if you were a Confederate in relative comfort and safety on deck. As an eyewitness recounted it, behind the cruiser were three burning ships drifting wildly among the huge ice islands, and ahead were the next victims, unable to escape despite their obvious danger.

Arriving at the site where the whalers lay, the *Shenandoah* went into action. The first victim was the *General Pike* of New Bedford, which had been under the command of none other than master Shadrach Tilton, formerly of the *Virginia.* However, before a reunion could be effected with Bulloch and some of the other officers from the *Alabama,* that prior February, death had interceded and removed Tilton from both command and life itself. (It was said the hapless master had after the loss of his ship been "completely broken down by the sad and painful experience.") Acting captain Hebron Crowell, formerly the first officer, apparently was no savvier than his predecessor. He watched the smoke rising from the *Nimrod* and the other whalers and thought it came from their try-pots. After the *Shenandoah* appeared under his stern and disabused him of that notion, he saw a way of making permanent his new position.

When Crowell was on board, the seated "pirate chief" said, "Well, Captain, your cruise has terminated rather more abruptly than you anticipated it would, but such is the fortune of war. I hope you will make yourself as comfortable as possible while on board my ship."

Clearly a quick thinking Yankee, he said: "If you ransom the *Pike,* her owner will think me so fortunate in saving her, he will give me a claim on them for command." Negotiations started. At first, Waddell proposed putting 160 men on the *Pike,* but as Crowell put it, "the brute" later crammed 222 instead, which, along with the ship's crew, brought the total number on board to a dizzying 252. In the meantime, the *Pike*'s officers became temporary guests on the *Shenandoah* as she steamed on to the next whaler, the *Isabella,* a large bark that two years before had put the Whaling City astern. Her captain was Hudson Winslow, a denizen of Freetown, a small village that boasted a brace of fine Federalist houses, sitting on the west edge of New Bedford.

Winslow was looking from his deck when he saw a ship without one sail set. Falling under that Siren-like spell that apparently prevailed so powerfully among the fleet, he decided she was just a whaler. By seven, he noted there were "three large black smokes" in the sky, and presumed this supposed whaler was towing a number of boats behind as she went alongside the *Pike*. As a last hint of her true identity, a Confederate boat crew materialized alongside the *Isabella* and delivered the gloomy news about the vessel being a prize. The officer then ordered him to the *Shenandoah* and the crew and officers to the *Pike*.

At 7:30 A.M. about two miles away, Orlando G. Robinson, captain of the *Gypsy,* was having a difficult morning. After all, a Confederate cruiser was steaming toward him and he was in dread for his very life. When the prize crew approached him, the captain was "as pale as a ghost and could scarcely return an articulate answer to any question addressed to him," said the boarding officer. It was clear Robinson thought he was going to be burned with his ship or hanged from a yardarm, and despite reassurance, he could barely accept the proposal that no personal injury was intended for him. This was, of course, war most civil.

But he stood liable to lose more than his skin. Luck had been reasonable on this voyage, at least up till now. Since leaving Massachusetts three years earlier, he'd already shipped cargo twice, and now the vessel held $10,000 worth of oil and bone. Robinson's luxurious cabin also held a two hundred book library, a writing desk, and fine furniture that "would have done credit to a well-appointed drawing room." For refreshment, he carried several cases of choice wine and liquors. Perhaps the one luxury he lacked was the company of his wife, whom he'd left behind this trip. The prize officer paroled the crew, sent them to the *Pike,* and subsequently appropriated a few trinkets and furs, as well as a couple of bottles of the choice spirits for the men. These tasks concluded, the "torch was applied."

Getting ready to create enough berths (to the degree there could be) for prisoners from seven vessels, the *Pike*'s crew threw overboard all casks, lumber, and iron hoops—normally indispensable, but now just so much worthless junk competing for space. Life in the forecastle was undoubtedly torture enough, but this miserable overcrowding was unbelievable even on a whaler. That wasn't all: The prisoners, petty officers included, had to submit to the indignity of having their captors search their pockets for prizes; some men even lost rings from their fingers. Although Waddell had promised otherwise, the masters weren't exempt from the pilfering, and they later complained of being robbed of anything of value, including their precious watches. For himself, Waddell took as much walrus ivory as he could, but left the baleen and oil to the flames. Perhaps to strike fear among the whalers, he also talked about arming another whaleship to ruin the entire fleet in the Sea of Okhotsk and in the Arctic Ocean. Facing this near penal trip, perhaps reminiscent of a Botany Bay transportation voyage, Crowell told the "pirate chief" he didn't think there was enough food to last.

"You should cook the Kanakas," Waddell said. "You have plenty of them." He also had a message for Crowell to deliver: The Union newspapers claimed "the Chivalry," as he called his officers, couldn't stand the cold. "You will soon be in San Francisco; give the naval officers my compliments and tell them we stand the cold first rate." He added that his men both had their mission and warm clothes to sustain them. (Circumstances later proved Crowell was indeed right about the inadequate provisions. The *Pike* was so low on water he had to pull into the whaleman's stop of Plover Bay for replenishment.)

On the twenty-seventh, the *Shenandoah*'s crew let her fires go down, collapsed the smokestack, raised the propeller, and beat northward under sail. Although the weather was cold and foggy, there was a good breeze and five tempting sails were in view. To ensure he would capture them all, Waddell decided to wait for the wind to die before striking. Day broke at 1:00 A.M., with the light shining on the coast of Siberia and the headland of East Cape. About twelve miles west through the strait lay the Diomede Islands, twins of dark towering rock standing their perpetual and gloomy watch over the black-colored tide that roared back and forth daily from the North Pacific into the Bering Sea. Although the channel between the mountain islands was deep enough for ships to sail very close to either of the brothers without fear of grounding, the rapid currents here could also be dangerous.

With the sun rising higher, the fog broke, creating what, for this region, would be a rare pleasant clear day, not to mention the busiest one for the *Shenandoah* on this last elongated spur of the Civil War. At 8:15 A.M., the lookouts made a ship passing the bow, heading southwest. She was the bark *Waverly* of New Bedford. Having nearly collided with her in the fog, Waddell decided she should be the first to go. The whaler's captain, Richard Holley, had just come up to the weather deck when a mate informed him that a steamer was approaching. Holley ordered flight, and after a two-hour chase, the cruiser fired a shot and brought the *Waverly* to. Her officers and captain were sent aboard the *Shenandoah,* along with the crew, from whose ranks the Confederates managed to recruit a black man. Shortly thereafter she was afire, along with her hard-won 500 barrels of oil and 6,000 pounds of bone. Holley was allowed to go up to the cruiser's weather deck, briefly, to watch the *Waverly* burn, the first in a series that day.

With Manning as pilot, the *Shenandoah* headed north; by 1:30 P.M. a number of sails of every type came into view; as Waddell put it, these were more of the "friends" from the South Pacific that he'd missed earlier in his voyage. In preparation for attack, he retracted the funnel and luffed sails, going as slowly as possible to keep the whalers from getting frightened. Like a good blubber hunter, he wanted to creep up as nearly invisible as possible and prevent the prey from gallying.

On this day of gentle weather, things were going badly for Captain Alden Potter of the New Bedford whaler *Brunswick*. The night before, she collided with ice, and in the cracked supporting timbers and crushed planks, the Bering Sea rushed inside through a hole as big as a bushel basket. The ship's ensign was raised upside down in the universal call for help, and although hardly a breeze stirred to make it flap, several masters rowed over to examine the damage. (To prevent any suspicion of potential fraud by insurers back home, it was a common practice to rely on a quorum of masters to decide if a vessel was in fact still seaworthy.) After verifying her state, the masters condemned the *Brunswick,* meaning, as custom dictated, pieces of the ship and her cargo would be auctioned. It also signified the adjudicating masters could get a damn good bargain.

One of the masters present was Reuben Cunningham of the *James Maury.* Cunningham was new to his estate, having been his ship's first mate until just the prior March. The *Maury* was sailing near Guam when bowel inflammation had taken the ship's master, Samuel L. Grey. Deceased Grey's wife and three children were on board, and with Yankee backbone, the widow had urged Cunningham to keep whaling till the casks were filled. She was part owner.

To continue the process of loading the *Maury*'s hold, Cunningham procured two unprocessed whale heads from the stricken *Brunswick.* The auction continued, with Potter selling off the cutting stage, compass, and a whaleboat, and during the Yankee give and take, two more ships appeared on the horizon, the *Martha* and the *Hillman.* Next from the south a black cruiser came into sight, provoking various opinions. The masters decided against her being a ship of war, they all had left port with the tottering Confederacy all but eliminated.

Hoping the cruiser might tow him to safety, or at least take his oil, which he was willing to sell for as low as twenty cents a gallon (a better price than his colleagues were offering), Potter sent off a mate in a boat to the steamer. After pulling under the vessel, the *Brunswick*'s party called up on deck and asked for a carpenter or two. The faces looking down from the *Shenandoah*'s rail were grave as an officer replied: "We are very busy now, but in a little time we will attend to you."

Captain Waddell overhead the exchange, and smiled.

"No hurry. The pumps will keep us afloat for a time," said the mate. Someone also told them their troubles were over.

The boat pulled back to the stricken *Brunswick.* Had the whalers paid attention to the cruiser's decks, they'd have seen the telltale signs she was readying for battle, with officers detailing boarding parties and arms being passed out. (These preparations weren't wholly dissimilar to those made on a whaler after sighting a leviathan.) Finally, the well-traveled great white flag of the Confederacy rose up into the quiet air, whose silence was disrupted by the explosion of a blank. The sound traveled over the water, catching the attention of the small fleet.

Seeing this new ensign rise on the cruiser and her boats pulling toward them, all but one of the crews struck their flags and the whalers' decks became confusion. To their amusement, the Confederates could hear the sound of an anchor chain rising, and the crew of one ship even sheeted her sails. The visiting captains on the *Brunswick* fled in their boats and pulled for their own vessels, but even if they'd arrived ahead of their pursuers, the wind had betrayed them with its absence, leaving them like "stranded whales to the mercy of the first enemy," as Hunt put it. "Had we known it to be the *Shenandoah,* not one of us could have escaped—it being a dead calm," noted the master of the *Isaac Howland,* Jeremiah Ludlow. On the *Howland*'s deck, with the prize crew pulling alongside, Ludlow realized he was in the "wrong pew" and that "John Bull had us fast." (Already the whalers were beginning to point the finger of blame for the raiders toward the island kingdom.)

Immobilized on deck, some whalemen looked up wistfully at their useless canvas. As they arrived at their targets, the dispatched prize crews told the helpless sea hunters they were now, as usual, prizes of the Confederacy and had to leave their vessels or face destruction. One by one, the masters made the pilgrimage to the cabin of Waddell. Captain Alden Potter of the *Brunswick* claimed that when he handed over his money to Waddell, he asked him if he wanted his watch, too. "No," said the commander, "keep it. You may think this hard, but we are simply retaliating for what the North has done to us."

The whalers' responses to capture varied. Waddell claimed some masters swore their sympathy for the South; others babbled incoherently of fire, insurance, and the cruiser. He later concluded: "A drunken and brutal class of men I found the whaling captains and mates of New England."

On the *Shenandoah,* Ludlow enjoyed a long conversation with Waddell, who pointed out that some of Semmes's own officers were now serving under him. Trying to impress the master with his ship's prowess, he said the cruiser could run under steam or sail and there was no escape from him. The commander, perhaps trying to win him over, gave Ludlow a handful of sovereigns and even helped him retrieve his clothing from the doomed *Howland,* from which a boarding party had relieved his revolver and nautical instruments.

It was a pathetic scene on board the *James Maury,* where Mrs. Gray tearfully begged the prize crew officer not to burn the ship that had been her husband's home for so long. As gently as possible, the Confederate said no harm would befall her by any act of the men of the *Shenandoah,* and he sent pro tempore master Cunningham over to see an expectant Waddell, who'd already heard the story of the dead master and his wife. The Confederate spared the ship, and after ransoming her for $37,000, sent Cunningham back with a message for Mrs. Gray to "cheer up." Cunningham also bore a note explaining that the "men of the South never made war on helpless women and children, although an example to the contrary had been set them by their Northern enemy we preferred the nobler instincts of human nature." There was more than Southern gallantry involved: The number of prisoners was running into the hundreds and he needed to get them out of the Arctic; thus he managed to serve honor and practicality at once. He also ransomed the *Nile,* a ship worthy of Jonah, that had seen six masters on her quarterdeck during a twelve-year voyage.

Before leaving, Manning offered some advice to Cunningham. "If I were you, I would go to Hakodate, turn the paroled prisoners over to the consul there and go into Okhotsk Sea, where you can have six or eight weeks good whaling and with every chance of a good voyage." Cunningham said he'd no desire to be nabbed twice; but Manning explained the *Shenandoah* wasn't going to the Okhotsk again, the coal was about used up, and the mission done. (Perhaps for once Manning told the truth.)

It was especially unpleasant for John Macomber, master of the *Hillman* of New Bedford. He'd been becalmed between the headland of East Cape and St. Lawrence Bay, whose inhabitants raised deer, and were known to be short, lazy, and fat. Macomber was taken by an armed party and hurried over the side and, despite promises otherwise, was left with only the clothes on his back. "I was taken on board the *Shenandoah,*" he later said, "and in a very short time I saw the ship in flames." After coming on board the *James Maury* in preparation for the long, hard journey back, he said, "we remained in sight long enough for me to witness her entire destruction."

The rather unlucky Captain Daniel Wood of the New Bedford bark *Congress 2nd* had the sort of record that gave owners and agents pause when considering whom they were going to hire. He'd managed to lose the *Fabius* on a reef off the coast of California five months before; four years prior to that, in May 1861, in the Sea of Okhotsk off Kamchatka, he'd lost the *Polar Star*—the first mate and his boat crew died in the landing. (*Congress 2nd*'s prior master, Captain F. E. Stranburg, had died earlier in 1865.) Now on board the cruiser, he was directed to the luxurious cabin full of plundered furnishings where Waddell held court with a clerk and another officer. Waddell made him "testify truly" about who owned the vessel and what she carried by way of cargo, instruments, and specie. After interrogation, he was paroled and allowed to go below for a couple of hours.

Given the sort of men that made up the officers and masters of the fleet, it was inevitable that at least one fought back. The mariner who redeemed the grizzled honor of the New England whaling fishery that day by refusing to strike his colors was Thomas Young, master and co-owner of the *Favorite* of Fairhaven. He'd sailed in her since 1836 over six voyages, twice as mate, and four as master. Approaching fifty-three (although for some reason thought to be twenty years older), Young hailed from York, Maine, and was described as a tough and grim old salt. He appears to have had something of a cool head: During the Civil War when running supplies in a schooner up the Potomac, he'd faced cannon fire—and perhaps learned that not every shell hits the intended target.

One habit clearly set him apart: He was a man of refined literary tastes and even knew French. As he said later: "I am fond of reading . . . to employ my mind, and we have plenty of spare time aboard a whaler to read." He'd assembled a 220-strong lending library on board, each book generally free from being "soiled or dogeared or partially injured." Among the titles was *Moby-Dick* (the white whale that had sunk its author's literary career). Young also kept a thirteen-volume history of France on his shelves, perhaps not the most common set of tomes on a whaler. The books were numbered and catalogued, and, at request, the cabin boy fetched and delivered books to the crewmen. Young was also a writer, and for thirty-five years, he'd faithfully been producing handwritten histories of his voyages in manuscript form, one volume for each year. "I could tell you where I was every day since 1829," he claimed.

The prior April, Young, with his library, had sailed from Japan and taken about five hundred barrels of oil and four thousand pounds of bone, and was beating up to the Arctic when he fell in with the doomed *Brunswick*. Around 2:00 P.M., Young caught sight of the *Shenandoah* and realized a disguised wolf had strayed among the sheep. At some point that day, Young had started drinking and, possibly buttressed by liquid courage, developed a clear idea about how to deal with this pirate. Moreover, as he later explained, "I have only four or five years to live anyway, and I might as well die now as at any time, especially as all I have is invested in my vessel, and if I lose that I will have to go home penniless and die a pauper."

Young loaded his bomb gun and mustered the crew, armed with muskets or handspikes, on deck. He waited on the cabin roof on the poop deck, carrying a cutlass in one hand and an old revolver in another. Waddell had already seen this potential threat and sent an armed party over to the *Favorite*, which arrived as fire and smoke began to rise from several of the captured whalers. The boarding party drawing near, Young bellowed: "Boat ahoy? Who are you and what do you want?"

"We come to inform you that your vessel is a prize to the Confederate steamer *Shenandoah*."

"I'll be damned if she is, at least just yet, and now keep off or I'll fire into you. Stand off!" Young yelled. He squinted down his bomb gun, and his crew, turned into makeshift marines, handled their muskets in a business sort of way.

At first, the officer thought this was a joke, but he realized the steady aiming of the bomb gun at him meant otherwise. He signaled the *Shenandoah* and ordered his men to row back to the cruiser, which steamed alongside the *Favorite*. Once again, a boarding party pulled toward the whaler, but the tough old shellback held his ground.

"Haul down your flag!" ordered the officer on the *Shenandoah*'s deck.

Young replied: "Haul it down yourself, God damn you! If you think it will be good for your constitution."

"If you don't haul it down, we'll blow you out of the water in five minutes."

"Blow away, my buck, but may I be eternally blasted if I haul down that flag for any cussed Confederate pirate that ever floated."

This farce did have the potential to become tragic, and an amused Waddell ordered a Whitworth cannon loaded, however, he was man enough not to want to cut down the defiant Yankee, at least not just yet. Not being made of the same stuff as their master turned commander, or at least not as drunk, Young's men began to tremble about the knees. With much less property but more lifespan to lose, the mock-marines dropped their weapons. Someone on deck explained to the master that "it was sure death for him to shoot."

"I die willingly, could I kill that wretch."

Leaving Young cornered and alone on his vessel, his officers and crew dropped the whaleboats from the falls and pulled from the ship. The forsaken Mainer lay on the cabin roof in his glory, sipping whiskey and preparing to die. "Fire, but fire low," someone said, but Young didn't bother to rise as he waited for a flash that never came. Looking at the water, he saw the boat pulling toward him again. The *Shenandoah*'s officer had decided not to risk blowing up his own men. Once alongside, the head of the prize crew ordered Young to strike colors.

"I'll see you damned first."

"If you don't I'll shoot you."

Waddell challenged the boarding party to take the deck of the *Favorite*. Whittle took a rifle from one of the marines in the boat and raised it at the "intoxicated" Young, and told him to leave his arms on the poop and go to the port gangway or he would kill him where he stood.

"Shoot and be damned."

In response, Young pointed the bomb gun and pulled the trigger. Had all gone according to plan, its feathered lance might have made quite a gory mess of Whittle and put Young first in line to be the final casualty of an already-ended war. But nothing happened. Unknown to Young, one of his mates, deciding just how much was the better part of valor, had intervened already by quietly removing the percussion cap from the bomb gun. The drunken master hadn't noticed until it was too late. Although the mate's act probably saved Young's life, it frustrated the master, who considered it nothing less than a shabby trick. It was tough enough to fight the Rebels to begin with, as he later noted, but lacking even a serviceable weapon sank any chance he had to succeed.

Once on the *Favorite*'s deck, the boarding party found Young leaning on or against the now useless bomb gun. Before the much-contested flag came down, the boarding party handcuffed the "royally" drunken master, who refused to leave his ship, and transported him into the boat by block and tackle. Now facing Young, the officer asked: "Would you have shot me?"

"Shot you! Yes, shot you like a dog!"

The crew plundered Young of his shirt studs, money, and watch, and helped themselves to his library. Not even needing to apply the rules of war, Waddell claimed the ornery Yankee had no ship's register and thus was on the seas illegally and not entitled to any protections. Alleging he was too drunk to take care of himself, he ordered Young thrown in the coal hold for a four-hour stretch and even told his guard to gag him if he got nasty. Seeing this, the other captive masters expected to be sent into the hold as well. When the oak-built *Favorite* was burned to the water's edge, so went whatever volumes hadn't been stolen from her extensive library—including Young's autobiography. This was an irreplaceable prize indeed. Young later requested $350 in compensation for it, although he said: "That is not one-sixteenth of the value to me. If I had the money and could get them, I would give $2,000 for them today."

Despite his humiliation, Young's blunt animal courage had won some admiration. As Hunt said: "He was at least three sheets to the wind from spirituous consolation, but voted the bravest and most resolute man captured." On shore, the press hailed him as belonging to the unyielding "John Brown stump of mortals"—referring to another lunatic who had, unlike Young, managed to successfully die in a harebrained scheme colored with the rosy hues of idealism. (Back in New England, Young remained unemployed for two years, until, possibly in consideration of his moxie, he was made assistant librarian for the state of Maine.)

Another account from that day, but somewhat suspect, was told by Horace Sherman, first mate of the *Congress 2nd*. He claimed his bark made a run for it, and boasted he even fired the stern cannon at the *Shenandoah*. The raider captured and burned the *Congress 2nd*. Later, while onboard the cruiser, a disgruntled slave named Sam helped Sherman escape the privateer to a nearby French whaler. The French vessel was short of hands and welcomed them aboard. While serving there, claimed Sherman, he helped take five whales, which paid his keep. He and Sam returned to America by way of Marseille.

Waddell claimed there was an awkward reunion between one of the captive whaling captains and his brother, Thomas Manning. After the two shook hands, any pleasure Manning's brother had in seeing Thomas soon faded when he discovered his Judas-like treachery. However, the two soon began to talk and the master developed a better humor as "he had gone over to the opinion of his brother that it was right to make a living whenever one can do so honestly." Waddell judged that was another example of the benchmark Yankees applied to their affairs and that "metallic virtue is the worship of his soul." (No Manning appears in the list of masters, and Waddell may have invented the story.)

Still in want of men, the Confederate officers mustered the whalers on deck to offer them a berth and a mission of glowing adventure. Most declined, but of the 336 men now liberated from the voyage—Kanakas, Portuguese, Anglo-Saxons, and even two African mates—only nine "intelligent soldiers" signed on to serve the doomed cause. Waddell claimed this was proof that no one really believed the war was over, but that assumes anyone naive or desperate enough to sign on to whale in the first place could've been trusted to make a better choice, especially under the circumstances then prevailing.

For the voyage back, the remaining men were divided equally among the cramped cartel vessels, the *Maury* destined for Honolulu, the *Nile* for San Francisco. Along with explicit orders to leave the Arctic on pain of destruction, Waddell also provided the masters with supplies and certificates to explain the lack of registers. In addition to the other vessels, Waddell also ordered the finishing destructive touch put on the *Brunswick;* he also burned the *Nassau, Favorite,* and *Martha,* as well as the *Covington* of Warren, Rhode Island, which had tried out six whales that season. Thus, in one eleven-hour span, Waddell had taken a blanket-piece sized chunk of profit out of the New England whaling fleet, worth about $478,000. On board the departing transport vessels, the men watched the smoke rise from the distance while the *Shenandoah* steamed fast into the southwest, where she vanished. A very long surrender lay ahead.

Presumably, it was a day to break the heart of an insurer—or a shipwright. Among the victims was the *Hillman* (see reference in book one); having once been her third mate, pilot Manning no doubt knew some of the vessel's key construction details. The crew of the *Shenandoah* hauled off a ways and dropped a kedge to stabilize the vessel and let them properly enjoy their pyrotechnic handiwork. It was an exquisite show: The burning fleet lit the horizon with a fiery glare, and the water was covered by billows of black smoke carrying sparks. To Waddell, it was "a picture of indescribable grandeur."

Powerfully touched as well was Lieutenant Hunt. "It was a scene never to be forgotten by anyone who beheld it, the red glare from the eight burning vessels shone far and wide over the drifting ice of those seas; the crackling of the fire as it made its devouring way through each doomed ship fell on the still air like upbraiding voices." In the light, Hunt looked over at the two weather-beaten "Noah's arks" and saw "the varied expressions of anger, disappointment, fear, or wonder, that marked the faces of the multitude on those decks, as their eyes rested on this last great holocaust."

Chew the Hapless wrote in his diary: "This day we gave the hardest blow that Yankee commerce has yet received; eleven more victims were to day added to our already respectable list. . . . A burning ship at sea is a grand sight, but what is it when two occupy the picture? What a destruction of property? At least half a million of dollars for ever gone." His elation—and that of his comrades, was short-lived.

Riding the Arctic water within a space of a few miles, the hulks in succession lit up the sky, then sank hissing and gurgling. Occasionally, gunpowder barrels exploded, sounding like artillery; liquid flames flew from the decks and ignited any flammable gear gone overboard into the water. So ended violently, but without the loss of life, the "last act in the bloody drama of the American Civil War."

However, at least two whalers made it away and avoided becoming Arctic hecatombs. The *Addison* had been sailing in the vicinity and even offered to help the stricken *Brunswick,* but had left Cape Thaddeus before the cruiser's arrival. The second day after the departure, her crew saw smoke and the long black ship came into sight. The men thought she was the cable vessel and were going to speak her, but ice separated them. A fog rolled in, and when it cleared, heavy smoke was coming from the direction of the ships, which was puzzling, as there hadn't been time to take whales.

The next day, the *Addison* turned back and the crew made out log books and other wreckage in the water. Unknowingly, they were sailing as fast as they could in the cruiser's wake. During an encounter with the

Jireh Perry, which had outrun Waddell, the *Addison*'s men divined the *Shenandoah*'s true identity, and they headed south. One mate even took the precaution of boring holes in his boots to hide some gold sovereigns, which proved an unnecessary measure.

Her victims still burning, the cruiser turned her bow briefly north for more prey. After poking into the Arctic Circle, on June 29, facing intractable ice, the *Shenandoah* headed back south, where the crew was able to see the fruit of their labors floating in sight—stove whale boats, casks, and other debris, noted Chew. One hulk had even gone adrift and was being swept through the Bering Strait by the strong current. Columns of smoke rose here and there, marking the location of the torched prizes.

That day, she chanced to cross paths with the Hawaiian whaler *Kohola.* Waddell hailed her captain, an Irishman named Barney Cogan, who asked: "Have you heard the news?"

"No, what is it?"

"Lee has surrendered, the North has beaten the South, the war is over, and you are done for."

"You go to hell," said Waddell.

The *Shenandoah* steamed on. Her crew had expected such news.

Yet another set of eyes may have beheld this scene. Stories came down from Eskimo elders who, during the walrus hunts, had seen the burning of ships. Perhaps it was mere legend, perhaps it occurred at this conflagration or one of the others—in any case, the stories claimed the hunters paddled away from the burning ships as fast as they could. There were more tangible signs of the connection between the natives and the whalers' disaster. For years later, whalemen prowling the region looked at gear the Eskimos carried and recognized lances and irons they had once wielded with their own strong, skilled hands.

12

---❧❧❧---

Terrible Havoc

For if you touch a Yankee you wound him in a sensitive and vital part.
This day we have destroyed property to the amount of $400,563 and
bonded property to the amount of $78,600. This will create an excite-
ment. I trust it will do our hearts good by encouraging our noble people.

—*William Whittle Jr., remarks, June 28, 1865*

W ord the privateer was "thinnin'" the ranks of the whaling fleet—
delivered by Cogan, Nye, and the master of the *Gustave*—began to
spread through the fleet's remnant. The mate of the ship *Congress* noted
he saw the bark *John Howland* with "his colors up run down"—upside
down. They spoke to the captain, who reported the Rebel warship was
running about the straits burning ships. The *Congress* raised all her colors
to draw attention to all the ships in sight, ensuring "a great enlightenment
among us all," as he put it.

Those lucky enough to receive the warning scattered—to Holy Cross
Bay, Mercury Harbor, Norton Sound, and Golovnin Bay. The *Oliver
Crocker, Cornelius Howland, Eliza Adams,* and *Louisiana* headed to
Kozebue Sound, where the *Louisiana* had the misfortune of running
aground. Her smashed hull became a landmark for the next decade, while
the other vessels successfully anchored at Chamisso Island for several
weeks. The *Gratitude,* also fleeing, was stove and sank without any Confederate assistance.

The natural barriers of the Arctic aided one ship. "Fortunately for us, it
was summertime up there," noted James Henry Sherman, on board the
Congress. "There was a great deal of thick weather, fog day after day. So

much so the decks were always wet. This condition enabled us to go just clear of the *Shenandoah* anchored off Plover Bay, outside Bering Strait. So we escaped her wrath and the fate of some twenty other whalers she burned to the water and sunk." Bad weather prevailed through the region. On July 3, the mate of the *Minerva* said: "Celebrated this day by cutting the fog with a knife cannot see a ship's length, wind N.E."

Even if unburned, these sogering whalers' unprofitable idleness was another victory for the now dead South. Their masters knew they were losing a valuable summer, as shown by a July entry in the logbook of the *Crocker:* "A fine chance to trade for furs if only we had something to trade with, such as guns, powder, caps and rum."

On July 1, having heard of the prowling *Shenandoah,* Captain Weeks of the whaler *Richmond* was waiting for a good wind to leave the northern seas and escape. As luck had it, he crossed paths not with the cruiser, but the bonded *General Pike,* which lowered a loaded boat that pulled toward him. As it came alongside, Weeks looked down in surprise at the faces of a cluster of dispossessed shipmasters—or to be more accurate, desperate beggars, who joined together to implore him for the "sake of humanity" to relieve them of their overcrowding.

After going on board, Weeks found they hadn't misrepresented the matter. The jamming-in was terrible, with the men unable to all find places to sleep simultaneously, and doing their cooking in the otherwise useless try-pots. On condition that the eight castaway masters draft a letter whose contents explained why the *Richmond* was losing a hunting season, Weeks agreed to take fifty-two of the Hawaiians; he then sailed back to Honolulu. The *Pike* pushed on to San Francisco with pleasant weather, and no events of note except two earthquakes, one of which lasted five minutes, causing "severe shock." (These cataclysms made a ship tremble violently from end to end, and pointed the surrounding water with small sharp waves, like a tidal rip.) No harm done, the *Pike* arrived in port. The Honolulu missionary publication the *Friend* noted that the crew was well supplied with clothing and that Waddell had been "rather partial to Hawaiians," as he'd recruited several of them against neutrality laws.

The other bonded ships plowed ahead, and on July 20, the arrival of the crews of the *Abigail, Euphrates, William Thompson, Sophia Thornton* and *Jireh Swift* created a stir in San Francisco. The same day, after going ashore, Williams visited the California State Telegraph Company and sent a message to Swift & Allen's offices on Middle Street in New Bedford: "*Jireh Swift* burned by *Shenandoah* off Cape Thaddeus. June twenty second— Four hundred barrels." The firm's optimism in Williams's prospects might truly have seemed a bit misplaced now.

He also wrote Eliza, whom he knew already had learned of the loss via telegraphed news stories. "I am very sorry such a fine ship should be Burned by an English Pirate and I hope our Government will make them pay every Dollar or sweep her Commerce from the Ocean," he wrote. He claimed he'd been well treated, although he'd lost half his clothes. Williams also had instructions for her regarding the Northern-living but Southern-leaning Copper Heads, were there in fact any around her. He wanted them to know "I do not care once cent about loosing my ship and my seasons work which is worth ten Thousand Dollars to me so long as we lick the Rebels and their English Friends with them which I consider we have all ready done[.] all I want now is to hang Jeff Davis and I will call President Jonston the man to wind up the war."

Oddly, Williams had learned his mother, in Wethersfield tradition, was growing onions to sell. He told Eliza to ask his mother what they were worth and pay her whatever she wanted for them. After that, "tel her [his mother] to let them go to the Devel. . . . I do not like to here of her working in the Onion Garden because I do not see any good reason for her to do so. . . ." He also promised: "I will tell you all about it [the *Shenandoah*] when I come home."

Williams and three other masters lodged protests and, after putting on suits, even had themselves photographed in a fine portrait to commemo-rate, if that is the word to use, the event. If the *Swift*'s loss had lanced his pride or self-confidence, Williams concealed it well in the photograph. In its frame, he sits serenely, larger than life, or at least larger than the other masters nearby, his face inscrutable. The caption described the Arctic de-struction as "the last act of expiring insolence." With the cargo of refugees passing the Golden Gate also came the stories, which the papers picked up on immediately. "Terrible Havoc by the Pirate *Shenandoah*—Eight Whaleships Destroyed" went one headline.

As could be expected, the off-loading of such and so much wretched flotsam caused intense excitement in the city. (Perhaps most shocking was the knowledge that white and black men and officers had been confined together.) In a humane mood, an editorialist suggested something be done for the vagabonds to provide them with funding home and to take care of their immediate wants. Idle, penniless whalemen were prone to become a nuisance. Ordinarily, he wrote, seamen can provide for themselves, "but when so many are in distress, it becomes our duty to lend them a helping hand." The editorialist also voiced his doubts about how Waddell could have readily believed Lincoln's death but not the war's, and he expressed the wish that the captor take care his neck "does not come within reach of Yankee rope."

One San Francisco poet even printed a rhyming ballad to Waddell, which included the line: "Sad, sad indeed, the day you were swaddled." The odd exodus—or perhaps more accurately, odyssey—of whalers proceeded. Twenty-two days after his encounter with Waddell, Jeremiah Ludlow, the late master of the *Isaac Howland,* told the Sag Harbor *Express* that it was no little surprise to his family and friends at having "circumnavigated the globe in the short space of ten months and five days."

The *Nile*'s arrival on August 2 dumped more homeless, broke, and hapless whalers into San Francisco's rough and seedy waterfront, but regrettably for the local tavern owners and whores, there was little or no money for them to extract from these usually reliable victim-patrons. One newspaper headline from August 14 concerned a group of fourteen riotous Hawaiians believed to be part of the wave of human flotsam beached by Waddell. Proving idle hands are indeed the devil's workshop, they engaged in a fracas in a below-street-level five-cent gin mill on Pacific Street, drawing the attention of a policeman. As the *Examiner* noted, the Hawaiians, "now bent on a free land-fight," offered stiff resistance to pacification—not surprising given the strength, courage, and girth of the average Sandwich Islander. Brother patrolmen chanced to come by the scene and managed to break up the brawl and arrest those who'd violated the city's tranquillity.

The brawlers, along with their friends swarming around them, turned the gin mill into a bedlam of yelling, hooting, and curses delivered in the musical thirteen-letter Hawaiian tongue. Their behavior, noteworthy given that it stood out even in the generally rough atmosphere of San

Francisco, was "like so many escaped lunatics." In court, one scrapper was sent up for assault and battery, two got misdemeanor charges, and the rest got the hand slap of a reprimand—"Promising to mend their ways and behave as respectable citizens during their stay in the city."

The news of the cruiser formed a tsunami-like shock wave that rapidly crossed the continent. Hearing of the disasters, an editorialist in New Bedford expressed his best wishes for Waddell, which was that he might be "wrecked upon an Arctic shore and left at the mercy of the whalemen he has robbed." If the disaster was hard on the crews, it wasn't pleasurable for the owners back in New Bedford, either, who only got wind of Waddell's mischief after he'd already fled the whaling grounds. They had expected something like this, having received news that a Rebel steamer had entered the Pacific and was reported in the neighborhood of San Francisco and Hawaii.

The newspapers had already publicized the inevitable danger: "Terrible Havoc Expected" was the headline in the *Shipping List* on July 26. Frightened that the apparition of the *Alabama* had again returned to haunt them, the merchants of New Bedford issued another letter to Welles in hopes that he might actually do something to protect their floating, faraway property. They said, "We earnestly hope it may be deemed right by our Government to give such protection to our vessels as may be sufficient for their security" and requested a force dispatched. As usual, the plea did little good, as Welles's ships, plagued with mechanical problems or bad timing, always managed to miss the *Shenandoah*.

Some owners had yanked war verbiage from their contracts in May, after getting assurance from the Stone Fleet architect Secretary Fox that he would protect the Pacific fleet. However, some owners took steps to protect themselves. New Bedford's Wing firm, the largest in the city, had sought to insure its vessels through New York underwriters, with other firms following suit, until $1 million worth of policies had been written at the cost of 15 percent of the ships' worth. The Atlantic Mutual Insurance had frantically crafted policies—in one day alone accepting $118,978, a record until the outbreak of the First World War. Eventually, they refused to write more policies. In total, something like a loss of $237,000 was incurred, but only $116,426 paid because of cancellations and limitations.

The *Shenandoah,* although feared, had by the time word leaked out become harmless and her leader confused. As Secretary Welles described her: "An erratic ship, without country or destination." After heading north on completion of his final and greatest holocaust, Waddell attempted briefly to keep up the hunt. The despised Manning, now promoted to acting master's mate, claimed that sixty whalers had passed the Bering Strait, and tempted by this prize, Waddell ordered they proceed through snow and ice. A collision with a floe stopped the ship in her path, which gave him pause. "In consequence of her great length, the immensity of the icebergs and floes, and the danger of being shut in the Arctic Ocean for several months, I was induced to turn her head southward," as he later explained it. He had achieved his primary task, and the decision to put the Arctic behind was a welcome one among the men.

The sojourn north over, some have argued, after the fact, just why Waddell turned around. It was probably a mix of motives—perhaps the most profound being that he realized the South had in fact collapsed, and he could no longer hide behind the flimsy motive of ignorance. It's possible that Waddell knew he was committing piracy. (Chew said they'd received newspapers telling them everything up to the twenty-second, a week later than the day Waddell claimed he had knowledge of, which would have indicated their noble cause was quite lost.) In any case, just as an ice field was closing up the gut of the Bering Strait, the *Shenandoah* safely passed by the Diomede Islands, heading for parts south and safe.

With the mission completed, the whalers destroyed or dispersed, and the *Shenandoah* in solitary command of these seas, deciding on the next move was a problem. Manning came up with an interesting idea. With the coal running out, he suggested they head to Hakodate, leave the men there, and go whaling. Waddell later claimed he briefly thought of steaming through the Golden Gate and laying siege to San Francisco until a ransom was paid by the "worst government under the sun." He abandoned the idea, to the degree he ever really entertained it, in August. After making the English ship *Barracouta* of Liverpool hove to, her captain confirmed the war had in fact ceased the prior April. Waddell was in command not of a cruiser of questionable legal status, but an outright piratical vessel, a legitimate target of any man-of-war and disallowed entry to any port.

The crew realized abruptly they were "bereft of country, bereft of

Government, bereft of ground for hope or aspiration, bereft of a cause for which to struggle and suffer," as one officer put it. The feeling was widespread. Surgeon McNulty, broken for drunkenness, said with Celtic melodrama: "We had been ordered to wipe out the whaling marine of the enemy; and now, after the government that had so ordered had been itself destroyed, we, unwittingly, were dealing the enemy our hardest blows—not our enemy, if we knew the facts, and we were making of ourselves the enemy of mankind." "We are exiles," said yet another officer.

Too late, Waddell reconverted the cruiser into a vessel of commerce. Gloomy crewmen took in the guns and stowed them below, then boarded over the ports and whitewashed the red funnel before collapsing it out of sight. Facing mutiny among the disgruntled officers and men, Waddell eventually made his way back up the Mersey to Liverpool on November 6, where the cruise had started thirteen months before. After dropping anchor, he gave the onetime *Sea King* over to the embarrassed authorities, in whose criminal exploits they were now accessories.

Although Lincoln had said the Union's victory would be with malice toward none, under Andrew Johnson's tenure, some persons possessed less "none" status than others. In that category were the officers of the *Shenandoah,* Waddell in particular. Despite the United States' demands to the contrary, the Crown released the last and perhaps least of the warriors of the Confederacy after brief detainment. This ensured freedom from prosecution for them, and embarrassment for Her Majesty.

After having executed possibly the most pointless mission of the Civil War, Waddell put the best face on his cruiser's run: "She never lost a chase, and was second only to the celebrated *Alabama.* I claim for her officers and men a triumph over their enemies and over every obstacle, and for myself I claim having done my duty." His reputation ruined, Waddell was even accused of having stolen prize money meant for the crew. Life was less than grand for the commander thereafter. So incensed were the Federals, they rather uncharitably placed his wife, still back in the now reassembled Union, under house arrest. A postwar letter of Waddell's appeared in the *Shipping List* for the delectation of the whaling barons whom he'd despoiled. "I am now in exile," he noted, "but far from being a ruined man." He cared nothing about the Union's feeling about him, although he acknowledged the imprisonment of his wife might humiliate her. "So ends my Naval career, and I am called a 'pirate'? I made New England suffer, and I do not regret it."

While he despised the Yankees he'd harmed, he felt something perhaps akin to regret about the ships his arson had cleared from the seas. Waddell admired whaling ships, noting once that many were a half century old, demonstrating just how skilled the shipwrights who had crafted them had been. Unlike an iron ship, made of a mineral plucked from the bowels of the earth, a wooden vessel was made of timber that "grew in sunlight, waved in the forest and heard the wind sing before bending to the breeze under top-sails." He believed: "There is life in the craft from the time she leaves the ways into the tide, to the hour when her timbers are laid on the sand or rocks, or, the saddest of all, in the ship-broker's yard."

A decade after the curtain closed on the tragicomedy of the *Shenandoah*, it was with some surprise that the citizens of San Francisco saw Waddell appear in public, now a captain in the service of the Pacific Mail Company. To employ the disgraced mariner, the firm had secured a pardon from the Republic of Hawaii for the illegal burning of the *Harvest*. Some of the whaling men in port waiting for a berth now remembered their sufferings at his hands. One paper claimed they "have arranged to abduct Capt. Waddell and give him a remarkably lively cruise in the Arctic before the mast of one of those self-same and much abused blubber hunters." As with nearly every revenge plot, this one was more hot air than substance.

The last leg of Waddell's career was as lackluster as the one previous to the war. After accidentally losing a vessel at sea to an inconvenient and un-charted coral reef, he eventually made his way to secession-loving Mary-land, whose governor set the former navy man's hand to the task of ridding Chesapeake Bay of oyster pirates. After several raids, he smashed them, and then proceeded to die with honor in Annapolis in 1881. In an act of kindness for the great bungler, the navy of a government he'd repudiated bestowed his name on a destroyer—the U.S.S. *Waddell*. (The ship is now retired.) As for the cruiser herself, like many of the principals of the Con-federacy, she didn't long outlast the war. After becoming the property of the Sultan of Zanzibar, in 1879 she embraced the floor of the Indian Ocean.

BOOK THREE

The Lance Strikes

13

Idle Wharves and Dismasted Ships

"What luck Captain? Clean or greasy," asked a New Bedford shipowner
as he was coming to the wharf to see if his ship had been lucky. Before
walking away, the master only said: "I didn't get any whales, but I had
a damned fine sail."

—*Post–Civil War whaling tale*

NEW BEDFORD, 1870

To the degree the whaling masters and officers could, they all signed
back on to blubber-hunt once more. One of them was Williams, who,
after losing the *Jireh Swift,* sailed from San Francisco to New York as a passenger in the vessel *Colorado,* which then was making her maiden voyage.
The New Bedford waterfront he beheld on his return must've given him
pause. The Civil War had been none too kind to the fishery. Anyone could
see the Commonwealth of Whaling wasn't what it had been before the eccentric editor of a self-published secessionist newspaper ignited the first cannon overlooking Charleston Harbor. Some hundred whaleships had been
lost in the Stone Fleet or to the cruisers.

With the consent of the moneyed class of New Bedford, the Stone Fleet
action had destroyed a considerable portion of the whalers. Without consent from New Bedford, the Confederate navy increased that number significantly. While in itself the operation had little effect on the outcome of
the war, or even the siege of Charleston for that matter, it did apparently
give the Confederate navy men an incentive to single out whaling as a
form of Yankee commerce particularly worthy of attention.

In effect, the Stone Fleet action was perhaps a tacit admission that whaling was no longer a going concern and that it would be better to recover some of one's investments rather than to continue to risk them at sea. A viable enterprise can be rebuilt—as whaling had proven again and again—but one that is a permanent cripple, short of a miracle, will be allowed to languish. Thus the capitalists by and large decided not to rebuild their ships. This reduced the opportunity to whale, and, in so doing, possibly helped prolong the fleet's existence. Fewer ships meant fewer catches. Also, that meant fewer ships needed to refit, so less cash to expend.

New Bedford harbor was no longer the bustling center of enterprise it had been when Williams ventured down there as a teenager. A photo of Merrill's Wharf taken at the time shows vessels tied to the docks gloomily idle and abandoned. Not only Charleston, but New Bedford, too, had suffered a defeat during the Civil War. As one historian glumly described it: "Our idle wharves were fringed with dismantled ships. Cargoes of oil covered with seaweed were stowed in sheds and along the waterfront, waiting for a satisfactory market that never came. Every returning whaler increased that depression."

New Bedford wasn't the only miserable party. The principals of the destruction of the whaling fleet, the Confederacy and in some cases, its partners, sympathizers, and agents, either were utterly destroyed or fared poorly because of the war. Raphael Semmes and James Waddell barely escaped being hanged, and though he avoided the noose or cell, James Bulloch never returned home. Even the Court of St. James's got a hand slap—in this case, for the Crown's connivance in the building and equipping of the cruisers. Eventually, under the Alabama Claims, an international diplomatic and legal action, the United States was permitted to sue Great Britain for the losses suffered by Confederate warships and privateers. The $15.5 million awarded in 1872 was eventually distributed to the shipowners, captains, and crews for both real and imagined or inflated losses. (For loss of clothes, nautical instruments, and other private effects from the burning of the *Jireh Swift*, Williams put in a claim for $13,634.98.) The money may have been a bit of a balm to the whaling industry for the stings of the war, but didn't revive it.

Ultimately, it's fair to say that the only party involved with whaling to have come out well from the Civil War was that of the hunted cetaceans. "It is entirely possible that the Confederacy's legacy may include saving the whales by hastening the end of a dying whaling trade," suggested one present-day Charleston historian. "Had the *Alabama* and *Shenandoah* never sailed, several species of whales might now be extinct."

By 1870, the rough, dangerous, and rather unsavory enterprise that the tough-minded Friends had birthed was old enough to be venerable, a sure sign its end was near. It had weathered two rounds of British wars and one homegrown conflict, survived the rise and fall of capital markets, the Gold Rush, and the westward migration. It had overcome all challengers, including Holland, France, Spain, and Russia. Yankee whaling seemed doomed, and the ports that conducted it were fewer. Nantucket had in November 1869 seen the *Oak,* the last of her whalers, slip over the accursed bar in her harbor, writing the final chapter in that long and tortured history.

Although in 1865 the prices of oil skyrocketed to $2.55 a gallon for sperm, and $1.21 for whale oil, and whalebone fetched $1.37 per pound, the prices gradually sank to their 1861 levels. To make it worse, not only was profit elusive, so was the supply. "Newly discovered whaling grounds, like gold mines, are soon overcrowded and worked out, the whales being either killed or driven away," as the naturalist Muir observed. The sperm had become inexplicably shy, and as its numbers apparently shrank, so had that part of the fleet devoted to slaying and flensing it, now a fraction of its size a few decades prior.

The whaling grounds that had been fished out two decades before weren't recovering. With the application of the invariable law that unrestrained greed will eventually destroy every resource that feeds it, these beasts were vanishing as well. The bowheads, which had almost single-flukedly supported the industry, were getting fewer and smarter, and thus harder to catch, and the general take was declining. Each year the ships sailed past the Bering Strait earlier, stayed longer, and ventured ever farther north, only to compete for a shrinking supply.

Moreover, the value of the products was as uncertain as spring ice. Although whalebone could support hoop skirts or be used as a buggy whip to snap at the rear of a steed, it was unable to support the profitability of the ever-lengthening voyages. The season of 1868 was poor, and 1870 an "un-remuneritive year," to use the ponderous phrase of the *Shipping List,* whose editorialist predicted—correctly—the next year would be worse. Even the owners of the great Wing Fleet, the largest in New Bedford, were charging double for the wares supplied in the slop chest.

If the Civil War had proved to be the first iron fastened to the victim, the stinking gases and liquids of the earth would lance its life. Though denounced by whalers because of their disagreeable habit of sometimes blowing up after ignition, the mineral illuminants camphene and kerosene were becoming the oils of choice. Bowing to the inevitable, even New Bedford had a gasworks and a kerosene distillery, and San Francisco housed a factory to distill camphene and refine whale oil, too.

Speaking metaphorically, the patient that was the industry was dying, and not just from external assault; he'd apparently also lost his internal will to survive. Without a return on investment any longer guaranteed, the owners' capital, the nourishing, life-sustaining blood of any enterprise, was not going back to underwrite the near slavery of the ships. Rather, it headed into other near-slavery concerns, such as factory cotton spinning, or it was flowing to the west, where ventures, legitimate or not, such as the railroads, were paying a premium. As the money left the industry like oil from a leaky cask, it ceased to pay for the slaughter of whales, and supported the killing off of what was most desirable and available in the west. (Even old Rodney French headed to Colorado to squeeze out the silver wealth in the region's guts. Reportedly, he also participated in trying to draft a state constitution, but so stuffed it with verbiage to elevate the status of Africans that he managed to block the document completely.) Some ships were left to rot at anchor, and the longer they sat idle, the more costly was the refitting, which ultimately became a prohibitive task.

The shrewd players were pulling out, men like the maniacally cheap Quaker "Blackhawk" Jack Robinson, also called "Napoleon," allegedly because of the way he ran his whaling business. His burly frame was a familiar sight on the waterfront and his booming voice, raised in yells at his men, was a regular treat for the ears. Married into one of the many rivulets of the Mississippi that was the Howland family, his father-in-law was Gideon Howland ("Uncle Gid"), who'd done some whaling in his youth. (He reportedly once pushed his shoulder against the side of the *William Hamilton* as the whaler was setting sail, and yelled: "I've sent her off.")

His fortune had started with Isaac Howland Jr., a diminutive ninety-five-pound illiterate, who had established his house as one of the most eminent in New Bedford, and began a fortune that eventually became one of the largest on the planet. With an eye for a bargain, he'd made his fortune by purchasing silk stockings from the men on his ships, washing them—presumably with great thoroughness—and after ironing them, reselling the garments.

At one point, the shrewd Blackhawk owned a piece of the *Charles Morgan,* the last Yankee whaler still afloat in the twenty-first century. Despite his wealth, he smoked five-cent cigars, and even once declined a free ten-cent stogie for fear it would spoil his taste for the cheaper brand. Among the precepts he shared with his daughter and business apprentice Hetty was to owe nothing—not even a kindness. The training paid off: While still a young woman, Hetty's lust for wealth inspired her to create a crude forgery of her aunt's signature on a fabricated will that left a suspiciously large amount of money to her. When caught, she left the country until the statute of limitations ran out—although the resentment of her cheated family was, apparently, eternal.

As the ship of whaling began to founder, Blackhawk decided it was time to pull out his precious money from the soon-to-be hulk. Hetty Green, through her marriage to Edward Henry Green, later turned that stake into a vast pot of gold. Even while expanding her treasure, which she defended and nurtured like a she-bear does a beloved cub, this Quaker woman with her vast investments in railroads and real estate managed to live in a dire poverty that could've been the envy of the purest and poorest Franciscan. It was almost sad: In a more normal family, she might have had a chance to achieve something like humanity. The mania of hoarding money not only robbed her of anything recognizable as normal human happiness, but even of fleeting pleasures, such as relief from pain. Despite her riches, she refused to hire a doctor to treat the hernia she'd developed from lifting heavy bank ledgers—or for an operation for her son's injured leg until amputation became inevitable. Her husband, doomed to die estranged from both prosperity and wife, was forced to pay for that grim procedure out of his own pocket. After her spouse's personal financial ruin, Hetty refused to bail him out. She obviously didn't believe in sending good money after bad.

To be fair, Hetty's awful lifestyle paid off in some sense: It made her—and her terrier, Cutie Dewey, under whose name she lived and hid her money—powerful. At the height of her financial reign, this black-garbed "Witch of Wall Street," crashed banks, played Shylock to New York City, and sent lethal financial tidal waves flying through the republic. At last, during an argument with a maid, death presented his bill for her to pay, and the much-swollen Howland fortune passed on to become probably the most undertaxed and least charitably distributed in history, according to one estimate. (As if in revenge, Hetty's one-legged son, the jolly playboy "Colonel" Green, managed to put a considerable dent in the estate, investing heavily in pornography and odd knickknacks—including the decrepit old whaler, the *Charles W. Morgan,* which he kept moored near his mansion at Round Hill, Dartmouth.)

In the same era, another Quaker had enough faith, however misplaced, to make a considerable reinvestment in blubbering. In 1867, high-minded George Howland Jr., the onetime mayor of New Bedford and employer of Frederick Douglass, wagered the unheard-of sum of $100,000 in fitting out a fine-looking new ship, the *Concordia.* Complicit with him in this act of near vanity and waste was his half brother Matthew, the ship's name being a tribute to their long partnership. Completing the rakish craft was the figurehead of the eponymous goddess herself, in whose grasp was both the horn of plenty—a mistake, given current conditions—and an olive branch. Despite this gesture, finances were in such decline in the Howland countinghouse that just a few years later, their chief clerk was enjoined to painstakingly slit the incoming envelopes so that accountants could later use them for doing computations.

After the Civil War, the competition to hunt down a command was fierce, and Williams had to bide his time until the familiar old *Florida* became available. Since he'd sold her in 1861, she'd proven an unsuccessful freight ship, and she was now his to take for a blubber voyage. After a trip back east to buy some whaling boats and gear, in April 1866, he put to sea from San Francisco, with Eliza and five-year-old Mary Watkins at his side again. In April 1867, while sailing in the Japan Sea, Eliza gave birth to another daughter, whom she called Flora. Later that same year, the voyage concluded and Williams returned to dock both the *Florida* and his family in California.

Whaling, as always, was changing, and acknowledging a Pacific-wards shift in the industry, Williams moved his family to the infant town of Oakland, which sat on the eastern edge of San Francisco Bay. After settling his affairs back east, late in 1869, he sailed to Hawaii to take command of the ship *Hibernia*. That same year Flora died, and an undoubtedly grief-stricken Eliza took Willie and Mary with her on a steamer to Hawaii to join her husband. The re-united family sailed out on the *Hibernia* on March 16, 1870.

After sailing from Hawaii and passing through the Aleutians, Williams had been forced to wait four weeks for the Bering Sea ice to break up so he could move farther north. Like other whalers, he was pressing up to Point Barrow to get at his quarry, thus increasing his risk. At least he had a good ship, the 550-ton *Hibernia,* possibly the biggest whaler in the fleet of 1870, and under full canvas, with double topsails on each mast and three royals, she was handsome. She was strong, but lacked reinforcement forward, so the crew shielded her bow with lashed-together mats of old hawsers and rafts of southern California ironwood.

Nevertheless, her weight and thus momentum made the measures useless—"everyone knew it when she hit a cake of ice," as his son Willie noted. She struck one such cake—a "submerged ram of an ice floe" off Point Barrow on August 28 and was condemned and auctioned off for a reported $150. (Men from the whaler *Helen Snow* salvaged the bone and whale oil off her in September.) Deprived of a vessel for the second time in a half decade, Williams was reduced to sailing back to Honolulu as a guest of Captain Barney Cogan of the *Josephine*. During what must have been for Williams a depressing voyage, an odd thing happened: One of the *Josephine*'s boat crews killed a whale. By the time they were taken up to the deck, the men, from the waist down, were frozen solid into the boat. After being freed from the craft, the men swallowed some liquor, and the coddling ended there.

14

Death Stared Us in the Face

When thy wares went forth out of the seas, thou filledst many people; thou didst enrich the kings of the earth with the multitude of thy riches and of thy merchandise. In the time when thou shalt be broken by seas in the depth of thy waters thy merchandise and all thy company in the midst of thee shall fall.

—*Ezekiel 27: 33–34*

Danger was ever present; Death and the whalemen touched elbows continuously.

—*Captain John Cook, on Arctic whaling*

OCTOBER, 1870, SHIP *JAPAN*, ARCTIC OCEAN, OFF THE COAST OF ALASKA

It was a rare thing to see—a completely jolly whaling crew. But then again, the final whale had been taken, the hatches battened by the carpenter, the gear declared snug and secure and the yards squared, and the Australian whaler *Japan* rode the stiff breeze of a northwest gale. Behind them was that section of Arctic Ocean called the "cowyard," so named because of the many bowheads slaughtered there, and the crew was going home. It had been with some relief the men had learned their master Frederick Barker had officially closed the hunting season they had waited so anxiously to end. After all, even the American whalers had already sailed home, some traveling 4,000 miles back to New Bedford. The bowheads that had lured the fleet up here had also left for their mysterious winter hiding place, and every day the *Japan* stayed in the Arctic, the less likely her crew would see Melbourne again. In relief, the mariners sang with a joy so intense it seemed they would be unable to belt out another tune, and happiness was "the order of the hour."

Leaving "the dreary regions of the north," the crew was already counting the days and hours it would take to escape, and the men entertained pleasant thoughts of home, friends, and family, noted one observer. There was no danger on the horizon—yet. The *Japan* was unique: Though her master was a Yankee, she had been the first English ship fitted through the "Victorian Agency" and had left the prior spring, with the well wishes of Melbourne to power her, and to that city she would return. At least they had some memories worth remembering: The summer had been grand, with the sun making the ice resemble "massive piles of burnished gold" that shone like rainbows, too painful to the eye.

Usually returning whalers headed down to the Aleutians, slipped through the channel between Onimack and Akontan islands, and sailed into the Bering Sea. Once in the North Pacific, a blubber hunter figured the dangers of the Arctic were behind, and it would be a short time before San Francisco or Diamondhead hove into view. The officers and captain no longer had to man the deck around the clock, because now all they faced were the ordinary challenges. Every face and conversation shone with gratitude.

In the *Japan*'s case, there was a lot to be grateful for, as the hunting had been rough all summer, particularly in the past weeks, when the conditions had become the wildest and most trying. During their labors, the fearful and anxious crew had watched great ice floes surround them, even threatening to bar their exit across the Bering Strait, through which they had slipped the prior March. Venturing into this region was like sticking one's head into a polar bear's mouth—one never knew when the jaws might slam shut.

That season had been rough going for the *Japan,* too. Gusts swept over jagged ice fields and down precipices with gathering force before striking the ship broadside, making her planks bend and creak. The "almost unbearable" wind was strong enough to cut right through jackets and shirts to tender flesh, and it made a disagreeable moaning song in the rigging, said one of the *Japan*'s crew. Sometimes the gusts drove ice floes together so hard, their motion and huge weight translated into a rolling thunder that drowned out even their own screams.

There was no way to predict what might happen in the course of a few hours in the Arctic. At the drop of a beaver hat, a wild shipwrecking gale might howl down from the top of the world. The conditions had become yet nastier after Barker had gambled on a push up to the well-named Icy Cape. Although he had already filled the lower holds with casks of oil, tons of whalebone, and a bounty of ivory from walrusing, he wanted yet more treasure, and anticipated more brisk and prosperous times farther north. Certainly the Old Man knew the chances he was taking, but as he put it, perhaps fibbing, "the weather had been so fine and the fishing so good," he'd prolonged the chase. (His assessment of the summer conditions was challenged by the testimony of another master in the fleet of '70, who noted the harsh weather had made this a rather unfavorable season.) Despite the danger of being jammed in, the crewmen had with the grim heroism of whalers kept the try-pots lit, and the boiling continued until Barker's high-risk wager with his and their lives paid off, they having in less than a trimester harvested two thousand barrels of oil.

Before he dropped anchor in Melbourne Harbor, Barker still had to get the *Japan* through some of the worst waters on the globe. The dangers of whaling up in the Arctic were so great, it was guaranteed that a ship or two would be lost each season, and a master could only hope it wouldn't be his. In this lottery, at least he had some odds in his favor, as the *Japan* was "as good a craft as ever entered Behring Strait," and "well found in every respect" and the crew was "as good, noble set of men as ever struck a whale." Barker himself was a proven captain, intelligent and well spoken—not necessarily prerequisites to being a whaler. It had been he, when he commanded the *Robert Towns* of Sydney at the close of the Civil War, who'd recognized the *Shenandoah* during her Arctic prowl and tried to warn the fleet of her presence. After the war had closed, Barker was one of those whaling masters lucky enough to be able to keep hunting.

As the bow plowed southwest from the coast of Alaska, the cold was already intense and ice formed on the shore. The change in weather made the voyage riskier, and needless to say, less pleasant by the day; the sun became obscured, making it impossible to calculate a position. By October 2, the *Japan* was far enough south to pass the great headland of Cape Lisburne, a popular spot for needy whalers to get wood and water or to repair a damaged vessel. To avoid the dangerous headlands and currents of the

Kamchatka Sea (the Bering Sea waters lying between the Pribilof Islands on the west and south of Cape Navarin), Barker now guided the vessel northward, which improved the ship's bad estate. But two days after passing Cape Lisburne, a gale blew in and a duel between heavy weather and the crew was joined. Ice cracked on bow and stern, and above the wind's scream was the dull thunder of colliding floes. Such a roar ended with a crack, followed by a splash, as chunks of broken ice crumbled into the sea.

Apprehensive, Barker scanned the horizon for another sail, but there was no one there to keep him company as he started his downward slide in earnest. On the seventh, the weather's anger grew to a fury that would have astonished anyone unfamiliar with these regions, with the masts bending and creaking with frightening violence. In response, the hard-laboring crew hove to under two lower topsails, and still, during one awful stretch, the *Japan* spent four hours on her beam ends. When morning arrived, the crew hoisted the whaleboats to the davit heads, lashed them securely, and cleared the wreckage off the main deck.

At dusk the next day, Barker saw something unexpected but reassuring through his spyglass on the port bow. Sailing before the wind was the whaleship *Massachusetts*. Barker, according to one account, decided to follow her, presuming the other master knew what path to take, and the two vessels lay to for the night. Before the dreary Sunday dawn, the wind got nastier, and a northerly gale blew in with snow. Fearing the *Japan* might be unable to weather the storm, Barker ran up a distress call on his mast, which the captain of the *Massachusetts* may not have seen. Just after signaling, the mountains of Siberia appeared on the starboard, and realizing how close he was to the coast, Barker tacked offshore, followed by the *Massachusetts*.

After breakfast, both vessels were put before the wind (with the wind to their aft), and the *Japan,* being the swifter, took the lead. It was rough going. She rolled from side to side, shipping water, and climbed up on boiling sea billows that next sent her bounding forward as if in flight, until she dropped into a trough to await the inevitable levitation again. To make it yet worse, the sea spray and puddled water on deck turned to ice, and a slip here could be fatal. At about 10:00 A.M., a thick fog closed over her and only the wailing of the troubled sea and the screams of the storm were audible. The stage was set for the *Japan*'s final act to draw to its close. "The next morning the gale blew harder if possible," as Barker recorded, and the snow came down so thick a crewman couldn't see half a ship's length. The binnacle and cabin lamps were lit to compensate. Although she ran only under lower topsails and storm sails, the gale pushed the vessel on at "racehorse speed." After ordering the helm put to starboard and the ship braced up sharp—turning the yards to the most oblique angle possible to lie best with the wind—breakers appeared off the weather bow. They were too close to shore to clear land, and the *Massachusetts* was still astern. After breakfast, the watch gloomily turned into their bunks to sleeplessly wait for the end, in a forecastle so penetrated by cold even the blankets were frozen stiff.

At noon, eight bells were sounded, reminding some men of a funeral dirge. Then there was a loud cry: "Land right ahead!" The dismal news traveled from one end of the ship to the other, working like electricity, and every man below took to his feet and clambered above, some only half dressed, others at least in boots and jackets. With Siberia looming before him, and the breakers just a few cable lengths off, from his spot by the mizzenmast Barker ordered the ship put hard to port.

The *Japan* answered the helm, but after the braces were let go to keep her out of the line of breakers, the headland of East Cape appeared rudely a few miles off to the northwest. He was heading for an accidental landfall. Seeing his true position, Barker countermanded himself with the order to sail to starboard. But now the *Japan* ignored the rudder and slipped within the line of breakers, and with that went all hope, for now she was doomed to run aground where the waves would smash her to atoms.

"Just then, to add to our horrors, a huge wave swept over the ship parting the whaleboats from the davits and sweeping the decks clean," recalled Barker. "Our situation was now most critical; death truly stared us in the face." The yards swung down on the deck, and a heavy wave rolled over the *Japan*'s stern, smashing the wheelhouse and washing overboard the steward, the blacksmith, and the carpenter, who alone made a brief reappearance before vanishing again permanently.

If the ship went to pieces here the outcome was clear. "No man could live a minute in the sea, which heaved and foamed around us and dashed with such fury upon the crags, which were but a biscuit's throw from our deck." Her sails in tatters, the now-unmanageable *Japan* careened so that those on deck clutched the halyards to keep their footing. Barker knew the ship was beyond saving, and possibly the crew as well. Every moment the danger worsened, and the embattled master knew that "what was to be done must be done quickly."

"Keep her head dead for the shore!" he called.

The *Japan* ran on past the "dangerous point" where the sea had struck her toward a small beach, that, optimistically speaking, offered them the slightest chance of reaching the shore on foot (as opposed to washing up there dead). The current and wind nearly pushed the *Japan* past the landing point, with the helmsman keeping the course as best he could. With "terrific force," the stern ran aground on an East Cape shingle beach, and as a finale, a breaker crashed into her starboard quarter and set the *Japan* on her side. She was beached.

"If ever a happy crew trod ship's deck it was that of the *Japan*. Our rescue had been almost miraculous, and the revulsion of feeling from the deepest despair to joyous hope was so great that for a moment not a man was able to move; but consciousness quickly returned and a general rush was made for the shore," Barker recounted. As long as they remained on board, their lives were in constant danger. A mate became fouled in the falls of a whaleboat and was unable to free himself. Grabbing at the ship's side in desperation, he begged a young Australian who was nearby on deck, "For God's sake cut the line." However, the youth was dressed only in flannel drawers and his limbs were already too numb for them or him to be of use, and, unaided, a backwater soon carried the mate to sea.

This wasn't the time to dwell on anyone else's death or to hesitate. Each man had to go overboard and slog through the surf up a steep beach in a temperature so cold it made the water freeze anywhere it touched the ship. Two men, apparently a bit squeamish, decided to stay on board and "miserably perished." The rest of them took their chances by plunging into the freezing soup and making it to the fogbound shore, where at least starvation would take a little longer to kill them than the climate.

Some of the castaways started getting comfortable on the snow-covered shore and became sleepy, drowsiness being one of the last stages of hypothermia. One wretch sat down long enough so that when his mates found and lifted him up, he went into his death throes. Luckier yet was another shipwrecked whaler who tried to lie on the ground to fall into a sleep that would most likely have been eternal, but who was stopped only by diligent friends. Two of the more vigorous mariners who literally wanted to keep their blood from freezing in their veins started running on the beach, and thus stumbled over something encouraging: a set of dog tracks in the snow. With the fog lifting, they followed the prints to a nearby village, or to be more exact, a wretched cluster of huts, populated by the Chukchi natives. Having chanced on this lifesaving prize, they returned to the beach to fetch their comrades.

These Chukchis were far-off kin to the Eskimos who lived across the strait, although described in the blunt language of the time as being more "Mongol" [Asian] in appearance. The coastline they inhabited was rugged and barren, with only moss and herbs thriving on it; beyond, there was a flat, dull interior. Being at the edge of the czar's vast and messy empire, they were unused to the presence of whites and were surprised by their sudden presence on this day. As these natives owned little, with the sea yielding up a bounty for them by way of the *Japan*'s wreckage, they headed to shore. But not only did they rescue the smashed bulwarks of the *Japan* now washing up on the beach, but her dislodged men as well. Hospitality being one of their virtues, the Chukchis gave the whalers skins to replace their ice-covered clothes and raw putrid walrus blubber to eat, this fare being a "great luxury" in the village. They were surprised the whalers turned it down.

While the crew worked to shore, Barker, still on board, went back down below to get his chronometer, log, papers, and provisions. He hoped another well-placed wave might put the ship on higher ground and out of the reach of the punishing surf, where she could serve as a shelter or at least let the crew unload her cargo. While carrying his goods back through the hatchway, another wave crashed over the *Japan*. Knocked backward, Barker dropped all his booty, which washed overboard, and so the persistent master scrambled belowdecks for another three hours trying to find clothes, food, and "spirits for the relief" of his men.

Peering to shore, he saw a few of his men struggling through the white-topped waves, trying to grab at the flotsam that had come loose from the wreckage—barrels, rope, staves, or tools—anything that might mean the difference between life and death on this forlorn tip of Asia. Carrying what few items he could manage, Barker made the deck, where he found only the foremast still standing. Although the mizzenmast had snapped, its backstays hadn't parted, and so taking these in hand to use as lifelines, he jumped overboard and worked to shore.

When on land, instead of dying on the beach alone, unmourned, and frozen like an icicle, Barker found the natives waiting for him, and they had even managed to find enough driftwood to kindle a fire. Learning the near-dead white was master of the ship, the natives loaded him on a dogsled and hauled him to their small village. His teeth chattering uncontrollably, Barker saw by the wayside the bodies of the *Japan*'s dead.

"To me it appeared hard that these poor fellows," wrote Barker, "after battling the storm so many days, undergoing such sufferings and facing death in so many forms, should be stricken down at the very moment when they had seemingly secured their own safety, and thus be frozen to death within the light of the very fires the natives had lit for their succor." Survival was not exactly a pleasure, as the whalers were badly frostbitten, and Barker in such agony he thought his teeth would freeze off. Just as he became certain he couldn't endure another minute of the cold, the sled halted in a cluster of huts in the village of three hundred.

Barker tried to pick himself up and run for the door of one of the crude dwellings, but his frozen legs gave way and he collapsed in paralysis. The Chukchis, unable to say anything that Barker might have understood, put him back on the sled, and to aid them, he kept still. While unable to move and feeling certain he was freezing to death, Barker was lifted off the sled and carried like a "clod of earth" into the chief's hut. Showing Chukchi hospitality, the headman's wife removed the master's wet boots and stockings and placed his frozen feet between her breasts to restore warmth, something that might have struck those in New Bedford as a bit carnal.

Barker passed out, but when he awoke, he learned eight of his thirty men were dead, and he and the survivors were now subject to the savages' tender mercies, which fortunately, were surprisingly considerable. The perceptive Yankee master later claimed that despite the harsh landscape here, "nowhere is the noblest of Christian virtue more generously displayed than among the ignorant, poverty-stricken tribes that live upon the borders of the frozen seas of the North." They shared all they had and did everything they could to relieve the hapless mariners' sufferings, which were far from trivial.

A more wretched place than this would be hard to find. The East Cape's landmark granite bluff, two thousand feet high, was capped with a crown of snow even in July. The dwellings were far from luxurious. The Chukchi huts sprouted from drifts of heavy snow near the on-shore breakers, and they offered the whalers little comfort. Descriptions of them say the exteriors were of skins stretched over erect poles in the shape of a peaked cone, about twenty feet in diameter by twelve feet high, with an inner chamber formed by hanging closely stitched reindeer hides over a small wooden frame. The inhabitants trod on floors of dirt mixed with hairy paste on which fires were kindled to cook what little blubber wasn't devoured in its raw state. From the ceiling dangled ivory-headed spears, arrows, and slabs of seal, walrus, and whale blubber. Inside was a tight universe wherein dwelt puppies and nursing bitches and children— human—snuggled in pots "making a kind of squalor that is picturesque and daring beyond conception." Not surprisingly, the air was stagnant and stank of smoke, rotting blubber, and humans packed closely together for months at a time—except when the Arctic sea wind blasted through the many holes in the hut's exterior and howled furiously through the driftwood rafters.

Nevertheless, being in the hut was better than being left outside to die, and this village was to be Barker's home for the winter—if he could last. He had a mother and sisters living on Maxfield Street in New Bedford. They'd be wondering if he was indeed lost at sea or might someday again come walking up Water Street, like Lazarus, a man back from the dead. Barker's wife in New Zealand would be scanning the horizon for his ship for a long time. As for the *Massachusetts,* she'd vanished and would or could offer no help. Apparently her master had decided not to follow the *Japan*'s example and moved on. The lottery of survival had been favorable to him that year, and there was no reason to push his luck further.

Thus closed, at least temporarily, another grim story of Arctic misfortune. One might wonder just why the blubber fleet was venturing so far north into places so undesirable. For good reason, the region had terrified Europeans for centuries. To get any idea of how badly, consider one example. In a move designed to bolster its northern whale fishery, the English Crown gave a group of condemned murderers the choice of commutation if they merely existed in Greenland for one winter. After their arrival at their camp, and seeing what they'd be facing, the men chose to go home and die quicker rather than slower. Nevertheless, to the north the whalers continued to go, and they managed to chalk up some impressive disasters. In 1777, 350 wrecked whalers and sealers trekked over the ice of Greenland toward safety: 150 survived. So lethal was Melville Bay, it acquired the moniker of the "breaking up yard," and at one point, there were a thousand men camped on the ice there. No one died, but in a drunken melee called the "Boffin Fair," they burned their ships.

The stories of Arctic misfortune were nearly endless. One of the grislier ones, which may be legendary but whose details are chillingly vivid and accurate, was from an English master named John Warrens. In August 1775, Warrens was sailing in the eastern Arctic in the *Try Again,* a type of whaler called a Greenlandman. While drifting among a pack of icebergs, Warrens came across a snow-covered derelict brig, sails tattered and yards swinging, floating aimlessly. He dropped one of his boats and pulled to the vessel, named the *Gloriana.* On approach, there was no answer to his calls, and he soon discovered this was a floating, frozen sepulcher. Down below in one cabin was a corpse with a green damp mold growing on the cheeks and still-open eyes; there was a quill frozen in one hand, as if it were about to write once more in the ship's log. The final entry, dated November 11, 1762, was: "We have now been 17 days in the ice. The fire went out yesterday, and our master has been trying ever since to kindle it again without success. His wife died this . . ."

Leaving the writer in his place, the whalers quickly entered the main cabin, where in one berth was a well-preserved female body. By the cabin stove was another corpse, holding steel in one hand and flint in the other, nearby was some tinder. The corpses of the *Gloriana*'s crew were frozen into their bunks in their blankets. Understandably, Warrens soon grabbed the log and fled off the ship to head for open ocean in the *Try Again.* Or at least he did in the yarn. Even if Warrens fibbed, he had accurately depicted what undoubtedly was the fate of countless lost whalers in the Arctic.

In 1832, the *Shannon* of Hull, England, smashed into an iceberg that ripped open her starboard side and sent her almost completely below in minutes, killing sixteen men and three boys. The rest of the crew survived in a part of the ship that was kept afloat by trapped air. While in this precarious state, three more men died. The rest drank each other's blood to survive. One despairing whaler went above to the deck to kill himself and happened to see two nearby Danish brigs that subsequently rescued them.

In 1866 the *Diana,* one of the small fleet of Scottish whalers, put off from the Shetland Island to Davis Strait where she vanished without a trace. So overdue was she, a reward was posted for information about her whereabouts. Next April, she hobbled into Rona Voe Harbor, a battered ice-crushed ghost ship, sails and cordage cut away, her deck covered with the dead and those soon to die. In all, ten corpses were awaiting disposal. Those few strong enough to dump them over had lacked the heart to do it. She'd been trapped in the ice, and despite the surgeon's constant efforts, scurvy had worked wonders to reduce the crew's number, the master himself being the first die. To survive, the crew had chopped up her boats and spars for firewood to keep alive.

Those still living weren't in much better condition than the dead. Thirty-five men were helplessly sick, and even with rescue at hand, the helmsman fainted. Just three men crawled on deck when the *Diana* arrived in harbor, and only two men were still able to go aloft. One wretch died in his berth as his would-be rescuers boarded. Another day in that state and the ship would have become a "common tomb."

Understandably, probing through the Bering Strait to hunt bowheads had been an intimidating proposition. It had taken until July 23, 1848, for the plucky Thomas Roys of Sag Harbor (a port at the eastern end of Long Island) in his bark *Superior,* riding a four-knot current, to manage to get a crew north across the Bering Strait. He planned to hunt the fatty and baleen-rich *Eubalaena mysticetus* (bowhead whale).

For pioneer Roys, the tale of the historic voyage through Bering Strait had begun during a hunt in the Sea of Okhotsk. A whale cut his boat in half with its flukes and dumped him into the frigid water, leaving him with an injured cheek, two broken ribs, and, apparently, a case of exposure. So bad were his hurts, after rescue, he landed in Siberia to recover. While recuperating, a Russian told him of seeing a large number of whales north of the Bering Strait in waters that had been so dangerous some called them the "River Styx." The presence of leviathans there was contradicted by the common wisdom of the blubber hunters of the time—but being a man to ask why not rather than why, Roys paid the huge sum of $100 for charts of the region, and decided secretly to see for himself.

On his first voyage to the region, neither the conservative firm of Grinnell, Minturn & Co., which owned the *Superior,* nor the crew knew Roys was going to this unknown and terrifying region. It was quite a gamble: He was facing the crushing power of the owners, the hostility of the officers and crew, and the danger and difficulties of working through the ice. He'd be yielding only to impossibilities, so to speak. If anyone on board had possessed an inkling of what he was doing, as Roys put it, "I should have been considered a madman and turned out of the ship."

A colorful and tough man in a colorful and rough time, he was taking a huge risk, which was nothing new for him. He had already probed farther south than any other whaler, nearly reaching Antarctica. Roys, whose red hair was prone to bristle when he was excited, once boasted of having been knocked out of a whaleboat after which he rode on the backs of two whales. A third whale knocked him back into his craft, after which he slew all three monsters with his lance, or so he said.

He was an inventor and while on the deck of the whaler *W. F. Safford* off the coast of France, in one of his endless—and largely fruitless—efforts to devise new whale-slaying weapons, he pulled the trigger of a bomb gun he himself had commissioned. There was an explosion that blew him backward without knocking him down. The gun had malfunctioned. He asked who'd been hurt and was awaiting a reply when he saw a finger on the deck, still encircled by a familiar ring. It was his own digit, now merely a fragment of his ruined hand. The wound was numb, and Roys ordered his mate to cut off what was left of the stump with a razor. His lower arm had to be amputated but despite the doctors' gloomy predictions, he survived to kill many more whales. Later, Roys, in a beaver hat and a suit, had his portrait taken facing the camera with his port side front, the sleeve revealing his stump.

Clearly, Roys was an uncommon man. Now, during his first stab at the Arctic Ocean, the sun finally appeared through steady fog and rain, and the mate realized they were at 65 degrees north latitude. "Great God, where is he going with the ship?" he asked. "I have never heard of a whale in that latitude before! We shall all be lost!" He collapsed, weeping, in his bunk. The secret was out and the men were ready to mutiny.

To ensure cooperation, Roys carried a Blunt & Sims revolver, although it was so dilapidated it was more effective thrown than fired. The master's hunch was justified when at last they saw the dark back of the polar whale on the surface of the water. "Clear away the boats," ordered Roys. "We will see what he is." His boat was even the first to fasten to these near-tame whales, and another chapter in Yankee whaling began.

The first whale died at around midnight—illuminated by the latitude's unique arrangement of perpetual lighting. A new field had opened to the whalers. Despite the dangers, the penetration of the Arctic paid hand-somely: Within three years, 250 ships were clogging the Bering passage to keep on with the harvest. With their arrival, in the normal course of bow-head hunting, the number of lost ships increased.

Not every Arctic ruin was spectacular. In 1865, after taking too much of a strain on her windlass during cutting in a bowhead in the western Arctic, the bark *Willis* was condemned, one of nine to be ruined in this re-gion that decade, showing there wasn't any need for Confederates to help reduce the fleet's numbers.

15

In the Topmost Frost-Killed End of Creation

Had it [the gale] not moderated as soon as it did, we should, by 10 A.M.,
have been shaking hands with our departed friends.
—*Captain Pease, master of the* Champion,
caught in a gale in the Arctic in 1870

NORTH PACIFIC, SPRING 1871

For each ship lost to the Arctic, another sailed in and caulked, as it were, the seam left open by her departure. Among those too stubborn to stop whaling, either from love or morbid need, was, of course, Thomas William Williams, whose quarterdeck now was the *Monticello* of New London. The master was again returning with the regularity of the bowhead itself to the Arctic and its attendant dangers. As he must have known, each trip he made increased the likelihood that at some point he wouldn't make it back. Despite his bad luck with the *Hibernia,* the prior November he had not only picked up another vessel to make war on the Arctic, but was even taking Eliza, Stancel, Willie, and Mary.

Maybe it was something in the family blood. After sitting out the prior season for school in Oakland, his son Stancel was serving under him, perhaps as mate. Although his father had destined him for a quite different and safer career on land, the young man wanted to follow the maritime life. It was too bad. His family knew he was too smart for whaling. He didn't have the luck for it, as he'd discover. Even so, sensing a sea change, Williams at last had begun expanding his investments into other businesses, including, somewhat traitorously, the rival coal oil industry in San rancisco. (An 1866 venture in woolen goods, undertaken with an inventor who made faulty machines, failed by 1868.) However, all these land-based enterprises he'd abandoned to prosper or wither on their own while he was at sea. Clearly what mattered most to him was whaling.

As was the custom, the *Monticello* sailed from Honolulu to the South Pacific for a "between season cruise" to break in the crew. She stopped at the picturesque port of Yokohama, whose entrance was a gut of water situated between two mountains, to take on provisions. Among them was a load of eggs, and of these young Willie ate so many he got sick of them. Too much of anything is a bad thing, as he later observed. That was the lot of a whaler: One moment you feasted on a single thing till you sickened of it, then you suffered famine. Williams next headed north, for the real work of Arctic hunting to begin.

The *Monticello* was a former Greenland whaler, well armored, with stout timber braces under the forecastle and before the fore hatch. In addition, she carried an extra course of oak planking several feet up, and, under the waterline, iron plating ran from the bow toward the back. Besides a good reliable ship, Williams had a seasoned crew of men who sang to every task—cutting in, working the windlass, raising anchor. It was known a song was as good as ten men; if so, he had as many as three hundred mariners on board.

A sailor couldn't sing and harbor a grudge, Willie recalled, and most of the men could belt out a yodel. The second mate even improvised songs, and when the ship was in port or by another vessel, the audience gave the crew new life as they worked. It was a joy to watch them snap to for an order, and the officers never had to beg for another pull on the rope or needed to tell them to belay before a line parted. On dark nights, when they were reefing topsails, every man would repeat orders like, "Haul out to windward," and they acted as one.

Either Willie was gilding the past in his recollections, or his ship was an exception, because the quality of the crews in other vessels was markedly inferior to the *Monticello*'s. This reflected a general slump in both the whaling and merchant fleets that had started after the war. The great spouter days were closing fast.

The most able men turned to other enterprises. "As the better types of Americans forsook the forecastles, their bunks were filled by criminal or lascivious adventurers, by a motley collection of South Sea Islanders known as Kanakas, by cross-breed Negroes and Portuguese from the Azores and Cape Verdes, and by the outcasts and renegades from all the merchant services of both the Old World and the New," as the lily-white whaling historian Elmo Hohman once wrote.

Of course, it had been a "motley" rough bunch that had served as the muscle of the fleet since the 1840s. Owners, agents, and captains regularly had been looking out beyond the cobblestone streets of Nantucket or New Bedford for labor, and long gone were the somewhat misnamed Golden Days when a man could look around in his whaleboat and see his boyhood friends, or a cousin or two from Holmes Hole or Dartmouth by his side. The great Nantucket blue bloods, so celebrated by Melville, had forsaken the harpoon. For decades, derelicts, outcasts, semicriminals, and lost souls had supplied the fishery with its fair share of incompetence, brutality, stupidity, and inefficiency, and they were becoming ever more prevalent and making it harder than ever for capable and decent men like Williams to succeed, given all the other mounting obstacles.

The bad pay was failing to attract new blood, and what little incentive there was for a neophyte with ability, explained ship owner Matthew Howland to a Canadian correspondent, was the chance to succeed. Although a green hand's first stab at whaling would net him something like $400 for his trouble—not figuring slop chest prices—no great fortune, he could use the experience to further his career quickly. "The promotion of an energetic young man, however, is rapid, since a large proportion of the foremost hands are ignorant blacks and men of mixed blood who have no ambition to rise," he wrote. That is, if the greenie managed to live long enough.

That 1871 season, the fleet headed to waters dangerous and stingy. As part of this human migration, early in May Williams entered the Bering Sea to the south side of Cape Thaddeus to meet the seasonal nemesis of the pack ice. He was one of forty masters from New Bedford, San Francisco, and Honolulu anxious to try their luck in the next-to-worst ocean in the world. Presumably he made good time. Williams was a fast sailer, who "never took things easy as with him time saved was time gained," as Willie observed. Whalers usually sailed through the "Seventy-two Pass"—the 172 meridian of longitude. After slipping through the Aleutians at the Amukta Pass west of the Islands of the Four Mountains, they beat to windward north into the Bering Sea. Some ventured up by Cape Olyutororski or through the Gulf of Alaska and Bristol Bay for northern right whales. Working northward from the Siberian side, they would usually meet the ice at 60 degrees north latitude.

As soon as the initial dazzle of the pack ice wore off, the master stared out at its fringes in the hopes of finding a crack or tear to enable him to penetrate its vitals. The view was of one sheer expanse of ice, broken periodically by small leads, and unless the wind blew hard, a ship hardly moved, which was at least refreshing for those who'd suffered the incessant pitch and roll of the Pacific. This year the wind was strong from the northeast, the ice closely packed, abundant, and uncooperative, and the *Monticello* remained in the floating city of whalers for two months. If the wind was favorable, the crew worked the rigging, although progress required many a detour and was never quick in this unusually heavy ice. Sometimes the bow was farther south than it had been on the day before.

The sailing here was, of course, extremely hazardous, if not, in fact, impossible. All the normal rules of navigation, to the degree there are any rules, ceased. A whaler might be held in the pack ice by an opposing current while his mates passed around him, in the meantime a welcoming corridor opened up overlooked. As part of the aquatic obstacles, there were black fogs so thick the rigging dripped, the decks remained wet, and rain and blinding snowstorms could wreak havoc for days at a time. "Just mention weather to any old whaler who has done service in the Arctic, sir, and he will cough scorn," noted one old whaleman. "It was terrible up there. . . . It would have been just as comfortable sailin' on a cake of ice." In July and August, all that could be exposed were one's hands.

And there was the ice, ranging from six to sixteen feet high, that moved with billions of tons behind it in deadweight, demanding wide-open eyes and a steady set of commands to the helmsman. Otherwise, one might hit a piece of loose ice hard enough to knock out "the ship's brains." According to Cape Cod whaler John Cook, the jobs of captains and mates weren't "sinecures," as they themselves, out of necessity, stood the monotonous watches in a crow's nest in biting cold, risking exposure, staying awake with cigars and coffee. The captain had to be awake, even more than the mates, and alert round the clock till he headed south, where he might as not meet gales. Only a fool ever let himself get comfortable, and certainly it must have been few that actually enjoyed it.

Sometimes a field of ice driven north by a strong, deep current collided with floes being pressured southward in a terrifying spectacle. "There was no escape of a craft that became caught between such battle lines," said Cook. For protection, the whalers, who usually hugged the land to be near the whales, worked behind a bar or shoal, and as the ice grounded, it would also pile up, "forming an immovable bulwark." However, if a whaler failed in this task, his vessel was pushed sideways and "ground piecemeal." Sometimes a master made friends with the enemy and fastened to a big ice floe and used it like a dock.

Because of the presence of the magnetic north pole, even a compass, so crucial to navigation in fog and foul weather, was unreliable, with variations of up to ninety degrees. The instruments sometimes took a whack to work properly; if not, one might direct the ship into a mistaken direction and fetch it up on a shoal or ground it. There were the frequent ice mirages that, siren-like, lured men into thinking the false horizon they saw was true, making accurate observations difficult. Only the south Arctic was charted at all, and those maps were crude and unreliable. Any lighthouse, guideboard, beacon, or buoy to mark shoals was thousands of miles away, and a master relied on years of experience overcoming obstacles "of which the navigator of warmer seas can have no adequate conception," as master Cook said. This was the hardest sailing imaginable, and when a "boner" entered the northern ocean, it was a "veritable tilt with Death" that only ended when the Arctic was in his wake. It seemed to one whaler the "great frozen ice fields stretching far down to the horizon . . . were placed there by Him to rebuke our anxious and overweening pursuit of wealth." No matter—the warning message never quite stuck, perhaps, because the lure of this greatest of sea lotteries was a strong one.

The coastline from the Bering Strait north was almost unyieldingly flat and rarely rose more than twenty feet over the water's surface. As for the vast interior, in March 1867, when America purchased Alaska, also called Seward's Folly or Seward's Icebox (after the secretary of state who negotiated the deal with Russia), about all that was known was that it was uneven, although some of the resources were already being all too successfully exploited. Before the Alaskan gold rush, among nature's harvest was the furry mammalian life, whose skins provided a valuable commodity. This enterprise was largely managed (or mismanaged) as a monopoly by the Scottish Highland–born officers of the mysterious and imperious—not to mention ruthless—Hudson's Bay Company.

After the inevitable decimation of those particular animals whose hides were the fur trade, just offshore, Alaska still offered the tempting prize of its "inexhaustible" fisheries. These included salmon, seals, walrus, cod, halibut, and, of course, whales. Thomas Roys's bold and foolish voyage through the strait had enabled the subsequent plunder of the Arctic bowhead whale population, not to mention all other available native and natural resources by whalers. Indeed, perhaps as much as anyone, Roys had helped set in motion those moves that led the booming post–Civil War U.S. government to invest in Seward's Icebox.

Sparsely populated then as now, Alaska's borders contained only about 10,000 people, of whom 6,500 were the various coastal and river-clinging aboriginals. Uneasily presiding over this great terra incognita was a military governor in Sitka, a modest town that boasted one street lined with log houses and a population of 500, including a garrison, some holdover Cossacks, and "Creoles." The administration appointed by Washington, D.C., was exceptional only in its corruption and incompetence. The faraway whites back in the United States wanted an ever-stronger hand applied to the region and the red men who inhabited it. At the same time, the soldiers responsible for law and order, Civil War veterans suddenly freed from the iron discipline that had once allowed them to defeat a not inconsiderable enemy, indulged in any excess with impunity.

Drunkenness plagued both officers and men alike, and the military presence actually posed a threat to the natives, who would have been safer left alone. These various ingredients, predictably, made for a volatile mix. For example, at this time, an egg transaction between an Indian and a U.S. soldier soured over the price and ended in a riot of natives, during which a military sentry was fired on. When the local major refused to retaliate by either arresting the man or opening fire on the nearby Indian village with his cannons, he was generally denounced as an "old granny." Another army commander, at the outpost in Wrangell, had more sand. On Christmas Eve 1869 he started a two-cannon barrage on the Indian portion of his village in hopes the natives would yield up a murderer. The incident's ultimate origin was the army officers' "debauch-ing" of the local women.

To break the idleness on board the *Monticello,* bomb guns and irons were always at the ready for aiming at any slick black head that chanced to pop into an open lead near the ship to spout or feed. When leviathan did actu-ally appear, there was a wild rush to the weapons in hopes of making valu-able this otherwise useless time. When conditions prevented any movement ahead for the ship, the whale hunters sometimes camped by the openings in the ice. However, even if someone managed to plant an iron firmly, the prey typically slipped under the ice of the sea, dying unprofitably in Neptune's clutches.

During the fleet's temporary imprisonment, the Eskimos paddled out from shore in their kayaks to trade. They also brought the bad news that winter was coming early that year: The evil spirit Toonok had decided it. The whalers, with their typical respect for natives, ignored the warning. Yet Charles Bryant, agent of the U.S. Treasury Department, an organiza-tion that passed as law and order in a place having no law and desultory order, once noted the 1870 winter had been unusually cold and long and said: "It may have been the Eskimos' knowledge of this that induced them to warn the vessels of their danger. Under ordinary circumstances, this is not likely to occur again."

The whalers couldn't have guessed that this year the weather was about to play tricks on them that happen only once or twice in a century. Typically, the spring warmth enabled the ships to sail to Point Barrow by early August, but this season there was a stubborn high-pressure system hovering over northeast Siberia that refused to budge, and cold westerly winds kept the ice from melting and pushed it to shore. Whether it was Tonook or a cantankerous cloud of gas over Asia to blame, by May's end, there was hardly open water north of the Gulf of Anadyr, and the whalers had made little headway through the cracks and gaps of the tortured pack ice.

June arrived with light and variable winds and a cloak of fog to clothe the ice's nudity. As the days ticked off, the pack opened up enough for the fleet to work within sight of Cape Navarin, and briefly its members had the pleasure of hearing the many bowheads spouting in the heavy ice, swimming north. Although largely untouchable, some of the luckier whalers managed to kill and render six. On the fifth, ships were putting in at the popular stopover of Plover Bay in Siberia, where the natives were willing to trade, and the crews could take in wood and water and make repairs. Among the native crowd was one especially unexpected face—that of Captain Frederick Barker, formerly of the *Japan*. Amazingly enough, he had survived the winter, and now made arrangements with several of the masters to save his remaining men, who still were eking out an awful existence among the Chukchis. (This simplified things a bit for Timothy Packard, the master of the *Henry Taber*, who, reportedly, along with several other captains carried orders to search for the *Japan*'s survivors, even to the detriment of whaling.)

Williams and the other masters shared their stores with the shipwrecked mariners, whalemen in distress always being treated like family. Along with the masters and mates of the fleet, perhaps during a gam in a cabin, Willie personally listened to Captain Barker's grim story of survival among the Chukchis. As the ill-fated Barker himself later related, those of his men who lived to make it to shore that unhappy October day had a hard stay in Siberia, with sufferings "beyond description," despite all that the natives did on their behalf. For eight months they'd lived in hopes of the first sail to appear on the horizon, and so had been "doomed to repeated disappointment."

According to various accounts of the disaster, after the bark's wreck, the wind dropped and the sea went calm and froze over, leaving the crew unable to get at the provisions still on board. Barker said his last square meal consisted of a few tallow candles that had washed up on the beach, and in desperation he began to feast on Chukchi fare: raw blubber, and boiled walrus meat with the hair still clinging to it. This was rough food even for a whaler, but eventually his digestive system transformed itself from one that had been temperate zone-conditioned to something more suitable for Arctic survival. It now demanded the consumption of proteins and fats to the exclusion of virtually all else. Willie was impressed by the story, and he wasn't alone: Barker offered an example for the other masters to consider.

The various survivors painted an interesting panorama of life on the tip of nineteenth-century Siberia. During the long, gloomy eight months following the shipwreck, the crewmen, looked on as "little short of deities," nevertheless were forced to share their exulted lives with the Chukchis in their caves. The region favored those patient enough to remain as still as possible for as long as possible. "No one who has not passed a winter in the Arctic regions can conceive the horrible monotony of such a life, and although we resorted to every means to amuse the men, they became restive," the luckless captain noted. To break this tedium, they joined their hosts in journeys for ice for fresh water, hunted polar bears and seals, and went dogsledding. One day ten of the castaways walked thirty miles to another settlement at Indian Point, where there was a village of maybe three hundred, although one of the pilgrims froze to death en route.

The whites found the copper-skinned Chukchis more European-looking than the Eskimos, and guessed they were perhaps a mix of the Russian and Tatar breeds. As they were of medium height and stockily built, the whalers concluded they were perhaps less of a "savage race" than the Eskimos on the other side of the strait. The Chukchis were a brave, untamed, and fierce people, who for years had fought with local rivals, the Eskimos, as well as the Cossacks. Known for savagery and stubbornness, they'd only submitted to Romanov rule in the late eighteenth century. As with the Inupiat across the strait, there was no formal law among them, but there were customs: For instance, a man who caught his woman cheating usually sliced off a piece of her nose as punishment. (The castaways noted many of the women went about so disfigured.) To preserve tranquillity, the Chukchis rarely argued, unless drunk on the alcohol they procured while trading. They were virtually never ill, and anyone sick for several days was doomed to have his neck broken in a violent ceremony, after which the man's best dog was sacrificed.

For food they relied primarily on the walrus, which species obligingly also provided them with materials for their summer huts, but they also hunted whales and polar bears. A single man was reckoned as able to kill one of the white bruins without much ado. On the other hand, in the warmer months, the brown bear was shunned, being apt to be particularly hungry and dangerous after waking up from his winter nap. For pleasure, besides drinking, both young and old enjoyed smoking a narcotic weed.

During his Chukchi sojourn, Barker had made a trip down to Plover

Bay and briefly taken quarters on the San Francisco schooner *Hannah B. Bourne,* which was wintering in the frozen ice to traffic in various goods, including whiskey, a useful tool to help assist the locals to part with their furs. With luck worthy of Jonah, after Barker boarded her, the *Bourne* sprang a leak, and her crew abandoned ship temporarily and made shelter on shore.

The fleet began the recovery of the other survivors. The next day at Indian Point, a speck appeared on the horizon beating up slow and clumsy against a light northerly breeze. Someone cried: "Sail ho!" and soon the whalers *Henry Taber* and *Contest* dropped anchor offshore and the natives, after giving them a round of cheers, took the handful of *Japan*'s survivors in their canoes to the waiting vessels. The men of the *Japan* were so weak and malnourished their rescuers had to assist them aboard; this kindness made eyes water. After rewarding the natives with some gifts, the whalers pulled up their anchors and beat to windward.

On the heels, or rather the flukes, of their prey on June 10, the *Taber* entered the Arctic Ocean with a fair wind and found pieces of broken field ice and anchored nearly abreast of another Chukchi village to retrieve more survivors. Again, the canoes appeared, the natives hugged their friends and wept, "unacquainted with the manners and customs of an enlightened people," as one observer put it. On June 16, some of the *Japan*'s refugees sighted the *John Wells,* which then proceeded to get lost in a dense fog for three days, requiring the Chukchis to launch a canoe to find her.

The whalers were surrounded by field ice, which got heavier the farther north they went, at times locking them in. Between June 18 and 30, the pack opened enough for Williams and the rest of the fleet to get past Cape Bering and through the strait. It was their intention to sail to the aptly named Icy Cape, which had earned its moniker from the redoubtable explorer Captain James Cook, who found the ice there impassable. It was a tough place to sail around, but with the thinning of the bowheads, breaching what had been impassable had become inevitable. From the Cape, the whalers were planning to push even farther northeast to Point Barrow, three hundred miles beyond the Arctic Circle. Most of the killing of leviathans had been done off Point Barrow in 1870, and the hunters expected them to oblige them by showing up to be slain this season.

On the way up to the hunting grounds, the blubber hunters were treated to one big event to give them a chuckle in what was a largely tedious time of the season. Being the first vessel to make it through the strait and get at the "spring catch" of migrating bowheads pushing farther north to the summer feeding grounds was a desirable and potentially lucrative prize. Captain M. Hayes of the bark *Oriole* was particularly eager for it. He commanded one of the newer whalers, with rakish beautiful lines that made her more a clipper ship than a spouter. (She'd already proven herself lucky six years before when she escaped the *Shenandoah,* "having run 50 miles off the chart" to safety.) On his way up to the straits, Hayes had sailed her to Plover Bay, coming across the *Hannah B. Bourne,* which he chartered for the whaling season. Away the two vessels went toward Bering Strait, and when the *Oriole* made open water off Siberia, Hayes, according to one of the more colorful accounts, said: "There, I guess we've got the best of them all this time."

The *Oriole* struck a submerged floe, and that night a boatsteerer removed the fore hatch to fetch an iron, and jumped into waist-deep frigid seawater. The crew covered the hole with oakum and canvas and took to the pumps, raising the distress signal. Among the respondents was Williams, who'd sailed through the main body of ice and was sitting with the rest of the fleet below St. Lawrence Island, a body of land whose most notable feature was that its location marked the halfway point between Asia and America. Assisted by the *Hannah B. Bourne* and the other whalers, Hayes managed to get his bark to Plover Bay, where the crew hove her down for repair. On June 14, when Hayes tried to get her afloat, according to one account, a hatch collapsed, and in minutes only the masts stood over the waterline. Hayes, with few other prospects, ordered the wreck broken up for gear and sold. The master who purchased her made a profit of $1,000 in resale. The *Oriole*'s crew reportedly had a grand time. With nothing better to do, they pulled onto the shore of Asia with rum and molasses and hunted, before they were redistributed among the rest of the fleet.

The fleet sailed on, but with the buffeting of the gales that closely packed the ice southward on the Alaskan side, they were forced to hug the shore. After a heavy fog set in, the fleet remained resident on the dark waves of the Chukchi Sea, wasting time, hardly seeing a whale until July

5. Once his eyes got used to the ice's dazzle, Willie was able to study the snow-covered ice packs. Unlike the eastern Arctic, there weren't any great icebergs, as there were no calving glaciers to spawn them. Rather, the ice of the western Arctic formed into a vast conglomeration of cakes that rarely rose more than ten feet from the water, but the rule of thumb was that ten times that visible bulk hid underneath, and that deception made them deadly. The wind might push the floes together into packs a mile or more long, like a train, with pressure ridges as high as ten feet. Water splashing off a floe here was often mistaken for whale spouts. So unpredictable was the ice's movement, it would have required a soothsayer—and a good one at that—to predict its course from day to day. The floes loved to make love to the shoreline, and a strong wind from the west was prone to pile the cakes up and send a ship caught between the ice and the shore on a beat to the south.

Hitting a floe was a toss of the dice with one's own life as the stake. When a vessel struck such ice, it might crumble, or as blue and impenetrable as granite, it could slice through the hull like a spade through blubber. In the smallest of forms, it was pancake ice, although a floe could be one hundred feet in size. A kind of frigid soil for algae, it lacked pure whiteness, but the extreme artistry of the Arctic sky could turn it a brilliant gold or dull lead. Such ice lives only a decade, and when it's melting, like a corpse decomposing, it's called rotten. Rough-hewn by the elements and endless collisions into an infinite variety of shapes and sizes, the individual floes were neither overwhelming in grandeur nor quite beautiful, said Willie. But: "There is within it a power which cannot be expressed and can only be partially comprehended," as he later explained.

Navigating in these latitudes was not for the faint of heart, as Willie learned. During the walrusing season there was plenty of opportunity to be nervous. The *Monticello* had frequent trysts with the ice, most often when heavy fog set in. Such encounters were announced by a telltale jolt that ran from stem to stern, after which came the order to try the pumps. A thump in the ice, he said, "always gives you a few bad moments when your breath doesn't seem to come just right and your heart wants to come up and see what the trouble is all about; but the pumps suck and with another addition to your regard for the 'good old ship' you get back to your normal mental condition only to get through the same sensation the very next time the ship fetches up good and solid."

The ship's closest call with disaster came after a fresh wind blew hard enough to move the pack, nearly shutting the ice door to open water. The single open lead available sat between two especially large ice floes, and toward that Williams sailed. There was a slight problem: The opening was not straight, but by the time anyone realized it, the vessel was plowing ahead with too much speed and momentum to do anything but sail through and pray. The ice struck a glancing blow to the weather bow before the *Monticello* ran into the floe on the other side, bringing her to a halt and dumping the forecastle watch off their bunks. After a few heavy rolls, she gathered headway and finally made the passage, although everyone was certain the hull was stove in. A crew manned the pumps, while other men went to the forepeak to listen for the telltale sound of water pouring inside. Luckily, the report came back that all was quiet, and the pumps failed to suck anything but air, meaning they had effected an escape from ruin, narrow though it had been. It was just one of a legion of near misses that season (One event of note was the family dog fell into the water and wisely became ice shy).

While waiting for the northern ice to break up in early July, with few whales nearby, the *Monticello*'s crew, like others in the fleet, put their idle weapons to use hunting the walrus. Once despised as unworthy of the iron, the sea horse had in just the past few years become a popular target for the whalemen to kill at this time of the summer. Weighing up to two thousand pounds, the relatively small-headed, fat-bodied, heavily blubbered walrus rendered oil that the market accepted just like leviathans'. Unfortunately for the walrus, he was as proportionately frightening looking as he was in fact harmless, and his great ivory tusks, much valued in the market, were not so much weapons of attack as tools to pry out mollusks from the ocean floor or to let him dine on vegetables. Grotesque not only in appearance, his snorting and grunting made whalers think of hogs, and hence pork, which didn't help his case.

With a few modifications to their killing tools, the blubber hunters stalked this prey from their boats in the same way they did whales, first fastening to them with an iron before finishing them off with the hand lance. However, the beasts were much easier to kill than their larger marine colleagues, and usually the *Monticello* crew towed the carcass onto the ice for skinning before trying the blubber out on the ship. So generally harmless was the ill-fated walrus, Willie was even allowed to join in the hunt, no doubt to start breaking him in for his whaling career. At first he found it unnerving to be in a boat and hear a bellow and turn around to see the dread walrus: the head peering out of the water with its sharp tusks, wicked black eyes, and signature long, drooping mustache. Willie soon learned that the beast was usually the more frightened of the two of them. So timid was the sea horse, when a whaleboat approached a herd of them encamped on the ice, they became frightened and fled, with the females pushing their young into the water. The sea became alive as if "bedlam had broken loose," said Willie.

Even walrusing had some risk, however, as did any activity in these latitudes. This summer the prey were wisely shy and rare, forcing the crews out as far as twenty miles away from the ships to kill them. Once, while Willie was hunting in the first mate's boat, a walrus put a tusk through its side, which prompted a quick response. First, someone dispatched the offending walrus with a lance thrust, after which the crew pulled to the ice and covered the hole in the boat with canvas—all done, said Willie, "in the same amount of time as it takes to tell it." In the second half of July, winds blew from the southeast and northeast, breaking up the ice on the American shore and ending the walrus season. At last the fleet had the opportunity to start thinking seriously about whaling. Walrusing over, the fragile whaleboats took a week to fix. Not a bad exchange: In under a month, working round the clock in four boats, the *Monticello* crew had killed five hundred of the brutes, yielding three hundred barrels of oil.

It should have been obvious to anyone interested that it was just a matter of time before this none-too-bright or -able opponent was cleared from the Arctic; and with it, the local natives such as the Chukchis, who depended on the walrus to survive. Not long after, the whalers hunting the animal disposed of the harpoon altogether in place of the rifle, and anyone who could make the proper head shot could kill a hundred at time without moving position. (Barker and his men did their native hosts one service to repay them: They relayed their complaint that the whalers were killing off the life-sustaining walrus. This prompted even the Hawaiian missionary publication the *Friend* to state in its pages: "Hereafter, walrus ought not to be wantonly killed, for ivory and oil." They might as well have been trying to outshout a typhoon. Between 1860 and 1880, perhaps 200,000 walrus were killed, not that whalers gave much thought to such things.)

The danger never ceased. On the seventeenth, caught in a fog, the *Contest*'s bow struck ice at the waterline, and she had to touch land for repair. The fleet worked north to below Cape Lisburne, which was emerging from its coat of ice. This impressive protuberance, with its smooth 850-foot sandstone hills and trickle of fresh water, offered the last high land on the America shore, as well as a poor type of coal that burned too quickly to be of much use. The local Eskimos there were friendly and known for their good humor. Now with the ice still heavy to the south, and the way northwest to Herald Island impassable, the fleet pushed northeast through open leads to a clear strip of water running parallel to the shore that ended a few miles south of Icy Cape. To the cape's northwest running along the coastline as far as ten miles out were the Blossom Shoals, ice-pressed shallow spurs that presented a hazard to ships. The ice was too thick now to proceed, and some vessels dropped anchor.

The wind blew strong from the northeast for several days, and as August 3 rolled around, the whalers still had a few miles to go to reach Icy Cape, and on the fourth, they even had to beat a retreat. Nevertheless, the ice began to disappear from the east shore of Cape Lisburne, but as Master Valentine Lewis of the *Thomas Dickason* noted, the ice was "fetching up against the ship often" and there was "Thick Fogg."

This location was where conditions were the most dangerous. The waters off that imaginary scimitar-blade edge connecting Icy Cape and Point Barrow were a fine place to be rid of fools. The crown of the axis was Point Barrow, a miserable tongue of Alaska that stuck defiantly into the Arctic, and a mariner could rely on it to always offer heavy, dangerous ice. This northernmost point of the United States was covered in snow year round and was "generally regarded as the top-most frost-killed end of creation."

Its beaches were of sand, and its seaward terminus almost flush with the ocean; the feeble tide here meant beached vessels in the shallows had a hard time coming back into the water. Offshore, the currents were powerful, and with a southerly wind, the sea could carry pack ice north at six knots. In winter, the temperature dipped as low as 56 degrees below zero, and the mercury was unable to top 40 degrees in the summer. Between

November 18 and January 24, the darkness is absolute. Not surprisingly, more whalers were lost at the lethal point than at any other part of the Arctic, which was no mean distinction. In just a few years after its opening as a whaling region, nearly fifty ships plying their trade here were crushed, imprisoned or taken north never to be seen again—forget the near misses.

The only signs of life on this barren tongue of land were the small Inupiat Eskimo villages dotting the cheerless coastline. Farther inland, the country was flat, with plenty of nothing to offer, as virtually no plant could take root in the soil because of the permafrost to a foot below the topsoil. In the summer, the tundra thawed out just enough to become an unstable mess of mud, and only light spongy moss, which bloomed to sustain the local caribou, defied the climate. Appropriately, the point bore the name of an English lord of the Admiralty who'd a fondness for squandering the lives of his otherwise idle men in pointless explorations. (There was little else for them to do after the fall of Napoleon; they probably would have been safer fighting the diminutive Corsican.) In 1831, one of those men, English admiral and explorer Frederick Beechey, found the cold intense enough to freeze his vessel in place during August, requiring the crew to cut through a quarter mile of ice to free her.

While a sane man would have been trying to get away from Point Barrow rather than approach it, ships were making Cape Lisburne by August 1. As always, there was a competition to sail farthest the fastest. The whalers raced as aggressively as if they were competing for a cup, and there were hairbreadth escapes from crashing. The old "square toes" (square rigged) manned by capable men sailing about here created a scene that would have been rare even for the "great traveled highways of the ocean," Willie later claimed. At one point, when the wind shifted to the west, it brought in the ice; thus stymied, the masters ordered the anchors dropped. It was time to waste some time gamming, which gave an anxious Willie the chance to get news and exchange books. When in the whaleboat paddling to the ship that was hosting the *Monticello*'s crew, the first mate even let Willie steer the boat and give the orders. He was, it appears, already filling with his small feet those very big shoes of his father.

At this time during the hunting, a situation that was nearly lethal became suddenly ridiculous. Williams was trying to kill a fastened whale running for the safety of heavy ice when his boat, linked to its prey, ran over a floe and capsized. The whale vanished with the line. Given the water's temperature, hypothermia could easily have picked the men off, but before anyone watching from the *Monticello* could make sense of what had happened, Williams's entire crew was sitting on the boat's keel. Luckily, the Old Man's line didn't catch, and no one was hurt, but "for some time it was not good judgment to discuss within the hearing of my father," as Willie noted. That wasn't the only close call. A wounded bowhead spanked one of the *Monticello*'s whaleboats with his great flukes several times, driving the crew to hug the bottom. However, as the bowhead wasn't much of a scrapper and this was probably more accident than intended attack, outside of a smashed oar or two, no damage was done, and the crew killed the whale, anyway.

The Eskimo tribes' settlements huddled along the coast to Point Barrow, where about a half mile away from the low, sandy beach, on a bluff about fifty feet high, their igloos occupied a site where their forebears had lived in squalor for centuries. To visit the whalers, the local northwest Alaskan Inupiat came out from their scattering of huts and "underground recesses" abreast the ships. Others arrived from farther inland where the native population was denser. They were a short people, with broad shoulders and muscular arms, making them look bigger when viewed sitting in their kayaks. They needed no formal judges or policemen, for they were orderly. The father was master of a family as long as he was the strongest and toughest hunter; when he grew old and his mind and body failed, he lost his privileges, and his lot was to sit with the women in the umiak. Their lives were nasty and brutish and, by white standards, short: Generally, the men didn't see the yonder side of forty. When someone died, his body was dragged away for the dogs to eat, and he was forgotten as an individual and became a dream-legend figure.

Their lifestyle had a perfect symmetry with the land they inhabited. It allowed no weakness, but their customs had allowed their forebears to survive for three thousand years. Their routine was tethered to the annual migrations of the prey, which included ducks, seals, walrus, and whales. Every Arctic resident unfailingly obeyed tradition. Unable to grow food, the Eskimo had hunted for it from time before memory. As a native here needed something like eight pounds of meat a day to survive comfortably, a whale clearly was a great resource.

To secure this bountiful prey, Inupiat hunters chased after the bow-heads in their umiaks (walrus-hide boats) and their stone-tipped harpoons carried lines attached to inflated animal skins, which helped tire out a fastened whale when it tried to sound. After the kill, the village headed to the ice to butcher it. So prevalent was whaling, at one point it became the basis for an entire prehistoric culture. It also was dangerous work. According to one story, during a whale hunt for the czarists—being forced to forage for the Russians was a common fate for the Eskimo—sixty-four men in two-man baidarkas (sea kayaks) drowned in one storm.

The various Eskimo bands showed modest variation in manners and temperament. For instance, those of Point Barrow were known to be peaceable and friendly; while those at nearby Cape Smythe, some twelve miles south, were bold and thieving. This season the locals spent a lot of time visiting the whaleships—perhaps too much—and as usual, they took trinkets from the whalemen, to some degree justifying their reputation as beggars. They liked the manufactured goods the whites brought, such as rifles and knives, which took some of the danger from their very dangerous, when not monotonous and bleak, lives. It was also customary for them to initiate bartering, and at least one captain in 1871 went on shore trying to bargain with them for whalebone to fill his holds the easy way. Barring trade, when the Eskimos' numbers were great enough and if emboldened adequately by liquor, they were inclined to take what they wanted by force, and thus some of the dealings with the whalemen became bloody.

Another popular commodity for trade was their women. Females were valuable for a number of very practical reasons not directly connected to venereal delight. They usually did most of the drudge work. In some tribes, the more wives a man had, the better his estate. The Eskimos and some of their counterparts across the strait were known to be willing to rent their wives and daughters—or at least the parts most interesting to a lust-ridden whaler—for the right price in an act called "puni puni" in the local argot. For the price of few bottles of spirits, a woman was placed at a whaler's disposal. Of course, this helped spread syphilis through the ranks of the people of the north, among the other illnesses the whalers so kindly introduced. (A man could even borrow a wife for a season, as proven in 1861, when the captain of the bark *Cleone*, fond of strong drink and domestic pleasures, began to live with a native in his cabin—prompting contempt among his men. That a white and a red could be something like a regular Christian couple was a bit of a stretch to imagine.)

Certainly the whalers brought to the Eskimo in particular and the Arctic in general little that was good. As one Alaskan historian put it, some were "as evil a lot of pirates as ever sailed with Morgan along the Spanish main or harried the coast of Louisiana under Lafitte." Assuming the whites had anything decent or useful to teach, they had poor learners in the Eskimo, and the only imprint of civilization they left appeared to be a fondness for tobacco and liquor, Willie decided. Alcohol was an especially lethal cocktail when mixed with their blood, and these so-called people of the whale "drank excessively from the first sip of liquor." Hard experience had taught them that after they had bargained for spirits, they had to hand their weapons over to the women before imbibing.

In addition to disturbing sea otter beds, burning the driftwood collected with difficulty by the Russian American Company, among their other acts of contamination, the whalers were known to be willing, even when it was illegal, to sell natives both liquor and firearms. Not surprisingly, between the destruction of the walrus and the whales, the spread of diseases, and the disbursal of alcohol, the Eskimos were in the midst of a decline that lasted into the 1880s—and the whalers of New England played a key part in that near genocide.

In addition to spirits, the Inupiat loved to consume tobacco, and when they couldn't get it, they smoked a herb called "Kilicanuck." (To whalers it was a substance so called because it was known to be potent enough to kill even a French Canadian.) To amuse themselves, in addition to story-telling, they made a type of music—but according to one white, "Their singing is not much better than a howl." Yet even their harshest critics had to admit the Inupiat had evolved to survive well in their inhospitable world. They were expert in reading wind and currents, and were artists of a most practical sort. With great detail they created accurate maps of their region using the materials of a sandy beach. They first would mark the coastline with a stick, and thereafter used stones to indicate hills and mountains and pebbles for islands.

Overall, the whaling men had mixed feelings about the Eskimos, which apparently ran the full gamut between contempt and amused disgust. The native presence was not exactly a comfort to Willie, who found them "extremely repulsive in looks and habits," and after the custom of the time, he considered them dirty, dumb, squalid, and helpless. Particularly distasteful to him was their custom of thrusting polished ivory and stone or brass cartridge shells into a hole in their cheek near the corner of the mouth; this makeshift jewelry sometimes worked completely through the lip. It was less than appealing to watch natives so adorned as they chewed tobacco. Although he thought them a fairly lazy bunch overall, the teen did have to admit their tanned sealskin and driftwood umiaks were fine watercraft. He also noted that while the men made the craft, they let the women paddle them.

Private property being a vague notion here, the whalers had to pay close attention to the natives, who were prone to stealthily relieve them of their possessions. A slow-moving Eskimo nabbed red-handed in the act of stealing often treated the situation as a joke, but thieving boldly was accounted an act of heroism. The appearance of Eskimos in large numbers was an ominous sign. One wary English explorer, Thomas Elson, whose barge was caught in the ice and driven broadside on the beach at Point Barrow, noted that the presence of suspicious natives increased the farther north he sailed. With his barge exposed, the locals started thieving openly, and he decided his fate as a shipwrecked white man wouldn't be pleasant. Rather than let the Eskimos take her, he got ready to sink the vessel in what was described as a nearby lake. A favorable change of the wind, coupled with the hard work of both the officers and men, had let him work his way free a few days later.

The whalers' frequent shipwrecks had let the natives hone their skills as wreckers, and they now knew by experience an abandoned ship was a floating tub of wealth, full of rigging, sails, lead pipe, bread, and other sundries that relieved their bare-bones existence. Ever the hunters, they often watched the struggle of a stricken whaler like "wolves scenting their prey from afar" before going in for the kill. Although the whalers may not have suspected it, given the aboriginals' skills in reading the weather, they may have been sizing up potential windfall all summer.

From the decks of the *Monticello,* Willie saw the hills of Cape Lisburne, and as his eyes still followed the land farther north, he noted the shore became a tedious stretch of low-lying marshes running for miles, with lines unbroken by so much as a shrub. Still farther north from there, the waters from the Bering Strait flowed on and eventually forked, forming a relatively fixed tongue of ice called Post Office Point. This was the northern boundary of navigation. There were no regular tides, and only the fickle wind's motions dictated the sea's rise and fall. Adding to all the other dangers were sandbars that ran along the coast, making the navigation especially dangerous. Here a master had to trust to his own skills and lead lines, and even with the best ships and men, a voyage in the Arctic was about as safe as a flight to the moon in the twentieth century—or even a bit less.

16

***

How Many Will See the Last
Day of Next August?

*One of the bravest and most successful of the shipmasters said to me,
"Capt. Pease, you may live to get out of this, but I never shall. If you do
live to get home, tell my family that I knew how to die."*
—*Testimony of Henry Pease, master of the ship* Champion,
caught in the 1871 freeze-in

On August 6, the wind moderated and offshore the ice formed a line five miles long. Five whalers passed Blossom Shoals, and within few days, most of the ships had sailed northeast to Wainwright Inlet. The pack opened to the south as well, and some worked to the northwest, whaling around the clock. With the improved weather, at noon on the seventh the whalers hit the limit of navigable water a few miles north of the inlet and were rewarded when the bowheads obligingly came into view. For example, on the *Seneca,* standing out perhaps three miles away from the Inlet and facing a "thick fogg" and a "solid ice barrier," the crew furled sails and broke out the cutting hook and falls to make the ship fast in the ice. Four bowheads appeared but soon vanished. Despite the obstacles, the prospects for the season looked good, and ships' cables rattled out to the bottom or were made fast to blocks of heavy ground floes with ice anchors. Men climbed to the sheltered watching places in the crosstrees called the crow's nests, boats were lowered, and the slaughter began, although as usual, more whales were lost in the heavily packed ice than were taken to the ship's side.

The fleet kept busy for the next several days plying its craft. By Thursday the tenth, twenty ships had made it to Wainwright Inlet and soon the whalers had the questionable privilege of broaching Point Barrow—only they would be minus a man who'd cleared out from the race. While on board the *Henry Taber,* a twenty-four-year-old (or "thereabout") *Japan* survivor, Lewis Kenney of London, proved death hadn't finished with the crew of his ship when he "departed this life" through "scurvy of the lungs." The log keeper grew poetic: "We are now called upon to witness on this solemn occasion the last tribute & respect paid to our fellow mariner & may we all bear it in mind that we have all got to go that way sooner or later. And from leaving this World of troubles and woe, he has entered Into a Heavenly mansion, where love & peace forever reins. . . . Oh death where is thy sting, Oh grave where Is thy victory."

They buried him halfway between Harrington's Inlet and Point Belcher, where at least the names were currently in English.

The whalers, so rudely interrupting the bowheads' routine of feeding and rather acrobatic, if awkward, lovemaking, were themselves rudely interrupted on August 11. The wind shifted into the northwest and sent the ice crunching toward shore with a deafening roar that must have sounded like biblical judgment on its way. The floes, thirty-five to fifty feet in height, formed around the ships, and the masters quickly dropped sails and cut lines to avoid having their ships jammed in. They worked inshore to the shoal water under the protective lee of the ground ice. It wasn't a smooth process and some sailed too close inshore and grounded, requiring the tedious work of refloating.

It was worse for the crews in the even more vulnerable whaleboats prosecuting their craft in the recently created open channel. "The ice closed up suddenly and we were forced to drag twenty-six boats over it," said Captain Edmund Kelley of the *Seneca,* now the northernmost ship. "Within half an hour from the time the ice began to move, we were solidly enclosed." Fourteen boats were frozen on a single cake of ice at once, like sprinkles on a cookie, with others being abandoned temporarily, and yet more dragged over long stretches of ice. While some were stove, all were repaired. On board the *Seneca,* the mate watched as the ice came down and closed her in, just one of "the fleet of ships unable to get out of the ice." It wasn't till the next morning at eight o'clock when Kelley himself appeared, having abandoned a whale line and sail to drag the boat what must have an unendurably "long distance." And still the ice started again.

On the thirteenth, after the advancing hordes grounded, a clear channel now existed up to Point Belcher, toward which twenty ships immediately made sail. The ice that had jammed the *Henry Taber* in for two days now began to open up, and after all hands were called to work her free, the pious log keeper said: "God be praised for his good & glorious works." The *Seneca*'s crew ran out blubber hooks and tried to warp out with all sail pressed on, but the ice was still packed too close for escape. In nature's own good time the ice loosened enough for her to get free under just mizzen and mainmast canvas.

The fat prey appeared again, lying tantalizingly out of reach in ice too deep for pursuit. Thirteen more whalers sailed up the open channel and dropped boats, although at this point, their occupation was primarily of a passive nature, restricted more to sightseeing than killing. Around the seventeenth, what little the Arctic had given it took away as the fickle ice moved again, forcing the fleet to squeeze closer to land on the outside edge of the shoals running from Wainwright Inlet to Point Belcher. Captain Edmund Kelley, who knew there was a path north in a place where there were no paths, only directions, wanted access to the deeper water behind the shoals fencing out the ground ice. Using a sounding lead, he navigated his way over the shoals in a whaleboat all the way to Point Belcher itself, dropping bundles of bricks tied to cordwood to act as marking buoys. Other whalers followed in his wake, although two ships went ashore doing so.

Patiently, the men of the fleet began anchoring behind the ice, ignoring the fact that if it was a fortress, it was also a prison. As persistent as a debt collector, the fog was thick most of the time and broke up only in short bursts, making it difficult for whaleboat crews on the hunt to navigate back to the protection of their ships. The whales knew by exceedingly painful trial and error they were generally protected by the heavy ice, like a crab in its shell, and that's where they stayed, making pursuing them harder. Even when wounded, they usually managed to die in the inaccessible ice floes, often taking with them an iron and line into the next world as if in final insult. At night, the men had to worry about colliding with ice cakes that ranged in size from "a country schoolhouse" to a "city block." On the nineteenth, the *Seneca*'s log recorded that there were "28 ships in sight."

They made the best of the situation. "Still fast in close packed ice.

Foggy part of the time. Saw three ships take whales today and we can't help ourselves. Leave one whale floating in the ice," wrote the mate of the *Henry Taber.* The reports of spouts up in those lumps of gravel and sand called the Sea Horse Islands at the mouth of Peard Bay prompted several masters, including those of the *Carlotta* and the *Seneca,* to mate their crews and send boats over the otherwise impassable shoals and ice for a strenuous two-day trip north. As in the Sea of Okhotsk, this sort of whaling was an especially tough job.

At last, on the twenty-fifth, the Arctic's rare good manners reappeared when the much-expected northeast gale blew in and rolled back the ice by as much as eight miles offshore. The open water provided an invitation to start whaling, just as if this was a typical Arctic hunting season, which it shortly proved not to be. After the storm, the ever-friendly if inscrutable Eskimos again warned the whalers to "get away with all possible speed as the sea would not open again." This was not what the whalemen expected or wanted to hear, so "they resolved to hold their positions." With the weather obligingly pleasant, during the next couple of days, hunting began in earnest and many a bowhead died on the twenty-seventh.

Confident the conditions were safe, on the twenty-eighth some masters sailed north, but on the next day, a southwest wind that had blown light in the morning freshened by evening. Once again, powered by strong northeasterly currents, heavy floes began to ground in shoal water, jamming ships ashore and sending the whalers scrambling to get behind the ground ice, with some slipping their anchor cables to do so. Those outside the barrier kept working in closer for safety. Some vessels even had to drop their anchors with only three to four fathoms of water between their bottom and their hulls. In all that day, some thirty-two ships were locked in the ice, with one unfortunate trio of whalers caught in the pack too close together to even swing at their cables. Yet the whalemen believed a northeast wind would intervene to save the season yet, and their chief fear was they'd lose profitable whaling time.

From Point Belcher to a few miles south of Wainwright Inlet, what remained of the clear water ran from two hundred yards to a half mile in width. The ice had two ramparts, one piled up on the shoals to seaward and the other grounded on the beach with smashed, uneven chunks visible everywhere. The whalers' predicament worsened when snow blew in from the northwest and south. Usually by the time the northwesterly winds came, the floes they blew were too small to be dangerous: Now the fleet retreated from the heavy drift ice running southward. The five north-ernmost vessels, *Roman, Comet, Concordia, Gay Head*, and *George*, were as imprisoned as if they'd been in the Tower of London. Before the ships was an endless expanse of ice that the southwest wind kept piling higher each day. The more southerly ships were in a safer position to watch the events unfold. While sailing about Point Belcher on the thirty-first, Captain Stephen Swift of the bark *Lagoda* saw a "large body of ice off to the north." The floes also began to fill in the empty water between the ships and the Alaskan shore.

The Williams family didn't come out unscathed from this meteorological turn for the worse. On the twenty-ninth, the *Monticello* was off Point Belcher working to Point Barrow when Williams, perhaps concerned for his family's safety, decided to turn south in a risky attempt to pass the shoals before the ice blocked them off. During a snowstorm, all hands were called on deck to assist as he beat to windward in short zigzag motions, movements necessitated because of the narrowness of the channel. Having made a few miles heading shoreward, the *Monticello* was almost into the wind. The leadsman in the chains called that there was still water below them, when, from out of the falling snow, ice suddenly loomed under the weather bow. She struck it, hung in irons (lay stopped) for a few minutes, and then went aground. Now onshore, there was little more to be done except take in the sail and lay an anchor to windward to keep from going on hard ice before all work ceased for the night.

August 31 was clear and fair, and most of the fleet was visible swinging at anchor. Taking note of the *Monticello*'s distress, other masters sent crews to help her refloat. It was a "gala day" with the *Monticello*'s deck covered with men executing orders with an energy and speed only sailors can muster when they're pleased to, claimed Willie. More chains were laid out astern and run to the windlass and hove taut; casks of oil were taken from the hold and rolled aft, and thus balanced, she floated free of the earth. Other vessels towed her backward till she could make it away from shore, and the task complete, she dropped her anchor for the last time with eighteen others, about ten miles south of Wainwright Inlet. The water was about three quarters of a mile wide between the pack and the shore.

As the pack ice swung in close to shore at Point Belcher and Icy Cape, the ships were divided into four groups, with the most northerly four vessels off Point Belcher. A few miles farther south were seven more ships, and just in sight of the lookouts in the mastheads, three more even farther south; the remaining seven whalers weren't visible. As long as the wind blew from the west, everyone prayed or whistled for the northeaster they felt was due to arrive, said Willie. Although the vessels crowded ever closer to the shore and the water on the ice edge was only twenty-four feet deep, they sent their boats out nevertheless. The *Monticello*'s crew caught a whale, and their colleagues decided they were lucky.

At the month's end the men on the *Eugenia* played out a farce as the ice pack drifted past. Her crew reportedly was a particularly rough one, with several men having tried to strike an officer with knives or fists. Even the cook was given a licking with a rope's end for refusing to clean his galley. As her log recorded on August 30, the crew had finished boiling down a whale when two men started fighting, and when the mate tried to break up the fracas, one of the brawlers, George White, said he wouldn't stop for "eney sun of a bich." The mate grabbed him, and in response, one of White's friends took up a crowbar and said "he wood punch his [the mate's] ies out with it if he did not lett his Chum go." Despite this resistance, the mates managed to get White into irons, after which he turned the air blue with curses against them and the captain, warning there would "be plenty of dark nights" before the return to Hawaii. The captain ordered White hung up in the mizzen rigging. Soon after, the master called aft his crowbar-wielding friend to answer for himself.

White and his companion appear to have been drawn together by a mutual brutality. Fond of picking fights with their shipmates, before this incident they'd warned "if thare was truble also that thay had the ship whare they wanted her, that the offersers were afraid of them and that they wood doo as thay pleased." Consequently, White's mate's call for help from the crew went unanswered, proving, as the mate wrote, "they have gut no more friends forward than thay have aft."

Not surprisingly, White's partner was "saucy and incelent" with the captain, and thus soon joined his chum in the rigging. Being triced up far off the deck in the Arctic night made even the nastiest Jack embrace peace and charity, and after twenty minutes, both transgressors repented the error of their ways and begged pardon. To overcome any lingering doubts over their conversion, the mate left them in the ropes another half hour in the same way a butcher might dangle a side of meat to ensure its quality. Allowed back on deck and told to take a walk to cool off, they backslid and made threats, after which they went back up in the rigging for another twenty minutes. This time they "promest to be good men."

Another scene played on the *Emily Morgan,* whose crew had both lost a line along with valuable hunting time. (One could say she was a lucky ship: During the *Shenandoah*'s brief reign of terror, the *Morgan*'s captain had managed to sail from the Arctic to relative safety in the Sea of Okhotsk and escaped capture.) Now with the ice driving down on her, the crew had to keep moving the vessel to avoid being crushed or locked in place. While catting the anchor (or raising it to its place on the bow) a talkative boatsteerer named Frazier, apparently had a little too much to say. Several times the first mate told Frazier to shut up; finally, the officer was "compelled to use force to preserve the discipline of the ship and in doing so, accidentally broke Frazier's jaw. This is not the first [time] Frazier has refused to keep silence when ordered. Otherwise, he is an excellent man."

Despite the precarious situation, there was no panic. As Captain Kelley stated: "I was stowing down oil and allowed no thought of danger to enter my head." The weather that framed the larger stage on which all the smaller dramas played out was still bad, and the wind blasted the *J. D. Thompson* onto the frozen shore. On other ships, between snatches of sleep, the men could listen to the reassuring sound of ice scraping against their hulls. By the morning, there was a coat of ice on the water, not a hopeful sign.

"Oh how many of this ship's company will live to see the last day of next August?" wondered Captain Packard on the ship *Henry Taber,* at the month's end. "God only knows. I will trust to his all wise hand." Having picked up some of the half-starved and ragged survivors of the *Japan,* he had seen for himself what the winter here was like. That same day Lewis wrote on the *Dickason,* "The ship still to anchor in the ice, the weather very changeable, plenty of snow . . . very cold, 4 boats in the ice after whales, no luck."

The beginning of the ninth month was no better, with the skies overcast and southerly winds blowing with sufficient force to slam ice into the

Eugenia's hull, squeezing off copper sheathing and snapping her anchor cable. Her mooring lost, she came perilously close to grounding, but the crew got a second anchor out and halted her progress three quarters of a mile from shore in about seven fathoms. "Some twenty six sail in sight," wrote her mate in classic nautical understatement. "All jammed in the ice close onto the beach. Things look bad at present." Mr. Earle, the log keeper on the *Morgan* noted: "The ice pressing in upon the land. All egress from our present position is cut off, both to the north and south, as the ice is driven up into 9 feet of water."

Commanding the northernmost of the whalers, Jared Jernegan, the unlucky master of the *Roman,* sat in a lonely spot by Point Franklin. The point bore the name, appropriately, of the gentle, elderly, and doomed English explorer Sir John Franklin, who'd met his bad end most famously in the Arctic decades before. Jernegan, after his first voyage, like other whalers, had faced the regular torture that was the whaleman's existence. While at sea, he missed the births of his children; in 1858, two weeks after his second daughter was born, he was not present at the death of his wife. A daughter also died, but Jernegan kept whaling, and though remarried, he felt despair.

"Truly my lot has been a hard one to bare and sometimes I feel as the quicker I leave this world the better it would be for me," he wrote. "But when I reflect on the future world I ask myself if I am prepared to meet my Angel Wife. I think I must experience a change of hart ere I am prepared to stand before our blessed Saviour." His mariner's career had its troughs, as well: in 1861, he lost the merchantman *Erie* in a storm. In 1865, he gave his new wife, Helen, some cryptic advice in a letter. "Sometimes I think you will wonder that we have Patience to stay away from home for so long a time. I will answer we are obliged to study patience."

Apparently unwilling to let his family out of sight again, he'd taken his wife and two children with him on the *Roman* for the 1871 tween-season cruise. During the voyage, he nearly lost the ship through a mutiny in Resolution Bay in the Marquesas Islands. At the head of the uprising was a "half cast" named Clark, whose brother Jernegan had promised to take off the island. After realizing the natives wanted to keep the brother in question just where he was, and unwilling to endure any bad will on shore, the master broke his covenant. It turned out to be a poor choice, for Clark "induced all my boatsteerers and a large part of my crew to assist him to take the ship."

The day he was to set sail some of the crew went ashore, where several hands and boatsteerers got drunk. Others on board, apparently wanting to join in the party, asked permission to row to the island and dance. "No, I didn't come to this harbor to give liberty to my crew," said Jernegan. That must have made the would-be revelers seethe, for when the drunken party pulled back to ship, the combined crew refused to obey orders. "This was a mutiny," as the master's wife later recalled.

Aware of the danger, Jernegan went down to the cabin to fetch his 1860 lever-action Henry rifle, a weapon that he admitted later was "rather unhandy to use in a row." Before he could even test the Henry out, one of the mutineers got a grip on the cabin's outside doorknob, preventing Jernegan from turning it and effectively making him a prisoner inside. Helpless, Jernegan listened to the rough scene unfolding on deck. First, the mutineers tied a rope around the neck of first mate, Mr. Apes, and dragged him about the deck before nearly killing him with a blow from a boat spade. (Jernegan considered him "a good man" with whom he got along "nicely," better than "some nabors at home.") To finish the job, they hung Apes in the mizzen crosstrees and nearly killed another officer.

The mutineers, thirteen hands and four boatsteerers in all, then stole three boats, whaling gear, and spare rowlocks, and headed to shore with plans to return the next day to run the *Roman* aground, recalled Jernegan's wife, who was relieved at their departure. "I expected then we would all be killed or that they would set fire to the ship," as she wrote. Luckily, the fourth mate returned from the island with his boat and another party of men, releasing Jernegan and taking Apes down from the rigging. The next day, the much reduced crew beat a retreat, hastily trimming sail to catch a fortuitous breeze away from the island. It was as close to a defeat as possible for a ship's master, and perhaps chastened, Jernegan left his family behind when he went bowheading.

During this Arctic hunting season, his men had caught whales up by the Sea Horse Islands and now were cutting in a stinker on deck. Unable to work to the ground ice because of a rising wind, Jernegan, in whaler fashion, had secured his ship to a floe. Unfortunately, a strong southerly wind forced the drift ice against the floe, loosening it from the bottom, and the ice and ship started to drift to Point Barrow. Looking for new shelter, Jernegan managed to get into a bight in the ice about 250 yards from shore, and dropped anchor to allow the crew to keep the try-pots boiling.

Next morning when Jernegan came on deck, he "saw the heavy drift ice had cracked the heavy point of ice that held our ship." If it broke adrift, he knew the anchorage would be lost and there would be trouble— and break it did. The ice point swung around; looming ahead was a pack of floes several miles in length. "Let go the lines to the ice anchors," Jernegan sang out too late, for the ice struck the *Roman*'s stern, fetching up the rudder and carrying away the pintles (pivot pins). The ice worked under the hull, nearly lifting her keel completely out of the water and shoving her into an immense grounded block. Three times the ice contracted and relaxed, acting like a massive hammer on an anvil, stoving in her side and finally smashing her to "atoms." The ice kept her upright till the two floes separated, and then she dropped headfirst to the bottom. A mere forty minutes had passed since the first blow. As one editorialist far from the danger later put it, the end of the "noble ship" must have been a "fearfully interesting" sight.

In minutes the panicked crew managed to drop the three port boats onto the ice and make it over the side. Lucky just to steal back their lives from the Arctic, they had no food or gear; they also left behind eight hundred barrels of oil, a small matter now. The new ice around them made it difficult for them to reach shore, but Jernegan kept his head and mobilized the crew. He assigned sixteen men to each boat, which they dragged behind them over the hummocky ice. A pistol in one hand, a blubber spade in the other to check the ice's depth, Jernegan took the lead. Reaching open water, they launched boats, raised masts, and sailed twenty miles to the protection of the nearest whaler.

The word rapidly went through the fleet. "The bark *Roman* is carried off in the pack," noted Earle of the *Morgan*.

September 2 got off to a bad start. At about 1:00 A.M., fate moved to eternally retire from the pursuit of leviathans the Hawaiian brig *Comet*, which given her name, had an appropriately spectacular ending. A storm blew in, creating massive waves that blasted icy spray over her decks so hard and cold that the water stirred up froze in midair. At about 3:00 A.M., the watch of the *Henry Taber* saw the motionless *Comet*'s ensign fluttering upside down at half-mast and the captain ordered one of his boats lowered to investigate.

Through a snowfall, the *Taber*'s rescue crew saw that two huge ice floes had caught the *Comet* between them; seesaw-like, her bow thrust help-lessly out into the air while her stern was submerged. By now, her anxious crew had made their way over the ship's sides into their whaleboats or onto the surrounding ice. While no one was hurt, it had been a close call. The massive floes had crushed the main timbers of the vessel into bits, pinching the stern so hard it had popped like an eggshell. The would-be rescuers ransacked the ship, which remained motionless in the ice, for whatever they could find. Packard himself relieved her of a whaleboat and a cask of flour, and even took her master, Joseph D. Sylvia, who joined him as a guest. They left behind the smashed hull of the *Comet* in her pre-carious position, half in and half out of the water. She remained that way for three days, but instead of resurrecting, when the actions of the wind and the tide finally parted the floes that had crushed and held her, the now-free vessel slid immediately a few feet to the shallow, muddy bottom. A subsequent auction fetched thirteen dollars, the cost of a slop chest out-fit, and with that, her economic life was over.

The *Taber*'s crew used their whaleboats to tow their vessel three miles to clear water and dropped anchor. After that, they broke up an old whaleboat for firewood, Packard having bought a new one from the wreck of the *Comet,* and then opened up a cask of bread, also from the same source. Things were gloomy elsewhere. "The main pack is slowly but steadily advancing toward the land, pressed in by the vast field to the northwest of us," wrote Earle, noting the arrival of the *Roman*'s crew. "The *Reindeer* was hard pressed by ice."

That same day off the mouth of Wainwright Inlet, a crew from the *Thomas Dickason* happened on a dead whale and cut it in. The mate of the *Eugenia* wondered just who'd killed it, noting, "coold not gett to him to see whose whale it was but rather suspicious it's ours." After the news came round about the *Comet*'s demise, as if preparing to fight back against the elements, the masters started to meet almost daily. As a precaution, Edmund Kelley and Williams launched a fruitless expedition south to find the open water that didn't exist, while other masters sounding the channels in the shoals in Wainwright Inlet found them too shallow for escape. The vanguard of the army of floes kept on the slow, inexorable advance over the shoals, pushed from behind by the main host of ice, tons of blocks full of the immeasurable latent energy that the Arctic was unlocking. As the floes grounded heavily ashore, the channel shrank again, perhaps as if being marshaled for the final invasion of the anchorage. It began to dawn on the whalers they were prisoners; but as faith is evidence in things not seen, the whalers had plenty to believe by way of the northeast wind's power to free them.

Looking from the deck, all one saw was ice as far as one's optic nerves registered. The fleet, strung along from Point Belcher to a few miles south of Wainwright Inlet, was now squeezed in a channel about a half mile wide at the greatest distance and a couple of hundred yards wide at the narrowest point. On the sixth, the bark *Fanny* recorded snow and that they were "shut in by the ice and 27 sails in sight. "

The weather was overcast and gloomy, but after seeing whales on the seventh, the crew of the *Emily Morgan* lowered their boats and the bow boat struck one before it could slip under the ice. The men in the waist boat bent a line on to the already fastened one for extra measure, but before they could take the whale's life, second mate Antonio Olivera, "while handling his bomb gun accidently shot himself the bomb entering midway of his lower jaw near the throat passing and coming out at the back part of his head, killing him almost instantly." The pursued soon joined pursuer in death, with one boat towing the stinker to the *Morgan* while another carried the dead mate. The *Taber*'s crew might have gotten some whales if the *Florida*'s mate hadn't whacked the water with his oar, sending a danger signal to any nearby bowheads' ever sensitive ears and stampeding them. "It looks like a poor show to get out of this season," the *Taber*'s log noted.

It rained and snowed most of the day, and "nearly every one in the fleet despairs of getting their ships south this fall, which is a cause of much uneasiness with everyone." There was yet more bad news: While sounding out the ground ice to southward, Captain Dexter had found a depth of less than eight and one half feet. The jail door was shut and the fleet was locked in. In places farther down the coast, the current ran northeast at the speed of a knot, and those ships able tried to work inshore to avoid the fate of the *Roman* and the *Comet*.

On September 8 the "brave mariners" finally started to notice what the Arctic was effecting under their noses. At about 4:00 A.M., a gale blew in and ice pressed down on the southern spur of the fleet, staving in and dismasting the *Awashonks*, grounding the *Julian*, and snapping the *Eugenia*'s rudder tackles, knocking her broken stock hard against the stern.

When the gale abated, the fleet had the pleasure of seeing the smashed *Awashonks* lying abandoned in the shallows, partly on the ice, and then receiving her now-dispossessed crew. The captain auctioned her off for the princely sum of sixteen dollars, and with another ship gone "there was no telling what a day or hour might bring forth."

(Like many, if not all whalers, the *Awashonks* had a long history not devoid of interest. The ill-fated ship, named after the equally ill-fated squaw-sachem of the Narragansett Indians of Rhode Island, was outfitted originally in Cape Cod. During one South Seas voyage, she was taken by natives who launched their attack on the unsuspecting crew by first decapitating the master with a blubber spade. Things might have gotten worse, but one enterprising crewman crept under the native-held deck armed with a keg of gunpowder, which he ignited. The resulting explosion scattered the intruders, allowing the crew to retake the ship and sail home as best as they could manage.)

The weather remained unpredictable. The wind canted from the southwest to the northwest, pressing the main pack dangerously close to the *Emily Morgan*. In response, the crew brought her closer to shore and anchored in three and a half fathoms, with one-eighth of a mile of water left between the "heavy masses of ground ice and the land," noted Earle. He observed, "The pack is still advancing. There seems to be little hope of escaping from our present position; to the north is simply impossible, to the south the greatest depth of water along the ice is 6 feet; and decreasing hourly."

The *Seneca*'s log recorded there were now thirty ships crowded together with "every prospect of being drove ashore." At 2:00 P.M. a party took the body of the unfortunate mate Olivera to shore and read the Bible over it before burial; unless precautions were taken, a corpse so laid to rest was likely to be dug up and eaten by hungry dogs, bears, or even the

Inupiat. Given the fleet's situation, the party must have wondered if Olivera was soon going to have company.

Open water was a shrinking commodity, and the situation was becoming a Darwinian game of roulette, with the ships needing all the speed and skill their crews could muster to keep away from the ice. For days vessels had been running aground. The *John Wells* beached, requiring the crew to fasten an anchor into a grounded floe and, pitting muscle and bone against the shore's grasp, heaved at the windlass to bring her off into the water. The *Elizabeth Swift* ran aground, taking an investment of man-hours to pull her off. The *J. D. Thompson* became fast attached to Mother Earth and required assistance to be refloated.

(The glum situation, however, didn't stop the crew of the *Victoria* from having some fun, according to one account. The men went hunting for the Arctic geese, which then were migrating south in such numbers there was scarcely a break in their procession large enough to see a church steeple through, supposing a church steeple had been there. So many did the crew kill and eat, they were eager to get back to their usual fare of salt pork and beef.)

From Point Belcher to Wainwright Inlet lay the ice-glazed vessels, some jammed in the floes, others in what little open water was available. The next day, as the dour news of the *Awashonks* traveled through the fleet, with the ice still closing in, *Morgan*'s mate wrote: "Offshore is one vast expanse of ice. Not a speck of water to be seen in that direction. All but three of the northern fleet have come down and anchored near us. There are twenty ships of us lying close to her. There seems to [be] but little hope of our saving the ship or of any of the other ships being saved. Commenced making bags for bread in case we have to abandon ship." Also on the ninth, Valentine Lewis wrote: "Ice bound on one side and land on the other. God have Mercy on this Whaling Fleet and deliver us from those cold and Icy shores."

Realizing their dire situation, the masters convened a meeting on Williams's old ship, the *Florida*, to continue pooling their collective centuries of experience. They realized they might have to abandon ship, a less than pleasant thought. Preparing for the worst, at forenoon on the ninth, Captain David R. Frazer headed south with three of the *Florida*'s boats to find the lower portion of the fleet, which they "supposed, or hoped, to be off Icy Cape." This was a considerable undertaking. While engaged in an exploratory mission of his own, Captain Packard spent fifteen hours to work through a mere ten miles of ice.

Desperate, the masters decided to float their two lightest vessels just below the *Victoria*'s anchorage over the mouth of the Wainwright sandbar, a spot which could accommodate a five to six foot draught. Under the command of Captain Edmund Kelley, crews spent an exhausting day hauling all the provisions and oil off the *Kohola* before taking her south along the coast to the channel, which was partly blocked by floes grounded in six inches of water. After all the hard work, the whalers discovered to their regret she had a hull too generously sized by three feet.

Things got nastier on the tenth of September with twenty-nine sails all jammed together. Young ice had formed during the night and there was a snow carpet on the land. This was a recurring harbinger of the season's end that usually sent the whalers fleeing. "There was every indication that winter had set in," said Kelley. Frightening words. The animals of the north would be changing to adapt. The short-tailed weasel would thicken its coat; the lemming's snow claws would curl out; and the local rodents would start doing their business during day, rather than in the darkness that was due to envelop the Arctic.

"Ice bound. The prospect looks dark," noted Lewis on the *Dickason*. The weather started clear and cold with a fresh wind from the northwest; gusts and snow squalls blew in. Around the ships, the ice's thickness varied from one to three inches as it became more solid by the day. Its growth seemed ever more irreversible, and, although the sun managed to reduce it to an inch's depth on the landward side, it was still difficult for the whaleboats to plow through. In the forenoon, the *Reindeer* and *Contest* weighed anchor, but were so tightly jammed, after an hour they'd hardly budged. Although it was difficult for the crews to seriously think about leaving behind their ships, they knew they had to act fast before they were completely locked in. They began boiling pork, making bags to carry bread, and ferrying provisions south, knowing that if their luck changed, they could carry them back to their ships. To prepare their whaleboats for the bite of the ice, the crews sheathed them in copper. As the boats would be beasts of burden and riding low, they put risers on the gunwales to keep them from shipping water.

At 6:00 P.M., the *Morgan* weighed anchor and worked her way about a mile southwest to get under a shoal's lee in nine feet of water. Earle observed: "There is no hope of saving the ship and we are preparing to abandon the ship. The only hope of saving our lives is that the ice in land water will break up." At the same time, the *Julian* had been "leeking quite bad." Still, no one from Frazer's party to the southern fleet had yet returned.

17

The Most Crushing Blow

Tell them all I will wait for them as long as I have an anchor left or a spar to carry a sail.

—*Captain James Dowden of the* Progress

MONDAY, SEPTEMBER 11, 1871, ICY CAPE, BARK *LAGODA*

Although the embattled whalers didn't know it, on Monday at 2:00 P.M. eighty miles to the south, below Icy Cape by Blossom Shoals, the whaleboat bearing Captain Frazer came alongside the bark *Lagoda*. She was sitting precariously with a "large body of ice off shore" when Frazer came on board and told of how "he had not any hopes of getting his ship out this season." In turn, he discovered the masters of the seven ships that made up the southern leg of the fleet had been fighting the ice in a "serious condition," battling a southwest wind that had locked them in for ten days. Indeed, the *Europa* had to slip her chain to avoid a collision, and several other vessels were still caught in place, although due to be sprung out.

After falling in with the other masters, Frazer made his case to men who now had whales spouting everywhere around them, but whose aid was needed to save 1,200 fellow seamen. The arrival of the news their brother whalers needed rescue when they would rather be killing leviathans wasn't exactly welcome. The alternative, however, was to sail back to New Bedford to endure the stares—or worse—of those whose brothers and fathers and sons they'd abandoned to fill their holds. But such an act of charity wasn't just a matter of risking the potential profits. Waiting there for the northern fleet meant they chanced their own survival. The longer they delayed, the greater the odds they'd be imprisoned all winter. To their credit, during this one skirmish in the eternal war of those that have versus those that don't, the southern whalers picked the part of humanity. As Alexander Starbuck put it: "It is a part of the whaleman's creed to stand by his mates."

According to one account, "The choice was made without a moment's hesitation. The masters, with the full consent of all the crews, decided at once to abandon their voyages and to rescue these men, entirely regardless of self and without a murmur." In this way these rough fishermen avoided "a cry of indignation" from the civilized world. Aware of the danger, some masters promised to wait only as long as was reasonable. However, the not-so-subtle Captain James Dowden of the *Progress* declared: "Tell them all I will wait for them as long as I have an anchor left or a spar to carry a sail." Willie Williams observed that "we all knew he meant just what he said."

The sky was overcast and rainy on the eleventh, and the ice was pressing upon the outer shoal. Crewmen continued to boil beef and pork in the otherwise useless tryworks and add the final modifications to their whaleboats. "Sets in rainy," wrote Earle. "Broke out bread and provisions. Boiled six barrels of beef for the boats. Two boats ready for a start. The ice is slowly narrowing the already narrow strip of water and rendering our position extremely dangerous.

"All of the ships are preparing to send provisions south to subsist on till some ship can be communicated with. Furnished two boats with provisions and clothing for the crew for a start southward." Some welcome news interrupted mate Earle's tedious recounting of the day's event's in the log. "As I write this, one of the boats that started two days ago has returned reporting that there are three ships in clear water and a prospect that four more will soon be in safety."

"Got news from ships to south'rd," wrote Nathaniel Ransom of the *John Wells*. "They seem to think they are safe enough as yet." These tidings apparently came none too soon, as on the twelfth, a southwesterly wind pushed the ice on shore so that "we have now just room to swing to our anchor clear of the land and the ice," as the log of the *Seneca* said. Unwilling to wait, at 4:00 A.M. Captain Benjamin Dexter told Earle he was taking his wife in the starboard boat to make it to "a place of safety to the south," promising to return if he wasn't rescued. He left orders to act according to circumstances, showing his confidence, no doubt well earned, in the mate. "If the other ships are to be abandoned to abandon ours at the same time to do as the others do," he said. "For my part, I will not cross the Arctic Ocean in an open whaleboat laden with men and provisions in the latter part of September and October. As far as Icy Cape, there is no danger, but beyond that, if all the ships' companies have to take to boats in Bering Strait, the sea is dangerous at this season of the year. Out of the twelve hundred, not a hundred will survive."

An hour later, Earle sent two more provisioned boats south, and for the rest of the day the crew, along with those of the other ships in the fleet, prepared to abandon the *Morgan,* "as all hope of saving this ship or any of the others has entirely vanished—we can only expect to escape with our lives if even that." Others in the fleet were of a similar mind. The *Taber*'s mate wrote: "Our beautiful *Henry Taber* lying at anchor close to the beach and close to the ice. . . . Finished fitting our boats and making preparations to flee for our lives."

The ice was in easy striking distance at any moment. Good news finally arrived with the return of Frazer in his damaged but still floating whaleboat at about 10:00 A.M. After waiting for what in their own private mental chronometers was ticked off as a long dreary while, the masters again convened. With the ice moving closer, the points of their compass were few. One alternative they were willing to employ was to wait here till near the bitter end, if need be, as long as there was one ice-free ship available for last-minute redemption. Barring escape, starvation and death were about the only two things they could look forward to. They had only to recall the miseries of the *Japan*'s survivors to get an idea of what life was like during a pitiless winter. They came to a decision, and drafted a document to seal it: They were all going to go down, as it were, together. They wrote:

Know all men by these presents, that we, the undersigned, masters of whale-ships now lying at Point Belcher, after holding a meeting concerning our dreadful situation, have all come to the conclusion that our ships cannot be got out this year, and there being no harbors that we can get our vessels into, and not having provisions enough to feed our crews to exceed three months, and being in a barren country, where there is neither food nor fuel to be obtained, we feel ourselves under the painful necessity of abandoning our vessels, and trying to work our way south with our boats, and, if possible, get on board of ships that are south of the ice. We do not think it would be prudent to leave a single soul to look after our vessels, as the first westerly gale will crowd the ice ashore, and either crush the ships or drive them high upon the beach. Three of the fleet have already been crushed, and two are now lying hove out, which have been crushed by the ice and are leaking badly. We have now five wrecked crews distributed among us, we have barely room to swing at anchor between the ice-pack and the beach, and we are lying in three fathoms of water. Should we be cast on the beach it would be at least eleven months before we could look for assistance, and in all probability nine out of ten would die of starvation or scurvy before the opening of spring.

Therefore, we have arrived at these conclusions after the return of our expedition under command of D. R. Frazer of the *Florida,* he, having with whaleboats worked to the southward as far as Blossom Shoals, and found that the ice pressed ashore the entire distance from our position to the shoals, leaving in several places only sufficient water for our boats to pass through and this liable at any moment to be frozen over during the twenty-four hours, which would cut off our retreat, even by the boats, as Captain Frazer had to work through a considerable quantity of young ice during his expedition, which cut up his boats badly.

Ship *Champion*
Off Point Belcher, September 12, 1871.

They prepared another document for the masters down south:

Gentlemen: By a boat expedition which went out to explore the feasibility of a ship's passage to clear water, report there are seven vessels south of Icy Cape in clear water sailing.

By a meeting of all the masters of the vessels which are em-
bargoed by the ice along this shore, as also those that have been
wrecked, I am requested to make known to you our deplorable
situation and ask your assistance. We have for the last fifteen
days been satisfied that there is not the slightest possibility of
saving any of our ships or their property, in view of the fact that
the northern barrier of ice has set permanently on this shore,
shutting in all the fleet north of Icy Cape, leaving only a narrow
belt of water from one-quarter to one-half mile in width, extending from Point Belcher to south of Icy Cape.

In sounding out the channel, we find Wainwright Inlet to
about five miles east north east from Icy Cape the water in no
place of sufficient depth to float our lightest draught vessel with
a clean hold, in many places, not more than three feet.

Before knowing your vessels were in sight of Icy Cape, we
lightered [lightened] the brig *Kohola* to her least draught, also
brig *Victoria,* hoping we should be able to get one of them into
clear water to search for some other vessel to come to our aid in
saving some of our crews. Both vessels now lie stranded off
Wainwright Inlet. That was our last hope, until your vessels
were discovered by one our boat expeditions.

Counting the crews of the four wrecked ships, we number
some twelve hundred souls, with not more than three months
provisions and fuel; no clothing suitable for winter wear. An attempt to pass the winter would be suicidal. Not more than two
hundred out of the twelve would survive to tell the sufferings of
the others.

Looking our deplorable situation squarely in the face, we
feel convinced that to save the lives of our crews, a speedy
abandonment of our ships is necessary. A change of wind to the
north for twenty-four hours would cause the young ice to make
so stout as to effectually close up the narrow passage and cut off
our retreat by boats.

We realize your peculiar situation as to duty, and the bright
prospects you have for a good catch in oil and bone before the
season expires; and now call on you, in the voice of humanity, to

abandon your whaling, sacrifice your personal interest as well
as that of your owners and put yourselves in condition to receive on board ourselves and crews for transit to some civilized
port, feeling assured that our government, so jealous of its phi-
lanthropy, will make ample compensation for all your losses.

We shall commence sending the sick and some provisions
tomorrow. With a small boat and nearly seventy miles for the
men to pull, we shall not be able to send much provisions.

We are, respectfully yours, Henry Pease Jr., with thirty-one
other masters.

Abandoning the thing that has been home, fortress, factory, protector
and friend cannot be pleasant. There had been many an accumulation of
memory inside these wooden frames wherein the whalers had enacted
their daily tragicomedies. They had lived, worked, slept, been sick, formed
friendships, spun yarns, boiled whales, and fought storms in these ships.
Some had made love, nearly died, been nursed to health, and even been
born on these floating villages. They read and composed letters here, conducted business, watched life and death struggles. Such an abandonment
to a sailor is an act of disloyalty. Nevertheless, before returning to their
ships, the masters agreed to it, unsure whether they had in fact already
waited too long, and aware they "stood in hourly peril of their lives."

Offshore, all one could see was a solid of body of rugged ice. From
Point Belcher to Wainwright Inlet, the ships were lying in every conceivable position in the inshore strip, some with their sides crushed, others
lifted from the water and tumbled like a child's toy and just as useless.
Nothing this grand had ever been seen before above the Arctic Circle. Despite the many tragic stories the English had managed to pen in a century
or more of pointless explorations, this was the greatest and most costly defeat to maritime enterprise yet.

The pack moved again that wretched Wednesday, stoving in the helpless bark *Fanny* (Lewis Williams's ship) and dragging the *George* past the
Gay Head, and smashing her jibboom. The weather became worse, with
new ice forming, a thick fog rolling in, and freezing rain pelting them. The
floes rose up into towers from thirty-five to fifty feet tall. The masters held
several meetings on the thirteenth and fixed the time of departure for 12:00

A.M. the next day. Now the crews faced a long trip south down a narrow strip of water between the ice and shore, much of it full of shoals. Prospects were particularly ominous, as perhaps as many as a hundred whaleboats had already been sent ahead carrying women, children, provisions, and some expendable private property, but none had yet returned to pick up their remaining human cargo. Because the trip south was eighty miles long, it was unrepeatable, and only the most essential items could go along. Virtually everything inedible or incapable of offering shelter, serving as fuel, or powering their boats had to remain. The fleeing crews would be exposed, vulnerable to the vagaries of floes and storms, and if blown off course, they were dead men. To prepare, men slipped on layers of pants and draped their backs with additional coats, while in their cabins, captains packed their precious chronometers.

On the afternoon of the thirteenth, accompanied by Eliza, Mary Watkins, and Willie, Williams abandoned the *Monticello* and became part of the exodus. His boat was so heavily laden with provisions and bedding the water reached the gunwales. For the safety of his family, the usually bold Thomas had decided to make this strenuous voyage over more than one day and so left before the general deadline. The Williams party made its way to the southernmost ship, the *Victoria,* to spend the night as guests of Captain Redfield before the final push to the southern fleet. Behind them, the *Monticello*'s colors were left in sight, and everything above and belowdecks remained in place as if the crew were returning the next day to go whaling. Williams had destroyed all the liquor on board, in keeping with an agreement among the masters, who knew the firewater might tempt the Eskimos to carouse, get violent, and perhaps damage the ships.

Thomas and Eliza managed a stoic demeanor, but as Willie wrote: "It was depressing enough to me, and you know a boy can always see possibilities of something novel or interesting in most any change, but to my father and mother it must have been a sad parting, and I think what made it still more so was the fact that only a short distance from our bark lay the ship *Florida,* of which my father had been master eight years, and where three of his children had taken their first breath." For once, a whaler was doing the unthinkable: leaving a completely sound vessel that hadn't sustained irreparable damage. It'd also been "our home 10 months and taken us safely through many a trying time." In cash terms, the *Monticello* was worth $45,000, and among the other incidental losses were the various knickknacks acquired in Japan and the South Sea Islands—as time went on, the abandoned trinkets seemed to grow in value, Willie recalled.

After passing an anxious night, on the fourteenth, as the *Seneca*'s log said, the ice was crowding the land, the barometer was falling, and, as the ship swung at anchor, the "rudder touches the ice." As planned, at noon the ships, some "as fine as any ever built," were abandoned, colors remaining at half-mast, and scores of whaleboats dropped down the falls into the water and their crews pushed off. (At least prospects were slightly better, as some of the advance crews had at last returned.) All along this stretch of Alaskan coast, officers made final entries into their logs. "God pleas send us a N.E. wind or all is lost," wrote Captain Lewis on board the *Thomas Dickason,* whose hands were about to abandon ship and whose provisions had already been sent to Icy Cape.

The gloom, if masked, was nevertheless present everywhere. Even Captain Edmund Kelley's big Saint Bernard seemed to fully comprehend the situation. After the boats were launched from the *Seneca,* Kelley went downstairs for a parting look at his cabin, and the dog trotted behind him, going below for the first time. To mark the time of departure, Kelley stuck a needle in the clock's face to hold its sweeping mechanical hand in place, while the canine put his forepaws on the table and eyed the master with a "most intelligent expression."

"Bos, we must leave the ship," said Kelley, and he and the dog went back on deck. After whimpering a bit, Bos nevertheless allowed himself to be lowered into a whaleboat with "perfect ease."

On the *Morgan,* the men assembled at 5:00 A.M. for breakfast before loading the boats. "If we save our lives, we ought to be satisfied, and that should satisfy the world," noted Earle, in his last entry on board. "To winter here might be possible, but not under the present circumstances. . . . We have neither the clothes nor the provisions, so to remain would entail an amount of suffering from cold and hunger and loss of life as would not justify anyone in attempting it. At twelve noon, paid out all of chain on both anchors and at 1:30 P.M., left with a sad heart ordered all the men into the boats and with a last look over the decks, abandoned the ship to the mercy of the elements. And so ends this day, the writer having done his duty and believes every man to have done the same."

Not everyone had been forced off board so gently. The *Julian* had a few days before faced a rough ice assault. The mate had called to master John Heppingstone to come on deck. "Well of all the rumbling, bellowing, grinding screeching noises I ever heard, it was then and there the worst," he said. To counter the ice, the mate suggested letting an anchor go, but the master decided it wasn't of any use. He was right, as soon, a cable length's away, the bill of an anchor appeared inshore: The ice was so powerful it had pulled it from the bottom. The ice crushed the *Julian,* she heeled over, the water reached the lower deck and the yardarms touched the beached ice. Understandably, Heppingstone's wife and daughter, then on board, were terrified. Finally, the master, his family, and crew walked over the ice and eventually joined in the exodus with the rest of the fleet— while the *Julian* went to "pieces."

Exits made, it was time for flight. Under those conditions, reaching the rescue ships safely required a miracle. Arctic whaling master Captain John Cook was once lost in an Arctic fog after becoming shipwrecked. After taking to the boats, his crew sighted another whaler in the distance about to leave the grounds for the season, and they made after her, successfully. Later, Cook offered a description of paddling for one's life through an impenetrable mist that hid everything that wasn't in spitting distance. Even ice easy to spot in clear weather appeared suddenly nearby in a "wraithlike way." Nothing but ice in sight to the starboard, down Cook went in a narrow strip of mostly shoal water. Pushed by the current, the ice moved quickly underneath them, and they heard the slap and gurgle of the water against it. To break a path ahead, his team used a lead boat, and every small stretch of open water it found had to be exploited. When large ice blocked the passage, a boat was swung squarely to the right or left and the crews paddled around it, however long a distance, to prevent collision. When the way was jammed completely, the men hauled the boats behind them. Despite these obstacles, they succeeded in making the ship, for as Cook explained: "But we were racing for more than life; we were racing to avoid the horror of starvation, long drawn out!"

The motive for the whalers in 1871 was the same, as away the boats went. At first the wind was light enough to allow the men from the *Morgan* to drop sails, although a slow boat in the group acted as a drag, said Earle. Ahead as far as he could see were hundreds of boats, making a sad parade past the ships, which were lying typically three to five abreast, all abandoned or about to be. Empty of men and animals, only the inverted Stars and Stripes fluttering at the mast was a sign of life on an abandoned ship. "As a stricken family feels when the devouring flames destroy the home which was their shelter, and with it the little souvenirs and priceless memorials which had been so carefully collected and so earnestly trea- sured, so feels the mariner when compelled to tear himself from the ship which seems to him at once parent, friend, and shelter," wrote Alexander Starbuck, whaling chronicler, of the abandonment.

At last, the "funereal procession" passed by the southernmost vessel in the northern fleet, the disabled *Victoria*, heeled over on her side. Behind it was a ghost armada stretching along the crescent linking Points Belcher and Marsh. As they made their way southward facing a harsh wind, the mariners discovered the progress and power of the ice were worse than they'd guessed. Had they idled longer, the ice might have kept even their whaleboats from passing.

The north was showing them no pity. This was by no means an easy voyage, and in some cases, it was miserable work, for in addition to en- during the bad weather, the crews had to portage the whaleboats. On the afternoon of September 15, the mate of the frozen-in *Eugenia* watched all the other ships' boats heading south. "Then I commenced packing boats and provisions [to cross] over the ice[·] A half mile to open water, and at 6:00 P.M., all hands left the good bark *Eugenia,* bound solid in the ice, with her ensign flying at the missen peak," he wrote in the log."

The whalers often struck bottom and frequently had to break through young ice. The conditions left little room for error here, as these bobbing boats, heavily loaded with men and provisions, rode low and were in con- stant danger of swamping. The wind blew so hard, men pulling in one boat couldn't hear the voices of those in the boats nearest them, and the snow made them invisible to one another. Yet: "These [hardships] were born with the endurance and perseverance for which our fishermen are noted," said one chronicler.

As the last men gave the region their backs, the natives, who'd camped nearby, waiting like ravens watching their prey, now boarded some of the ships. Because of recent idleness, their plundering may have been an act of necessity, a way to survive; the argument that they'd been counting on the fleet's demise is strong. With their typical agreeableness, they'd even lent a red hand to some of the whalers loading their goods into the whaleboats. A chief's wife gave Captain William H. Kelley a sleeping bag of fox skin, moccasins, and deerskin mats. Their acts of charity completed, the natives started moving the whalebone and anything else they wanted off the ships for their own disposition.

At 3:00 P.M., some of the whalers stopped to eat on a grounded ice floe. When he was ten miles from his abandoned ship, Earle met with some of the *Morgan*'s own boats heading north; after loading them with provisions, he ordered their crews to head back toward Icy Cape. As night came, the wind increased and heavy black clouds "seemed to rest over us and it was not possible to see more than a few feet and we were in constant danger of coming in collision with the many fragments of ice floating in the narrow passage between land and the main pack."

The first evening, some of the whalers dragged their boats over the sand hills near the beach, turned them over, covered them with sails, and kindled driftwood fires. Among them was Earle, who at 10:30 P.M. landed his boat with several others and brewed coffee. The wind blew even harder with rain, forcing them to double-reef their sails and single-reef the jib before shoving off into the dark an hour later. "The navigation was difficult and dangerous; we kept the land well aboard [in clear view] and sounding continually," he said. Earle eventually stopped to rest, but some boats kept going till morning. "The sleet and snow were flying all around us, and the blasts of wind that swept across the ice fields made nothing of flannels and oil skins; but there was nothing else to do but pull away at the oars, as best we could, the whole night long," said a mate named William Davis, noting the boats were strung along like geese in a procession.

At daylight, Earle broke camp on the beach and prepared for the next leg of the trip to Icy Cape. A fresh breeze from the south blew till 1:30 A.M. through a near-total darkness, and as it died, one of the *Morgan*'s boats struck a small floe above the waterline, staving a hole in the bow. They hauled the boat up on the beach, quickly repaired the damage, and cast off again. At 3:00 A.M., Earle sent up rockets, assembled his boats, and proceeded again for five hours, till he was about twenty miles northeast of Icy Cape.

On this final day of flight, the rainy, foggy weather went from bad to worse. By 10:30, some thirty whaleboats had beached on Icy Cape—several of them, Earle discovered, were from his own ship—making the number of the *Morgan* fleet seven in all. With the wind picking up and knowing they would be facing it directly after rounding Icy Cape, they double-reefed sails. Earle ordered the boats to weigh and proceed. They beat, tacked, and rowed until 3:00 P.M., when south of the Cape they dined, a long sliver of ice serving as table.

Ahead was the goal. The mate of the *George,* whose boat contained two sick men along with the provisions, said: "We suffered some from the cold, and were in danger of being cut into and sunk by the thin ice that was forming." Approaching Icy Cape, the open leads of water, which had been smooth, with the wind's help became "very rugged." When the procession reached Blossom Shoals, the rescue vessels, five miles offshore, started to come into sight. The fleeing whalers discovered there was yet another challenge: The southern fleet lay behind a peninsula-like tongue of ice that stretched south ten miles, and the exhausted crews still had to pull round this before they made good their escape. As they made their way to open water, the southwest gale blew against them with a force "that would have made the stoutest ship tremble." The sea seemed angry about having to give up its prey, and it gave the rescue ships a "pretty rough usage" that parted the chains and cables of several ships. When the *Lagoda*'s anchor cable parted, she lost her port anchor and fifteen fathoms of chain, and she ran offshore with 153 passengers until the next day to pick up more of the fleeing whalers. The *Arctic*'s port anchor chain also parted, but she was brought up again with her starboard anchor, which held until the fleet was ready to sail.

The passage was none too gentle on the whaleboats, as the cold wind kept a coat of fresh ice on the surface of the ever-shrinking channel. Where the seas were free, tall waves tossed the boats around like bits of cork, and water rolled over the sides, drenching passengers with freezing brine and ruining the carefully packed bread, water, and flour. With their lives at risk, the men in the boats bailed madly to keep from sinking before making good their escape. For one crew it was a marathon. Nathaniel Ransom, a mate of the *John Wells,* claimed that for twenty-four hours he pulled and signaled through hail and rain. To ease the burden on the boat, he even dumped over the side his costly bomb gun and lances and Eskimo wardrobe. Despite these awful conditions, as Captain Preble noted, the "hazardous journey had to be performed and there was no time to be lost in setting about it." Everyone showed "becoming cheerfulness," with even the women and children "smothering their apprehensions as best they could." The refugees felt gratitude "to that Providence which had guided them, and preserved means for their rescue from the frightful perils and hardships through which they had passed."

As the boats arrived off Icy Cape and approached the waiting whalers, there was the ticklish problem of boarding in a rough sea, which meant running the risk of smashing one's boat to bits against the rescue ship's hull. After a search, Earle's party found an opening in the ice, and with a fair wind, "delivered" the whole of the *Emily Morgan*'s crew to the *Europa* of Edgartown. He'd already received letters from Captains Dexter and Thomas Mellen, the *Europa*'s master, the latter "nobly offering the hospitalities of his ship to any and all who might come." Another passenger on the *Europa* was the log keeper of the *Taber,* who, having "left our home for parts unknown," had with his mates made it on board there "as shipwrecked mariners." He finished his entry with "so ends the log, journal, voyage & also the end of the Bark *Henry Taber.*"

(Captain Mellen, along with the other masters of the southern fleet, himself had barely escaped disaster on the thirteenth when the ice attacked. "[We] got into clear water at dark by cutting the chains and letting the anchor go with forty five fathoms of chain attached and then heaving her through the ice with cutting falls," said Mellen. Captain Norton of the leaking and stove in Australian ship *Chance* was unsure if his vessel was even seaworthy.)

Similarly, it was a somber journey for the Williams family. Early on the fifteenth, leaving the hospitality of Captain Davis behind, the Oakland master rowed and sailed to Icy Cape just before the Arctic night fell. After landing on shore, his party set up a tent for the women and children and kindled huge fires. Rain was falling and the wind was blowing, and the party passed through what, at least to Willie, was an unforgettable night. Eventually, the rain stopped, and after the party finished breakfast, Williams dropped sail to catch a fresh breeze that conveniently rose up and headed to his destination: the *Progress.* Dowden had put a lookout in the mast with instructions to announce the arrival of the escaping whaleboats. When they were sighted, he raised his colors as a signal that he knew they were coming.

Even with several reefs in Williams's boat's canvas, the final dash over several miles of open water in the heavily laden craft was a hair-raiser. The pitching of the *Progress* at anchor made it seem impossible that any-one, forget a woman with small children, could make it over the ship's side alive, yet Williams, in a boat manned by his own whaling crew, managed the feat without so much as "the wetting of a foot," said Willie.

The boarding routine was repeated again and again with the other boat crews. A shipwrecked party clambered on deck, his baggage was hauled up, and with no room for spares, each boat's painter (securing line) was cut. The waves would pluck up the now empty whaleboat, twirling and tossing it like a toy and finally smashing it on shore.

If there were separations, there were also reunions. One ship's mate, William Davis, claimed he pulled alongside the *Progress,* went up her side, and said to her master, Captain Dowden, whom he'd known since his school days: "Hello, captain." "Hello, Bill," was the reply. "I guess you want to stay, don't you?" Dowden said there were better ships to sail on than his, but Davis told his men to board and push their boat away, and the waves, running masthead high, smashed it on the ice. Davis told Dow-den, "I was just down to the rail to see about going off to the other ship, but someone had cast off the painter and there she goes now."

The ordeal was harsh for the crews, who, in fear and anxiety for their lives, had paddled and dragged their boats over seventy miles of water and rough ice. Sleep had been irregular, if enjoyed at all, and sometimes there was no food for a day at a time. The men looked worn-out and many complained they felt sick, but now their accommodations were neither luxurious nor commodious. The cubic volume of this cargo being taken aboard required some displacement. To make way for the new passengers, their hosts cleared out blubber rooms and the tween decks, and spread extra sails over the deck, giving them a "snug and comfortable" look. Decks were crowded with men and baggage, and clothes and nautical in-struments lay in every direction. On board the *Progress* alone were 188 people who required the placement of rough berths between decks. Noth-ing like this had been seen in the fleet since the days of Semmes and Wad-dell. A generous Dowden played landlord to Williams, two other captains, and their families, including one babe in arms. Williams and the captains and officers took the forward cabin; a grateful Willie was stuck in the after cabin. One man took the transom, and two others and himself slumbered on the floor. He never figured out where Dowden slept. (In gratitude to his host, Williams and the other lodgers on board the *Progress* later presented Dowden with a gold watch and an inscribed medal made from a twenty-dollar gold piece.)

Thus the entire tribe of whalers made ready to leave; the mariners "pushed together as bad as any Irish immigrants"—clearly, a bad situation, indeed. By 4:00 P.M. on September 16, the last crewman was on board and the final whaleboat was cut loose to its destruction, and what was left of the fleet sailed on to Plover Bay for water. Passing East Cape on the afternoon of the twenty-sixth, one former member of the *Japan* looked over the strait to the very slope in Asia, which, while a temporary member of the Chukchi race, he'd roamed the prior autumn. What exactly he thought he didn't record, but perhaps no one else on board appreciated the view as he did.

The presence of a whaler at the coral reef off the mouth of Honolulu Harbor on October 23 lured a pilot out to guide her in, and when he came aboard, he was surprised to find a crowd of three hundred men on deck, lounging or moving about within the tight confines. After standing momentarily bewildered, the pilot listened to the story of the fleet's ruin, and even more astonished, he walked the quarterdeck, clearly agitated. This scene didn't bode well for him or the port, because whaling still was one of the enterprises that seeded Hawaii with money. The natives crowding down to the wharf had something to talk about, and soon the news created a sensation through the city—not to mention "a depression of spirits to those deeply interested in whaling matters." At least the forlorn survivors of the *Japan* had a chance to be treated by doctors, even if the quacks of the time more often than not functioned as recruiting agents for the Angel of Death.

Yet, as with everything, it could have been far worse, as was evidenced by the fate of the *Shelekov*. Her only survivor, the captain, arrived the same day as the whaler, as a passenger on the San Francisco ship *Moses*

Taylor. A cattle transport brig, the *Shelekov*'d put out of Honolulu only to sail into a cyclone that left her waterlogged and disabled and killed everyone on board except, perhaps scandalously, her master. Contrariwise, only one Kanaka had perished in the flight of the whaling fleet (dying en route to Honolulu), a remarkable feat, indeed.

Nevertheless, indictments against the masters were issued almost immediately. "Did you not quit your vessel too soon, ought you not have waited a little longer?" someone asked the disgorged vagabonds, according to one newspaper account. A proven and weathered first officer replied: "We left not one minute too soon," and most of the other masters concurred with that statement. A mate of the *George* said: "I have made several voyages to the Arctic seas in whaling vessels, but never before encountered just such weather as that which drove the fleet to its destruction. It was very unusual, and defeated every calculation by which it was at first thought the vessels could be saved from the ice and got inside the open seas."

(One of the more amusing, if probably legendary, anecdotes of the abandonment concerns a whaler that was carrying some rare Madeira and Manila cigars. On the return of the master to port, the owner asked about the fate of the cargo. The captain reassured the owner that he'd saved all of it, and when the owner asked where it was, the master replied: "Well, you see, I drank the wine and Mr. Jones, the mate, he smoked the cigars, and they certainly done us both good.")

That they had toiled like Trojans to save their ships and property was beyond doubt. Nevertheless, those capitalists enjoying the seductively bright sunshine and 80 degree weather of Hawaii, as one writer for the *Friend* pointed out, would find it very easy to ask just why the masters had so readily left "behind their hard earned wealth." The editorialist continued: "We have no doubt that the owners and agents of whaleships in New Bedford, seated before a good coal fire, will express their deliberate opinion that the fleet was abandoned too soon. The idea that 33 shipmasters and their crews abandoned their ice-bound vessels, except from stern and fierce necessity is not to be entertained for one moment." The choice to flee came "in connection with their united experience in those waters."

Such an event didn't escape the attentions of a verbose Honolulu preacher, who saw an opportunity to use this near tragedy as a sort of bait to fish for men's souls. Preaching in the Seamen's Bethel, he noted the deeds of the "manfully brave men" and "braver women." He said, "your deliverance resembled that of the Israelites when passing through the Red Sea. . . . The signal deliverance of so many from their perilous situation, affords a not inapt illustration of the deliverance of so many from that greater and more fearful destruction which awaits all who are unwilling to escape by the passage which has been opened up from the City of Destruction to the gates of the Celestial City." (On the other hand, one master who'd returned from the wreck took a dimmer view of it and decided it "was a judgment for killing the walrus"; another whaler claimed it was a punishment for giving the natives rum.)

Whalers, like all seamen, were superstitious, and now there were many Jonahs in the fleet's ranks to finger as the cause of bad luck. Williams's station and own personal disasters of late made him an object of special notice. One journalist praised him with a faint damn. Naming both the ship and the captain, he said Williams, who "bears an excellent reputation as a navigator and successful whaleman has been remarkably unfortunate. One fine ship he commanded and had interest in was turned into a torch by the *Alabama* [actually the *Shenandoah*]. Last year he lost the *Hibernia*."

Unsurprisingly, the news of the greatest punch yet to land in the eye of the already reeling whaling industry caused a stir back in the City of Light. Whaling, once a sensible investment, now seemed a foolhardy venture, and the $2 million (worth a great deal more in today's money) that had just been lost in its prosecution was virtually irreplaceable. Looking for perspective, a Boston reporter paid a visit to New Bedford and called upon Mr. J. Swift Jr. at the offices of his three-decades-old firm, Smith & Allen. Inside its walls was a neatly arranged countinghouse that spoke of business and symmetrical accounting. Sitting on the shelves over the door were metal boxes that contained ships' papers, each identifiable by the names printed on their sides: *Fanny, Massachusetts,* and *Elizabeth Swift,* three of the lost whalers. While inside his private office, the fifty-year-old Smith, flecks of gray in his sideburns, answered questions with that defensive elusiveness and unjustified optimism characteristic of businessmen talking to the press, then as now.

"It is a hard blow for us to bear and though there is no cause for any alarm concerning the future, some people think we have been doing a business that was altogether unsafe and that the risks were more hazardous than any insurance company should take," he said. Swift claimed the whalers did more favorably than the merchant marine vessels that plied the waters of the Indian Ocean and faced its particularly dangerous and mysterious currents and shoals. And although this was the fourth time since 1842 the business had been flat, "We have built it up every time," he said. He commented on Provincetown's sperm fishery: Although Semmes had made the small town suffer by burning several of its whalers, he'd failed to utterly kill it off as a blubber port, perhaps to his disappointment. "Lately the market had been crowded and the price kept down," claimed Smith. "If Provincetown had never gone into the sperm oil trade, we would have sold for enough to make a handsome profit."

He ventured an interesting if cold observation about the risks: "We expect about once a year that one or two ships have been crowded in the ice or have been lost, but that's a very small proportion of the whole fleet."

A couple of idle whaling captains on hand told the reporter that the ice massed northerly opposite Point Barrow in the Polar Sea, but enabled whalers to travel back and forth with no more "risk than one undergoes in traveling by sea between New Bedford and Boston." They took a rather cheery view: "The disaster was merely one of those deviations from natural laws against which all precautions are futile; such an event would not probably occur again in a lifetime." (They spoke too soon.)

Yet the loss was not absolute, as whale oil's price soared from forty-seven cents to seventy-five cents a gallon—for use by steamboats, engines, and "other strong works" as a lubricant. Back in the Arctic the local economy was also due for enrichment. "Bad very bad for you. Good. Good for us. More walrus now," said one illiterate Plover Bay native, whose words eventually found a permanent and concrete form in the pages of the *Whalemen's Shipping List*. On November 14, the publication also noted that over the past year "a series of disasters on land and sea, such as was never before known in this country; and the calamity which has been swept from the ocean in a single season, will be seriously felt by the community. This is the most crushing blow which has ever fallen upon the whale fishery."

Back in the Arctic, under gray skies and lying in freezing brine with winter fast approaching, breaking up into its constituent parts near the flat desolate shores of Alaska was the Yankee whaling fleet. It had been a great instrument crafted with skills learned over centuries of hard trial and error, and manned by the bravest and most able seamen of their time, possibly the best ever. At least the fleet wouldn't decay alone, for there was a sympathetic witness to its unraveling. As a rumor swirling about the boats during the escape had indicated, there had, in fact, been one man in the fleet, a boatsteerer, willing to risk his life for the estimated $1.5 million in salvage. Clearly he'd little idea of just what an awful and potentially lethal mess he'd headed back into, but for a time he successfully became both the captain, crew, and single passenger on the *Massachusetts*. He'd live to regret this adventure.

BOOK FOUR

Rolling Out on the Fin

18

Enough to Fill a Book

Once more unto the breach, dear friends, once more.
—*William Shakespeare,* Henry V

Even if Williams's reputation had been stove in by his recent collisions with the Arctic's uglier side, he was still ready to, in a sense, strike back at those forces that had conspired against him. He wasn't the sort to become introspective or dwell on failure, and the prior year's misfortunes offered a unique chance to take a kind of revenge and increase his worth simultaneously. "A rich prize in whalebone awaited anyone who should be fortunate to find these deserted vessels, if still afloat, when the ice broke up in the following summer," as one contemporary put it. Williams, among some of the other masters present at the fleet's abandonment, was aware of the beckoning wealth there for the taking for any man with the moxie to retrieve it. It didn't require any actual whaling: He'd catch what'd already been caught. The enterprise wouldn't even require the tedious prospect of the hunting itself. Making the best of this very bad situation, Williams needed to simply rescue that poor unfortunate oil and bone, lost as it was on the coast of Alaska.

At some point, using what remained of his reputation as captain and man of business, Williams was able to get the ear of the mayor of his small city of Oakland: big, booming, and bearded Sam Merritt. He had a six-foot-three frame populated by 340 pounds of flesh and fat. He possessed a loud voice that could carry over a ship's deck and a voluminous laugh to match. Hizzoner was one of the most luminous fixtures in the sparkling firmament that was California as it had been reborn after years of indolence under the moribund rule of Spain. A Yankee transplant, Merritt had, unlike the mostly luckless forty-niners, actually found gold here. If not the yellow metal itself, then the equivalent.

Merritt's route to prosperity had been a circuitous one after he left staid, stagnant old Plymouth, and its elongated impractical harbor, back in the Bay State. He'd originally trained in the then-questionable practice of medicine, but after gold was accidentally discovered at Sutter's mill, like many others looking for an easy fortune, Merritt elected to head west. After all, in this seemingly new Pacific frontier, men could more readily bribe, steal, and bully their way into a great fortune than in the old East, which had already been overrun by those who'd made their fortunes, and had devised means to block others from doing the same.

The Old Colony sawbones sold what he owned and made plans for the great voyage to far-off California. Perhaps realizing the truism that there was more money in peddling to gold miners than in trying to extract the metal oneself, he started assembling a cargo. He missed a fortune more than once. While provisioning, a messenger brought Merritt news of an accident as he headed to Duxbury to buy tacks, and so the fasteners went unpurchased before his ship put New England behind. On dropping anchor in Frisco Bay, he discovered not only were tacks selling for five dollars a paper, but he'd managed to let another bundle slip through his fingers en route by neglecting to buy potatoes in Valparaiso, Chile, of which staple the Californians currently had none. The rest of his goods lacked a market, and desperate, he resorted to earning a living as a doctor, amassing a scandalous $40,000 treating the woeful prospectors. Luckily for Merritt, sick and hurting argonauts awash in mineral wealth were willing to pay a premium for the extortionate doctors of the City of Saint Francis to misdiagnose and mistreat their ailments and injuries.

Looking to cast his bread upon the waters, or at least his money, and increase it, he sent a ship up to Puget Sound mistakenly thinking he would find ice, but instead his vessel arrived back with trees for precious wharf pilings. Next, he sent a captain out with Puget Sound piles for Australia with orders to bring back coal, but somehow the cargo became even more valuable Society Islands oranges. Rising ever higher in estate, eventually

Merritt closed his office on the peninsula and headed east across the cold, wide bay to found on land he owned there the city of Oakland. A mayor, a millionaire, and owner of the finest yacht on the coast, his trip to California had been one of the few of the 'niners that actually had been worthwhile.

It was less than surprising that another big man from the east—the famous whaler Thomas Williams—chanced to meet Merritt and talk business. Williams already owned a vessel, the *Florence,* but he needed partners to help him outfit her. Sage businessman Merritt was game and put up some money, as did a couple of other partners. The redoubtable captain from Oakland would also serve as master of the salvage vessel. The small group of adventurers had a target whose cash value was commensurate with its own considerable capacity for greed. And as it was clear whaling had truly taken a turn for the worse, this venture was probably the best bet for one's money, even if the fleet's demise had given a short boost to the value of whalebone.

In fact, there was enough of a lift so that instead of yielding "supinely" to this nasty turn of weather, some merchants decided to risk yet more property and cash (their own) and lives (others') in the less-than-friendly polar regions. This season, they sent twenty-seven more ships to the Arctic, outfitting five sperm whalers for the north, as well. While the Atlantic sperm fishery remained a fair one for the small fleet that still prowled its choppy grounds, it was unable to sustain a sizable, let alone a grand, industry anymore.

Nevertheless, these efforts were just prolonging the inevitable. The San Francisco insurers on California Street who'd underwritten every Arctic voyage prior to 1871 now viewed the industry as a fatality and refused to issues new policies; anyone looking to launch a ship had to scramble for an underwriter. Back in New Bedford, the "blanket piece" of insurance money paid for the lost fleet went into raising factory smokestacks rather than masts, pressing forward the inevitable reshaping of the once low skyline of the Whaling City. Few of the crews of 1871 had bothered signing back on, and only 60,000 barrels would be harvested in 1872, as compared to the prior year's 110,000 barrels. Of the thirty-four vessels swinging at anchor on the Acushnet, half were for sale, and some of those arriving back would change hands before they even had a chance to be refitted.

On May 25, the *Florence*'s bow pointed north toward the dangerous seas that had already claimed two of her master's vessels. This vessel had a raised poop from whose deck the cabin protruded several feet, ensuring superior ventilation but generally inferior heating during cold weather. She sailed stiffly, which meant she rolled into the wind, and her deck was usually wet. Nevertheless, she was well fitted for this voyage, with plenty of tools, rope, and sails and whaling gear, and was manned by a "sturdy gallant" crew of twenty-six men, who'd the perhaps contradictory qualities of being "both energetic and cautious." Also on board was Thomas Stancel Williams.

It was unsurprising, given these gloomy circumstances, that Williams wasn't the only man to sail through the Golden Gate with big ideas about striking it rich in salvage. The Alaska Commercial Company fitted out the schooner *Eustace,* commanded by Elija Everett Smith, onetime captain of the *Carlotta,* lost the year before; another enterprise launched a bark, the *Francis Palmer.* In contrast with the other wreckage hunters, an ancient Santa Barbara otter hunter named Kimberly was more comic relief than anything else. Reportedly, as eagle-eyed Mexican and "half breed" hunters had killed off most of the native Californian sea otter herds from which he'd been deriving a rough living, Kimberly decided to take his chances in the Arctic.

Short of money, he outfitted the schooner *Cygnet*—not elaborately— and sailed northwest with a half dozen men and a few muzzle-loading Kentucky rifles, planning to ferret out new sea otter rookeries in the North Pacific en route. After passing by Japan to the southern Kurile Islands, he discovered fertile beds full of nearly tame prey that offered themselves as easy targets. In a few weeks, Kimberly slaughtered two hundred, and soon returned to part another hundred sea otters from their expensive skins. Having thus made a bundle from these heretofore unknown rookeries, he never bothered to risk his life salvaging in the Alaskan ice.

Sharing the dangers, if not the spoils, of the wreckers were men on twenty whalers who'd returned to the "precarious sea." The blubber hunters observed this season that the bowheads appeared to be coming east from the Beaufort Sea above Canada into ice that was just slightly less thick than the prior year. In case anyone had forgotten just where they were, the elements were quick to remind them by picking off a few of these whaleships. For instance, on August 18, ice surrounded the aptly named *Helen Snow* and carried her north in a type of Arctic rape. The crew, not liking this situation, over the orders of Captain George Macomber (who'd already lost a vessel to Raphael Semmes), decided to abandon the *Snow* and dropped whaleboats to find open water.

The salvagers engaged in a typical whalers' race to make it through the strait and to the hunting grounds as fast as possible. Speed would determine whether one's venture made any money at all, because the winner would take everything. As later retold, there was nothing worth mentioning about the *Florence*'s voyage until her bow was eighty miles from the strait, still more than four hundred miles from where the fleet was abandoned. On August 19, one of the Arctic whalers, the *Roscoe,* was crushed, and after being gripped by the ice, another, the *Sea Breeze,* was abandoned, and then reoccupied after the ice released her—although when Williams passed her on August 22, she was still on beam ends and he wrote her off as lost.

(At the same time the ice relented on the *Sea Breeze,* the *Helen Snow* also broke free, and three other whalers were stove in. But it wasn't all bad, at least for one captain, Leander Owen of the *Jireh Perry,* for whom this turn of events proved valuable. He'd lost the *Contest* the prior year, and now evened the score against the Arctic by taking the *Snow* back to San Francisco after she'd come free.)

On through the dangerous region ventured the companies. As Williams later recalled, while sailing under the northern lights, he was only able to make his way slowly through the ice. As was typical of the season, at midday the sun beamed almost horizontally on the water, making it sparkle and giving the men warmth, at least till the temperature dropped again at night. As they pushed north, the natives who traded with them had plenty of baleen on hand, and it wasn't hard to guess the bone's origin. After passing Icy Cape, the locals even relayed the promising news that three ships of the fleet were still floating. By July's end, it appeared the race was not going well for Williams, as the other salvors, the *Eustace* in the lead, had made it to Icy Cape; trailing behind was the *Palmer,* just off the *Florence*'s stern.

Knowing a small head start could pay large dividends, Williams outfitted two whaleboats with gear and a month's provisions and sent them up the coast under first mate Edward "Ned" Perry Herendeen. This "lion

hearted stalwart man" had been the master of the *Mary,* lost the prior year
with the other ships. After lowering, the party took to their oars for some
hard pulling, and in a reverse of the exodus of the prior September, they
piloted through a maze of ice, until after about eighty miles, along the
frigid sandy beaches, they started finding relics that had been spit out from
the fleet's bowels. These "promiscuously" scattered artifacts—including
spars, timbers, planks, staves, casks, hoops, soap boxes, and bread—if not
sacred, were at least sometimes valuable. This mess must have appeared the
work of an angry giant. Launching to the small, nimble whaleboats proved a
wise move, for at last they saw the ships, now little more than a line of hulks
adorned with smashed spars and slack lines, running twenty-five miles north
from Wainwright Inlet. To aid in the destruction caused by the ferocity of the
weather was the ineptness of the natives. Thousands of barrels full of oil had
washed ashore, where the Eskimos carelessly smashed them open for their
contents to run out and be reclaimed by the ocean.

A gloomy thing for a whaleman to lay eyes on, this twenty-mile-long
ship's boneyard was a sweet sight for a wrecker. Here was Herendeen's
own *Mary* of Edgartown, crushed and lying ashore in latitude 76 degrees,
40 minutes. Next was the *Minerva,* on her beam ends in the shallows by
Wainwright Inlet, down a few sails, copper chafed, but her hull still intact.
Although her hold was full of ice, along with 130 barrels of oil, she was
seaworthy. The natives, Herendeen observed, given how little they'd
picked at her, apparently just wanted to find out of what she was made.

The bark *Thomas Dickason,* once the property of the high-minded
Howlands, was grounded on her side on a bank, bilged (i.e. damaged
bilge pumps) and full of water, unsalvageable and uninsured, but with
hundreds of barrels for the taking. The *Kohola* was a ruin ashore, and a
stove-in and bilged *Reindeer* lay aground on her beam ends, her innards
encased in ice that wouldn't allow anything to be pried loose. The remains of the *Awashonks* lay in two feet of water. After Williams arrived
with the *Florence,* he recognized the two iron-plated ends of his own
Monticello, the bow and stern sundered by a half mile and frozen into a
cake of ice. Carrying 150 barrels, the *Emily Morgan* had a hole large
enough to let what passed as the Arctic tide run in and out of her. The
Seneca, dragged onshore by the ice, lay twenty-five miles north of the
main pack; although her masts were standing, the bowsprit, jibboom,

and rudder were gone, and the bulwarks crushed. Her hull was sound, but currently welded to a floe.

The wreckers received the grim news that the natives had taken the *Florida* north to the Sea Horse Islands before lighting her up to the water's edge. To the north were two hulks with side timbers poking up, and it was only a guess of whose whole these constituent parts had once been part. Others, such as the *Champion, Gay Head,* and *Concordia,* had gone up in smoke, the latter's destruction perhaps demonstrating that the Howlands hadn't been so clever after all. In consequence of their arson, some of the local natives, fearing revenge, had hidden inland.

The party also found a living remnant of the Fleet of '71: the boat-steerer who'd reversed course the prior September and stayed the winter in the *Massachusetts.* He looked a wreck himself, and his story wasn't exactly an inspiration. Four days after the whalers left, as the boatsteerer observed, the ice froze completely, providing a platform for the Eskimos to safely walk out to the ships and help themselves to whatever hadn't already been plundered. The natives, usually deprived of the comforts most whites took for granted, were having a grand time. Freely, they trod on the whalers' decks in their sealskin boots, prying loose wood and iron, or climbed into the rigging to cut away sails for use as hulls in their umiaks or to cover their summer huts. One Eskimo, whose taste ran to the finer things, even helped himself to some wood paneling to decorate the interior of his igloo.

Although the masters had before abandonment destroyed their spirits, they neglected to dispose of their medicines, which could be more lethal than alcohol, then as now. (According to legend, one Nantucket captain who carried his medicines in numbered bottles found a sickly mate was in need of bottle 13, which was empty. In a burst of inspiration, he combined the contents of bottles 6 and 7, which he fed to the mate, who promptly was cured of life itself.) The Eskimos drank the whalers' medicines, and instead of euphoria, they became sick; some possibly died. In response, they torched any ship where there'd been a poisoning, possibly either to purge a supposed taboo or for revenge. These arsons also provided some spectacle. After all, there was sufficient wood in the body of a whaler carcass to supply them with fuel to light up their feasts for a long time to come. Perhaps they even created a fire they wrote a song about.

There was another irony: Fourteen days after abandonment, in one of God's small jests, an eastern gale struck so hard it drove everything but the ground ice away. "Of all the butting and smashing I ever saw, the worst was among those ships, driving into each other," said the anonymous refugee. "Some were ground to atoms, and what the ice spared, the natives soon destroyed, after pillaging them of everything they pleased." The submerged hulks remained in place, keeping each other company for that long dark winter, along with one white man and a scattering of natives.

The boatsteerer's prospects were, at first, favorable; the Eskimos even helped him stack the abandoned baleen. Then for some reason never made clear, perhaps the violation of some taboo, they later turned on him, stole his stolen bone, and decided to be rid of him eternally. The tribe's women had intervened to save him, and some old chief then lent him his protection. Later, the current carried the *Massachusetts* around Point Barrow. That summer he abandoned her for the second time, and after a five-day trip reached the fleet's original resting spot around Point Belcher. When the wreckers found him, he was about used up, but was able to offer some sage advice, earned through hard experience: "A hundred and fifty thousands would not tempt me to try another winter in the Arctic." When he went home with the other refugees of that season on the *Florence,* it's not clear what—if anything—of his foraging he took with him.

Having outraced their rivals, Williams's crew worked to also beat the end of the season by flensing the remains of the hulks as rapidly as possible. The men had the double incentive to work hard: It helped keep them warm in the cold air while increasing their profits. Getting oil into the *Florence* required the crew to roll the casks into the surf and tow them out to the bark. They got the ice out of the *Minerva*'s hold. When the tide rolled in, they managed to get her afloat, and once again she dropped anchor. The salvors outfitted the vessel with new sails and gear, and according to one account, Williams even appointed his son Stancel as her master.

As the operation progressed, the company relieved the *Reindeer* and *Contest* of the burden of their cargoes as well. With all this success, it became clear that Williams would "do well," as one clearly envious observer wrote from the deck of the whaler *Live Oak.* The writer also claimed in his letter home the winter was mild, with only small ice, thus making salvaging easy, but he may have been exaggerating. After all, he was stuck earning his lay the old-fashioned way and probably wanted to downplay the salvors' efforts. However, Williams wasn't alone in the plundering. The *Eustace*'s Captain Smith also managed to help himself to what had been the beached and unsalvageable *Thomas Dickason* and was the first to get his hands on the *Seneca*.

As most of the oil wasn't in the hulks, but in barrels on shore that had been landed by the natives, the deft trader Williams started swapping guns, ammunition, blankets, and trinkets to recapture it and the bone. (Liquor wasn't reported as part of his commodities, to his credit.) About a month after his arrival at Point Belcher, and the season closing with the late summer thaw, the ice began to move, giving Williams's crew the chance to make a vigorous bid for the *Seneca*, which was now coming free of the floe that had imprisoned her. They rigged her with a rudder, fastened her to the *Florence*, and on September 5, the tiny fleet headed south with a fine northwest breeze in their sails. On the eighth, Williams made East Cape, finding ice spanning half the distance across Bering Strait.

About this time the Arctic tapped him on the shoulder. A strong southwest gale blew in, which belted the mated ships and moved the field ice. Suddenly faced with life or death for his own flagship, Williams had to cut loose the *Seneca*. She crashed ashore and was ruined—finally, this time—not that he could waste time to worry about that. He only was able to save the *Florence* by standing her in half-hour tacks. The next day, he made Plover Bay for water, and from there sailed to San Francisco weighed down with a catch of 1,500 barrels of whale oil and 80,000 pounds of bone, along with some of the grateful crewmen from the whalers that'd been wrecked that season. He was again lucky. Having lost three ships in the Arctic, he'd managed to recapture one. Fortunate indeed: Although Williams had escaped without any major accident, if anyone needed reminding that the rules of the Darwinian lottery were still in effect, that same winter, the *Ansel Gibbs* (a ship we have met earlier) had the misfortune of being locked in at Hudson's Bay in eastern Canada; unable to return home, scurvy picked off fifteen of her crew.

The *Minerva* herself also proved a good catch, and by order of the U.S. Court, she was sold on Front Street for $5,350 on behalf of "whom it may concern," with the reporter who was covering the transaction noting that the vessel went cheap. The buyer was an old whaler who planned to take a cargo of rail ties south and then outfit her to "search for the oily monsters of the deep." With a few repairs she could last many years.

Naturally, these goings-on were of great interest throughout San Francisco and Honolulu. Shipowners and insurance agents wanted to reclaim what they could of their oil and bone. A spirit of suspicion prevailed. Rumors flew about whalers in the Arctic sneaking oil back on the sly; coopers examined ships' casks for their markings to see what vessel they'd originated from. Inquiries and claims about the original ownership of the goods were made. (One whaling master, looking to avoid sharing his salvage with the owners, craftily poured oil from the old ship's casks into his own, then burned the old staves to prevent identification. He later claimed he'd found the barrels as wreckage and didn't know what ship they were from.)

Accordingly, Williams also faced "tedious lawsuits" from the original owners. One Sunday, after his arrival home, an uninvited and unwelcome stranger presented himself at Williams's door in Oakland. He claimed to be a reporter, then, as now, a sordid profession, and he was snooping around for yet more information on the successful voyage. This pesky scribe put Williams on his guard, and he said, "I have reported everything there is to report, and you have it all in the *Alta* [a California newspaper]."

The reporter asked, "Do you claim salvage?" (That meant perhaps Williams would only net something like 75 percent of the goods' value.)

"Salvage! No! We intend to claim all that we have got." When the *Alta* reporter persisted, Williams said: "There, that's all I intend to tell you." While the reporter was apparently as greedy for knowledge as Williams and Co. had been for wreckage, the master thought he sniffed an incognito detective or insurance agent. "I don't know what your motive is in coming here, and I don't intend to take your for word for it."

"Golly," the reporter said, perhaps realizing he had collided with an obstacle as hard as an ice floe. He described it as just one of the many "difficulties thrown with rude hands" to men of his particular craft. Faced with what, coyly, the reporter was to call Williams's "inexplicable modesty," he decided to tack more obliquely. Rather as Williams stalked unsuspecting whales, he approached stealthily, asking innocuous questions and eventually sparking interest in the "bluff heart of the Arctic wrecker." He queried about the Polar Sea, asking if the east and west Arctic Oceans were one body. The whaler known as having pushed farthest north said, with what appears to have been professional pride: "No: I believe there is a continent of ice, possibly with a current of water underneath. I believe there is ice up there that never did come and never will. I've been up to latitude 73 degrees, almost as far as Captain Long went, and I know there was solid ice ahead."

The reporter (apparently referring to the British naval explorer Sir William Parry) said, "But Mons Pary holds a different opinion. He says—"

"Pary is a [damned] fool, and you may say that I said so. He don't know what he is talking about." As for passing through a Northwest Passage: "It is impossible. You hear of folks talk of taking dogs and reindeer and crossing the country, but it's all theory." Concluding the impromptu chat, he said, "Well, I might give you a very interesting account of our voyage— perhaps I will some time."

"Oh! thank you; but I think I've enough for the present."

"Enough! Why I haven't told you much, I'm sure." The reporter said there was a column's worth, amazing the old whaler. "A column! I'd like to see you make a column out of what I have said. I'm sorry I can't oblige you to-day. I could tell you enough to fill a book; but I object to doing so now. It will all come out by and by, if there is any suit brought to recover the property. Then it will be shown whether we had a difficulty or not."

19

Appreciable Deterioration

Some day a cleaner craft than the Yankee whaleboat may be evolved; some day man may fashion a machine more beautiful than a full-rigged ship; but I doubt if ever there will be a braver or a sturdier race of men bred in this world than the officers of that vanished fleet. There is one other thing that I hold certain: If ever there is to be fairer and better hunting than the chase of the sperm whale, man will have to voyage to other worlds to find it.

—*Clifford W. Ashley,* The Yankee Whaler

WHALER *FLORENCE,* CHRISTMAS DAY, 1873, GOLDEN GATE

Teenaged Willie Williams watched his fifty-four-year-old father take his place at the main hatch to give the opening speech to christen this ill-fated voyage. Oddly enough, Willie was one of the more seasoned hands on board, and upon completion of this trip, as cabin boy, he'd be entitled to a one two-hundredth lay. Even the youth's relatively untrained eye saw that the crew, such as it was, now assembled in the waist, was a nondescript gang of landlubbers and semisailors. Privately, he wondered if they could be converted into competent mariners before the ship made it to the Arctic and back this season.

One can only guess what the very practiced eye of the Old Man, who owned and captained the vessel, made of what he saw in front of him. While the mix of men had always varied from ship to ship, there was getting to be a preponderance of the worst and least desirable material. The agents doing the recruiting had gotten less picky, if that was possible, about their prospects, and the overall quality of the manpower in the fleet was perhaps worse than ever.

As Willie learned, the *Florence* had her fair share of less than seaworthy human flotsam: Two of the crew had signed the ship's articles in the belief they were going for a short fishing trip to the Farallon Islands; by now the wretches had realized they were on the biggest fishing trip imaginable, for the biggest fish ever. Naturally, such hoodwinked green hands lacked any gear, let alone the kit to let them survive the Arctic, and this meant having to dip into the slop chest. They weren't alone, as most of the other green hands had nothing either, and needed clothes. They were warned not to trade these items with natives when they put into port, presumably for trinkets or the temporary use of a certain female anatomical part of great interest to sailors.

Given the awful pay and food and the other miserable conditions, not to mention the fact that hunting the biggest animals in the world had no great correlation to longevity, it wasn't surprising how few men now signed on at all. In San Francisco, recruiters soon resorted to kidnapping their green hands.

(Dubbed crimps, the men engaged in this calling drugged their victims, and while they were in a stupor, hauled them on board ship. One legendary San Francisco crimp, Nikko the Lapp, even resorted to delivering dummies stuffed with straw into the ship's berths. Sometimes, to make them seem like men suffering from delirium tremens, he stuffed a few rats into the arm for special effect. One tavern keeper named Miss Piggot, also of San Francisco, reputedly served up a spiked drink, not unsurprisingly called Miss Piggot's special, and dropped the soon-to-be mariner through a trapdoor to the waiting crimp.)

Given the motley crews of unemployed ragtags pumped out of the Golden Gate every season, ultimately, the only question was why the officers were so relatively gentle. After 1871, very few able men who signed on made mate or captain—soon, almost none rose to a master's position—and that meant there was little incentive left. Whalers such as Thomas Williams had gone to sea not out of despair or fear of the debtor or the law, but because they wanted to succeed at the profession. They'd wanted get out of the shadow of their birthplace and didn't need to be drunk to join a crew, nor be forced up into the shrouds for fear of the belaying pin—although that probably helped from time to time. These were the men who had obeyed orders because they were necessary to succeed at their profession.

Among the *Florence*'s crew, it later proved, was a dreaded sea lawyer, whom Willie seemed to consider as dangerous to the ship's progress as a reef. Such lawyers, by repute, could raise a stink with any U.S. consuls they met with and hold up the voyage with litigation, although the magistrates they protested to over real or imagined legal infractions by the captain and mates usually were ineffectual. The roster got still worse. Defying reason, there was an eighteen-year-old gangster in steerage whom Willie dubbed of the "Frisco type," not in flattery, and the lowest variety of that type, to boot. Nobody knew why he was there, except that perhaps his gang, settling some grudge, had managed a double cross to land him on the *Florence*'s deck. If so, it must have been a considerable slight they were avenging. So bad was the young thug, the Old Man ordered—and his mother Eliza implored—Willie to avoid any contact and contagion with him. After all, he was officially a member of the after gang that managed the ship, and only half a whaler. The other half was occupied with being a young, respectful boy of the Victorian era. No point in mixing with the deckhands.

As bad as it might have been for the after crowd, it was probably not much of a Christmas for the forlorn and apprehensive green hands, either. They faced the great empty ocean, and once the glow of the Farallon lighthouse had faded from sight, that was largely the end of any civilized illumination, except what they carried, for many a league. As always, the greenies also had to contend with seasickness and the attendant torture the more experienced men inflicted on them. As one green hand tried to pass through the small lubber hole—an opening in the top platform of the mast—the deck had some entertainment. Willie found the greenies both exasperating and funny, depending on their ignorance. Despite being young, he'd the advantage of being ship born and raised.

No doubt making it worse for the green hands was the way the *Florence* rolled, which made sure the decks were always wet and potentially dangerous. Even the hogs, animals known to be great mariners, found themselves skidding as they wandered across deck, until they learned to lie safely in the lee scuppers. Yet even equipped with knives and clothes from the slop chest, the crew still lacked something more important than any tool: the ambition and courage to succeed at a job that demanded both. Hence, in shaping and directing them, the very capable mates on board had to compensate for the lack of the men's enthusiasm with profanity and energy. More than ever, the crew had to fear the officers more than the dangers they were commanded to dare. This schooling was a touch brutal, but even if the end result of the process wasn't an able seaman (the age of miracles having passed), at least by voyage's completion, these sailors might know how to slack a lee brace, coil a rope from left to right, and hand-reef and steer. Above all, they'd know better than ever to go whaling again.

As at the beginning of all voyages, the officers and captain began to divide the ship into watches. During the ritual, Willie heard his father say: "I will take my boy for the stroke of my oar boat." Like other young boys, Willie was fascinated by the world of men, and now he was prouder than ever to be included in it at last. The child being the father of the man, Williams must have shared his son's pleasure. (It's also likely he had his own private reasons for this choice. His wife had probably urged him to keep the boy in sight, and needing to make sure the whaleboat was perfectly balanced, the relatively small and light Willie could serve him on the stroke oar.)

As cabin boy, Willie was assigned second table on the second watch, which he shared with the cooper, while his father presided over first table with the first mate, Eliza, and Mary Watkins. Although the fare back there was certainly preferable to the forecastle's slop bucket, it was still monotonous, unless his mother intervened and cooked a real New England dish for the afternoon tea. Accommodations, of course, were far from luxurious for Willie, whose berth in his family's staterooms in the starboard side of the cabin was so tiny, if he wasn't careful, he was prone to hit his elbows or head on the deck beams above. As long as the cabin door was closed, there was no ventilation, and for nighttime diversion, there was the song of the *Florence* to listen to; he learned her rhythms so well that when she creaked, he knew what part of the twenty-year-old girl was under stress and limbering up.

The educational opportunities on a whaler were limited, but at least Willie could, if he wanted, learn what life course not to sail. For instance, during the voyage, he observed the dissolute mate Frenchy, whose memory of his mother country was so dim about the only bit of his native tongue he could manage was "La Marseillaise" when drunk. This mate, in the tradition of so many wretches wedded to debt and the sea, had before shipping out squandered a lay of $1,000 twice over, along with his advance for this voyage, on rum and women in one of San Francisco's Bay's cheap waterfront rooms. He already owed the *Florence* $500. The fourth mate was a "Gee"—a large black man from Brava in the Azores—not likely to do better than make third mate, maybe. Then there was the steward, who reputedly had been a revolutionary in China but, loving strong drink, had failed in all but keeping his head on his shoulders. Also dipsomaniacal was the flamboyant cook, and in between cruises, the kindly Eliza would herself supervise him at the family home in Oakland to keep him from lapsing back into inebriation. (It proved a lot of fuss for someone who was before the decade's end going to endure what must have been a lingering awful death on the wreck of the Arctic whaler *Mount Wollaston*.)

Willie knew that if he strayed, he'd be facing a rope's end wielded by his father, and that kept him on the proper tack. For instance, like all sailors, the boy wanted a tattoo, but the Old Man had warned him of the tattooing job he would do on him if he found his body carrying one. With no doubt his father was in earnest, Willie obeyed the order. Unlike most other young men at sea, from another point of the compass, his gentle mother was present to exert a civilizing influence on him.

But a boy will always be a boy. After the sea lawyer on board demanded limes to help stave off scurvy, Williams was forced to anchor at Guam to procure them. To his chagrin, he'd chosen to visit this most Catholic of islands during Lent, and the local priest decreed there would be no commerce that day. Although Williams turned the air blue with cussing, he failed to get his fruit and had to wait for the holiday to pass. While stuck on shore, Willie drank just enough wine to prevent his father from detecting his drunkenness, and even bought a gamecock, which he smuggled on board. While he bragged about its presence to the crewmen, and after they had assembled to watch, he pitted the vicious fowl, armed with spurs on its talons, against his family's Oakland rooster. The professional fighting cock quickly dealt the domestic-bird-turned-sea-traveler his fate with one precise leap. With the evidence of his mischief fairly blatant, Willie knew he was due a licking from his father.

When he told his mother, who especially despised cockfighting, her only reply was: "Willie, how could you be so cruel?" The words hurt more than the beating, which he never received.

The early part of the voyage was uneventful, and the first whales sighted turned out to be illusory. To break the monotony, Willie did go on a hunt of his own, fishing for the sharks that swam near the *Florence*. One he managed successfully to hook was about to yank him overboard when he released the line. The Old Man had some ambition for him, and began to steer him toward a nautical vocation that followed his own. As three of the *Florida*'s mates didn't know how to read, and as the fourth, not planning to rise to captain, hadn't bothered to learn the crucial skills to determine latitude and longitude, one day Williams told Willie:

"Boy, I am the only man on this ship that can work out a sight and you must learn how, so that if anything happens to me, the ship can be navigated back to San Francisco."

So, as many a budding young mariner had done for decades, it was time for Willie to study Bowditch's *American Practical Navigator,* the not always accurate, if indispensable, bible of seafaring Yankees. Learning the navigation calculations, he was able to determine direction, but without, to put it mildly, complete precision. During one of his afternoon celestial observations held daily between two and three, Williams checked a set of his son's calculations and realized they would have landed the *Florence* on a beach. Casually, the Old Man said if the same mistakes were made the next day, it meant a licking with a rope's end. Knowing his master and father's threats were never idle, Willie's memory was braced, and the mistakes were never repeated. In fact, he became so good a navigator his work later exposed a malfunction in his father's chronometer. Looking to further his whaling career, he also began preparing his weak and probably cracking teenage voice to boom by calling out the watches. Clearly, it would have looked foolish for him to take his turn at the mast only to let all that precious lard and bone swim away because of the inability to cry out loud enough to alert the crew.

In his writings, Willie never mentioned competing with his older brother, Stancel, for success or their father's respect, and the absence of reference to a rivalry makes it seem conspicuous. They weren't the only children in the family business: Sister Mary Watkins was also put to use in the service of the *Florence*. Her job was to heave overboard a line with knots tied in it at regular intervals. As the rope paid out, its speed was measured using an hourglass to determine the velocity of the ship. As she pointed out, it was something a girl could do as well as a man.

The voyage continued, one mate's bellow at a time, and as it did, the green hands became something like decent mariners. Willie observed, as the two ends of the ship got to understand each other a bit better, they both became mellower. Although under orders not to mix with the crew, nor even go forward of the tryworks, Willie managed a taste of the forecastle life. There in the nose of the *Florence,* he saw how the men spent their spare time, mostly telling lewd stories or describing in detail love affairs, presumably some of which'd actually happened. Through his observations, Willie realized the kind of crew that'd sailed under his father in the *Monticello* was composed of different and better material than this one. It was, he realized later, more evidence that somehow the Civil War had led the best men out of the fishery and there was an "appreciable deterioration" in the minds and bodies of those who took their places.

The maritime habits were fading away as well. Outside of one straight-haired, stiff-backed Kanaka who could yodel, this crew was unable to sing. The men couldn't even do the simple call of "yo-heave-ho"; of the few ditties they learned on this voyage; the only one they sang with zest was "Whisky Johnny," belted out in hopes of getting the master to tell the mate to dole out spirits. Just a few years before, the *Monticello* had no green hands, and the men all sang. These not-so-capable hands, cruder and less ambitious than their predecessors, weren't improving the industry's chances for survival.

Predictably, given the materials the *Florence*'s crew was made of, there was a near mutiny when a gang of men decided to turn this voyage into a passenger cruise. Looking to disembark during a port stop, they picked up their bundles and went on deck, with plans to take a boat and try their luck on shore. The second mate took note of the goings-on and warned the master, who climbed on deck amidships and asked the would-be deserters where they were going.

The response was, "We have gone as far as we intend and we're leaving the damned old hooker before she drops beneath us. Step aside if you don't want to get hurt."

That was all it took. Without replying, Williams plowed into the crowd, his long arms working like pistons and the men flying like tenpins. Despite his age, the Old Man had maintained his potency, and the officers and boatsteerers watching in the waist knew enough not to interfere as he made a hash of the gang. The fracas ended when one man, seeing the plot foiled, tried to run for it, but stumbled, giving the master a chance to stretch out his long arms and take him by the ankle with one hand and the pants' seat by the other. Tossing him into the forecastle hatchway, he crashed into the fleeing rearguard trying to squeeze down inside. Williams had a "fine time" while navigating around this particular obstacle. When three other deserters were recaptured from shore, as punishment they were forced to pound rust off the anchor chain and listen to the gibes of their shipmates.

It was unfortunate the *Florence* had so poor a crew, for this turned out to be a not propitiously favored voyage; the ship needed able seamen. While approaching the line of the equator, St. Elmo's fire appeared, a bad omen. It wasn't surprising that even Willie had his own mishap; like his father on his first trip, he incurred moon blindness, his eyes weeping involuntarily. The teen attributed it to sleeping on deck in an effort to avoid the heat of his tiny berth. Bad luck wasn't limited to him. At Pleasant Island, which must have lived up to its name, one man went over the side to become a beachcomber. Willie noted that, like other deserters, he would stay there till the natives became bored with his presence and made him vanish. In any case, his absence was filled by two stowaways who appeared suddenly when the *Florence* was several miles from shore. One was a vendor of hats, two of which he'd been unable to peddle; these he placed on his head before jumping over the side to swim home. The other, who would be known as "Sam Kanaka" and had a "Malay" look to his face unique to this island, remained on board and signed on as replacement.

On the *Florence* went in her tween-season cruise, and it proved that as bad as her crew was, the ship's master and mates were correspondingly outstanding, and their acts permanently etched in Willie's brain images of daring and skill. He admired the helmsman's ability to gently maneuver the ship close to speak to another whaler and arrange for a gam without a collision. He noted the complete trust his mother had in the skill of the men protecting and surrounding her. After a gam ended, when being rowed back on board, the *Florence*'s crew lowered a boat for her to the surface of the water and the men below transfered her into it. Once she was in the lowered boat, the crew hoisted it and Eliza up to the rail. Once there, she, small and surefooted and completely obedient to the crew's instructions, stepped out safe and dry on deck. Nothing ever went wrong during these transfers, but Willie was sure everyone breathed a sea of relief when they were concluded. It wouldn't have done to dump the Old Man's wife into the ocean.

As with many other sons, to Willie his father was a god. More than once he saw the Old Man at his best, beating off a rocky and destructive lee shore during a storm where even a small mistake would be fatally uncorrectable. As Willie recalled, the tall master was on the lee side of the quarterdeck, one hand holding the mizzen shrouds, his trained eyes looking forward at the white foam under the *Florence*'s bow. All hands were on deck, spray was flying along the entirety of the *Florence*, her scuppers had sunk underwater, and it seemed she was going to run ashore. As the sea lifted the vessel, a rifle crack of a voice called: "Hard a-lee!"

Thunder rolled back in answer, but the men obeyed, adjusting the sails and rigging, and although the decks were covered in water, the "old girl" swung offshore, as the skilled Williams had intended. It was just another day in the whaling life.

As this was a blubber trip, you could safely lay your money down a number of people on board were not going to make it home. Death stalked this voyage like all others, as a polar bear stalks a man, keeping its distance and striking at will. The question was just when. Once, as Willie watched, the boatsteerer in charge of Williams's whaleboat lost control of the lines attached to the sail. The wind ballooned the canvas to the head of the mast and capsized the boat, a potentially fatal situation, but, luckily, the entire crew survived.

Anything might happen: once, during the hurried unhooking of a boat's falls to pursue a bowhead, a mate's bomb gun, propped up against the craft's stern sheets, mysteriously went off. The fired lance cut the mate's face from chin to over the eye, fracturing the bone above the brow, and he fell back into the arms of the officer behind him. Though blinded with powder and blood, he was still conscious and made his way back up to the deck almost on his own. Lacking antiseptics or the perilous anesthetics of the time,

Williams had to ply his sometime craft of surgeon to sew up the ruined face. The nature of the injury made the situation especially troublesome, as the big strong mates trying to hold the wounded man in place couldn't stomach their gory task till the end of the operation. It was up to blood-repulsed little Eliza to show her "nerve and grit" and keep the head steady. With her husband plying the needle and thread, they succeeded. After four weeks, the wound healed, and eventually a silver plate was inserted where the bomb had fractured the brow, after which only a slight scar remained to serve as reminder of the accident.

Even before the crew took their first whale, one warm day the new crewman, Sam Kanaka, was on deck, excited and talking fast in what appeared to be his own language. This was just the latest episode of odd behavior. He'd been acting so queerly some thought he should be in irons. However, when brought before Williams, outside of a worried look in his eyes, he looked healthy and made no complaint of the crew. The Kanakas from Ocean Island, which was near Friendly Island, didn't understand his language and decided he was just homesick. It was left at that—until the day when, in his odd state, he grabbed Willie's wrist. The teenager pulled it back, and Sam gave him a wild look and went aft, leaving him squatting on the deck. Although he sensed all was not right, he knew mentioning the incident to the mates would have just provoked their laughter.

But Sam was lethal indeed. He next headed toward a young German crewman just awakened from a sleep on deck. The youth carried a sheathed knife, and when in reaching distance, Sam pulled the blade out and slashed him fatally before attacking another Kanaka, who fled into the rigging with only a cut shirt. Someone shrieked, and the other men on deck scattered while Sam headed to the forecastle, where on the steps sat an unsuspecting mariner reading a book. Sam cut him twice and the victim made it up the stairs only to fall lifeless on the deck. Later, Willie realized that day he'd been his closest ever to dying. During his encounter with Sam, the section of rail that had been nearby was only a foot high from the deck: The madman could have tossed him overboard easily. By the time a rescue boat was launched, it could easily have been too late.

Sam continued his rampage. Finding no one below, he came back up on deck with the bloody knife before heading aft. As he did, Harry, a boat-steerer, was coming out of the hold, and assessing the situation, he grabbed a harpoon lying on the carpenter's bench that was awaiting sharpening. He drew it back to spear Sam, but coming behind him was Captain Williams. "Don't dart," he commanded.

Thus spared, the madman went back to the forecastle, and needless to say, there were no volunteers sick enough of life to follow him down. Nor, predictably, did Sam obey Williams's orders to come back up. As for Willie, after hearing the shriek, he knew someone had been murdered, and ran down to the cabin and procured the Old Man's Spencer rifle and brought it back up on deck, loaded. Wisely, the first mate took it away from him, noting the combination of this teen and the weapon could prove more dangerous than a lunatic. Disarmed, Willie helped the white-faced young German, whose bowels were hanging out but who was still walking erect, lie down on a bulkhead. Eliza also came on deck, behaving as coolly as any man there, and over the mate's objections, refused to return to the cabin. Taking command on her own, she sent Willie and the dipsomaniac steward down to fetch pillows and a shawl while she bathed the German's head and face. The son marveled at his timid mother's self-control, and he voted her "superb."

It was time to bring Sam's tragedy to its ultimate conclusion. Armed with rifles, some of the crew went into the forehold and used tools to break open the forecastle bulkhead, while a guard remained at the scuttle to catch him if he came on deck. Still wanting to help, Willie fetched another firearm, a pepperbox self-cocking revolver that carried caps in all six barrels, allowing it to fire automatically, like a miniature Gatling gun. This time it was the unarmed second mate who took it from him. With Sam moving from berth to berth in the dark, empty forecastle, the suspense on board was terrible. As he moved among the bunks, someone's rifle bullet found its mark, and he dropped dead. Willie's revolver malfunctioned during the melee, and shot only once.

After the crew were certain Sam was dead, the hunting party passed the body up to the deck, and without ado slid it over the rail into the Pacific. That done, the crew breathed a sigh of relief. After setting colors at half-mast, all hands mustered onto the waist to hear Williams read the service of the dead for the slain forecastle reader, now sewn up in a weighted canvas bag. The ceremony completed, the corpse was slid down a plank into the sea. The next day, the corpse's solitude was interrupted by the presence of the young German, who had died without a whimper. While the ugly event itself was closed, in that compressed universe of the whaler, a depression hung like a dark cloud over the ship, and took some time to dissipate.

There was a somewhat comic addenda to this grim story. Another islander on board told the first mate he feared for his life, and Williams ordered an eye kept on him. The situation worsened when, during the dog watch, the Kanaka, sputtering out his own jargon, fell down on his knees before Williams, who assured him no one wanted to hurt him and sent the man forward. A few days later, the native repeated the scene, leaving Willie amazed at his father's restraint. Yet again, the Kanaka made it to the raised poop deck and prostrated himself before Williams, who was taking his exercise by walking back and forth. The master apparently decided some rough medicine was in order to doctor the ailing crewman. He stretched out a long arm, grabbed the sailor by the collar with his right hand, and lifting him up, spun him around and shoved him forward, putting a boot in his rear for good measure. The Kanaka was airborne for ten feet, and after landing didn't stop moving till he was ahead of the tryworks—a considerable throw, akin to something a modern professional wrestler might have executed. Whatever the cause of his ills, the Kanaka thereafter ceased his prostrations.

There were other comical moments, too. When in Saipan, the crew adopted a small but feisty goat, appropriately named Billy; young Willie had some knowledge of such bucks, having owned one in Oakland. (That relationship had ended when the beast took over the house verandah and barred Eliza from entering until Willie had arrived back home from school. Thereafter the goat had been banished.) Not surprisingly, Billy became popular with the men, who for laughs harnessed his aggression and taught him to butt anyone in the rear who happened to bend over. This was an effective way to break up the ship's discipline. Growing larger, Billy started writing his ticket off the ship when he ate a pan of dough from the galley. Later, he sealed his fate when the first mate leaned over to pick up a dropped match to light his pipe. Butting his rear, Billy nearly sent him through the cabin bulkhead. The goat suffered a licking and thereafter became a gift to some natives who'd come on board.

The bad mood created by mad Sam evaporated like a morning fog when one lucky Kanaka caught the first sight of a spout and won a precious reward of twenty pounds of tobacco. Boats lowered. Ordering Willie to follow him, like a general might watch a battlefield, Williams climbed into the rigging with his spyglass to view his men as they attacked the whale, a sperm. Even at this distance from the actual fight, the old hunter was excited. Initially, it was like a normal fastening: A spout appeared just in front of one of the boats, the boatsteerer stood up, white water began to churn . . . but the prey neither sounded nor ran.

"He has either missed the whale or the iron has drawn," said the master. Willie expected that the boatsteerer was due to be broken and forced back to the forecastle, with someone else taking his place. The Old Man then announced he was lowering his own boat and climbed down the shrouds to get ready for battle. Willie remembered he was pulling the stroke oar in that boat and felt a little differently about the job than at the moment when his father had first chosen him. Although in no hurry to join the fracas, as the teenager threw off the after grip to swing the boat clear of the cranes, he knew it was too late for regrets. Over the *Florence*'s side and down the shrouds he went to join his Old Man and the rest of the boat crew on the water. As the crew started rowing, he wished that the whale was twice as far away—until he'd been pulling for fifteen minutes without arriving at the destination.

"Put your back into it," his father commanded from behind him, managing the long steering oar with his left hand while he heaved against the stroke oar with his right. Not wanting to catch a crab (not clear the water with the oar), without fully turning his head around, Willie managed to cast his eye over his shoulder just enough to see they were nearly on the fastened boat. Finally, Williams said, "Way enough," and Willie and his fellow whalers freely looked over their shoulders to view the messy scene the leviathan and his persecutors had wrought. They might have preferred to have kept their backs to the whale.

Willie saw that the boatsteerer had struck the big sperm in the spout hole, preventing him from sounding, and he was now swimming in a circle. A second boat fastened to the whale, making it worse, and the beast had rolled over a couple of times, fouling the lines of the two boats, and the mates had exhausted their vocabularies of every cuss word to drive their crews to paddle into bomb-lance range. Before the action got nasty again, the bow of one boat struck the steering oar of the second mate, lifting him up in the air and dumping him into the water, giving Willie a good laugh. Now it was Williams's turn to attack the sperm, and as the distance between them and the monster closed, the boatsteerer, who was also the ship's cooper, stood up. He then put his leg in the clumsy cleat, took his iron from its place in the bottom of the boat, and got ready to strike. "Give it to him," Williams ordered. The boatsteerer darted, sinking the iron to the hitches.

"Stern all" came the order, which the crew executed raggedly, and the bow struck the whale, who proved very large indeed. The boatsteerer changed places with Williams, who took up the lance, his well-known refusal to fire bombs for the kill was a joke among his men. The crew started hauling in the fastened line, which Willie kept taut to avoid a kink. Aiming for the life, Williams stabbed behind the whale's fin, prompting some violence in the water.

"Stern all," ordered the master again. Although everyone wanted to flee, including Willie and the other green hands, for all their efforts to pull away from the melee, they remained nearly on top of the whale. The beast settled down in the water and then snapped his jaws within an arm's length of the boat; Willie had never seen anything like this. It so frightened the nervous steerage boy, also in Williams's boat, he decided with the curious logic of panic that it was wiser to jump overboard than stay inside. He managed to get his leg on the rail before Williams, whose practiced eye had been on the most frightened of the crew, jumped over a few thwarts, took the lad by the collar, and threw him to the bottom. Overboard men trying to get back into a boat had a knack of grabbing only one side, causing the boat to capsize.

The whale's head came down to the surface again, shipping water in the boat, and when he started running slowly, the men discovered they were quite close to the great flukes. As he swam, the lines connecting him to his tormentors went taut and the ride began, with Williams's boat bringing up the rear, where it remained even as the whale towed them under the *Florence*'s bowsprit. When one of the mates managed to fire a bomb lance into the wretched creature, he spouted blood and died; it was now the whalers' turn to pull the whale.

Thus closed out Willie's first day as a whale killer.

• • •

The 'tween season refused to end without yet another tragedy. Before reaching the Arctic, the *Florence* put in at Ponape so Williams could visit the Reverend Doane. While there, the steward, weary of the world, jumped overboard with shells tied around his ankles to weigh him down and drowned. This was too bad for Eliza and her daughter, because he'd been kind to them, and domestic tranquility in such a tight place was crucial. The family later took on a new steward who looked Chinese, thus earning the hatred of Willie. Back then, as he pointed out, no California boy liked the look of the hardworking and thrifty "Chinaman," whose business skills rendered him enviable monopolies in San Francisco industries such as laundering. As one San Francisco paper of the time noted, they were even beyond Christian salvation, as they had no souls.

The *Florence* reached the North Pacific at last, with the crew switching from their usual civilized garments to native-wrought skin clothing, thus making them look Eskimo-like. Even Willie padded around in a pair of sealskin boots that had a thick bottom layer of oakum. This year Arctic whaling was again evolving, as the captains realized a voyage might only pay at the very end of summer. After some preliminary hunting south in Bristol Bay or the Gulf of Alaska, most of the whalers sailed right to Point Barrow for the brief but hopefully profitable end-of-season hunting in August and September. Some of the bolder masters actually pushed through the dangerous waters off Point Barrow 150 miles east to Harrison Bay, Canada, largely virgin territory to blubber hunters. Some began to even consider pushing on to what they believed were rich grounds between Point Barrow and Banks Island. As it turned out, a sail to Alaska that year probably wouldn't have been worth the risk for Williams: Although the ice was light, the whales were shy and refused to make their expected appearance around Point Barrow.

Expecting poor hunting off Alaska, Williams decided to try his luck in the Sea of Okhotsk. His brother Lewis, under a Russian flag, was also whaling, the single captain to be doing so legally; but rather awkwardly for him, he was unable to catch a whale. As the diversions were few, Willie wanted to go ashore at Okhotsk City, where, as an ailing infant during his first voyage, his mother had taken him for a poultice. Although the governor—a position apparently won by incurring the czar's displeasure—was an old family friend, Williams chose not to risk any contact with what passed for authority there, so avoided landing.

Bad luck dogged the voyage here, as well. After arriving in Shantar Bay, Williams sent out a crew to try shore whaling with little success. He also had a disagreement with the cooper, and replaced him as boatsteerer with Willie. Understandably, the boy felt he'd earned the promotion: He was growing quickly and had some of the Old Man's strength in his young limbs. Moreover, when anyone had been too sick to hunt, Willie took that man's place in the boat. To use Melville's terminology, Willie wasn't merely a squire, he was becoming a knight of the ship. "Life took on a more interesting and important outlook and I prayed for an opportunity to show that I could dart an iron as far and true as any of the boatsteerers," Willie said. Although the mates joked about his new status, when they tested him, the youth proved he could throw the line in a neat coil on deck and ship his oar properly.

To the teen's disappointment, not long afterward, Williams judged he wasn't quite up to the task of joining him in a battle with two devilfish. In part this was because the Old Man was lowering with a darting gun, a weapon comprised of an iron with a bomb lance attached. When fastened to the whale, the bomb was ignited with a fuse triggered as the lance passed into the blubber. After the charge exploded, hopefully the whale was immediately translated into the afterlife. As the darting gun was unwieldy and the blow had to reach a vital area for the bomb to be of any use, the still-too-green Willie had to remain safely on the deck of the *Florence* while his father hunted without him.

Things that day didn't quite go according to plan, as Williams only managed to badly injure his whale but failed to kill it. This at least gave him a chance to indulge in his great love of the lance, which he sank immediately into the stricken beast, who soon spouted blood, rolled fin out, and sank. Luckily, the stinker rose again, and the crew got a chain into its fluke for towing. The other devilfish was more lucky. After the mates in the other two boats had fired every bomb they had into him, he just ran faster, and they didn't want to face such a dangerous opponent at night, so they cut their lines before sunset. On their return, Williams couldn't resist saying, "I expected you would get run away with, you had too many bomb guns."

Eventually, the master decided to cut his line, so to speak, and during a spell of bad weather ran up the signals into the rigging to recall the boats for the last time. This put an end to a poor season that had increased the family wealth by a mere 200 barrels of whale oil and 2,000 pounds of whalebone. As the word spread from the mates to the boatsteerers and crew, the men didn't bother to hide their considerable joy. In fact, Willie thought they were unusually pleased. Still looking for whales, Williams ran the ship under short sail through the Kurile Islands Strait; during this passage, she began to shake and the smooth water nearby became choppy. The elder Williams explained to the younger that someone was facing an earthquake in the islands. Even after entering the Pacific, there was no climactic respite for the *Florence*, and the wind blew hard and raised waves that broke on the bow and swept the entire ship's length. Every morning after a rough night, a nervous Willie counted the rate of strokes of the pump and compared them to those from the night before to make sure they hadn't increased. If so, the ship was taking on water.

This unlucky voyage had yet another tragedy to add to its credit. Spoiling the sail home, just days before reaching San Francisco, a "frenzied" crewman, for reasons unknown, struck the second mate in the head with a blackjack, nearly killing him. Williams put the culprit in irons and sent the mate ashore for doctoring after they sailed through the Golden Gate on November 12. That was to be Willie's last voyage: His ambitions as a whaler, to the degree he had any, were done. The lad whose first sight was the father that delivered him on the *Florida* soon turned his back on the industry. He'd had a full gulp of the sea, having spent three years in five ships. It was for his elder brother to carry on. Stancel had hopes, as ill founded as they were.

20

ↀↀↀ

Looking for a Modern Joshua

Anyone can make history. Only a great man can write it.

—*Oscar Wilde, from "The Critic as Artist," 1891*

WALTHAM, MASSACHUSETTS, MARCH 1877

During March in New England, winter (at least before the current heating trend worldwide aided by whale oil's successor, petroleum) often fights hardily against the flowering of spring. The snow sits lazily on the hard ground or hangs from bare branches. Lakes and ponds are still frozen and just beginning to soften into a slush. The air is crisp, cold, and wet. It was during just this month that a local Homer, bespectacled Alexander Starbuck, was finishing his own *Iliad,* the *History of the American Whale Fishery.* In many ways, it was also the history of his ancestral home of Nantucket—like Siamese twins, the island and the enterprise couldn't be pried apart.

Born in 1841, Starbuck grew up amidst the desolate moors, wild cranberries, heather, and roses that gave the sand spit its stark haunting beauty and made it seem, in comparison with the rest of the Bay State, as if it were from another planet. He himself bore a name synonymous with whaling—in *Moby-Dick,* Melville named Ahab's first mate Starbuck. Indeed, Alexander had ancestors among the island's first settlers, who had subsequently become wreathed in a mist of veneration, deserved or otherwise. Despite young Starbuck's past, like so many other enterprising islanders, he'd left behind the decay amid the low rounded hills of sand and gravel to find his fortune on the mainland. He arrived at the city of

Waltham, whose not accidental position on the Charles River had allowed its denizens to enslave enough water power to fuel factories during
the industrial revolution. Manufacturers were able to make more than
candles here: For the first time on the continent, workers performed under one roof all the work necessary to process fabrics or even assemble an
entire timepiece.

In this modern city, Starbuck worked first as a watchmaker and jew-
eler before his transformation into that architect of exaggerations and sup-
pressions, not to mention chronicler of daily life, that is, a newspaperman.
Although ultimately his desire was to conquer blank pages rather than
whales, he'd a sympathy with the antique Nantucket industry even while
he saw it dying, and wanted to preserve it in some sense. Thus he'd com-
piled the *History;* a massive catalog of the industry that listed the whalers'
voyages, their catches, the ships that came back, those that didn't, the
masters, and the owners. Others had tried to break ground ahead of Starbuck, in the same way men such as Roys had extended the reach of the
whaling fleet itself. One of them was the editor of the Nantucket *Enquirer,*
who'd launched his venture with little encouragement or materials and
eventually abandoned the quest in a less than greasy voyage. Meanwhile,
time had moved on, the newspapers were crumbling, the whaling men
passing on, and the mist of history was closing around the fishery. The
sands dropping quickly in the hourglass, Starbuck pursued like a hunter
the various yellowing documents held by the collectors of the ports of
Boston and New Bedford.

He studied these papers and the voyages they described as if they
might render the secrets of a universe, and, at last, a big picture emerged,
like a painted cloth panorama. (A precursor to celluloid films, a panorama
was a long painted roll of cloth with a sequence of images that told
stories—among their subjects were whaling voyages.) Unlike the whalers
or other men of action of his time who measured success by what they
built or broke, he measured his achievements with another scale, in the
filling up of pages, not barrels. His story described an arc—the rise of a
small people from the blasted and barren moors and sands of his island
from poverty to great wealth, all on the leviathan's broad back. The *History* covered the pursuit of the monsters from the earliest days—back
when the race of small red men, doomed to be dispossessed and dispersed,

chased whales in Massachusetts Bay from canoes with stone-tipped harpoons. It would end with the fall of New Bedford's fleet.

Desolate Nantucket, Martha's Vineyard, and Cape Cod were, for a time, rivals of New Bedford in whaling. Cape Cod, for instance, had little choice—landlubber Thoreau, who walked the coastline of the outer Cape three times, said it was like "traveling a desert." Consider Provincetown—a near miss village whose location was where the Pilgrims had first landed before they debarked at Plymouth. The early colonists who actually did try to survive there so viciously raped the soil by ripping up the local flora and planting crops they awakened a veritable monster. The town turned into a virtual desert, and in its environs, scraggly grass and grotesquely twisted scrub pine and oaks engaged in a precarious and permanent war with the ever-growing sand dunes. These massive golden piles of sand started on the Atlantic's edge at Race Point and ran inland, threatening to devour the rest of the town and even the Cape itself, like a leprosy.

As for what was inland of the Cape, the sharp-eyed prig Thoreau wondered if this "elevated sand-bar in the midst of the ocean can be said to have any interior." It wasn't a surprise that the men here, who dwelled within hearing of the ceaseless crash of breakers on shore, looked to the sea by the 1700s. Whaling, in a variety of forms, was part of this seaward push. These were the days when whaling was a great secret; the method of transmuting the corpse into oil was a valuable and rare skill. The Puritan settlers wooed teachers from Long Island and other places, and, eventually, the art had spread like the Gospel. Cape Cod taught Nantucket to whale, and Nantucket later tutored New Bedford.

At first, farmers took up the iron as a way to fatten their purses in their off season. They waited for the prey to beach themselves—which was frequent. As Thoreau observed: "The restless ocean may at any moment cast up a whale or a wrecked vessel at your feet." Stranded or sickly monsters, blackfish especially, were common sights on the desolate white beaches; a fortuitous mark on a beached blackfish signifying ownership made a man rich. There were fights between the town and the crown over not just who owned the carcass, but the oil, as well. Plymouth, ever with an eye on the heavenly as well the earthly kingdoms, demanded a hogshead from each stinker found. Drift whales being a gift from the Almighty, Eastham and Truro used the oil to pay their ministers.

The rudimentary fishery was profitable enough so that many men in Wellfleet on Cape Cod chased blubber (the whalers even drank in their own tavern, safely separated from the rest of the village). When an unsuspecting leviathan ventured too close to shore, the whalers leaped into the water, making noises to galley and trap their prey. The cry of: "A whale in the bay!" was enough to clear out a town meeting. Using this desultory method, the primitive hunters managed to kill or frighten off the once abundant right whale herds that traditionally had swum just offshore.

Lacking coastal prey, the whalers in the hardscrabble villages dotting the Cape and islands changed their tools and methods. They turned from relying on nets and small craft to costly ships capable of sailing the open ocean. For multiple reasons, not all the towns could build up and out, and the rival ports began lagging in the race of whaling till only Nantucket, Martha's Vineyard, and Provincetown remained in the running with their modest fleets. For instance, during the American Revolution, the English navy blockaded Wellfleet's harbor sufficiently to bottle up its whaleships, and by the time the contract for independence was inked, the old vessels were unseaworthy hulks. As no one had deep enough pockets to build new ships, this killed Wellfleet as a whaling port—leaving its inhabitants to rely on their harbor's reserve of fat tasty oysters till this day.

Nantucket endured the longest as a major island port. One might actually pity the mighty that had fallen. The Faraway Island, as its name meant in Wampanoag, had produced an exceptional race of ornery, morbidly pious, and enterprising mariners the likes of which the world had never before seen—nor would see again. Nantucket, with its sandy, moor-ridden face, was at first a place of Quaker outcasts clustered together near the waterfront, who, until whaling and prosperity came, had lived for generations in pretentious unpretence in their unassuming shingle shacks. They were renowned, justly, for looking askance at off-islanders—with the possible exception being Cape Cod's or Martha's Vineyard's men—the rest of the race they called "coofers [off-islanders]."

Yet it was no great privilege to be from Nantucket. The island's sandy infertility was so dire it had for centuries forced its men to take up the rough work of monster hunting rather than tilling the soil. It did so with a vengeance: At the fishery's peak, nearly all activity on that terminal moraine, doomed some day to be reclaimed by the sea from which it had stolen so much, had bent to the gravity of whaling. Even the cows, some said, came to watch the waterfront's bustle. The ranks of Nantucket's whalers had their share of dour steely men, whose gloomy countenances were often matched by their ponderous names, ripped directly from the King James Bible: Seth, Barzillai, and Obed. They braved innumerable perils and strong rivals to make the scraggly dot of sand, for a time, the greatest whaling port in the world. They had enjoyed some fleeting glory days, to the degree the grim inhabitants celebrated such vanities: It was a Nantucket man who'd first started deep-sea whaling in the pastures of the great open ocean; another had first stumbled on, then killed, the sperm whale, opening a new chapter in the industry's long saga. Trail-breaking Nantucketers began to harvest the mid-Atlantic off Brazil and also rounded Cape Horn. Accordingly, the women were exceptional specimens as well, known for their long-suffering patience, level business heads, and addiction to loneliness-easing opium. Stories abounded of the islanders' whaling-created peculiarities: One boy became famous for trying to harpoon his house cat with a fork; there was even a rumored sorority of maidens who'd marry only a man who'd killed a whale, thus proving his eligibility as breadwinner.

Like Homer, Starbuck had great figures and scenes to depict, ones he'd probably seen with his own eyes: the dour blubber barons carrying on their business, men who dressed in black, ate drably, and found ways to deny themselves every worldly pleasure, yet wrung every cent from their ships and exploited crews. There were the great captains and mates walking erect and strong on the docks, making sure every detail in fitting out the ships was seen to. They were heroes, demigods on that island: In their youth, the boatsteerers were recognizable by the chock pin dangling from around their necks. (This small rounded piece of wood was placed in a small opening in the bow of the boat and kept the line from flying free as it passed out—it also served as a sign of eligibility for marriage.) Inevitably, as in all wars, there were victims and hostages: the tortured women, bonnets hiding their hair, and children, bidding farewell to brothers and fisherman fathers. The sight of a vessel's stern as she rounded Brant Point might be the last glimpse one had of a loved one. As the men plied the waters of the globe, their wives looked forlornly out from widow's walks in fine houses, searching for a sign of a ship, often in vain.

The dead whales offered prosperity. The shacks the first settlers had huddled in gave way to houses that grew ever larger on Main Street, brick by brick, pillar on pillar. The fashion of the world changed, the Quakers eventually left their meeting houses empty, and Baptists and Methodists supplanted them. The former erecting a church on Summer Street, the latter, one on Center Street with pillars in the scandalous Greek Revival style. Starbuck himself was a Unitarian—a wise hedge to all wagers religious. During Nantucket's height, in 1765, one of its sons, Joseph Rotch, sealed its fate. Rotch, like some sort of aquatic mammal about to take an evolutionary leap by returning to dry land, sailed from Nantucket back to the mainland and established the industry in Old Dartmouth—moving whaling's center from his birthplace.

Nantucket's eminence lasted for decades, through two destructive wars, until a sandbar at its ever-shifting harbor mouth began to block ships from passing in. Whalers were ever increasing in size to accommodate longer voyages and greater catches. These larger ships had as much difficulty broaching the bar as did the heavily laden camels going through the needle's eye in Christ's parable. The harbor obstruction had help in ruining the enterprise from other quarters, including, oddly enough, the island's habit of combating fire with separate and competing fire brigades. These incompetent rivals were unable to adequately cooperate to extinguish a wharf blaze before it had destroyed the waterfront. The last blow came by way of a Quaker merchant who had an itching palm. He embezzled enough of his bank's money to crash the institution—the resulting financial shock waves were massive and lethal to the island.

With Nantucket in no condition to fight back, it faced a fierce competitor in New Bedford, which had a deep harbor and whose location enabled direct links overland. For twenty years, from 1859, the year when Starbuck began to work as a clerk, the island's population began its contraction down to three thousand residents and Nantucket took on a "body-o'-death appearance," as one observer put it. On the decline, by the end of 1860s, the harbor was empty, and the only fruits of the sea disgorged there were the fish a few old men caught offshore and sold on the wharves. The offspring of the great whaling men transformed themselves into brave and fierce salvagers of shipwrecks. Left behind were grand stories; nearly every whale voyage could provide the stuff of a dozen romance novels. Yarns for the telling included that of the doomed *Essex,* sunk by an angry whale and her men cast adrift to die or eat one another, the taking of the *Awashonks;* the bloody mutiny of the *Globe;* and many others. And that had been the end of Nantucket.

Now, as Starbuck observed, New Bedford was following in its parent's footsteps. The owners of the whaleships would have sold their ships off if there were buyers, but in the meantime, they had to keep sending them off with as little outfitting and transportation costs as possible to recoup their investments. Thus it was, perhaps, appropriate to look backward at this industry rather than forward to make a projection about its future. This kingdom was doomed to fall. One indicator stands out: Few ships that sailed north failed to return without carrying a scar, making a vessel somewhat resemble a sperm whale that had survived a tussle with a giant squid. "Disasters were the rule and immunity from them the exception, thereby incurring, when the vessels were not lost, heavy bills for repairs, besides the ordinary ones of refitting," Starbuck wrote.

At that time, that great nurturer of industry, the federal government, had become as treacherous and unreliable as the whales and the marketplace. That was ingratitude: The whaling fleet had emptied its ranks to supply the Union Navy with some of its most able mariners in the Civil War. It had been whaling men who'd put out the waterfront blaze in Hawaii—started by whalemen themselves, a fact Starbuck didn't add in his narrative. Now the government's policy was to use coal oils in its lighthouses. This would, he suggested, "further hasten the ultimate abandonment of a pursuit upon the resources of which it draws so heavily in the day of its trouble." The federals should ask themselves if this, the only small subsidy the industry receives, might still continue at the expense of a few dollars more per year.

Not that a few pennies from Uncle Sam was going to help. The industry was clearly headed for some far-off point where it would cease to exist. Even Starbuck queried if the fishery's sun would finally drop into the western horizon. Or, as he put it: "Whether some modern Joshua shall command it to stand still, or whether it shall move still nearer its full setting, is yet uncertain. Some oil will still be used until a perfect substitute is produced at so low a rate that the expenses of whaling will entirely absorb its profits."

As Starbuck was closing his great solitary work, he'd yet another disaster to chronicle, as if he were a storyteller who was informed of a sudden change in plot in midbreath. He'd discovered that thirteen more ships were ruined, the ambergris of the fleet, and fifty men yet to return from the Arctic. This was almost like 1871, except that whalers were dead, and others were still in danger. He held out hopes, noting that unless the whalers faced attack by the "avaricious natives," they might survive the winter comfortably. He observed: "These men are still there, and there seems no feasible way to communicate with them until the summer of 1877."

Starbuck didn't know it, but there never would be a feasible method that summer to talk to those fifty whalers, as there was no way then, as now, to reliably speak to the dead.

21

—◦◦◦—

A Dreary and Uncertain March

There was given an illustration of what man can accomplish in an
emergency.

— *Arctic whaling man John Cook on the events of the autumn of 1876*

WESTERN ARCTIC, SPRING 1876

Things went bad fast in 1876, with disasters that didn't require the end-
of-season finale. In May, before passing through the Bering Strait, the
Marengo collided with the *Illinois,* which sank in fifteen minutes. The remaining twenty vessels of the now-tiny Arctic fleet continued to routinely
whale in the Bering Sea. Contrary to the whalers' hopes, there was plenty
of ice to the north, the weather was cold, and few whales were available.
They took only eleven. By June 1, the crews were walrusing in the Chukchi
Sea, which proved so profitable for the men of the *Norman* and *Northern
Light* they didn't bother to stop, which proved a blessing later.

A south wind began to blow on July 1 and refused to stop till the sixth,
when the next disaster struck. The *Arctic,* an alumna of the class of '71,
was getting an early start to Point Barrow by riding the offshore winds to
Point Franklin. When about eighteen miles off the Sea Horse Islands, the
wind changed direction, surrounding the vessel with heavy ice that pummeled her hard enough to make the *Arctic*'s master heave anchor and drift
along with the pack to keep from being stove in. The ice was a rough companion, rolling her from side to side, and even working under her bottom
and lifting her hull up and, perhaps immodestly, removing her copper
sheathing.

It got worse on the July 7 when she was tied to a large floe. A cake collided hard under the counter, that part of the stern that rises just out of the water. A loud crack exploded through the ship as the wood ends of the sternpost tore loose. After sounding the pumps, the crew discovered two cataracts pouring inside, one on each side of the sternpost, six feet above the waterline. The water level rising sixteen inches every ten minutes, already there was some three feet of Arctic Ocean in the hold. With so discouraging a sign, the crew started retrieving what provisions they could and getting them and the whaleboats onto the ice that was grinding hard around her. By the eighth, the only thing keeping the *Arctic* afloat was the adhesion of the ice itself. When the pack broke up the next day, she fell over on her side, smashing the fore-topmast and topgallant mast. By 8:00 A.M., just one half of the port side even remained above water, and the master decided it was time to run for shore. They took one boat and a dingy, but because of the ice hummocks, it was slow going hauling the boat, so rather than add days to their trip, after making two miles, they abandoned it, taking only what provisions they were able to carry on their own backs.

After a thirty-hour march and "pretty well used up," they made land at Wood Inlet, about halfway between Point Barrow and Franklin. Fortunately, the *Onward* and other whalers were nearby and sent out boats to rescue the unfortunate mariners, each of whom came with only a single shift of clothes and few provisions. One enterprising *Arctic*-er made his own way south, found open water, built a raft, and for the price of his rifle, hired the natives to ferry him to the *Onward*. Shortly afterward, ten more castaway men arrived for redistribution, with the *Arctic*'s captain going aboard the *Rainbow* as a guest of Irishman Barney Cogan.

Between July 20 and August 1, with the ice still clinging to shore, the remaining whalers crept up to Cape Lisburne and east of Point Barrow. Among them were the brothers Williams, Thomas and Lewis. Although they were still prosecuting the family trade, Thomas had left Eliza back home, not for fear of danger, but so she could attend to the education of her children. There was a new ship under Thomas now, the *Clara Bell,* while his brother Lewis walked the quarterdeck of the *Florence,* of which Thomas remained the agent. The elder Williams was coming off a greasy voyage. The prior season, a seven-month hunt had netted him 1,250 barrels of oil with a value some other masters might have taken four years to secure. The whaling had been good overall for the three years prior, and some of the more optimistic dared hope the industry might rise up like one of Christ's healed lame and walk. In fact, during the mild weather of 1875, some of the whalers had ventured three hundred miles east through the Beaufort Sea to Barter Island, making them the second party of mariners to do so since the H.M.S. *Enterprise* had touched there two decades earlier.

Before July closed, the whalers were finding the ice still heavy at Point Barrow. However, after fourteen ships had arrived, on August 1 the prevailing southeast winds ceased, and a northerly wind gusted enough to blow the ice offshore and break it up. Yet the wind remained fickle, the currents strong, and the ice moved rapidly; several times the floes settled back onshore, forcing the fleet to get under way to Point Barrow for safety. Despite the risks they took, no whales appeared until August 14, when a breeze rose from the northwest and stirred up and separated the ice. Bowheads began spouting north of the point and the whaleboats and gear finally were put to the task they'd been made to do. The wind was often westerly until August 18, when it began to blow fresh from the northeast. The ice began to drift with it, forcing the vessels into shore, some anchoring in as little as three fathoms. On the nineteenth, the eastern wind strengthened, and hauling to the north, caused the ice to ground on shore. Threatened, the whalers sailed to the south side of Point Barrow for a few hours before running eighteen miles farther south to the protection of Cape Smythe. The clear space around the ships extended to seven or eight miles offshore. Although the crews took whales, the wind was now blowing from the west, causing an "uneasy feeling" as the area of open water closed steadily.

On August 23, the wind freshened from the northwest, forcing the drift ice in toward shore and around the entire fleet. The masters elected to run for open water or at least get under the shelter of the Sea Horse Islands. The ships included the *Acors Barns, Desmond, Clara Bell, Florence, Josephine, St. George, Marengo, Cornelius Howland, Java, James Allen, Camilla,* and *Onward.* Only two vessels, the *Rainbow* and *Three Brothers,* whose crews were busy cutting in whales in a bight under Point Barrow, remained safely anchored in place.

On the *Marengo,* Captain William H. Kelley bent on all sail and headed southwest, making the "fatal mistake" of beating against the strong northeast current—he only realized his error after it was too late for correction. It must have been a heartbreaker for Kelley, as the *Marengo* had managed after ten hours to make it the farthest south of the fleet, about thirty miles. In fact the *Marengo* was within a few ship's lengths of open water before being caught in the ice and "completely beset."

By sunset, after the ice and northerly current had stopped the progress of the fleet south, navigation ceased. In the morning, a fog set in, and with all leads shut by heavy ice, the whalers began to drift north with the pack. The ships were caught with the drift ice in a narrow strip of water between the grounded ice toward shore and a barrier of heavily packed ice that blocked them from open water.

Eventually, the ships became locked in solidly and were subject to the tender mercies of the floes—some of which were miles in size—that imprisoned them. "I had never seen such ice before and each succeeding day increased the barrier," said Kelley. He later recalled the ice piled higher than any whaler had ever seen, and by season's end, mountains of it towered over the masts of the ships; these peaks persevered against wind and weather for two years.

The brothers Williams both found spots in relative safety in their separate ships. The ice nipped the *Clara Bell* while Thomas Williams was tacking her about twenty miles south of Point Barrow, leaving the ship helpless with a broken rudder. Thomas managed to run the *Clara Bell* near shore and drop anchor as the pack ice closed in around her. Luckily, a barge—that she had been presumably towing—grounded behind her, and formed a makeshift breakwater against the floes. Lewis drifted up to Cape Smythe and managed to sail under the protective lee of a grounded berg—which "proved her salvation."

The rest of the ships ran helplessly north—these were the cream of the New Bedford fleet. For instance, among them was an unlucky bark called the *Desmond,* of Hawaii. Formerly she had been the New Bedford bark *Helen Snow,* till her abandonment and recovery in the Arctic four years prior. She'd been renamed *Tugur*—then, finally, the *Desmond.* She'd taken her last whale on the twenty-fourth and was carrying 830 barrels of oil, 9,000 pounds of bone, and 3,500 pounds of walrus ivory when the southwest wind started blowing. She had worked south to Wood Inlet, but by the twenty-sixth, was a solid fixture in the ice five miles offshore and drifting north about twenty miles a day.

As the runaway ships neared Point Barrow, they were caught in a slack current for two days and moved slowly. They were facing two alternatives here, as the current forked at the Point. One outcome was that they'd be taken by the prevailing easterly current and drift along the shore into the Beaufort Sea. By 1879, some thirty-three vessels in the fleet would have been carried away in drifting pack ice to the northeast, never to be seen again.

On the other hand, if the ships were caught in the northwesterly current, their destination was deep into the Arctic Ocean—and unable to sail back, their passport to the next world would certainly and irrevocably have been stamped.

Either way, it was a bad situation to be in. Expert Arctic survivor Captain Ebenezer Nye once questioned an explorer named DeLong, who was heading for Wrangel Land. He asked about DeLong's strong ship, and the plentiful provisions and coal he carried; DeLong claimed he had everything necessary to survive. "Then, put her into the ice and let her drift, and you may get through or you may go to the devil, and the chances are about equal." (DeLong, incidentally, did go to the devil, as, eventually, did Nye himself.)

The *Acors Barns, Marengo,* and *St. George* sent boats to shore with provisions in case the crews had to abandon ship, but the drift ice blocked them. Jammed in place but protected, the crews on board the *Rainbow* and *Three Brothers* could only watch as their fellow blubber hunters floated by. On the twenty-sixth of August, however, in an act of kindness, the first officer of the *Three Brothers* dropped a boat and crew to fetch the wife of Captain S. Hickmott of the *Acors Barns* on board. The woman had to cross over three miles of ice to meet the rescue party.

On the twenty-seventh, the ten-strong fleet was passing, helpless, by Point Barrow and the situation was clearly desperate. That day, during one of their attempts to get a boat ashore, the crew of the *St. George* was caught in a fog, forcing the men to go on board the *Rainbow* and *Three Brothers* or return to their ship. One unlucky man froze to death on the ice, but the next day, thirteen crewmen attempted to return to the *St. George.* They failed, and two men paid for the bid with their lives; the crew of the *Three Brothers* rescued the survivors.

The drift continued rapidly to the northeast, and luckily, by the twenty-eighth, the fleet was caught in the easterly current to the Beaufort Sea. The *Rainbow* and *Three Brothers,* still at anchor at Point Barrow, faded completely from view. Although the two stationary vessels were protected by a barrier of grounded ice, as the *Three Brothers'* Captain Leander Owen noted, they were still packed in by a "heavy and impenetrable body of ice," extending far away to the northwest, north, and northeast. Days passed at Point Barrow with "nothing but ice, ice, ice to seaward; our situation began to look serious."

But for the drifting ships heading east, the situation "was worse than ever," according to one chronicler. The fleet's only hope was that a northeast gale would erupt to free them and reverse the current—at least before they got to too far east of Point Barrow and the easterly wind starting piling up the ice on the land there.

On the twenty-ninth, the whalers were off Point Tangent, perhaps forty miles east of Point Barrow. Some of the masters planned to work their way out; others decided the situation was hopeless. The enterprising Captain Kelley took fifty men, mostly from his own crew, and dragged a boat over the ice, then launched it through an open lead to shore. It was slow going as he had only a compass for guidance, and a thick fog set in with snow. The ice inshore opened as well, creating a strong current to work against, and after a few hours, the sailors became exhausted, and he abandoned the attempt, having made a mere five miles. After a rest on the *Java,* the party returned to the *Marengo* after twenty-four hours with nothing to show for their effort except fatigue.

On the thirtieth, the masters held a council, where the opinions of which tack to take varied. Some masters recalled how events in 1871 had turned out; others wanted to avoid the example of the once-abandoned, then salvaged *Helen Snow.* A few ships were already "badly crippled" by the pack. The ice had knocked the foreboot off the bark *Camilla* and split her rudder head; the *Josephine*'s rudder was damaged, and this was only a "touch of what was most likely to be the result if they remained on the ice."

Worse, the water along the shore was already frozen, and that solid state would soon expand out to the ships. Then, even their whaleboats would be useless and escape would also cease to be a choice. A wall of ground ice lay between them and the clear water inshore, requiring "extraordinary forces brought to bear upon it" to break through. After realizing there was no hope of extricating the ships, they faced a "dreadful lingering death." Thus, as one of them later wrote, taking a Darwinian tone, "we should be compelled to abandon our ships and face unknown hardships and danger in a struggle for life."

If nothing improved, they fixed September 5 as the final day for flight; in the meantime, the masters met frequently. For extra precaution, Kelley had two whaleboats reinforced and coppered over in case he needed to make a hasty departure, and the crew began sewing canvas into tents. Through the fleet, the beleaguered masters doled out clothing and provisions to their men, and by the appointed day, everything was ready. By the fifth, all the vessels were from twenty-two to twenty-eight miles from land, abreast and east of the west head of Smith Bay, perhaps sixty miles from Point Barrow. Ahead was a long and dangerous journey to find open water and navigate it to any free ships that could carry them away. Because of her position relatively westward, the *Onward* served as a makeshift headquarters for operations. When the signal was given, three hundred some-odd men marshaled on to the ice, and at their head was Captain Kelley, acting as land pilot, a less than enviable task given what little they knew of the ice's condition. At 3:00 P.M., the retreat southwestward began. Each ship's company took two boats and twenty-five days' worth of provisions, including bread and wheat, clothing, blankets, and guns. The rest of the food remained behind, along with fifty men, mostly Kanakas, who chose to stay, perhaps hoping to claim salvage. (One sick man was abandoned on the *Camilla*.) Those who pressed on must have, at least once during their journey, envied the sogerers.

It was rough going from the start. At least in 1871 all the fleeing whalers had to do, by and large, was drop their boats and pull. Not so this time. The ships were miles from open water and their crews faced a brutal and potentially lethal overland haul before they could even reach an open channel, assuming one existed. Because the combined weight of the boats and provisions would have required a Hercules to haul, the men moved them separately. First the crews dragged their boats ahead a half mile over the rough, uneven ice, then they walked back to fetch the provisions. Adding to the difficulty, in some places the ice surface was very thin and some men crashed through into the cold water below. Those unfortunate enough to have wet feet here were facing the beginning of the end. At the front of the column, Captain Kelley twice fell through and nearly froze to death. To save him, men broke the small boats into kindling to light a fire so he could dry his clothes, and allowed him to rest before starting again.

As night fell, having made about four miles, the whalers camped on a "convenient iceberg" and, turning over their boats, crawled underneath them to steal some sleep. Before morning dawned thick and gloomy, wind and rain blew in from the northeast, and after a hastily eaten pork and hardtack breakfast all hands started again on their "dreary and uncertain march." Rather than prolong their suffering and "endure the hardships they supposed were in store for them," several men, sick of their brief taste of Arctic overland travel, decided to desert. Those continuing on assumed they wouldn't see the deserters again.

To remain on the ice was death, so the officers and captains cheered on the men who remained in the exodus. After a hard journey, during which they stopped only to eat, at 5:00 P.M. they sighted a strip of open water and headed toward it. As if to confound them, a southwest wind blew strongly enough to move the ice they were on, breaking a floe off and separating boats and provisions. They launched toward the coast, and after two hard miles they made a grim discovery: Young ice had frozen over all the leads to open water and they "must lose no time." As the darkness enveloped them, they found a large cake of ice grounded in twelve fathoms, hauled up to it and spent a "most dismal night" on it under their boats. The wind was setting to the east, the cold extreme, and some men forced to lie on the ice suffered terribly even by the standards of that pain-tolerant age. In dread that the young ice was spreading, they passed what even Kelley later said was "one of the most miserable nights I ever experienced."

As light dawned over the fog, the men quickly ate a frugal meal and launched into a freezing wind that was already moving ice inside the floe's lee. To escape, they used spades and axes and whatever tools were at hand to break the young ice. To keep moving, they rocked the boats as hard as possible to force passages in the ice, keeping them tethered together end to end to prevent any one boat from getting cut off from the others. After several hundred yards, they reached a floe, which they pulled the boats over. They repeated this process over and over again, although sometimes crews stepped out and pulled the boats behind them in the open leads. At noon, they stopped to eat again, and ever at the lead, Captain Kelley crawled to the top of the tallest floe and swept the horizon with his spyglass to the south-southeast. He delivered some good news: "Land ho!"

Others picked up the yell, making it re-echo a hundredfold. The party then ate lunch with "heartfelt thanks and all hands took hold with new life." They knew the land was perhaps four miles away, and there were even some open leads where they could use oars to power their boats. They pushed on, but at 3:00 P.M. they faced a crevasse, fifteen feet deep, twenty wide, and very long, directly in their path—another one of the Arctic's little jokes. They halted, but, facing death, instead of wasting time circling around the crack, they bridged it with their whaleboats, and by 5:00 P.M. they reached a narrow strip of open water. They stepped their masts and set sail, carrying along some melted ice water to drink.

Three hours later, they landed at a beach two miles west of Point Tangent, and in fifteen minutes they'd hauled up boats and unloaded stores. Using driftwood and smashed boats as kindling, the beach was soon strung with a necklace of fires. After the harsh trek, the pleasure of making camp, resting, drying clothes, getting warm, and eating was considerable. They were so hungry after their exertions, even the wisest sailor wolfed down with abandon a "hearty meal" and made "motley messes"—a saucepan here would have been a luxury—of anything they could get.

More tolerable weather gave them a respite the night of September 7, and even better, when they awoke "there was a fair prospect of escape," as Kelley put it. Although the provisions were low, again they all ate like hungry sailors, "as if they had a year's supply" of food. At daybreak, they launched with their backs to the rising sun against a northwest wind, into cold severe enough to freeze their breath in their beards, making the knotted strands of hair resemble the dipped candles for which they toiled. Unable to make much headway by sail and looking to keep their blood flowing, they landed on a beach and towed their boats behind them as if they were in a canal. They made perhaps fifteen miles when the shore ice forced them back into the water and they pulled again.

The party made camp on a sandspit eighteen miles from Point Barrow, despite the low temperature. They were in the company of the local Eskimos, who, lacking food and showing "disregard for our pitiable condition," begged the whalers for some of theirs. Had there been more of them, the natives might have taken what they wanted without the formality of asking, said Kelley.

The awful cold prevailed on the ninth as they launched, and with no wind to break it up, the young ice kept forming. Despite their considerable misery, by 9:00 A.M. they made what they called a bay, but might have been part of the Elson Lagoon, just southeast of Point Barrow. They set sail from its southern shore. When within two miles of Point Barrow, they landed on a low-lying sand spit covered with wild ducks, who rapidly were in rifle sights. Those who first got to the slain birds ate them raw before the marksmen were able to manage so much as a bite. At 12:00 P.M. the refugees laid eyes on the *Three Brothers* and the *Rainbow,* still locked in place. Working through icy lagoons, they landed by an outlet and rested before the final push. Before night, they made it to the dubious safety of Point Barrow and the stranded vessels there, from whose decks the crewmen had been watching the crowded whaleboats approaching. The men received the vagabonds kindly, this treatment was common from even the roughest of blubber hunters.

Although this leg of the voyage was done, the situation was largely unimproved, as the ice here was frozen solid, and the exit was another 130 brutal miles distant. A meeting convened, and the men leading the party deemed it best to continue the dozen or so miles south to Cape Smythe, the site of an Eskimo village. The eleventh was breezy as the rear guard of the party— including the crews of the *Acors Barns* and the *Java*—arrived, finding their mates jury-rigging large sleds to carry the whaleboats and provisions on. Away they went, and the evening of the second day out, they'd made six miles to reach the *Florence,* where the Williamses gave them a cordial reception. The *Florence* was still in comparative safety behind ground ice, but beyond that barrier, the pack was tighter than a Quaker's fist around his money, and wouldn't suffer even the passage of a whaleboat. The elder Williams's *Clara Bell* was locked in place six miles to the south.

Before the party sledded on in the freezing weather, they chanced on a northward-traveling band of Eskimos who gave them yet more bad news: The pack ice was solid all the way down to Icy Cape. With no open water on the landward side, their fragile whaleboats would never last the journey. One master, Fred Tilton of Martha's Vineyard, had some choice comments on traversing the Arctic coastline. In 1897, after the stranding of eight whalers, Tilton made a near-impossible 1,700 mile run by foot and dog to get help on the mainland. "The surface of the table and low lands from a distance may appear quite smooth and even," he later wrote, "but when approached it is very rough and full of hummocks large and small of various heights, so that a man is never able to find an even footing. It's difficult traveling here in the summer when there is no snow, but when snow covers this uneven land the imagination of one who has not spent a winter in the arctic can scarcely conceive the terrible conditions which exist. There where it is cold the snow falls dry and flakey, and even after it has lain for many months it does not pack sufficiently hard to support a man's weight much of the time unless he has native shoes or webs. Upon the steep slopes and in the mountains the same conditions exist, but even worse, for here large, jagged rocks and deep crevices make much of the country impassable."

Back on the *Florence,* the whalers held yet another conference, with the '71 freeze-up much in mind. With overland travel a proposition no longer on the table, the southern expedition died early. The masters realized that outside of a welcome gale from the east, the best chance to live was to prepare for the oncoming winter. This was a prospect ugly indeed. Nevertheless, Lewis Williams, with the peculiar generosity whalemen were capable of, promised he would either take the castaways with him if the ice opened, or barring that, share of the "last biscuit" on board. Given the circumstances, that was quite a pledge. As he put it, the fleet "had reached the end of the rope."

Williams's guests returned to Point Barrow to form a sort "Co-operative Union to make a common stock out of all the scanty stock." They erected tents of old sails to inhabit near the site of the Eskimo village while they prepared two huts for winter lodgings. Food was placed in casks, and to supplement what they had, they kept a "strong party" of men, the best of each ship, out in nine boats hunting leviathans round the clock "to help us to live and support life." Here was a new wrinkle for the whalers: They now were hunting for survival, as opposed to profit. If they failed and came back clean, the time to starvation could be ticked off on a calendar. Other less skilled whalers took Eskimo dogsleds to hunt for wood and turf to kindle fires. With the natives showing their customary and inscrutable helpfulness, the crewmen worked away with enthusiasm, and the first hut began to rise.

Things improved on the twelfth when a light breeze transformed itself into a northeast gale, which, nevertheless, didn't open up any channels. The next day, a shore party received "glad tidings" from Lewis Williams: If the weather allowed him to work free, he would signal the men working on shore to come on board. With each increasing gust, hopes rose accordingly, said Captain Kelley. The gale blew through the evening of the thirteenth. The ice began to move, slowly but surely, and eventually only the grounded cakes remained behind. The icy fence around the *Florence* shrank to a narrow strip, about a quarter mile wide and running from thirty to fifty feet deep. If they could just open an exit, there was an opportunity to escape. Armed with spades, the crew laid into the barrier and opened a swift current of cold water wide enough to match the ship's beam.

On the fourteenth, the men managed to warp the *Florence* out through the ground ice, and once freed, she dropped anchor and raised colors to signal a welcome to her soon-to-be guests. The stranded whalers on land looked out with their spyglasses and noticed the message from Lewis Williams. After the news of the ship's deliverance spread, with a shout the men stopped their labor, and not even bothering to collapse their tents, they ran pell-mell for the boats. In minutes, a small fleet was under way to the *Florence*. After taking on his passengers, Lewis steered the *Florence* south toward the *Clara Bell,* whose mate came on board and told him his brother Thomas, if unable to work his way out, planned to abandon ship on the seventeenth and that Lewis should head farther south and wait. Lewis left behind a whaleboat and, accidentally, two officers and two captains who had been heading to the *Florence.* While congregating on shore in the middle of a group of Eskimos, they became virtually indistinguishable from the natives to the men aboard the *Florence,* and so were abandoned. Presumably they made their way to the *Clara Bell.*

Hugging the ground ice until she was blocked from further sailing, at 8:00 P.M. Lewis dropped anchor six miles north of the Sea Horse Islands. As the wind kept blowing, on the fifteenth, the ice moved enough for him to make it south of Wainwright Inlet to take on water and wood and await Thomas. The cold wind blew into a gale, harrying the task of loading the water casks onto the ship. Wary that the other ships might be unable to free themselves from Point Barrow and bring with them more provisions, the masters kept their men's rations to a spartan level, with a measly piece of pork or beef and a pint of bread daily.

To the north, the *Clara Bell* remained in her ice jail, and as a northeast wind pushed the floes and the vessel away from shore, "we began to wish then that we had gone aboard the *Florence*," as one mate put it. Perhaps getting a bit nervous, Williams sent out two parties in boats, one to go south to the *Florence*, another north to the *Rainbow* and *Three Brothers*. First, the crews had to rescue the whaleboat the *Florence* had left behind, which was now a mile at sea, inconveniently riding on a floe that had broken off and scudded fast to leeward. Under the command of a Captain Keenan, the two crews dragged the *Bell*'s bow boat over the rough ice, staving her in. Though their boat took on water after launching, the crew maintained their pursuit for the *Florence*'s wayward craft. By the time they recovered it, the gunwale of the their boat was an inch from the water.

After patching the *Clara Bell*'s boat up with canvas, the party set sail— Captain Keenan in the sound boat—with both craft keeping close, in case the damaged boat foundered. One crew worked halfway to Point Barrow before the mast was carried overboard, and the men pulled four hours against a headwind to reach ice and shore. There bad luck still dogged them, as the local natives wouldn't lend out any tools to repair the mast, and they had to drag the boat to camp for repair. After a hard journey against wind and over ice, they reached the *Three Brothers,* their mission now fulfilled. The other party traveled fifty miles south, but unable to find the *Florence,* they abandoned the boat and walked back to the *Clara Bell,* now frozen in eight miles out to sea. They had spent several days risking their lives for nothing.

With the *Florence*'s escape, Captain Owen and his men began to hope that the easterly gale blowing would free the *Three Brothers* as well. "As day after day passed and did not spring one trap, and the young ice was making freely, it began to make us again view the prospects of an Arctic Winter here, with no pleasant thoughts," recorded Owen. After six days of waiting, they had "really begun to despair" when, on the seventeenth, "the same invisible Hand opened for us a narrow passage 50 feet in width, and we sailed out, thankful, indeed, but I fear not in such a manner as we ought."

The *Rainbow* also sprang free, and together, Owen and Cogan went south to consult with Thomas Williams on the *Clara Bell*. The captains of the two free vessels insisted that by now the *Florence* was halfway to the Fox Islands in the Aleutian chain, although Williams assured them his brother wouldn't leave without getting word to him of it. While Cogan wanted to keep hunting, Owens was sick of whaling and, understandably, wanted to return to Honolulu. He negotiated a deal, releasing the *Rainbow* from the obligation of shipping home any of the shipwrecked crews, while demanding in turn the payment of one hundred barrels of oil and two thousand pounds of whalebone—the equal of one good whale. "This was agreed to by all and each expressed himself perfectly satisfied," said Owen.

Preparing to abandon ship on September 17, Williams opened the slop chest and brought up clothes and other gear and let the men take what they wanted. The crew filled their bags with biscuit, and each man received twenty pounds of tobacco, probably with an eye to giving everyone something to trade with the natives if things got bad enough. Before the crew had even left the *Clara Bell,* the scavengers of the north had climbed over the side to rummage around—among the prizes was the ivory of a thousand slain walrus. When the first mate tried to interfere with this friendly pillaging, one of the natives tried to cut him with a knife, but the whaler blocked the attack with a pistol. Ending hostilities, Williams drove the Eskimos back to the ice. The crewmen left in two boats, which they dragged over two miles of ice before launching for the *Three Brothers*. Needing extra provisions, Williams sent a party back to his ship for twenty-one barrels of beef. When on the *Bell,* the party discovered their unwanted guests had returned, gotten drunk, and stripped the sails and rigging. One had even climbed the main-topmast, plummeted, and split his skull open on the taffrail and died, probably causing a few snickers among the *Bell*-ers.

On the eighteenth, the *Three Brothers,* carrying Thomas and the *Bell*'s crew, came in sight of the *Florence* off Wainwright Inlet, and Lewis stood his vessel out to meet her. Giving Owen half the people on his ship, he then sailed down to St. Lawrence Bay to make final arrangements and secure the provisions needed for survival till reaching home port. After parting with the *Three Brothers,* while sailing home, the *Florence* met a storm that pushed her off course 630 miles.

Once again, the bulk of the fleet was ruined, although the brothers Williams had saved one ship and all their men. The extreme conditions of confinement, near starvation, and worry created a hell for the crews and finished off the job that consumption had been working for months on the body of one sailor, who died en route. When the *Florence*'s bow passed the Golden Gate, as Kelley put it: "The last piece of meat was in the copper [try-pot] and the last loaf of bread in the oven." Another account said they were down to a few sacks of flour, and even allowing for the typical whaleman's exaggerations, it was probably close to the truth.

The toll on the survivors was severe, and they presented a grim sight when arriving at the Merchants Exchange. Some had lost up to twenty-five pounds, and recovering proper weight and health wouldn't be swift. About all the disgorged men could spit out was that a dozen vessels had been lost. Although the exhausted officers only made a brief statement, their sunken eyes and hollow cheeks apparently told the story quite well. One whaler said it made him sick just to think about the subject, much less discuss it. The masters, perhaps to defend themselves, opined that the men who were wintering over in the Arctic hadn't "the remotest chance" of getting free—unless there was a commotion in the ice that a good crew could exploit. "In conclusion, we would say that we abandoned our ships to save life, and not until fully satisfied that we could not save our ships, by our delay running a great risk of losing our lives and never reaching a place of safety."

The whalers, recognizable by their native-made fur vests and bearskin blankets, wandered from the waterfront to beg for food and lodging. They'd no possessions but the exotic clothes on their backs, and as one editorialist ventured to say, they "must be somewhat discouraged," having also lost a year with nothing to show for it. The abandoned crewmen parading the streets in their "handsome fur coats and pants" proved a rather attractive sight to many of San Francisco's ladies—"but we cannot say if their feeling was pity for the men or a longing for the furs." The captains who lived on the East Coast cleared out as soon as possible.

There was no shortage of comment in the press. One writer offered a wry comment about the long-lived *Desmond,* noting that the present indications were that her name "will not be changed again." A local editorialist contrasted Lewis Williams's generosity to Barney Cogan's behavior, saying, "We praise Williams for never stipulating any compensation in consideration of carrying a company of shipwrecked seamen." For her part, the *Three Brothers* arrived in Honolulu after a relatively safe voyage carrying 190 passengers—"all well, but deserving of much charity." As if to be symmetrical with the *Florence,* there was one casualty: a man, who also died of consumption and was buried at sea.

When on October 21 shipowners in the New Bedford Merchants Reading Room received a gloomy dispatch from San Francisco, they didn't want to believe its contents and hoped for further advice "in some measure to alleviate this disastrous calamity." According to the *Shipping List,* these late fall disasters "cast a cloud of sadness over the community" as once again the Arctic became the scene of a great disaster: Of twenty vessels, twelve were gone. "But the sad and fatal result of pushing too far North, will, we hope, be a lesson to our whalemen in the future, not to venture where there seems hardly a chance of escape when opposing circumstances arise." The loss of ships and cargoes ran to some $2.5 million.

"No one needs be told that the business of whaling is a dangerous one," noted the once venerable but now defunct *Alta* (a California Newspaper). "The continuous pursuit of the poor whales have so thinned their numbers and sharpened their intelligence that they have sought safety and peace within the arctic seas and circle." Sucking up the reservoirs of oil in the bowels of Pennsylvania might make these risky ventures of whalemen avoidable, the editorialist concluded.

It wasn't just money, either, that caught the attention of commentators. There was the price in human life. Those men who'd returned to the ships during the trek to Point Barrow had dim prospects, indeed, unless they got to some friendly natives. Even if they did, the vessels, which lacked the protection of a harbor, would probably be destroyed the same way as those in the fleet of 1871 had been, and observers decided that the fifty-three "will probably perish." That was an excellent guess.

By 1877, when the Arctic whalers of New Bedford's much reduced fleet reached Point Barrow for the summer hunt, they received somewhat murky and contradictory reports about the fate of the fifty men and the ships left behind. A letter from the San Francisco schooner *Newton Booth* indicated that the *Clara Bell* had been stripped, but she was otherwise sound, and the *Booth*'s crew salvaged her and towed her to San Francisco.

The Inupiat locals claimed that two ships abandoned in 1876 had drifted near shore during the winter. Among the various testimonials of the whalers, five men had made it to shore at Point Barrow; three had survived, the others died. The *Acors Barns* was one of the ships that had drifted ashore on Point Barrow, and on her resided for a time two live Kanakas and some dead ones. They torched her before winter's end.

The few men who survived were taken in by the Inupiat and generally received kind treatment. However, depending on how drunk and potentially dangerous the Eskimos were, the marooned whalers had to move from igloo to igloo. As for the rest of the half a hundred men, along with the ships, they vanished without a trace—more anonymous victims of the Arctic.

---·∞∞∞·---

The Clear-eyed Men of the Sea

Leave her, Johnny, ye can leave her like a man,
Leave her, Johnny, Leave her!
Oh, leave her, Johnny, oh, leave her while yer can.
An' it's time for us to leave her
> —*Old mariner's song*

The history of whaling as it is being written today is irritating
to me. . . . The truth itself, I think, would prove far more interesting than these "dreams."
> —*Willie Williams*

The 1876 freeze-in killed virtually all that had been left of the ailing enterprise of Yankee whaling. For any of the industry's advocates still
remaining, here was yet another rejoinder of why the high investment was
not worth the considerable risk. Correspondingly, the flow of whaling
ships to and from New Bedford became a trickle, and within a few decades dried up all but completely.

The sort of whaling the Williams family had practiced faded—like a
painting exposed to the sun—with any of the gritty elegance and adventure largely dissipated. A handful of ships from San Francisco, for a time,
replaced New Bedford's fleet. There were differences as the industry and
technologies changed again, however. The tween-season cruise was abandoned completely, and the ships, now powered by steam-driven screws,
headed straight to the Arctic, and often deliberately wintered over. There

were empty places in the boats. The dangers of the job, the low pay, and the hardships involved effectively guaranteed no one remotely sane would bother ever signing back on unless drugged and dragged on deck unwillingly by crimps. The quality of the crews dropped below bottom. If the earlier whalemen had been a bit rough about the edges, the final generation of them was made up of outright thugs and ne'er-do-wells. One ship from San Francisco actually freighted a particularly rough customer who proved to be an escapee from San Quentin sought by the authorities. After an attempted desertion, they rearrested him.

"The men who had created a great industry, and who had become the finest body of mariners the world has ever seen, passed on with the ships and left no successors," as Willie Williams glumly noted in his old age. The fleet's management, too, was willing to sacrifice what had been best about the trade. More than ever, it had become money mad, in Willie's opinion. After capture, the whalers decapitated the bowheads for the baleen and dumped the bodies and even the blubber overboard for the delectation of the *Ursus maritimus* and other local carnivores. Despite this gross profligacy, the industry, Willie was sure, was less profitable than it had been prior to the freeze-ins.

For those who wanted to continue hunting blubber, it was a losing war, and surrender was no longer cowardice. Synthetics, such as plastics, and metal springs eradicated the need for baleen. Petroleum completely erased the need for whale oils, which were too scarce to have supplied the modern world with fuels needed for automobiles and electricity, not to mention enabling mankind's accelerated baking of the planet. About all one could trust in was that the dangers of whaling were getting greater and the value of the whaling products less.

One example may do. In October 1879, Captain Ebenezer Nye, who had expertly piloted an open whaleboat two hundred miles through the ice to warn the fleet of the *Shenandoah*, finally drew the wrong straw. While whaling on his vessel the *Mount Wollaston*, a northwesterly change of wind drove his and another ship, the *Vigilant*, into open Arctic water. This was accompanied by pack ice drifting up from the south and closing the exit to the Bering Strait. Unable to escape, Nye was frozen in—with lethal consequences. Judging by his black, shrunken corpse—temporarily found, then lost at sea—his death was most likely slow, hard, and awful. All that was recovered of him, reportedly, were his spectacles. (Despite his shaky past, he was eulogized as one of the "oldest, bravest and best men in the service.") With him died the dipsomaniacal cook from the *Florence*'s 1874 cruise as well.

There were still amazing stories written by the whalers. In 1898, the freeze-in of eight undersupplied ships resulted in one of the most amazing overland journeys of all time. Looking to reach help before the crews died, George Fred Tilton, using a dogsled, made a thousand-mile excursion worthy of a Scott or a Franklin—except that he both survived and succeeded, at least in a sense. When he finally got to civilization and sent a telegraph off begging for help from the shipowners, they didn't believe it was Tilton contacting them. In any case, the stranded whalers had been supplied by the government with reindeer, rendering superfluous Tilton's most risky of feats.

One after another, the old whaling traditions were abandoned. One bellwether occurred when the *Whalemen's Shipping List* ceased publication in 1914. The final issue quoted sperm oil as selling at forty-five cents a gallon; as for whalebone, it declared "that we do not learn that any sales have been made." The annual New Bedford harbor Fourth of July whaleboat races, lacking skilled hands, ended as well. Arts such as sail- and candlemaking and shipbuilding were forgotten. Lacking younger apprentices, ancient graybeards climbed into the rigging and bent sails to the spars of the few active ships. Virtually all that remained of the fleet were the warehouses, lofts, ships, and casks of whale oil by the acre, covered by a layer of seaweed. The oil awaited buyers that never came.

The bones of the whaling ships lay everywhere: the Arctic, off Point Barrow, Charleston Harbor, and on and on. Other vessels, still more or less whole, sat idle in the Acushnet River or in San Francisco Bay or the Sacramento River, dying slow and hard, offering a floating playground to the local children. Tied up at dock, they rotted, and along with the smell of unsalable "ile" from the leaking casks onshore, they also served as a reminder to some of the graying pedestrians strolling the waterfront of a youthful blubber cruise. Eventually, all the ships vanished. One whaler was scuttled in New Bedford Harbor by her owner; another was burned as a holiday evening treat in the Acushnet for a crowd of silent onlookers.

Some of the doomed hulks had truly been lucky in their day. Take, for example, the whaler *Mayflower*, whose keel was laid in Plymouth around

1820. In 1849, she had sailed to the tent city of San Francisco as part of the gold fleet, was dismantled, and became a store ship with a great hole cut in her port side, the cabin serving as the proprietor's quarters. Given her name, the miners asked if she was that original *Mayflower* and cut slivers from her as keepsakes. She was refitted for a failed whale hunt from which she came back leaking, and then was converted to and from Puget Sound, with the pump being the only thing between her and the bottom. Even that proved too much, so she was relegated to carrying lumber to Victoria. Finally, after four decades, she was completely disassembled and her hull broken up. The last whaler afloat is the *Charles Morgan,* which sits prettily in the muddy waters of the Mystic River, Connecticut. But she now hunts with greater reliability, if less glamour, for tourist dollars, rather than whales.

New Bedford, the onetime mecca of whaling, continued its evolution through decline and rise and decline again. The 1876 disaster broke the House of Howland. Onetime mayor George Howland had to sell his family home to pay his debts, and the bloodline, rather like mercury on a cold day, never rose very high in public life again. Other families replaced the Howlands in eminence as smokestacks continued to crowd out ships' masts in the City of Light. The rocks on Cuttyhunk's shore eventually claimed its last active whaler, the *Wanderer,* in 1924. New Bedford, briefly, became a textile center, along with nearby Fall River. Eventually, the spinning factories closed or moved south, where labor was cheaper. Fishing for scallops still continues in earnest in the city, with tough mariners—many of them of Portuguese descent—providing crews. But as the tale of whaling itself shows, fishing is at best a precarious vocation.

A whaling park was established to hold the last vestiges of the old city to the public eye, which was fortunate. Nevertheless, the downtown was paved over with a highway that divides the waterfront in two and the planners have turned the Acushnet's edge into one of ugliest waterfronts in the state. Today, when New Bedford is in the news, it tends to be because of sordid crimes, such as the notorious gang rape in Big Dan's bar in 1983. Where it does lead, it's in the negatives: in poverty, illiteracy, and drug abuse. The city couldn't even keep its last whaler, the *Morgan,* tied at her own docks. Its excellent whaling museum, surrounded by some of the same churches and banks that Williams was familiar with, can give one a sense of what has been lost, if one imagines hard enough.

The whaler was ever the vanguard of the American empire, and the fleet's effect is undeniably still felt wherever its members sailed. It was, allegedly, a whaling captain who noticed the presence of oil in Alaska, a discovery that has been a curse and a blessing to that state. In Hawaii, the brief spur to the economy that whaling provided ceased. However, the demand to sweeten palates while softening teeth was vast, and by 1877, cultivating sugar had become a "perfect fervor." A half interest in one plantation sold for half a million dollars, and it was said that planters were "coining money out of their crops." The handful of natives still alive were free to toil in near-slave conditions, under contract to whites, for twelve hours a day doing the back-breaking work of clearing, planting, and harvesting sugar cane. Eventually, improbably, Hawaii, like Alaska, became a state, and Pearl Harbor the site of the North Pacific's fleet base for the U.S. Navy.

Although America-based whaling ceased, as the nineteenth century passed through into the twentieth, the industry, like a vampire, left its coffin to keep stalking. This time it took a completely different form as the whale became a source of meat, fertilizer, and other products. It required a killing technology shift that was by no means easy or smooth. Sag Harbor master Thomas Welcome Roys had kept experimenting with his rockets and harpoon guns and managed to slay the heretofore unharvestable blue whales and other rorquals by the dozen. Regrettably for everyone except aquatic bottom-feeders, after being killed, Roys's victims only sank uselessly to the ocean floor. He'd yet to devise a way to keep them afloat for flensing. Failing in his task, the once-celebrated Arctic pioneer eventually had died a cuckold, broke in wallet and mind.

It remained for the inventive Norwegian Sven Foynd to devise a more effective explosive harpoon. Now the most massive and swift whales could be hunted to near extinction just as the sperm, bowhead, right, and other leviathans had been. This newer enterprise, as practiced by England, Japan, Russia, Norway, and others was as ruthlessly efficient in paring down blue, minke, sei, and other whale populations as it was absolutely unnecessary. Even now, the ban passed by the International Whaling Commission appears fragile and permanently endangered through poaching. It seems not only regrettable that Norway, Russia, and Japan wink at the rules in the name of profit, it's a downright poor use of a maritime resource. Today there is almost certainly more money in watching whales than in killing them. Moreover, the abundance of toxins such as mercury in the whale's flesh makes it a lethal, not to mention stinking, staple on the sushi market.

As for Thomas Williams, in 1879, he took the bark *Francis Palmer* for an eight-month voyage to the Arctic. On the deck was an innovative precursor of things to come for whaling—a small steamboat similar to a tug. After lowering the craft, he hunted in the ice for days at a time. The exposure out among the floes was hard on his aging frame, and this proved his last voyage. The next year, it was son Stancel at her helm, although his father had set him up safely onshore in the carriage business in 1875. Stancel had even married the daughter of his father's partner. No matter, young Williams had the fever and awhaling he would go.

Stancel did well on his voyage, but in an odd reversal of roles, just as his father had come home to find him born, he came home to find the old man deceased. Death, the master hunter that turns everyone and everything into prey, finally had ensnared Thomas at his home in Oakland on August 26, 1880. The year his tide ran out permanently, Williams was acting as the agent of the bark *Dawn*. (Reputedly, he was arming his vessels with rocket harpoons. One ad even boasted Williams wouldn't go whaling without the apparatus.) The bad food and water that was a whaling man's fare, and the worries over the risks had gotten to him. Every man is perhaps killed by the thing he loves, and Williams, who had left a factory to better his health, had become a whaling casualty. As with any passage, it was the end of an era. One local obituary noted his achievements, and how his name had become synonymous with the Arctic fleet.

Ultimately, he wasn't destined to remain a Westerner: his body was sent east for burial in a Wethersfield Church cemetery. Taking her daughter, Mary Watkins, Eliza returned to Connecticut, living another five years before her death and burial in 1885. For once, it was Thomas who had to wait for Eliza to return to him. Although one writer dubbed the Williams family a whaling dynasty, that's not entirely accurate; it really spanned only a single lifetime. After his father's death, Stancel wanted to sailor on, but he lacked the Old Man's luck. Eliza allowed him to sail out until the estate could no longer support the costs of outfitting, and after his final voyage in 1884, his whaling days ceased. After two years of lying in the Oakland Estuary, the *Palmer* was sold off. Stancel retained with him a lifelong memento of his voyages: His leg had been ruined by a bomb lance and a wooden prosthetic had usurped its place, ruining his chances at the maritime career he coveted. He died on July 9, 1917, in San Francisco; he lies with his parents in Connecticut.

Thomas's brother Lewis Williams kept whaling, losing the *Florence* in 1878, but saving the cargo, which was worth $11,500, a decent take. He kept whaling till 1906; his last voyage was on the ship *California,* owned by the whaling juggernaut William Lewis & Son of New Bedford. (Captain William Lewis had launched the steam whaler *Mary and Helen* in 1879, the first such vessel in the Arctic.) Lewis Williams died in Oakland on December 16, 1906.

Whaleship-born Mary Watkins Williams, who had faced with her family the shipwrecks of the *Hibernia* and *Monticello,* married Edgar Lewis, son of William Lewis. After her husband's death, she returned to New Bedford after a sojourn on the West Coast, and lived with her nephew, Thomas William Williams, until her death in 1938.

Having cast off from whaling completely, Willie Williams headed to Columbia University to study a different type of extraction that was, ecologically speaking, perhaps even worse than whaling: mining. He married an Oakland girl, had four children, and served the mining industry for several years. Eventually sickening of life out west, he moved east to become the first city engineer for New Bedford. He built a bridge to Fairhaven, became a state engineer, and even lent a hand in the creation of the much overdue Cape Cod Canal. After his death in 1929 at his house in New Bedford, his body was sent to the family plot in Wethersfield.

He left behind something of a testament to his father's days of blubber hunting—a memoir that went unpublished in his lifetime. As Willie grew old, he'd lamented that the whaling chronicles then being published were tipped askew, leaning toward recording only the brutality and sadism in the fishery. He wanted to right the public's perception by writing his own memoir. It would show just what sort of men the whalers had been. So high an opinion had he of them, they provided the scales he weighed all other endeavors by. As he put it: "My mind often drifts back to those clear eyed men of the sea when I am obliged to listen to the lurid description of the terrible fights some man thinks he has had to reach his goal, and I wonder what is his conception of a fight."

Bibliography

Aldrich, Herbert L. *Arctic Alaska and Siberia, or Eight Months with the Arctic Whalemen.* Chicago and New York: Rand McNally and Co., 1889.

Allen, Everett S. *Children of the Light: The Rise and Fall of New Bedford Whaling and the Death of the Arctic Fleet.* Boston: Little, Brown, 1973.

Allen, Arthur J. *A Whaler and Trader in the Arctic, 1895 to 1944: My Life with the Bowhead.* Anchorage: Alaska Northwest Pub. Co., 1978.

Ammen, Daniel. The *Navy in the Civil War,* vol. 2, *The Atlantic Coast.* New York: Charles Scribner's Sons, 1883.

Andrews, C.L. *The Story of Alaska.* Caldwell, Ida.: Caxton Printers Ltd., 1940.

Ashley, Clifford W. *The Yankee Whaler.* Boston: Houghton Mifflin Company, 1926.

Bockstoce, John R. *Steam Whaling in the Western Arctic.* New Bedford, Mass.: Old Dartmouth Historical Society 1977.

————. *Whales, Ice, and Men: The History of Whaling in the Western Arctic.* Seattle: University of Washington Press in association with the New Bedford Whaling Museum, Massachusetts, 1986.

Bodfish, Hartson. *Chasing the Bowhead.* Cambridge, Mass.: Harvard University Press, 1936.

Boeri, David. *People of the Ice Whale: Eskimos, White Men, and the Whale.* New York: Dutton, 1983.

Boss, Judith A. *New Bedford, a Pictorial History.* Norfolk, Va.: Donning Co., 1983.

Boykin, Edward. *Ghost Ship of the Confederacy.* New York: Funk & Wagnalls, 1957.

Browne, J. Ross. *Etchings of a Whaling Cruise, with Notes on a Sojourn on the Island of Zanzibar.* New York: Harper & Brothers, 1846.

Bullen, Frank. *The Cruise of the "Cachalot" Round the World After Sperm Whales.* New York: D. Appleton and Co., 1899.

Burns, W. N. *A Year with a Whaler.* New York: Outing Publishing Co., 1923.

Chaffin, Tom. *Sea of Gray: The Around-the-World Odyssey of the Confederate Raider Shenandoah.* New York: Hill and Wang, 2006.

Chase, Owen. *The Wreck of the Whaleship "Essex,"* ed. Iola Haverstick and Betty Shephard. New York: Harcourt Brace & Co., 1965.

Chestnut, Mary. *Mary Chestnut's Civil War.* Edited by C. Vann Woodward. New Haven, Conn.: Yale University Press, 1981.

Clark, Henry W. *Alaska: The Last Frontier.* New York: Grosset & Dunlap, 1939.

Clayton, Barbara, and Whitley, Kathleen. *Guide to New Bedford.* Montpelier, Vt.: Capital City Press, Inc., 1979.

Cloud, Enoch Carter. *Enoch's Voyage: Life on a Whale Ship, 1851–1854.* Wakefield, Rolo: Moyer Bell, 1994.

Cochran, Hamilton. *Blockade Runners of the Confederacy.* Indianapolis: Bobbs-Merrill, 1958.

Colby, Barnard L. *For Oil and Buggy Whips, Whaling Captains of New London County, Connecticut.* Mystic, Conn.: Mystic Seaport Museum Inc., 1990.

Cook, John A. *Pursuing the Whale: A Quarter Century of Whaling in the Arctic.* Boston and New York: Houghton Mifflin, 1926.

———. *"Thar She Blow": Experiences of Many Voyages Chasing Whales in the Arctic.* Boston: Chapman & Grimes, 1937.

Cookman, Scott. *Ice Blink: The Tragic Fate of Sir John Franklin's Lost Polar Expedition.* New York: Wiley, 2000.

Creighton, Margaret S. *Rites and Passages: The Experience of American Whaling, 1830–1870.* Cambridge: Cambridge University Press, 1995.

Dana, Richard Henry, Jr. *Two Years Before the Mast.* New York: Penguin Books USA, 1981.

Davis, Charles H. *Life of Charles Henry Davis, Rear Admiral, 1807–1877.* Boston: Houghton Mifflin, 1899.

Davis, William, M. *Nimrod of the Sea; or, The American Whaleman.* New York: Harper Brothers, 1874.

Decker, Robert Owen. *Whaling Industry of New London,* York, Penn.: Liberty Cap Books, 1973.

DeKay, James Tertius. *The Rebel Raiders: The Astonishing History of the Confederacy's Secret Navy.* New York: Ballantine Books, 2002.

Dow, George Francis. *Whale Ships and Whaling: A Pictorial History of Whaling During Three Centuries.* Salem, Mass.: Marine Research Society, 1925.

Druett, Joan. *In the Wake of Madness: The Murderous Voyage of the Whaleship Sharon.* Chapel Hill, N.C.: Algonquin Books of Chapel Hill, 2003.

———. *Petticoat Whalers: Whaling Wives at Sea, 1820–1920,* Hanover, N.H.: University Press of New England, 2001.

————. *Rough Medicine: Surgeons at Sea in the Age of Sail.* New York: Routledge, 2000.

Dulles, Foster Rhea. *Lowered Boats; A Chronicle of American Whaling.* New York: Harcourt, Brace, 1933.

Editors of Time-Life Books, *Voices of the Civil War: Charleston.* Alexandria, Va.,: Time-Life Books, 1997.

Ellis, Leonard Bolles. *History of New Bedford and Its Vicinity, 1620–1892.* Syracuse, N.Y.: Mason and Co., 1892.

Ellis, Richard. *Men and Whales.* New York: Knopf, 1991.

————. *The Book of Whales.* New York: Knopf, 1985.

Ely, Ben-Ezra Stiles. *"There She Blows": A Narrative of a Whaling Voyage in the Indian and South Atlantic Oceans.* Middletown, Conn.: Published for the Marine Historical Association by Wesleyan University Press, 1971.

Fleming, Fergus. *Barrow's Boys.* New York: Grove Press, 1998.

————. *Ninety Degrees North: The Quest for the North Pole.* New York: Grove Press, 2001.

Foote, Shelby. *The Civil War: A Narrative,* 3 vol. New York: Vintage Books, 1986.

Fox, George. *Some Principles of the Elect People of God who in Scorn are called Quakers.* London, Printed for Robert Wilson, 1661. [http://www.qhpress.org/texts/gfprinc.html]

Gibson, Gregory. *Demon of the Waters: The True Story of the Mutiny on the Whaleship Globe.* Boston: Little, Brown, 2002.

Grover, Kathryn. *The Fugitive's Gibraltar: Escaping Slaves and Abolitionism in New Bedford.* Amherst: University of Massachusetts Press, 2001.

Haley, Nelson Cole. *Whale Hunt: The Narrative of a Voyage.* New York: Ives Washburn, 1967.

Hall, Daniel Weston. *Arctic Rovings.* New York: William R. Scott, 1968.

Hammond, Tomas W. *On Board a Whaler.* New York: Putnam's, 1901.

Hare, Lloyd C. M. *Salted Tories: The Story of the Whaling Fleets of San Francisco.* Mystic, Conn.: The Marine Historical Association, 1960.

Hart, Albert B., ed. *Commonwealth History of Massachusetts.* New York: Russell & Russell, 1966.

Hearn, Chester G. *Gray Raiders of the Sea.* Baton Rouge: Louisiana State University Press, 1992.

Heffernan, Thomas Farel. *Mutiny on the Globe: The Fatal Voyage of Samuel Comstock.* New York: Norton, 2002.

Hess, Bill. *Gift of the Whale: the Iñupiat Bowhead Hunt, a Sacred Tradition.* Seattle, Wash.: Sasquatch Books, 1999.

Hohman, Elmo P. *The American Whaleman: A Study of Life and Labor in the Whaling Industry.* Clifton, N.J.: Augustus M. Kelley, 1928.

Horn, Stanley F. *Gallant Rebel: The Fabulous Cruise of the C.S.S. "Shenandoah."* New Brunswick: Rutgers University Press, 1947.

Horwitz, Tony. *Blue Latitudes: Boldly Going Where Captain Cook Has Gone Before.* New York: H. Holt, 2002.

————. *Confederates in the Attic: Dispatches from the Unfinished Civil War.* New York: Pantheon Books, 1998.

Hughes, Robert. *Fatal Shore.* New York: Vintage, 1986.

Hunt, Cornelius. *The Shenandoah; Or, The Last Confederate Cruiser.* New York: G. W. Carleton & Co., 1867. Reproduced by Eastern Digital Resources, Clearwater, South Carolina.

Hurd, Hamilton D., ed. *History of Bristol County, with Biographical Sketches of Many of Its Pioneers and Prominent Men.* Philadelphia: J. W. Lewis & Co., 1883.

Hutt, Frank Walcott, ed. *A History of Bristol County, Massachusetts,* 3 vol. New York: Lewis Historical Publishing Co., 1924.

Johnson, John J. *The Defense of Charleston Harbor.* Charleston, S.C.: Walker, Evans & Cogswell Co., 1890.

Jones, Virgil C. *The Civil War at Sea,* vol. 1, *The Blockaders.* New York: Holt Rinehart, Winston, 1960.

Kell, John McIntosh. *Recollections of a Naval Life, Including the Cruises of the Confederate State Steamers "Sumter" and "Alabama."* Washington: Neale Co., 1900.

Kittredge, Henry C. *Cape Cod: Its People and Their History.* Boston: Houghton Mifflin, 1930.

Lewis, Arthur. *The Day They Shook the Plum Tree.* New York: Harcourt, Brace & World, 1963.

Liversidge, Douglas. *The Whale Killers.* Chicago: Rand McNally, 1963.

Lopez, Barry. *Arctic Dreams: Imagination and Desire in a Northern Landscape.* New York: Bantam, 1986.

Lund, Judith Navas. *Whaling Masters and Whaling Voyages Sailing from America Ports.* New Bedford, Mass.: New Bedford Whaling Museum, 2001.

Luraghi, Raimondo. *A History of the Confederate Navy.* Translated by Paolo Coletta. Annapolis, Md.: Naval Institute Press, 1996.

Macy, William F. *The Story of Old Nantucket: A Brief History of the Island and Its People from Its Discovery Down to the Present Day.* Boston: Houghton Mifflin, 1928.

Marsh, Daniel, ed. *The Story of Massachusetts,* volume 2. New York: American Historical Society, 1938.

Mawer, Granville Allen. *Ahab's Trade: The Saga of South Seas Whaling.* New York: St. Martin's Press, 1999.

McDonald, Christopher. *The Military History of New Bedford.* Charleston, S.C.: Arcadia Publishing, 2001.

McFeely, William. *Frederick Douglass.* New York: Norton, 1991.

McPherson, James M. *Battle Cry of Freedom,* 3 vols. New York: Oxford University Press, 1988.

Melville, Herman. *Moby-Dick.* Edited by Harrison Hayford and Hershel Parker. New York: Norton, 1967.

————. *Typee.* New York: Dodd, Mead, 1968.

Merrill, James. *DuPont: The Making of an Admiral.* New York: Dodd, Mead, 1986.

————. *The Rebel Shore: The Story of Union Sea Power in the Civil War.* Boston: Little, Brown, 1957.

Miller, Pamela A. *And the Whale Is Ours: Creative Writing of American Whalemen.* Boston: David Godine, 1979.

Montgomery, Richard G. *Adventures in the Arctic.* New York: Grosset and Dunlap, 1932.

Mooney, Robert F., and Andre Sigourney. *The Nantucket Way.* Garden City, N.Y.: Doubleday, 1980.

Morgan, Murray. *Confederate Raider in the North Pacfic: The Saga of the C.S.S. Shenandoah, 1864–65.* Pullman: Washington State University Press, 1995.

Morison, Samuel Eliot. *The Maritime History of Massachusetts, 1783—1860.* Boston: Northeastern University Press, 1961.

Muir, John. *The Cruise of the Corwin.* Edited by William Bade, Boston: Houghton Mifflin, 2000.

Musicant, Ivan. *Divided Waters: The Naval History of the Civil War.* New York: HarperCollins, 1995.

Newcomb, Raymond L. *Our Lost Explorers: The Narrative of the Jeannette Arctic Expedition.* Hartford, Conn.: American Publishing Co., 1882.

Norling, Lisa. *Captain Ahab Had a Wife: New England Women and the Whalefishery.* Chapel Hill: University of North Carolina Press, 2000.

Olmstead, F. A. *Incidents of a Whaling Voyage.* New York: D. Appleton, 1841.

Parker, Hershel. *Herman Melville: A Biography.* Baltimore: Johns Hopkins University Press, 1996.

Parry, Richard. *Trial by Ice: The True Story of Murder and Survival on the 1871 Polaris Expedition.* New York: Ballantine Books, 2001.

Pease, Zephaniah Walter. *A Visit to the Museum of the Old Dartmouth Historical Society.* New Bedford: Old Dartmouth Historical Society, 1957.

————. ed. *History of New Bedford.* New York: Lewis Historical Publishing Co., 1918.

————. *New Bedford, Massachusetts: Its History, Industries, Institutions, and Attractions.* Edited by William Sayer. New Bedford, Mass.: Board of Trade, 1889.

Philbrick, Nathaniel. *In the Heart of the Sea: The Tragedy of The Whaleship "Essex."* New York: Viking, 2000.

————. *Sea of Glory: America's Voyage of Discovery.* New York: Viking, 2003.

Ricketson, Daniel. *The History of New Bedford, Bristol County, Massachusetts: Including a History of the Old Township of Dartmouth and the Present Townships of Westport, Dartmouth, and Fairhaven, from Their Settlement to the Present Time.* New Bedford: Privately printed,1858.

Robertson, R. B. *Of Whales and Men.* New York: Simon & Schuster, 1954.

Robinson, Charles M. *Shark of the Confederacy: The Story of the CSS Alabama.* Annapolis, Md.: United States Naval Institute, 1995.

Robotti, F. D. *Whaling and Old Salem,* New York: Bonanza Books, 1950.

Rodman, Samuel. *The Diary of Samuel Rodman: A New Bedford Chronicle of Thirty-seven Years, 1821–1859.* New Bedford, Mass.: Reynolds Printing, 1935.

Scammon, Charles Melville. *The Marine Mammals of the Northwestern Coast of North America; Described and Illustrated, Together with an Account of the American Whale-Fishery.* Introduction by Victor B. Scheffer. New York: Dover Publications, 1968.

Scheffer, Victor B. *The Year of the Whale.* New York: Charles Scribner, 1969.

Schmidt, Frederick P.; De Jong, Cornelis; Winter, Frank H. *Thomas Welcome Roys, America's Pioneer of Modern Whaling.* Charlottesville: The University Press of Virginia, 1980.

Schneider, Paul. *The Enduring Shore: A History of Cape Cod, Martha's Vineyard, and Nantucket.* New York: Henry Holt, 2000.

Schooler, Lynn. *The Last Shot: The Incredible Story of the C.S.S. Shenandoah and the True Conclusion of the American Civil War.* New York: HarperCollins, 2005.

Semmes, Raphael. *Memoirs of Service Afloat During the War Between the States.* Introduction by John Taylor. Baton Rouge: Louisiana State University Press, 1996.

Severin, Timothy. *In Search of Moby Dick: Quest for the White Whale.* New York: Basic Books, 2000.

Sinclair, Arthur. *Two Years on the Alabama.* Boston: Lee and Shepard, 1895.

Slack, Charles. *Hetty: The Genius and Madness of America's First Female Tycoon.* New York: Ecco, 2004.

Smith, Kathleen Lopp, and Verbeck Smith, eds. *Ice Window: Letters from a Bering Strait Village, 1892–1902.* Fairbanks: University of Alaska Press, 2002.

Snow, Henry James. *In Forbidden Seas: Recollections of Sea Otter Hunting in the Kuriles.* London: E. Arnold, 1910.

Spears, John R. *The Story of the New England Whalers.* New York: Macmillan, 1910.

Spence, Bill. *Harpooned: The Story of Whaling.* New York: Crescent Books, 1980.

Sparkes, Boyden, and Moore, Samuel Taylor. *The Witch of Wall Street, Hetty Green.* New York: Doubleday, Doran, 1935.

Stackpole, Edouard A. *The Charles W. Morgan, the Last Wooden Whaleship.* New York: Meredith Press, 1967.

———. *The Sea Hunters: The New England Whalemen During Two Centuries.* Philadelphia: Lippincott, 1953.

Starbuck, Alexander. *History of the American Whale Fishery from Its Earliest Inception to the Year 1876.* Secaucus, N.J.: Castle Books, 1989.

Stevens, Peter F. *The Voyage of the Catalpa: A Perilous Journey and Six Irish Rebels' Flight to Freedom.* New York: Caroll & Graf, 2002.

Stevens, William O. *Nantucket: The Far-Away Island,* New York: Dodd, Mead, 1936.

Swanberg, W.A. *First Blood: The Story of Fort Sumter.* New York: Meridian, 1957.

Taliaferro, John. *In a Far County: The True Story of a Mission, a Marriage, a Murder, and the Remarkable Reindeer Rescue of 1898.* New York: Public Affairs, 2006.

Thomas, Sylvia. *Saga of a Yankee Whaleman.* New Bedford, Mass.: Trustees of the Old Dartmouth Historical Society, 1981.

Taylor, John. *Confederate Raider: Raphael Semmes of the Alabama.* Washington: Brassey's, 1994.

Thompson, Robert Means, ed. *Confidential Correspondence of Gustavus Vasa Fox,* vol. 2. New York: Printed for the Naval History Society by DeVinne Press, 1920.

Thoreau, Henry David. *Cape Cod.* Boston: Ticknor and Fields, 1866.

Tilton, George Fred. *Cap'n George Fred Himself.* Garden City, N.Y.: Doubleday, Doran, 1928.

Verrill, A. H. *The Real Story of the Whaler.* New York: D. Appleton, 1916.

Waddell, James I. *C.S.S. Shenandoah: The Memoirs of Lieutenant Commanding James I. Waddell.* Edited by James D. Horan. Annapolis, Md.: Naval Institute Press, 1960.

West, Richard S. *Gideon Welles: Lincoln's Navy Department.* Indianapolis: Bobbs-Merrill, 1943.

———. *Mr. Lincoln's Navy.* New York: Longmans, Green, 1957.

Whipple, A. B. C., and the Editors of Time-Life Books. *The Whalers.* Time-Life Books: Alexandria, Va., 1977.

———. *Yankee Whalers in the South Seas.* New York: Doubleday, 1954.

Whiting, Emma Mayhew, and Hough, Henry Beetle. *Whaling Wives.* Boston: Houghton Mifflin, 1953.

Whittle, William C., Jr. *The Voyage of the CSS "Shenandoah," a Memorable Cruise.* Tuscaloosa: University of Alabama Press, 2005.

Wilkinson, David. *Whaling in Many Seas and Cast Adrift in Siberia: With a Description of the Manners, Customs and Heathen Ceremonies of Various [Tchuktches] Tribes of North-Eastern Siberia.* London: Henry J. Drane, 1906.

Williams, Harold. *One Whaling Family.* Boston: Houghton Mifflin, 1964.

Withington, Sidney. *Two Dramatic Episodes of New England Whaling: The George Henry and the Salvage and Restoration of H.M.S. Resolute. The sinking of the Two "Stone Fleets" During the Civil War.* Mystic, Conn.: Marine Historical Association, 1958.

Wood, Virginia. *Live Oaking: Southern Timber for Tall Ships.* Boston: Northeastern University Press, 1981.

Yergin, Daniel. *The Prize: The Epic Quest for Oil, Money and Power.* New York: Simon & Schuster, 1991.

Magazines and Newspapers

Boston Globe

Boston Herald

San Francisco *Daily Alta California*

The Economist

The Eskimo Bulletin

Honolulu, *The Friend*

Frank Leslie's Illustrated Newspaper

Liverpool Mercury

New Bedford Mercury

New Bedford Republican Standard

New Bedford Standard-Times

New York Times
New York Tribune
Harpers Weekly
Sacramento Daily Union
San Francisco Daily Examiner
Scribner's Monthly
Vanity Fair
Vineyard Gazette
Whaleman's Shipping List and Merchant's Transcript

Articles and Reports

Bockstoce, John. "History of Commercial Whaling in Arctic Alaska." *Alaska Geographic* 5, no. 4, 1978.

Flude, Anthony. "Whaling in New Zealand." In *Pioneers in New Zealand* Web-site, (http://homepages.ihug.co.nz/~tonyf/whale/whaling.html), 2001.

Gordon, Arther. "The Great Stone Fleet: Calculated Catastrophe." *United States Naval Institute Proceedings Report*, Dec. 1968, 780, Vol. 94. No. 12.

Hoole, Stanley H. "Letters from a Georgia Midshipman of the C.S.S. *Alabama*." *Georgia Historical Quarterly* 59, no. 4 (Winter, 1975).

Jared Jernegan. "My First Whaling Voyage." *Dukes County Intelligencer* (Martha's Vineyard Historical Society), February 1964.

Kamiya, Gary. "Sex, Sin and the Gangs of San Francisco." *Salon*, Dec. 20, 2002.

Magune, Frank, "The Great Stone Fleet." *Yankee*, April 1960.

Mason, John T. "The Last of the Confederate Cruisers." *Century Magazine*, August 1898.

McKibben, Frank. "The Stone Fleet of 1861," and the "Whaling Disaster of 1871." Both published in the *The New England Magazine* 24, no. 24, June 1898.

McNulty, F. J. "The Shenandoah: Her Exploits in the Pacific Ocean, After the Struggle of 1861–'65 Had Closed." *Southern Historical Society Papers* 21, 1893 (Reprinted at the Confederate Navy Research Center, Mobile, Alabama at: http://www.csnavy.org/mcnulty,shenandoah.htm).

Nash, Howard P., Jr. "The Ignominious Stone Fleet." *Civil War Times Illustrated*, June 1964.

Poole, Dorothy Cottle. "Capt. Jared J. Jernegan, II." *Dukes County Intelligencer*, November 1972.

Potter, James A. "The Voyage of the Diana." *Shetland Life*, April 2000.

Roach, John. "Rare Whales Can Live to Nearly 200, Eye Tissue Reveals." *National Geographic News*, National Geographic.com, July 13, 2006.

Williams, Harold. "Whaling Wife." *American Heritage*, June 1964.

———. "Yankee Whaling Fleets Raided by Confederate Cruisers: The Story of the Bark *Jireh Swift*, Captain Thomas W. Williams." *American Neptune* 27, October, 1967.

Other Publications, Dissertations, Documents

Francis Thornton Chew Diary, Francis Thornton Chew Papers, University of North Carolina, Chapel Hill.

Crawford, Richard W. *Whalers from the Golden Gate: A History of the San Francisco Whaling Industry, 1822–1908*, Thesis, M.A., San Diego State University, 1981, Reference Department, San Diego Public Library, San Diego, Calif.

Forbes, Allan. *Whaling Ships and Whaling Scenes*, as portrayed by Benjamim Russell. Boston, Second Bank-State Street Trust Co., 1955.

Frances, Joseph F. Remarks about the ship *Milo*, 1865. New Bedford Whaling Museum.

Hassey, Catherine. "The New Bedford Whalers and the Civil War." Thesis, M.A., Bridgewater State College, August 1971, Bridgewater State College Library, Bridgewater, Mass.

Heppingstone, John. "Remarks" in Agard Papers. Box 5, American Antiquarian Society, Worcester, Mass.

Memoirs and Christian Conversion of James Henry Sherman (transcribed for him when he was 89 years old). Kendall Whaling Museum, New Bedford.

State Street Trust Company. *Whale Fishery of New England: An Account, with Illustrations and Some Interesting and Amusing Anecdotes, of the Rise and Fall of an Industry Which Has Made New England Famous Throughout the World*. Boston: Printed for the State Street Trust Company, 1915.

Strout, Robert Bruce. Diary from the *Cleone*. G. W. Blunt White Library, Mystic Seaport, Mystic, Conn.

Williams Papers, Collection of William H. Tripp (Coll. 58), G. W. Blunt White Library, Mystic Seaport, Mystic. Conn.

Ships Logs and Scrapbooks

These include items in the various museums and libraries. The following is a list of some of the logs used.

New Bedford Free Public Library, New Bedford, Massachusetts
Brunswick
Emily Morgan
Eugenia
Fanny
James Maury
Leonidas
Martha
Milo

New Bedford Whaling Museum
ODHS:
Almira
Eliza Adams

Florida
Gay Head
Henry Taber
John Wells
Lagoda
Mercury
Northern Light
Seneca
Splendid

KWM

Cape Horn Pigeon
Congress
Eliza Adams

Paul C. Nicholson Whaling Collection
Providence Public Library, Providence, Rhode Island
America
Governor Troup
L. C. Richmond
Minerva

Government Publications

Case of Great Britain as Laid Before the Tribunal of Arbitration Convened at Geneva, 3 vols. Washington, D.C.: U.S. Government Printing Office, 1872.

Correspondence Concerning Claims Against Great Britain, Transmitted to the Senate of the United States in Answer to the Resolutions of December 4 and 10, 1867, and of May 27, 1868, 7 vols. Washington, D.C.: Government Printing Office, 1869–71.

Imprint of the Past: The Ecological History of New Bedford Harbor. U.S. Environmental Protection Agency, Oct. 23, 2003.

Alabama Claims/In the Court of Commissioners of Alabama Claims, 12 vols. Washington, D.C.: Gibson Brothers, Printers, 1883.

Official Records of the Union and Confederate Navies in the War of the Rebellion, 31 vols. Washington, D.C.: Government Printing Office, 1894–1922. (Contains an abstract of the *Shenandoah*'s log)

Web sites

New Bedford Whaling Museum
  http://www.whalingmuseum.org/
Mystic Seaport Museum, Connecticut
  http://www.mysticseaport.org/

Index

Abigail, New Bedford whaler
  alcohol trading from, 217–18, 220
  crew turncoats from, 225
  Waddell's capture/burning of, 219–20
Acushnet, 11, 13–14, 101, 107, 230
Acushnet, 26
Adams, Charles, 186
Adams, John, 186
Adams, John Quincy, 76
Addison, Waddell escape by, 254–55
Alabama, 260. *See also* Semmes, Raphael
  Bulloch's invention of, 154–55, 183
  as Confederate raider, 152, 154
  crew of, 153, 156–57, 163–64, 182
  Kearsarge's sinking of, 180–82
  secrecy surrounding, 152–53, 155, 186
  Semmes's command of, 152–57
  Semmes's rescue from, 182
  ship hunter design of, 154–55
  whaling fleet's proximity to, 152–53,
    156, 232
Alabama Claims, 268
Alaska (1871)
  fur trade in, 291–92
  soldiers v. natives in, 292–93

Alaskan Inupiat, 302, 397. *See also*
    Eskimos
  lifestyle of, 303
  whale hunting of, 304
Albion, 25
alcohol trading, with Eskimos, 217–18
Alert, Semmes's catching/burning of, 167
Alexander Barclay, 24
Alice Frazer, boat crew, 67
Alina, Waddell's scuttling of, 196–97
alligators, 81
ambergris, 42
Ansel Gibbs, 1, 353
Archer, scuttling of, 143–44
Archer, William, 197–98
Arctic, ice floe's destruction of, 381–82
Arctic Ocean whaling
  dangerous weather in, 277–78, 298,
    309
  dangers of, 276–77
  disaster stories of, 283–84, 320–38
  ice floes/packs in, 298, 309
  Japan's deadly voyage of, 274–82
  Roys's opening of, 284–86
Arctic whalemen, 4, 48, 325

Arctic whaling fleet
  Eskimos' winter warnings to, 293, 311
  grouping/regrouping of, 313, 320–21, 322
  ice locking/grounding of, 311–12,
    314–15, 319, 321
  ice/weather battles of, 308–11, 314–15
  ship losses/ice fears of, 318–19, 321
Arctic whaling fleet abandonment
  Arctic region impact of, 341
  lone holdout's aftermath report of,
    351–52
  media support for, 339
  ships' captains indicted for, 339
  whaling industry impact of, 340–41, 347
  Yankee whaling fleet impact of, 342, 347
Arctic whaling fleet, 1871 freeze-in, 320–38
  abandonment preparations in, 322,
    326–27 ·
  captains' abandonment agreements in,
    326–28, 330, 331
  Eskimos and abandoned ships of,
    333–34, 351
  families' departure south from, 329–31
  northern fleet abandoned in, 330–31
  southern fleet aid in, 321, 324–25,
    327–29, 336
  southern fleet's dangers in, 324–25, 335
  survivors' arrival from, 338–39
  whaleboats' dangerous voyage, 332–37
Arctic whaling fleet, 1876 freeze-in, 381–97
  Clara Bell stripped by natives/salvaged,
    383
  coastal ships ice-locked in, 390
  crews prepare to winter-over, 387–89, 391
  crews trek ice for open water/rescue,
    382, 387–89, 390–91
  fleet devastated by, 383
  Florence freed, heads south to wait, 392
  gale-driven ice closes open water, 383,
    386
  helpless/hopeless ships abandoned in, 387
  ice imprisoned ships drift north/east,
    384–86
  ice pack blocks Arctic Ocean exit, 384

  media response to, 395–96
  men refuse trek, remain behind, 382
  owners' losses/human life costs in, 396
  Rainbow freed, heads south to wait, 394
  ship disasters early in season, 381–82
  survivors' arrival from, 395–96
  Three Brothers freed, heads south to
    wait, 394
  whales appear late, 383
Arctic whaling fleet salvage, 345–55
  abandoned ships' conditions in, 350–52
  owners v. wreckage hunters in, 354
  salvage ships' destroyed in, 349–50
  Williams's success in, 349–50, 352–54
  wreckage hunters bound for, 348
Ashley, E. R., Nye's warning and, 239
Awashonks, 320

Baja California, 81, 89
Baker, George, Edward Carey captain,
  204–16
Banderas Bay, Baja Mexico, 79–81
Barker, Frederick. See also Japan,
    Australian whaler
  Chukchi natives rescue of, 281–82,
    294–95
  as Japan captain, 274–82
  risky gamble of, 276
  as Robert Towns captain, 228
Barker, Joseph, Nye captain, 180
Bartlett, Ivory H., & Sons, 101, 103, 179
Basques, first whale hunters, 50
Bay of Islands, in New Zealand, 48, 58.
    See also Maori natives
Benjamin Tucker, 170
Bering Sea, 226–27
  navigation unreliable in, 290
  sailing hazards in, 290
  weather/ice dangers of, 290–91
Bering Strait, 13, 226, 255, 257, 307
Blanquilla, Venezuela, 175–76
blockade runners, of Charleston, 102, 146
Blossom Shoals, 301, 308
blubber. See whale blubber

bomb gun, 50, 250, 285, 293, 319, 364
bomb lance, 38, 45, 50, 371–72. *See also*
    harpoon(s); irons
bonded ships, 244, 257
Botany Bay, 244
Bourne, Jonathan, 29
bowhead whale. *See* right whale
Brava, *Florida*'s visit to, 46, 47
Brown, John, hanging of, 119, 252
Brunswick, New Bedford whaler, 245
  ice damage, condemning of, 245–46
  Waddell's capture/burning of, 247–48,
    253–54
Budington, James, 4
Budington, Sidney O., 3–4
bull sperm whale, 35, 42, 46, 95
Bulloch, James Dunwoody, 268
  Alabama construction by, 154–55, 183
  Bienville commanded by, 184
  character of, 184
  command v. diplomacy for, 185
  commandeering skills of, 184–85
  Fingal commanded by, 184–85
  Mallory's relationship with, 185
  negotiation/diplomacy of, 186
  Sea King purchase by, 187
  Waddell's orders from, 194
  Yankee whaling fleet impact of, 183,
    186
Buzzards Bay, 11, 16, 55, 94
  mariners' graveyard of, 19–20
  nautical hazards in, 105

cachalot. *See* sperm whale
Cahawba, 136, 138
Calhoun, Confederate privateer
  John Adams captured/sold by, 169–70
  Mermaid captured/sold by, 169–70
  Parana captured/sold by, 169–70
cannibalism, 5–6, 49
Cape Chidlay, 3, 4
Cape Cod
  Bourne of, 29
  early whaling on, 375–76

  Nantucket's impact on, 376–78
  whalers' sailing reputation and, 51–52
  whaling ports' emergence on, 376
  whaling v. farming on, 375, 376
Cape Cod whalers, sailing reputation of,
  51–52
Cape Lisburne, 301, 306
Cape Thaddeus, 227, 254, 258, 289
Cape Verdes, 46–47
capitalists
  petroleum investing shift of, 95
  textiles investing shift of, 270
  of whaling industry, 26–27
cargo ship, 31–32
castaway whalers, 164, 166, 167, 170–71,
  215–16
  from Arctic fleet, 244, 248, 253, 257
  San Francisco arrivals of, 257–59
Catherine, Waddell's capture/burning of,
  241–42
Catholic mission, Guam, 73
caulkers, skilled craft of, 120
Cavalier, 30
Charles Morgan, last Yankee whaler, 271,
  401
Charleston, 134
  blockade runners from, 102, 146
  Confederate's harbor defense of, 138–39
  economic decline of, 140
  physical characteristics of, 139–40
  siege of, 141
  Stone Fleet rendezvous at, 135, 138–40
  Stone Fleet scuttling at, 141–49
  Yankee whalemen's hate for, 139
Charleston Harbor
  channels remaining in, 146, 147
  Stone Fleet scuttling at, 141–49
  Stone Fleet's improvement of, 148
  Yankee whaling fleet graveyard of, 146
Charleston Harbor blockade
  British protest over, 147–48
  Southern media on, 151
  by Stone Fleet scuttling, 141–49
  whaling fleet consequences of, 150

Chase, Amos, *Harvest* captain, 204–16

Chew, Francis, 205, 208, 212, 234, 254

Childs, William, 170

Christopher, of Nantucket, 14

chronometer(s), 104, 121, 330
  landmarks checking of, 163, 177, 227
  prized booty of, 228, 234, 235

Chukchi natives, of East Cape. *See also* Eskimos
  food of, 282, 294, 295
  hospitality of, 281
  Japan castaways and, 280–82, 294–95
  lifestyle of, 282, 295

City of Light, 12, 95, 114, 230

Clara Bell, 383, 384, 393

Clark, James, 241
  Nimrod captain of, 241–42
  Ocean Rover captain of, 165–66, 173
  parole request by, 241

Clark's Point, 16, 20, 94, 100, 107

Cleone, 54, 304–5

cockfighting, 360–61

Coffin, Seth, self-amputation of, 53

Cogan, Barney
  Josephine captain, 273
  Kohola captain, 255
  Rainbow captain, 382

Comet, ice floe's destruction of, 317–18

Committee of Vigilance, 117

Condor, 54

Confederacy, arms procurement
  from Europe, 102
  from Yankee merchants, 127

Confederacy, ports of, 100

Confederacy's legacy, saving whales as, 268–69

Confederate raiders, 96, 152, 154. *See also* *Alabama; Florida,* Confederate raider; Semmes, Raphael; *Sumter;* Waddell, James Iredell

Congregationalism, 118, 122

Congress 2nd, New Bedford bark, 249
  Waddell's capture/burning of, 252

Cook, James, 48, 52

Cootey, S. M., 240–41

Cortoreal, Miguel, 119

countinghouses, of whaling fleet, 28–29

Courser, whaling schooner, 170

Covington, Waddell's burning of, 253

crew's quarters. *See* forecastle

Crocker, Oliver, 256

Crowell, Hebron, 242, 244

Cuffe, Paul, 32

Cunningham, Reuben, *James Maury* captain, 246

Cuttyhunk island, ship wreckers of, 19–20

Dana, Charles Henry, 31

Dana, Richard Henry, 88–89, 167

Daniel Webster, 1, 2, 7, 137–38

Davis, Charles H., 137
  Stone Fleet and, 136–38
  Stone Fleet scuttling plan of, 142, 148–49

Davis, Hiram, 4, 7

Davis, Jefferson, 102, 210, 214, 221
  as Confederacy president, 74
  resignation speech of, 75

Davis Straits, whaling grounds, 1

Dawn, 403

deserters, 362–63

desertion insurance, 90

devilfish. *See* gray whale

Dexter, Benjamin, *John Wells* captain, 325

Diamondhead, 82

Diana, Arctic disaster of, 284

Dighton Rock, 119

Diomede Islands, 244–45

Doane, Edward T., 205, 370

Douglass, Frederick, 28, 120

Dowden, James, *Progress* captain
  Arctic fleet promise of, 324–25
  generosity of, 337–38

Dowden, John, *Abigail* turncoat of, 225

duck pen, for tryworks cooling, 40–41

Duddy, James, 104–5, 108

duff, nautical confection of, 22, 160, 180

DuPont, S. F.
  second Stone Fleet and, 147
  as U. S. Navy Admiral, 106, 136, 147
Dutton, William, 3, 5

Eben Dodge, 125–26, 129
  booty from, 130–31
  Confederate raider *Sumter* and, 126,
    129, 146
  Hoxie's surrender of, 130–31
  Semmes and captain/crew of, 131–32
  Semmes and crew of, 154
  Semmes's burning of, 132
Edward, capture/burning of, 198–99
Edward Cary, capture/burning of, 204–13
Elisha Dunbar
  Semmes and crew of, 174
  Semmes's capture/burning of, 174
Elizabeth Islands, dangerous channels of,
  19
Ely, Ben-Ezra Stiles, whaler, 92–93
Emigrant, 54
Emily Farnum, neutral ship, 174
Emily Morgan
  accidental bomb gun death on, 319
  Arctic abandoning of, 320, 331
  crew-officer altercation on, 314
Empire State, Federal steamer, 145
England
  neutrality laws of, 155, 156, 186, 191–92
  Waddell's criminal exploits and, 262
English shipyards, spies in, 152–53, 186,
  187, 190–91
Eskimos, 255, 293, 301–2. *See also*
    Alaskan Inupiat; Chukchi natives, of
    East Cape; Inuit
  alcohol trading with, 217–18, 305
  Arctic fleet's abandoned ships and,
    333–34, 351
  differences between bands of, 304
  severe winter warnings from, 293, 311
  whaler crews' feelings about, 305–6
  whalers' negative impact on, 305
  women trading by, 304

Essex, 35
Eugenia
  Arctic abandoning of, 333
  crew fighting on, 313–14
  gale's damaging of, 320
Euphrates, capture/burning of, 227–29

Fabius, Wood's loss of, 249
Fairhaven, Massachusetts, 27–28
Favorite, of Fairhaven
  lending library of, 249, 251
  Waddell's capture/burning of, 249–53
Fernando de Noronha, Brazil, 177–78
Fish, Robinson & Co., 11, 81–82, 96
Fish, Roland, 11
Fish, William ("Willie"). *See also* Williams,
    Eliza Azelia; Williams, Thomas
    William
  cockfighting and, 360–61
  early whaling career of, 356, 359, 371
  Florence's whaling voyage of, 356–72
  Florida birth of, 47–48
  life aboard *Florida* for, 81
  Monticello voyage account of, 287–89,
    298, 302–3, 312, 330–31
  post whaling career of, 404
  ship navigation education of, 361
  whale kill of, 367–69
  whaling memoir of, 404
Fisher, Joseph, 3, 5, 7
Fisher, Samuel, 3, 5
Flanders, Stephen, 177–78
flensing, of whale, 39, 62, 80, 81, 352, 402
Florence, Arctic whaling voyage of, 382,
    392–93. *See also* Arctic whaling fleet,
    1876 freeze-in
Florence, as salvage vessel
  Merritt's investment in, 347
  precarious voyage home on, 353
  Williams's success with, 352
Florence's whaling voyage
  crew v. *Monticello* crew, 362
  disreputable crew members of, 358, 360,
    362–63

Florence's whaling voyage (*continued*)
   Eliza's role on, 359, 365, 366
   Mary's role on, 359, 362
   murder/death on, 365–67, 370
   Ponape island visit on, 370
   poor whaling season on, 372
   stowaways as crew for, 363
   whaler crew of, 356–58, 362, 367
   Willie's whaler training on, 356, 359,
      361, 367–69, 371
Flores island
   captured crews cast off to, 164, 166, 167,
      170–71
   chronometer checking at, 163
   Ponta Delgado on, 171
Florida, Confederate raider, 181
   crew v. yellow fever on, 186
   Golconda whaler taken by, 186
   Wachusett's sinking of, 186, 202
Florida, New Bedford whaler, 11, 17, 321,
   330. *See also* ship(s); whaling ship
   captain's living space on, 20–21
   crew's food on, 21–22
   crew's quarters on, 21, 24–25, 29
   near disaster of, 85
   officers' food on, 21
   physical description of, 15, 19, 32, 60–61
   pilot's incompetence on board, 72
   planning sale of, 96
   Reed's death/burial on, 68–69
Florida's whaling voyage. *See also*
   Florida, New Bedford whaler;
   whaling voyage
   Banderas Bay visit on, 79–81
   Brava island visit on, 46, 47
   1861 final docking of, 93–94
   island natives' visits on, 72
   Japan visit on, 56–59
   MacAskill Island visit on, 73
   Maori natives on, 48–49
   Ponape island visit on, 69–72
   Sea of Okhotsk visit on, 59–62
   season's end whale kill on, 85–86
   settling last affairs of, 90–91

forecastle, 21, 24–25, 29
Fort Sumter, 122, 138
Fortune, New London's flagship, 111–12
Fox, George, looser Quaker sect of, 118
Fox, Gustavus V., 102
Foynd, Sven, 402
Francis Palmer, 403
Franklin, John, 4
Frazer, David R., 321, 323, 324, 326
French, Rodney, 99, 101, 105
   background of, 118–19
   career of, 119–20
   Margaret Scott and, 123
   New Bedford Africans and, 122
   New Bern, North Carolina v., 121–22
   personal traits/characteristics of, 113
   slavery's opposition by, 119, 121–22
   as Stone Fleet Commodore, 106, 108–9,
      124, 150
"Friends." *See* New Bedford Quakers;
   Quaker(s)
Fullam, George Townley ("Hell-Fire Jack"),
   178

gams, of nearby whaling ships, 64–65, 111,
   363–64
Garland, Stone Fleet flagship, 99–100, 103,
   106
Gay Head, 22–23
General Pike, of New Bedford, 242, 257
   prisoners' transportation on, 244
   Waddell's capture/paroling of, 242–43
General Williams, capture/burning of, 240
George Henry, 3, 8
George Howland, 65
Gloriana, Arctic disaster of, 283
Golconda, Confederate raider taking of,
   186
Gold Rush, 89
Golden Gate, California, 87–88
government protection
   Pacific Mutual Insurance petition for,
      175
   whaling fleet owners petition for, 174

Governor Troup, 239

Gray, Rufus, *Altamaha* captain, 170

gray whale
  females v. males danger of, 79
  hunting/killing dangers of, 79–80

Great Britain
  Civil War lawsuits against, 268
  Confederate warship building by, 268

green crewmen
  breaking-in of, 17–19, 33, 358–59, 362
  ill-prepared, 357
  seasickness of, 20, 32, 33, 34, 358
  whaling voyage maturing of, 91–92

Green, Hetty Howland, 271–72

Greener gun, for whale killing, 49

greenhorn/green hand. *See* green crewmen

Greenland, 2, 149, 283

Grey, Samuel L., 246

Grinnell, Minturn & Co., 285

Gustave, French whaler, 238–39, 256

Gypsy, capture/burning of, 243

Habana, as Confederate raider *Sumter,*
  127–28

Hae Hawaii, 229

Hakodate, 56, 57, 261

Hall, Charles Francis, 4

Hannah B. Bourne, 296, 297

harpoon(s), 402. *See also* bomb lance
  dangers of, 37
  Temple toggle, 32–33
  types of, 35–36

harpooners, 21, 23, 36–37, 39–40

Harrocke, Thomas, Ponape pilot, 205–16

Harvest, Honolulu whaleship, 229
  Waddell's capture/burning of, 204–13

Hathaway, Jonathan, 114

Hathaway, Thomas, 114, 228

Hawaiian Islands, 82
  sandalwood forests of, 83
  whaling/maritime impact on, 83–85,
  338
  Yankee whaling fleet port of, 82–84, 85,
  92, 338

Hawaiians
  male/female dress of, 82–83
  missionaries' exploitation of, 84

Hawes, Jonathan, *Milo* captain, 230
  San Francisco destination of, 236–37
  Waddell's ransom acceptance from, 231

Hayes, Isaac, 149

Hector, capture/burning of, 204–13

Henry Taber, 294, 296, 309–10, 320

Heppingstone, John, 229, 332

Hercules, 183

Hibernia, 273

Hillman, of New Bedford, 60, 246
  Waddell's capture/burning of, 248, 253

Hillman, Zachariah, 60

History of the American Whale Fishery
  (Starbuck), 373–80

Hobson Bay, Australia
  Confederate sympathizers of, 202
  U. S. Consul and *Shenandoah* in, 202–3

Hokkaido, Japanese island of, 56

Holley, Richard, *Waverly* captain, 245

Honolulu, as whaling port, 82–84

House of Howland, post-whaling fortunes
  of, 401

Howland, Abraham, 113

Howland, George Jr., 122–23, 272

Howland, George Sr., eminent Quaker,
  117

Howland, Gideon, 115, 270

Howland, Isaac Jr., 271

Howland, Joseph, 108, 110

Hoxie, Gideon C.
  Confederate raider Semmes v., 129–32
  Eben Dodge surrender by, 130–31
  Semmes's treatment of, 131–32

Hudson Strait, 3, 4

hula, as scandalous dance, 82

human heads, commercial traffic in, 49

Hunt, Cornelius E., 210, 219, 221, 223,
  254

insubordination, of crew, 93

Inuit, 6–7

irons, 35–36, 38. *See also* bomb lance;
    harpoon(s)
Iroquois, whalers rescued by, 201
Isaac Howland, capture/burning of,
    247–48
Isabel, blockade-runner, 146
Isabella, capture/burning of, 243–44
Ish-y-paw, Ponape king
    Waddell's negotiations with, 209–14
    whaling ships' plundering by, 213

J. D. Thompson, 321
James Maury, 246
    Honolulu orders for, 253
    Waddell's capture/paroling of, 248
Japan, Australian whaler. *See also* Barker,
    Frederick
    Arctic whaling disaster of, 274–82
    Barker's risky gamble with, 276
    Chukchi natives, and castaways of,
        280–82, 294–95
    East Cape beaching of, 279
    heavy weather attack on, 276–78
    hypothermia, and castaways of, 279–80
    survivors of, 294–95, 296, 326
    whaling season of, 274–75
Japan, *Florida*'s visit to, 56–59
Japanese people, 57–59
Jernegan, Jared, 24
    mutiny against, 315–16
    Roman's loss to ice by, 316–17
    whaling v. family life of, 315
Jernegan, Nathaniel, 50
Jireh Perry, escape of, 255
Jireh Swift
    construction of, 158–59
    at Flores Island, 173
    Mount Wollaston's collision with, 232
    Shenandoah v., 234
    Waddell's catching/burning of, 231,
        234–35
    Williams takes command of, 157–60
John Howland, raider warning by, 256
John Wells, 321, 325

Johnson, Andrew, 262
Johnston, Joseph E., 242
Julian, Arctic destruction of, 320, 332

Kaiser Wilhelm II, Semmes and, 182
Kamehameha, of Hawaii, 83
Kamehameha V, 216
Kanakas, 24, 54, 83, 198
Kate Cory, Semmes's capture of, 177–79
Kearsarge
    Alabama's sinking by, 181–82
    as Union navy gunboat, 169
kedge off, freeing whaling ship, 85, 312
Kelley, Edmund, *Seneca* captain, 309, 322,
    331
Kelley, William H., *Marengo* captain,
    383
Kingfisher, Semmes's capture/burning of,
    168, 176–77
Kohola, Hawaiian whaler, 255, 322
Korean junk, *Florida*'s encounter with, 59

Labrador, 3, 6, 7
Lafayette, Semmes's capture/burning of,
    177–79
Lambert, Thomas, *Kingfisher* captain, 168
Laurel, English steamer
    Confederate Navy/guns on, 191–92
    Sea King rendezvous with, 192, 194–96
lay, 17, 27, 90–91
Lea Harbor, 70
Lee, Robert E., 123, 147, 241
Leonidas, 101, 108
    scuttling of, 142
    stone cargo tossed by, 110
letters of marque, 102, 169
Levi Starbuck, Semmes's capture/burning
    of, 175
Lewis, William, *Lafayette* captain,
    177–79
Lincoln, Abraham, 102, 228
live oak trees, prized wood from, 119
Liverpool, waterfront spies of, 152–53,
    186, 187, 190–91

Lizzie M. Stacey
  Shenandoah v., 197–98
  Waddell's capture/burning of, 198
Louisa Hatch, as *Alabama's* supply ship,
  178–79
Louisiana Purchase, 89
Ludlow, Jeremiah, *Isaac Howland* captain,
  247

MacAskill Island, 73
Macomber, John, *Hillman* captain, 248
Madeira, Portugese island, 192
Maffit, James, *Florida* raider captain, 186
Maffit's Channel, second Stone Fleet and,
  146
Mallory, Stephen
  Bulloch's relationship with, 185
  Confederate Navy Secretary of, 185
  Yankee whaling fleet and, 187
Manet, Edouard, 181
Manifest Destiny, 89
Manning, Thomas, 235, 248, 253, 261
  Abigail crew turncoat of, 219, 224–25
  Shenandoah's new pilot of, 225, 245
  turncoat crew recruiting by, 225
Maori natives, 48–49
Marengo, Arctic fleet whaler, 383–84
Margaret Scott, 101, 123, 138
Martha, Waddell's capture/burning of,
  246, 253
Martha's Vineyard, 22, 24, 160
Mary Garland, English brig, 179–80
Massachusetts, whaleship, 277, 282
masters. *See* whaling captain(s)
Maury, Matthew Fontaine, 194
Mayflower, 400–401
McClellan, George, 101
Mellen, Thomas, capture of, 175
merchant mariners, whaler crewmen v., 17
Mercury, Nye's warning to, 239
Merril's wharf, 29
Merritt, Sam, 345–47
  earned prosperity of, 246
  Williams's salvage investment by, 247

Mexican War, of 1846-1848, 89
Milo
  capture/paroling of, 230–31
  San Francisco destination of, 236–37
  vagabond crews on, 236, 237
Minerva, 352–53
missionaries, Hawaiians exploited by, 84
Missroon, J. S., 100, 135
Monticello
  Arctic abandoning of, 330–31
  Arctic Ocean whaling voyage of, 296–300
  Bering Sea whaling voyage of, 287–89
  disaster close calls of, 299, 302–3
  grounding/kedge off of, 312
  ship/crew of, 288
  walrus hunting on, 299–300
  whale hunting on, 293, 296–97, 313
moon blindness, 93, 363
Moravian mission, Okak Island, 6–7
Morgan, George D., Stone Fleet and, 103
Morgan, Samuel, 19, 20, 23, 37, 40
mosquitoes, 70, 82, 84, 128
Mount Wollaston
  Jireh Swift's collision with, 232
  Nye's freeze-in death on, 399–400
Mustang, coal transport, 203
mutiny, 93, 315–16

Nain, village of, 7
Nantucket sleigh ride, 37, 85
Nantucket whaling port
  Africans/blacks refuge of, 118
  rise/decline of, 376–78
Narragansett Bay, 22
Nashville, Confederate vessel, 190
Nassau, burning of, 253
natives, 62–63, 70–72, 292–93, 383. *See*
  also Alaskan Inupiat; Chukchi
  natives, of East Cape; Eskimos; Inuit;
  Maori natives
naval weapons prototypes, 137
neutrality, laws of
  in England, 155, 156, 186, 191–92
  in Ponape, 211

New Bedford, 1, 7
  anarchy in, 116–17
  description of, 13–15
  1859 holocaust of, 94
  favored development of, 115–16
  population mix of, 26–27
  post Civil War in, 268
  post-whaling fortunes of, 401
  Quakers and whaling in, 114
  San Francisco compared to, 89
  slavery's opposition by, 118–19, 119
  wars' impacts on, 100–101
  as whaling capital, 11–12, 16, 27–28,
    109, 379
  whaling region of, 46
New Bedford Quakers. *See also* Quaker(s)
  Revolutionary War and, 122
  wealthy lifestyles of, 113, 117, 118
New Bedford waterfront
  ship leaving/arriving ceremony at, 12
  sight/smells/sounds of, 13
  whaling commodities stored on, 13
New Bern, North Carolina, 121–22
New London, Connecticut, 25
New London whalers, and Stone Fleet,
  111
New Orleans, 170
  Union blockade success in, 127–28
New York slave trade, 123
Newport, Rhode Island, 23
Nile
  San Francisco orders for, 253, 259
  Waddell's capture/paroling of, 248
Nimrod, capture/burning of, 241–42
Northern Light, Semmes's encounter with,
  175–76
Nye, Ebenezer, *Abigail* captain, 217–24
  Arctic freeze-in death of, 399–400
  Eskimo alcohol trading by, 218
  prisoner behavior of, 220–21, 223–24
  turncoats v. loyal holdouts of, 223, 225
  Waddell danger, warning raised by, 237
  whalers warned by, 239
Nye, Semmes's capture/burning of, 180

Ocean Queen, Federal steamer, 145
Ocean Rover, 241
  Clark's arguments for, 165
  crew's parole and, 166
  Semmes's capture of, 165–66
Ocean Wave, loss of, 66
Ocmulgee
  captured crew of, 162–64
  Osborn's fight for, 161–62
  Semmes's capture/burning of, 161–63
Ocracoke Inlet, 142
Okhotsk City, 59–60
Old Man. *See* Williams, Thomas William
Olivera, Antonia, death/burial of, 319–21
Oneida, 181
Onward, Arctic fleet whaler, 382
Oriole, 297
Osborn, Abraham, *Ocmulgee* captain, 160,
  161
Ottawa, gunboat, 141–42

Pacific Mail Company, 263
Pacific Mutual Insurance Company, 175
pacifism, 122
Packard, Timothy, *Henry Taber* captain,
  294
Parrott, E. G., second Stone Fleet and,
  146
Pearl, capture/burning of, 204–13
Pease, Henry, Jr., 329
Peck, Titus, 117
Pelin, boarding of, 201
Penniman, Edward, 239
Perry, Matthew, 56
petroleum, 94, 95, 187, 399
petroleum industry, whaling industry and,
  82, 187, 399
Pilgrim, 88
Pocahontas, steamer, 143–44
Point Barrow, 301–2
Polar Star, Wood's loss of, 249
Polk, James K., 89
Polynesian peoples, 82, 84
Pomeroy, George, 65

Ponape island, South Pacific
  castaway whalers on, 215–16
  Florence's visit to, 370
  Florida's visit to, 69–72
  natives/trading on, 70–71
  neutrality laws of, 211
  Shenandoah's arrival at, 205–6
  Waddell's diplomacy on, 209–14
  Yankee whalers destroyed at, 204–13
Port Royal, 134–37
Porter, David, 180
Portuguese slave settlement, 46
Post Office Point, 307
Potter, Alden, *Brunswick* captain, 245–47
Potter, Andrew, 55, 93
prisoner(s), 220–21, 223–24, 231, 244. *See
    also* castaway whalers
Progress, Arctic fleet whaler, 325
Provincetown, *Calhoun* and schooner fleet
    of, 169–70
Puritans, Quakers v., 117

Quaker(s). *See also* New Bedford
    Quakers
  beliefs/values of, 113–14, 116–17, 122
  as blubber barons, 26, 115
  pacifism v. slavery for, 122
  Puritans' special hate for, 117
  slavery opposition by, 101, 112, 118, 120,
    122

Randall, William P., 67–68
Rebecca Sims, scuttling of, 143
Reed, Tim, 32–33, 68–69, 94
Resolute, H. M. S., 4
Resolution Island, 4
Rice, John ("Bony"), New London
    commander, 111–12
Richmond, castaways and, 257
Ricketson, Daniel, historian, 116
right whale
  Arctic Ocean plundering of, 292
  characteristics of, 43–44, 66
  commercial value of, 43, 45

  hunting of, 62, 66, 274
  overhunting of, 48
Robert Towns, of Sydney, 228
Robin Hood, torching/sinking of, 145
Robinson, Jack ("Blackhawk"), 270–71
Robinson, Orlando G., *Gypsy* captain,
    243
rock oils. *See* petroleum
Rodman Candleworks, 28
Roman, ice floe sinking of, 316–17
Roosevelt, Theodore, 185
Rotch, William, 113, 119–20
Roys, Thomas Welcome, 61, 225–26
  Bering Strait pioneer whaler, 284–86
  fortunes of, 402
  personality of, 285
rules of etiquette, nautical, 19, 25, 35, 58,
    65

San Francisco. *See also* Yerba Buena
  Dana's impact on, 88–89
  history of, 88–90
  New Bedford compared to, 89
  sailor-friendly port of, 78
  ship jumping frenzy in, 89
San Francisco Bay, 88–90
sandalwood forests, of Hawaii, 83
Sandwich Islanders, 84
Savannah, 100, 134
  blocking harbor of, 102–3
  Stone Fleet rendezvous at, 135
Scammon, Charles Melville, 65
scarlet fever, 232
Scott, Winfield, 101
scurvy, 2, 93, 177, 226, 284, 309, 327, 360
Sea King. See also Shenandoah; Waddell,
    James Iredell
  Bulloch's purchase of, 187
  Confederate Navy crew of, 191–92
  Madeira rendezvous for, 192
  sail and/or steam power of, 187
  secrecy surrounding, 189–92
  as Shenandoah, 195
  war cruiser conversion of, 187–88

Sea of Okhotsk, 56, 81, 223, 226, 370
    deadly ice in, 60–61, 222–23
    discomforts/dangers in, 59–61, 221–22
    Florida's near disaster in, 85
    Shenandoah navigating in, 216, 222–23,
        225
    whale killing in, 62, 85–86
sea otters, hunting of, 348
seasickness, 20, 23, 32, 33, 34, 47
secession, of southern states, 74–75, 81–82
Semmes, Raphael, 74–77, 241, 268. *See*
        also Alabama; Sumter
    Alabama command by, 152–57
    Alabama's sinking, rescue of, 182
    Charleston's revenge desires of, 156–57
    Confederacy joined by, 76–77
    as Confederate fighting man, 126–29
    as Confederate navy captain, 152–54
    description of, 75–76, 126
    as Kaiser Wilhelm II inspiration, 182
    pro-Union wife of, 76
    slavery beliefs of, 165
    Somers, Mexican War loss by, 129
    Stone Fleet response of, 152–57
    as U.S. Navy Commander, 74–75
    Union's ships/shipping targets of, 77, 126
    whalers' non-resistance to, 168–69
    whaling fleet decimated by, 180
    whaling fleet knowledge and, 156
Semmes's Yankee whaling fleet
        destruction
    Alert's catching/burning in, 167
    Eben Dodge's burning in, 132
    Elisha Dunbar's capture/burning in,
        174
    Kate Cory's capture in, 177–79
    Kingfisher's capture/burning in, 168,
        176–77
    Lafayette's capture/burning in, 177–79
    Levi Starbuck's capture/burning in, 175
    Northern Light's encounter in, 175–76
    Nye's capture/burning in, 180
    Ocean Rover capture in, 165–66
    Ocmulgee's capture/burning in, 161–63

    Virginia's capture/burning in, 171
    Weather Gauge's capture in, 170
Seneca, 309, 310, 331, 353
Seward, William, 148
Shannon, Arctic disaster of, 283–84
Shantar Bay, night whaling in, 66–67
sharks, 38, 42, 46, 88
Shelekov, disastrous voyage of, 338–39
Shenandoah. See also Sea King; Waddell,
        James Iredell
    Abigail's alcoholic plunder and, 220
    Australia, repairs of, 201–2
    Australian U. S. Consul and, 202–3
    Bering Strait navigation of, 226
    commercial vessel reconversion of, 262
    crew lacking on, 195–98
    crew's ship-burning methods, 199–200,
        235
    disallowing any port entry by, 261
    Emily Morgan's escape from, 314
    Indian Ocean graveyard of, 263
    Ish-y-paw's tour of, 212
    Jireh Swift v., 234
    Liverpool turn over of, 262
    Lizzie M. Stacey v., 197–98
    Mustang's torpedo attack on, 203
    North Pacific navigation by, 226
    Ponape arrival of, 205–6
    Sea of Okhotsk navigating by, 216,
        222–23, 225
    stowaways as crew for, 203
    turncoat crew recruiting for, 225, 253
    Waddell takes command of, 195
    war orders of, 189
Sherman, Horace, 252
Sherman, James Henry, 256
Sherman, John Henry, 218
ship(s). *See also Florida,* New Bedford
        whaler; whaling ship
    built for whaling v. speed, 15
    custom-built whalers, 60–61
    kedge off/freeing of, 85, 312
    leaving/arriving ceremony of, 12
    whaler v. cargo, 31–32

ship jumpers, 70–71, 89, 90, 92

Sinclair, Arthur, 182–83

Skinner, Samuel P., slave trader, 101

slavery, 23, 46, 84
   New Bedford's opposition to, 119
   Quakers' opposition to, 101, 112, 118,
      120, 122

slop chest, 90

Small, Samuel C., *Weather Gauge* captain,
   169–70

smallpox epidemic, *Delta* caused, 70

Smith, Francis, 228

"smoked ship" for rat control, 43

Sophia Thornton
   plunder from, 234
   vagabond crews and, 236
   Waddell's capture/burning of, 231,
      233–34, 237–38

South Boston, 29, 31, 55

South Pacific missionaries, whalemen and,
   71

South's capitulation, Waddell's refutation
   of, 227, 229, 236, 238–39, 241–42

sperm whale, 35, 42, 45, 46, 95

sperm whale oil, 42
   petroleum erased need for, 399
   war's most precious fuel, 77

St. Elmos's fire, 363

Stancel, Thomas, 21, 187, 287, 361, 372
   bomb lance accident and, 404
   father's salvage voyage with, 348, 352
   Francis Palmer captain of, 403

Starbuck, Alexander, 333, 373–80
   early career of, 374
   whale fishery research of, 374–75, 377

Stone Fleet, 99, 100, 101
   aging whaling fleet as, 100
   as Civil War footnote, 149
   finding crews for, 105
   New Bedford and, 107, 149–50
   New Bedford departure lithograph of,
      149–50
   New Bedford departure of, 107
   New Bedford pride in, 149

"Rat Hole Squadron" as, 125
   second wave of, 138
   as Waddell/Semmes warrant, 267
   as Yankee whaling milestone, 149

Stone Fleet captains
   final reluctance of, 137–38
   French's orders ignored by, 108–9, 124

Stone Fleet scuttling
   burning sails/cordage after, 145
   Charleston Harbor blockade by, 141–49,
      175
   Davis, Charles H., plan for, 142
   escort ships support in, 141–45
   expedition bad luck during, 143
   Lee's anger over, 147
   media coverage of, 141, 143, 144–47
   officers/crews return home, 145
   private wreckers stripping of, 144
   stripping/scavenging after, 144
   Vanity Fair's ridicule of, 147

Stone Fleet, second fleet, 146, 147

Stone Fleet ship(s)
   Charleston, scuttling of, 141–49
   final stripping/scavenging of, 144
   painted Fiji ports on, 112
   reshaping/refitting of, 104
   sloppy repairs on, 104, 108
   unbalanced stone cargo and, 105, 108

Stone Fleet voyage
   Charleston final rendezvous on, 135,
      138–40
   Corea's waterspout battle on, 134–35
   escort ships and, 138
   greatest danger during, 110, 137
   initial luck in, 109
   New York media coverage of, 107, 112,
      134
   outfitters' safety concerns for, 109–10
   Port Royal rendezvous on, 135–37
   Savannah rendezvous on, 135
   Timor's wretched luck on, 112

Stoughton, Massachusetts, 7

stowaways, 203, 363

Street, William, 14

Sturges, Albert, Ponape missionary, 71–72,
205
Sullivan, John F., 2, 4
Sumter. See also Semmes, Raphael
armaments installation on, 128
Confederate raider/warship, 101, 126,
128
Eben Dodge v., 126, 129, 146
New Orleans blockade escape by, 128
ship/crew of, 133, 154
Superior, as Bering Strait pioneer,
284–86
Susan Abigail, burning of, 238
Sutter's Mill, 89
Swain, William, 14
Swift & Allen, of New Bedford, 158, 183,
258–59, 340–41
Swift, Rudolphus N., 100
Sylvia, Joseph D., *Comet* captain, 317–18

Temple, Lewis, 32–33
Temple toggle harpoon, 32–33
Tenedos, scuttling of, 141
Thompson, J. W., 234
Three Brothers, Arctic whaling voyage of,
386, 390, 393, 394
Tilton, George Fred, 50
Tilton, Shadrach
General Pike captain of, 242
Virginia captain, 171–73, 174, 242
Treaty of Kanagawa, 56
Tristan da Cunha, stranding whalers on,
200
tryworks, for blubber boiling, 15, 35, 40
Tucker, Moses, 232, 233–34
Two Years Before the Mast (Dana, Richard
Henry), 89, 167

Unitarianism, 118

Victoria, 322, 333
Virginia, 242
Semmes and crew of, 171–72, 174
Semmes's capture/burning of, 171, 242

Wachusett, 186, 202
Waddell, James Iredell, 268. *See also Sea
King; Shenandoah*
background/career of, 193–94, 263
character of, 193
as Confederate raider, 183
England's complicity with, 262
Harrocke's relationship with, 205–16
Ish-y-paw's negotiations with, 209–14
media coverage of, 250, 258
Pelin boarding by, 201
physical characteristics of, 193
piracy of, 261–62
Sea King, taking command by, 192
Shenandoah, taking command by, 195
war orders of, 194
whaler crews treatment by, 200, 209,
214–15, 219, 231, 235–36, 244, 248,
253, 257
whaling maps' capture by, 207
whaling ships' plundering by, 212–13,
220
Yankee whaling fleet overall impact of,
253, 256, 257, 260
Waddell's Yankee whaling fleet
destruction
Abigail's capture/burning in, 219–20
Addison's escape in, 254–55
Alina's capture/scuttling in, 196–97
Alina's scuttling in, 196–97
Brunswick's capture/burning in,
247–48, 253–54
Catherine's capture/burning in, 241
Civil War's pointless mission of, 262
Congress 2nd's capture/burning in, 252
Covington's burning in, 253
Edward Cary's capture/burning in,
204–13
Edward's capture/burning in, 198–99
Euphrates's capture/burning in,
227–29
Favorite's capture/burning in, 249–53
General Pike's capture/paroling in,
242–43

General Williams's capture/burning in, 240

Gypsy's capture/burning in, 243

Harvest's capture/burning in, 204–13

Hector's capture/burning in, 204–13

Hillman's capture/burning in, 248

Isaac Howland's capture/burning in, 247–48

Isabella's capture/burning of, 243–44

James Maury's capture/paroling in, 248

Jireh Perry's escape in, 255

Jireh Swift's catching/burning in, 231, 234–35

Lizzie M. Stacey's capture/burning in, 198

Martha's capture/burning in, 246

Milo's capture/paroling in, 230–31

Nassau's burning in, 253

Nile's capture/paroling in, 248

Nimrod's capture/burning in, 241–42

Pearl's capture/burning in, 204–13

Sophia Thornton's capture/burning in, 231, 233–34, 237–38

Susan Abigail's plundering/burning in, 238

Waverly's capture/burning in, 245

William C. Nye's capture/burning in, 240–41

William Thompson's capture/burning in, 227–29

waif flag, whale carcass ownership and, 38

waist, of ship, 18–19

walrus hunting, 299–300, 381

Waltham, Massachusetts, 373–74

Wampanoag Indians, as New England whalers, 22–23, 32

waterspout, 134–35

Watkins, Mary, 78, 87, 272, 287, 359, 362, 403–4

Waverly, capture/burning of, 245

Waverly, of New Bedford, 245

Weather Gauge
Semmes's capture of, 170

Welles, Gideon, and Stone Fleet, 102

Wellington Island, natives of, 72

Wethersfield, 25, 29, 30–31

whale(s), 3, 12, 14, 17–8. *See also* right whale
age of, 42
baleen, 35, 43
blackfish/pilot, 33–34
blue, 49
hearing acuity of, 36, 39
humpback, 45
killer, 35
sighting of, 33
sulphur bottom, 49

whale blubber, 34–35. *See also* flensing, of whale
"bible leaves" of, 40, 41
extracting oil from, 41–43, 375
natives eating/drinking of, 62–63
stripping/boiling of, 40

whale carcass, 34, 42. *See also* flensing, of whale
legal rights to, 38
night whaling and, 66–67
processing/trying out of, 39–40
sharks v. crew on, 80–81
smells of, 39

whale killing
dangerous profession of, 33, 35–37, 45–46, 66
description of, 36–37
Eskimos' survival by, 304
kill logging after, 42
"Nantucket sleigh ride" while, 37, 85
sperm cows/calves, 45, 46
technology developed for, 37–38

whaleboat(s), 3, 6, 33
Arctic Ocean dangers in, 309
Okhotsk Sea hunting with, 61–62
provisions in, 36
whale killing with, 36–37, 62

whaleboat crew(s), 33
boatsteerer role in, 3, 23, 36–37
duties of, 18–19, 35–36
selection of, 18, 359

whaleboat crew(s), (*continued*)
  whale hunting dangers to, 37, 66–69, 309, 364
whalebone, 1, 8, 13
whaler. *See* whaler crew(s); whaling ship
whaler crew(s), 12
  blubber boiling impact on, 41
  Eskimos favor with, 305–6
  forecastle life of, 21, 24–25, 29
  kidnapping men for, 357
  merchant mariners v., 17
  professional whaler v. vagabond, 357–59
  quality decline of, 288–89, 356–59, 362, 399
  recruiting of, 2, 17, 18–19
  recruits typical for, 16–17, 24
  sea lawyer among, 358
  shipboard life of, 16, 25, 32, 362
  on shore life of, 90–93
  wages/compensation of, 17, 90–91
whaling captain(s), 35. *See also* Semmes's Yankee whaling fleet destruction; Waddell's Yankee whaling fleet destruction; Williams, Thomas William
  battle-less surrendering by, 130
  as brutal/cruel, 53–54, 92, 93
  complex tasks of, 52
  kidnapping natives by, 72
  medical responsibilities of, 48, 53, 365
  precarious life of, 51–52
  responsibilities of, 51, 55, 66
  on secret mission, 99
  as Stone Fleet captains, 106, 107
  Waddell protests lodged by, 258
  whaling alternatives for, 95
whaling fleet, 30. *See also* Arctic whaling fleet; Yankee whaling fleet
  Alabama's proximity to, 152–53, 156
  Charleston blockade consequences to, 150
  countinghouses of, 28–29
  media and devastation of, 258

New Bedford's region, 46
North's greatest weapon as, 77
Semmes brutality rumors in, 169
whaling-related industries, 12, 28–29
whaling fleet owners, 28
  government protection sought by, 174
  Waddell's impact on, 260
whaling industry
  alcohol trading in, 217–18, 305
  Arctic fleet abandonment and, 340–41
  capitalists of, 26–27
  decline of, 94–95, 109, 146, 269–70
  Eskimos, and impact of, 305
  odds game of, 66, 276, 298
  petroleum industry and, 82, 187, 399
  trading and, 70–71, 73, 217–18
  valuable summer hunting lost by, 257
whaling officers
  as brutal/cruel, 54–55, 92, 93
  punishment of, 56
  on shore leave for, 91
Whaling Schooner, whaleboat loss of, 67
whaling ship(s). *See also Florida*, New Bedford whaler; ship(s)
  abandoning of, 329
  auctioning whaling gear from, 104
  blacksmith and, 52, 56, 57
  boarding skills needed for, 16
  cargo ship v., 31–32
  characteristics of, 15, 130
  coopers and, 51, 58
  daily life aboard, 16, 21, 24–25, 29, 32, 64–65, 359–61
  fighting whales v. ships, 130
  harpooners and, 21, 23, 36–37, 39–40, 51
  onboard pleasures of, 32, 64–65
  punishment/discipline on, 55–56, 93
  rat control on, 43
  rules of etiquette on, 19, 25, 35, 65
  sail v. steam powered, 398
  San Francisco's derelict, 90
  Savannah sinking of, 102–3, 135
  scattered remains (bones) of, 400–401
  wartime outfitting costs for, 184

whaling voyage, 28. *See also Florida's* whaling voyage
  cargo ship voyage v., 31–32
  greasy/success of, 12, 42
  traditional starting ceremony of, 18, 19, 359
  whalers changed by, 91–92
whaling/maritime impact, on Hawaii, 83–85, 338
White, Dave, Semmes' teenage slave, 169
Whittle, William, Jr., 189–91, 221, 256
  turncoat/information fishing by, 223–24
  as Union blockade runner, 190
William C. Nye, San Francisco whaler
  officers/crew of, 240–41
  Waddell's capture/burning of, 240–41
William Gifford, 238
William Thompson, burning of, 227–29
Williams, Eliza Azelia (wife), 11. *See also Florida's* whaling voyage; *Monticello;* Williams, Thomas William
  Connecticut relocation of, 403
  daily onboard life of, 63–64
  family's California relocation of, 273
  Fish, William's birth by, 47–48
  Flora's birth/death and, 272–73
  Jireh Swift voyage and, 159–60
  personality of, 31, 34
  physical characteristics of, 30
  seasickness of, 32, 34
  second whaling voyage of, 272
  Watkins, Mary's birth by, 78
  whaling voyage of, 16, 31, 34–35, 63
Williams family. *See also* Fish, William ("Willie"); Stancel, Thomas; Watkins, Mary; Williams, Eliza Azelia (wife); Williams, Henry; Williams, Thomas William
  Arctic whaleboat voyage of, 330, 336–37
  Dowden's generosity to, 337–38
  Monticello's abandoning by, 330–31
  sibling rivalry in, 361–62
Williams, Henry, 21, 232

Williams, Lewis (brother). *See also* Arctic whaling fleet, 1876 freeze-in
  Florence captain of, 282
Williams, Lewis (brother), *Florence* captain of, 282
Williams, Thomas William, 11, 30, 231. *See also Clara Bell; Florida,* New Bedford whaler; *Florida's* whaling voyage; *Hibernia; Jireh Swift; Monticello;* whaling captain(s)
  Arctic fleet salvage voyage of, 345–55
  Arctic salvage success of, 349–50, 352–54
  background of, 25–26, 52, 93
  Civil War losses lawsuit of, 268
  early career of, 29–30
  final voyage/death of, 403
  as fishy whaleman, 50, 52
  fleet owners v. salvage success of, 354–55
  land-based investments and, 287–88
  Monticello abandoned by, 330–31
  New Bedford return of, 267
  personality of, 18, 34, 51, 55–56, 95, 234–35, 258
  physical characteristics of, 17–18, 51, 81
  Potter's friendship with, 93
  San Francisco return of, 258
  son Willie and, 81, 364
  Waddell challenged by, 234–35
  whaling alternatives ignored by, 95
Winslow, Hudson, *Isabella* captain, 243
Winslow, John A., *Kearsarge* captain, 181
Wood, Daniel, *Congress 2nd* captain, 249
Worth, William, 106

Yankee merchants, Confederate armaments and, 127
Yankee whalemen
  hate for Charleston by, 139
  port behavior of, 58
Yankee whaling fleet, 32. *See also* Arctic whaling fleet; Semmes's Yankee whaling fleet destruction; Waddell's Yankee whaling fleet destruction; whaling fleet

Yankee whaling fleet (*continued*)
  Arctic whaling fleet loss and, 342, 396
  Arctic whaling maps of, 207
  Bulloch's impact on, 183, 186
  Charleston Harbor graveyard of, 146
  death of, 398
  Hawaiian Islands port of, 82–84, 85, 92,
    338
  Mallory's wiping out of, 187
  nature's protection of, 256–57
  of North Pacific, 183
  recovery of, 268
  scattering of, 256
  Stone Fleet milestone of, 149
  Waddell's overall impact on, 253, 256,
    257, 260
  Waddell's war orders against, 194
yellow fever, 186
Yerba Buena, 88–89. *See also* San Francisco
Young, Thomas, *Favorite* captain
  prize crew confrontation by, 250–52
  35-year autobiography of, 249, 252